International Practice
for Architects

INTERNATIONAL PRACTICE FOR ARCHITECTS

Bradford Perkins
FAIA, MRAIC, AICP

WILEY

John Wiley & Sons, Inc.

Copyright © 2008 by John Wiley & Sons, Inc. All rights reserved

Published by John Wiley & Sons, Inc., Hoboken, New Jersey

Published simultaneously in Canada

For general information about our other products and services, please contact our Customer Care Department within the United States at (800) 762-2974, outside the United States at (317) 572-3993 or fax (317) 572-4002.

Wiley also publishes its books in a variety of electronic formats. Some content that appears in print may not be available in electronic books. For more information about Wiley products, visit our web site at www.wiley.com.

Library of Congress Cataloging-in-Publication Data:
Perkins, L. Bradford.
 International practice for architects / L. Bradford Perkins.
     p. cm.
 Includes bibliographical references and index.
 ISBN 978-0-471-76087-0 (cloth)
 1. Architectural practice, International. I. Title.
 NA1996.P35 2007
 720.68'4—dc22
                                        2007030205
Printed in the United States of America

10 9 8 7 6 5 4 3 2 1

To the many friends I have worked with overseas
and to my family who have shared my interest
in international travel, culture, history, and cuisine.

Contents

Contents

Acknowledgments

Special thanks to my research assistant and daughter, Rachael Perkins Arenstein

Thanks to the many people who assisted me by providing insights and material for this book:

Alan Baldwin, Freeman White (India and outsourcing);
Shawn Basler and Ibrahim Mosa (Egypt);
Jim Bell, BeltCollins;
Paul Bello and Federico Bernal, Atkinson Koven Fineberg (Mexico);
Sherry Caplan, William J. Higgins, and John P. Sheehy, Architecture International, Ltd. (Philippines);
Chris Choa, HLW and now EDAW (China);
Ellen Delage, director, International Relations, The American Institute of Architects;
Stephen Forneris, TPG Architecture (Latin America/Ecuador);
Michel Franck (Luxembourg);
Thomas Fridstein, Hillier and SOM (United Kingdom);
Don Goo, George Berean, David Moore, and Robert Zheng, WATG (Asia, Australia, and the South Pacific);
Scott Kilbourn, RTKL (Japan, China and Hong Kong);
Charles "Chuck" Legler;
Ted Liebman, Liebman-Melting Partnership (Russia);
Herbert McLaughlin, KMD;
Peter Moriarty, Burt Hill (Dubai and the U.A.E.);
Tom Vonier, for the material he collected for a potential book on this same topic, which he generously provided to assist me.

Thanks also to the principals and staff at Perkins Eastman, some of whom are from the over 50 nationalities represented at our firm:

Anthony Belluschi
Paul Buckhurst (Brazil)
David Hance (Japan)
Shuping Hou (China)
Georges Jacquemart (Luxembourg)
Paul Johnson (Bermuda)
Jihoon Kim (Korea)
Douglas King (Bahamas)
Gilles Le Gorrec (France)
Nicholas Leko (New Zealand)
Peggy McGrath
Sarah Mechling (images coordinator)
Carl Ordemann (Korea)
Horacio Repetto and Alejandro Knopoff (Argentina)
Meena Singh (India)
Janette Sutton (graphics)
Victor Tesler (Russia)
Michael Thanner (Germany)
Ron Vitale (China)

Jules and Barbara Demchick for providing beautiful settings in Barbados and Italy, where parts of this book were written.

Chapter 1

Introduction and Historical Overview

INTRODUCTION

Virtually every aspect of the North American economy has been affected by globalization. Design professionals—architects, engineers, planners, interior designers, and more than a dozen other design disciplines—are currently engaged in countries around the world. For a few, international projects are an essential part of their practice; but for most, such work is an interesting—but secondary—part of their workload. For many, international work has been both professionally challenging and profitable, but for others it has been a serious drain on their firm's human and financial resources.

This book is intended as an introduction to international practice. Because of the author's direct, personal experience, the primary focus is on the issues facing architects, planners, landscape architects, and interior designers, but much of the material applies to other design disciplines as well.

Specifically, this book was written primarily for six groups:

1. North American design professionals as well as students and interns who have no, or very limited, international experience but who are interested in exploring foreign work.
2. Architects and others who do not work overseas and who are looking to confirm their decision to stay near home.
3. Firms that have international experience and that are interested in building overseas work into a significant part of their practice.
4. Firms with international experience in one or more regions that are looking for an introduction to the issues they will face in new countries or regions.
5. International firms looking to the experience and advice of other firms to strengthen their international practice.
6. Firms looking for an introduction to issues they should be considering on specific international practice issues: setting up an overseas office, managing an international practice, outsourcing, etc.

Of course, this book is not a comprehensive analysis of the issues facing design professionals in each country around the globe. Instead, with the help of experienced principals from dozens of firms, this book introduces interested professionals to the major issues most firms face in the international markets for design services.

The book is organized into six parts:

1. An introduction.
2. A second chapter that covers the issues that should be considered prior to seeking work outside of the United States.
3. A subsequent chapter that discusses issues related to running an international practice.
4. A chapter, which makes up the greater part of the book, that provides an introduction to over 190 countries and

overseas territories around the world—many of which have used North American design services. This section, Chapter 4, includes expanded descriptions of some countries to highlight issues that a North American design professional might face while working in the regions and countries that have most frequently employed international architects for significant projects.

5. A final chapter that discusses issues and trends that could impact international practice in the future.
6. Appendices with supplemental material.

While the majority of the fee volume earned on projects overseas is earned by the larger firms, many smaller firms are actively engaged in international projects. According to the *Business of Architecture: 2003 AIA Firm Summary*: "More than a quarter of the firms overall are currently working on international projects or are interested in doing so" (p. 44). Few firms are actively working in more than two or three countries at a time, and most of us who work internationally have experienced how quickly conditions can change. Thus, this book is intended as both a guide for firms contemplating international work as well as a current overview of the international market—as of 2007.

Some of the material in this book will, undoubtedly, be made obsolete by the rapid changes that are occurring in the world economy, but much of the material is as relevant today as it was at the beginning of my career thirty-eight years ago. Firms contemplating international work or expansion into new countries should find guidelines—many of which

have been provided by others as noted above—that are a useful starting point for their planning.

AN HISTORICAL OVERVIEW

When my grandfather's firm designed the original campuses of two universities in China—Shandong and Nanjing—the required travel was a commitment of months. Years later, when I was growing up in the 1950s, I remember going with my father to the airport because it was a special event; he was flying to Germany to start Perkins & Will's first international project—a school for the children of U.S. Army personnel in Frankfurt, Germany. Except for the architectural divisions of large engineering and design-build organizations, international practice was not a major part of most firms' practice at that time. Today, my children and the children of hundreds of my contemporaries find nothing extraordinary about their parents taking another flight to another foreign project.

In the 1960s, the rapid expansion of international air travel, as well as many other factors, began to change design professionals' view of international practice. A growing number of firms—such as The Architects Collaborative, which was retained to plan and design a new technical university in Baghdad—began seeking and receiving major commissions from clients other than the U.S. government and North American corporations with operations overseas.

It was the great U.S. recession, as well as the Organization of Petroleum Exporting Countries (OPEC)–related shift of wealth, in the mid-1970s that permanently changed things for the architectural profession in North America. During those years many sought internation-

Fig. 1–01: *Nanjing University, Nanjing, China. Perkins, Fellows & Hamilton, 1917.*

al work due to a sharp drop-off in domestic commissions (particularly in such major centers as New York City) and the availability of huge new commissions in countries with limited domestic architectural resources. In that period, many firms made major commitments to international practice, and large numbers of my contemporaries got a taste for both the rewards and the strains of working overseas.

The OPEC countries became a less important part of international practice when Europe, Hong Kong, Japan, and other countries opened up to North American architects in the 1980s. In addition, North American clients, such as Olympia & York, Disney, and IBM, as well as international clients imported many firms for their expertise in those most American of building types: high-rise office buildings, shopping centers, and mixed-use and corporate interiors. The draw of major projects in such glamorous places as London, Paris, and Madrid was irresistible, and many firms even committed to permanent offices overseas.

When the real estate boom of the 1980s hit the wall at the end of the decade, a large number of firms had developed the skills, organization, and need to continue to seek work overseas. Just as the European and Japanese firms finally caught up with us in our traditional areas of expertise, a new real estate boom took off in Asia.

The Asian boom—and the steep North American recession that lasted into the early 1990s—drew more firms overseas, this time to the overheated economies of Indonesia, Thailand, Korea, Taiwan, Malaysia, Singapore, and the emerging giant, China. North American firms continued to work in the Middle East and, if a firm had a local office or marketable design reputation or expertise, in Europe. A reduction in barriers to foreign design firms also opened markets in South America, Eastern Europe, and Russia.

Many of these markets crashed in the mid 1990s, just as the U.S. economy was recovering. Some firms reduced their commitments to work overseas; but the majority of the large firms, as well as many smaller firms, now regarded international practice as a basic part of their strategies for their firms' futures.

At the time this book was written, North American firms are engaged in projects in dozens of countries around the world. China is the hottest market, until their own domestic design capabilities grow to meet the demand; but the United Arab Emirates and several other regions have also become big markets. Hundreds of firms now work in these as well as dozens of other countries around the world.

The *Engineering News Record (ENR)* annual "Top 500 Design Firms Sourcebook" records the steady increase in international practice. The 1965 version does not refer to international work even though many firms had started to work outside the U.S. and Canada. The 1975 issue, on the other hand, noted the rising importance of international work, particularly the emerging market in the Middle East. Reported projects there tripled from 1972 to 1974. Central and South America, in the 1970s, still accounted for the largest number of projects, followed by Africa and a growing number in Indonesia. By 1985 the top 500 had over $1 billion in foreign billings and almost half of that came from the Middle East. Overall, 210 of the 500 firms were working

Table 1-1. International Practice at *ENR*'s Top 10 "Pure" Designers

Firm	Total Revenue from International Practice (%)*	International Offices**
HOK	43	Hong Kong, London, Mexico City, Ottawa, Shanghai, Toronto
Gensler	12	Dubai, London, San Jose, Shanghai, Tokyo
SOM	36	Hong Kong, London, Shanghai
Leo Daly	1	Hong Kong
HKS	6	London, Mexico City
Perkins & Will	10	Shanghai, Vancouver, Victoria
Heery International	18	London, Scotland, Germany, Spain
NBBJ	23	London, Beijing, Shanghai, Dubai
EDAW	37	Beijing, Brisbane, Edinburgh, Hong Kong, London, Manchester, Melbourne, Shanghai, Shenzen, Singapore, Suzhou, Sydney
RTKL	31	London, Madrid, Shanghai, Seoul, Tokyo

Source: *"The Top 500 Design Firms," Engineering News Record,* April 18, 2005. Firms listed in order of gross revenue.

**Firm web sites*

abroad—89 of which had projects in Saudi Arabia. By 1995 Europe, which had been a busy market, was now according to some "a very mature market," and Asia had become "the top attraction for international design firms."

By 2005 over 20 percent (almost $11 billion) of the revenue of the *ENR* "Top 500 Design Firms" came from international assignments. Even taking out the huge international design revenues of the larger engineer-architect-contractor firms, such as Fluor or Bechtel, it is clear that overseas work is a permanent and important part of many firms' practices. This is particularly true for the largest architectural firms. Most of the 10 largest architect, architect-engineer, or architect-planner firms on the list derived a significant percentage of their revenue from international projects, many of which were managed out of overseas offices as illustrated in Table 1-1.

While many of the smaller firms on the list did not have overseas work in 2005, firms of all sizes are working internationally.

The 2006 American Institute of Architects (AIA) Firm Survey in "The Business of Architecture" noted that about 12 percent of the total respondents had been involved with international work in the last three years. For firms with 20 to 99 staff members, the figure was 24 percent and firms with more than 100 staff members, 59 percent had recent international work. Billings, for this work, while still a small percentage of the respondents' total, doubled between the 2003 and 2006 surveys (p. 53).

Ten years from now the focus of international practice will undoubtedly have shifted again. The design professions in North America are now—and will continue to be—integrated into an increasingly globalized world economy.

Chapter 2

Getting Started

WHY CONSIDER AN INTERNATIONAL PRACTICE

International practice sounds glamorous and fun, but is it something that your firm should consider? As noted in Chapter 1, the cyclical nature of the North American economy was one of the factors that stimulated international practice at many firms. A growing number have used overseas work to balance periodic declines in domestic workload. This, however, is a rationale that is typically used after a firm has already committed to pursuing international work. Few firms have been able to anticipate the periodic North American recessions, and even fewer have been able to shift their practice from domestic to international on short notice.

Eight Reasons To Consider International Practice

While a balance of domestic and international work can be a valid long-term rationale for pursuing an international practice, most firms begin their involvement overseas for other reasons. Eight of the most common reasons are the following:

1. *A strong personal interest:* Most firms are a direct reflection of the personal interests and capabilities of the senior principals. If one of those interests is international work, it can be a valid basis for pursuing work overseas. Because of this interest, one or all of the principals may have developed a network of relationships overseas that eventually leads to project opportunities. In my own case, an undergraduate degree in Latin American studies led to a lifelong interest in the region and several of my first international projects.

2. *An influential foreign friend or business associate:* Many of us have been drawn overseas by an individual who claimed to have access to international projects, and most of us have found that this is not always true. Unfortunately, most of us have stories about con men who convinced us to fund unproductive business development efforts overseas. As I describe in later chapters, however, this approach is valid often enough to be one of the major starting points for many firms' international practice. Nevertheless, learning to judge who can, and who cannot, really help you get work in a country is an essential and hard-to-learn international practice skill.

3. *Introductions from friends and family:* Many North American architects or their firms' employees are foreign-born and educated, or they have friends and family overseas. Many of the first projects may start with requests for assistance on or introductions to overseas opportunities from these relationships.

4. *A client who takes you international:* All firms owe a good part of their success to a few clients who give them the projects that become the foundation of the practice. This is true for international practice as well. Many firms have been taken overseas by clients (including the U.S. government) who

> **Common reasons to start working internationally**
>
> 1. Strong personal interest
>
> 2. Influential foreign friend or business associate
>
> 3. Introductions from friends and family
>
> 4. Clients who take you overseas
>
> 5. International clients seeking expertise
>
> 6. Foreign design firms seeking expertise
>
> 7. Targets of opportunity
>
> 8. A planned effort

they met and worked for in North America.

5. *International clients seeking specific expertise:* Some firms establish a reputation that attracts international interest. In some cases it is a reputation for design innovation and creativity; but in most cases it is a demonstrated track record in a building type or service that is perceived as relevant and needed by international clients.

6. *Foreign design firms seeking expertise:* In this increasingly global world, overseas design firms also seek out U.S. and Canadian firms that have the experience needed for their projects.

7. *Targets of opportunity:* Many firms' first overseas opportunities happen by chance. A principal meets someone at a conference, a college classmate makes an introduction, and so forth, and it eventually leads to a first project.

8. *A planned effort:* Possibly the least-followed start to an international practice—but the one strongly recommended in this book—is a plan. Some firms plan the effort that leads to their first project.

International practice, however, should not be justified by the cliché used by some mountain climbers to justify their dangerous sport—"because it is there." Overseas work can be expensive, disruptive, and a serious distraction. Some firms have even destroyed their domestic practice by diverting too much energy and too many resources to foreign work. The Architects Collaborative (TAC) of Cambridge, Massachusetts (and my first architectural employer), is just one of the more prominent examples. TAC, once one of the country's leading firms, had many problems in its

later years; but its heavy commitment in the Middle East left it overextended when Saddam Hussein's invasion of Kuwait brought a sudden halt to several large projects.

Since international practice is inherently riskier, why do it? Interest in foreign culture, a desire to travel, and other personal motivations can be valid justifications; but there are some typical business justifications as well. Among the most often cited are the following:

1. *Growth:* Some firms are committed to growth; they see it as a way to keep the firm challenging and profitable for the principals and staff. At some point in the development of these firms, a number of the better growth opportunities were outside of North America.

2. *A hedge against North American economic cycles:* As noted in Chapter 1, an interest in international work has often been stimulated by an economic downturn in the United States. Few firms can shift from domestic to international work on short notice; but with planning, overseas work can be a healthy way to balance changes in domestic workload. In addition, if one takes a long view, some projections suggest that the majority of the world's design and construction activities will shift from the developed to the developing countries over the next two decades.

3. *A new market for a specialized capability:* Some of us have specialized practices, and we are always on the lookout for clients who need that expertise. SOM and KPF are just two of the firms whose commitment to high-rise office design makes it logical that they pursue opportunities overseas where many

of the most challenging high-rise projects are being planned.

4. *Creation of an interesting practice:* I used to refer to our initial international projects as "yeast"—they helped make the dough (our practice) rise. This might be a clumsy analogy, but creating a challenging and interesting practice is a valid objective. Interesting practices attract better staff, media attention, and clients. As Burt Hill's CEO, Peter Moriarty, noted, "The prospect of overseas travel and international work could and should be a recruiting and retention assist—especially since so many of our staff in the future will be immigrants or their children—many of whom will retain ties to their country of origin."

5. *Building credibility for future domestic opportunities:* Some firms find that they can get projects overseas that enhance their ability to get similar work back home. Because international clients are often not as focused on demonstrated expertise in a particular project type, it is often possible to get projects that can be used to convince a more focused North American client that you are qualified to design their project.

6. *The scope and challenge.* The scope and challenge of some overseas projects is unmatched domestically. For those who find the opportunity to design multimillion-square-foot, mixed-use developments, entire new university campuses, and new cities exciting, most of these opportunities are overseas.

7. *Profit:* Some international work can be extremely profitable. The 2006 AIA Survey on "The Business of Architecture" found that the surveyed firms reported that, while the cost of doing business internationally is higher, "profitability is comparable" (AIA 2006, 57).

8. *Mission:* Some of us believe in the old-time religion—that our design expertise can change people's lives for the better. In our case, our professional commitment to the belief that the physical environment plays a part in the health and health care as well as the housing of the frail elderly has helped support our involvement overseas. We—and many other firms—believe we can make a meaningful difference in people's lives, and that alone justifies the effort to work overseas.

9. *Globalization:* National boundaries are becoming less relevant each year. Firms are not only working internationally but using international resources to carry out the work. Each year more firms are outsourcing drafting, rendering, and other tasks to the highly talented, low-cost resources developing in countries like India and China. Thus, as the *AIA Handbook of Professional Practice* article, "Practicing in a Global Market," states: "International practice has become a reality for American design firms" (Williams and Meyer 2001, 100).

Reasons to Be Cautious

All of the above are valid reasons to pursue work outside of the U.S., but these rationales should be balanced by a clear understanding of the risks. International practice is far more difficult and risky than working near home. The *AIA Handbook* explains some of the issues: "Differences in language, privacy, trust, and accessibility all make the foreign design project quite different from the U.S. project, and

---

Reasons to Have an International Practice

1. Growth
2. Hedge against domestic downturns
3. New markets for specialized expertise
4. Creation of an interesting practice
5. Building credibility for future domestic opportunities
6. Scope and challenge
7. Profit
8. Mission
9. Globalization

"[The firm] had completed several first-rate, widely recognized equestrian training and boarding centers in the eastern and western United States, mainly for race and show animals. The firm loved doing the work, and I think we had become the best in the country in this niche market. But the domestic market for that kind of work had become pretty saturated, so I started researching where else in the world there were racehorses. Then I wrote lots of letters, enclosing examples of our work. We got new work very quickly in Europe and the Middle East. It was very lucrative, and [the firm] is still internationally recognized as a leader in the field,"

Architect who asked not to be named.

all can have negative impacts that at times appear insurmountable" (Williams and Meyer 2001, 100). There can be good reasons to pursue work overseas, but one should do so with eyes open to these risks. In addition, the economic, political, and social volatility of many countries means that conditions can change rapidly. Among the most frequently cited concerns, however, are the following:

1. *Drain on senior resources:* Most international practices are built on the efforts of the firms' most senior personnel. The *AIA Handbook* chapter on this subject correctly states that "working with clients abroad will demand more time than most architects expect, so be prepared…People [in many foreign countries] spend more time with each other and can be quite offended by the American 'gotta go' working methods" (Williams and Meyer 2001, 106). During the peak years when I was building our practice in China, I spent as many as 100 days per year there. Not only did that leave me slightly vague about what time zone I was in, but it also meant I was often unavailable for important presentations, meetings, and decisions back home.

   One should be realistic about these issues and not commit to more than is good for both your own health or the health of your firm. As one of my friends noted, he knew he was traveling too much when on his return from a trip, he went to the movies with his family and tried to find the seatbelt after he sat down.

2. *Financial risk:* Many of the first international efforts are very expensive. It is not uncommon for firms to find they have invested hundreds of thousands of dollars before they get their first project. Even after the work begins to flow, the risk of substantial loss is at least equal to the potential for profit. In addition, as emphatically stated in the *AIA Handbook*, the "greatest risk for the architect overseas is the risk of not being paid" (Williams and Meyer 2001, 107).

3. *Impact on domestic clients:* At first, some domestic clients are impressed and supportive. Over time, however, their tolerance erodes when you are not available for key meetings. The rapid improvement in international communications has reduced this problem, but I have had many overseas trips cut short by the need to be back in the U.S. to deal face to face with an important client. This is in addition to the phone calls I am expected to take at two in the morning when I am in China.

4. *Lack of legal recourse:* In most foreign countries, if a client does not pay, the only recourse is to stop work. Therefore, if your payments do not cover the work to date, the normal options— liens, legal action, etc.—are not avail-

able. Almost every firm working internationally has stories that reinforce the basic advice: "Do not let them get ahead of you!" As almost every firm will acknowledge, however; that it is easier said than done.

5. *Physical risk:* Many countries are as safe as the U.S. and Canada, but many are not. I stopped going to Lebanon in the 1970s, where I was working on a plan for the American University of Beirut, when the dean of the architectural school was shot and killed 12 hours after I had dinner with him in his home in East Beirut. In some countries the risks are more likely to be the food and water, but physical risk should be a consideration—particularly for people with young children.

6. *Professional compromises:* Getting a project built that is consistent with the original design intent is even harder in most overseas locations than it is in the U.S. Very few countries have the commitment to quality seen in Japan and some European countries. In too many cases, the design drawings done in North America are just a general guideline.

7. *Lack of recognition:* If a tree falls in a forest and no one is there to hear it, does it make a sound? Many firms active in the Middle East during the 1970s complained that their years of effort resulted in projects no one ever saw or acknowledged.

8. *Challenges to integrity:* It is rare for any firm working overseas not to come up against some moral—and sometimes legal—choices. The Arab states' enforcement of a boycott of Israel was one such issue in the past, but the more common problem both then and now are situations where payments are

expected that look too much like bribes or kickbacks. Some of these are governed by the Foreign Corrupt Practices Act (see Appendix E), but many fall into a gray zone. For example, is a payment to an agent a payment for professional advice, or is it a payment to influence a potential client to hire you? For those who do not want to be faced with frequent moral and ethical judgments, avoid international practice.

9. *Limited control:* Many international practices require the commitment of staff to overseas offices. Managing domestic branch offices is a difficult task, but managing offices in a foreign country is even harder. Firms really have to trust the managers of their foreign offices and projects because detailed oversight is usually impossible.

10. *Currency and tax surprises:* Most firms with international practices experienced sudden currency devaluations, inability to convert local currency, and/ or unexpected taxes. All can be very unpleasant and expensive surprises.

If, on balance, these risks do not outweigh the positives, the effort to build an international practice can be a worthwhile investment in a firm's future.

PLANNING AN INTERNATIONAL PRACTICE

Many firms—mine included—stumble into their first international project. It is not uncommon to react like a dog that chases a bus and, to its surprise, catches it. Then what?

Most experienced firms agree that any international practice should be governed by a plan—even if it is developed after securing the first one or two projects. The

---

Reasons to Be Cautious in Pursuing Work Overseas

1. Drain on senior resources
2. Financial risk
3. Impact on domestic clients
4. Lack of legal recourse
5. Physical risk
6. Professional compromises
7. Lack of recognition
8. Challenges to integrity
9. Limited control
10. Currency and tax surprises

costs and risks of international practice are too great to just play it by ear.

There is no standard format for a plan, but there are at least six basic issues that should be addressed: market analysis, goal setting, analysis of strengths and weaknesses, development of a marketing plan, management and operations, and a financial plan.

Market Analysis

The first questions should be:

- What makes working in this country of interest?
- Is there a need for our services? For how long?
- Are good design and quality building valued?
- Who else is there?
- What does it take to be competitive?
- Are the prevailing fee levels adequate?
- Can the fees be paid in American dollars? Are there tax issues?
- What special skills, resources, and advisors are needed?
- What have the major risks and rewards been for the firms already working in the country?
- Are there local resources that can help us get and do the work efficiently?

Often the best sources for answers to these questions are other firms with experience in the country. Some of this is shared in conferences, some comes from friends in other firms, and some advice comes from other firms in related disciplines—engineers, builders, and consultants. Useful information can also be obtained from the commercial section of the country's U.S. Embassy; a variety of book, magazine, and online sources; and the firsthand impressions gained in an exploratory trip.

The *AIA Handbook* chapter on "Practicing in a Global Market" also recommends that "you can learn a lot about the history of a nation and the values of its people from literature, guidebooks, travelogues, and by attending seminars, all before you go abroad" (p. 103). Some combination of these sources is usually enough to develop preliminary answers to the questions listed above. Only firsthand experience and a constant effort to learn about working in a country will result in the answers needed to be really successful.

Setting Goals

Setting realistic goals is an important part of any plan. Some of the goals should be set in a firm's discussions of the issues raised in this chapter. Others should be more specific:

- What country or countries will be the primary focus?
- What projects or project types will be targeted?
- How much time and expense will be budgeted?
- What results (new projects, types of projects, sales revenues, profits, etc.) make the effort worthwhile?
- What results will trigger abandonment of the effort?
- Does the long-term strategy involve a commitment to a permanent presence in the country? Will it be a marketing or representative office, a local technical liaison and support office, or an office able to offer services on its own?

An Evaluation of Strengths and Weaknesses

The first step toward achieving international goals is often a realistic evaluation of the firm's strengths and weaknesses. A recognized specialty, size, strong contacts overseas, an able local partner, management depth, and spare financial resources are all important strengths. Even with some or all of these, a firm must ask itself:

- Are my services needed in the target country?
- Are we competitive with the international and local firms we will be competing with?
- Do we have the contacts, knowledge, and local relationships to operate effectively in the country?
- Can we communicate effectively?
- Can we spare the senior management time required?
- Do we have the financial resources to ante up for the initial effort?

If the answer to any of these questions is no or maybe, the plan should include proactive measures to compensate for the perceived weakness(es). The right local adviser, a specialty consultant, and/or a joint venture partner or team with complimentary skills and resources are just some of the ways to deal with a gap in the firm's capabilities.

A Marketing Plan

This part of the plan should cover all of the major issues in any marketing plan:

Who are our target clients? The *AIA Handbook* essay on Practicing in a Global Market provides an overview of the range of client types to consider (see below).

Range of Client Types

"**An existing American client expanding its business to overseas markets**. The client in this case is a known entity. With a relationship of trust between client and architect, the American architect should have an advantage in pursuing international design work for this client. Examples of client categories and international building types include:

- **Corporations**—regional or foreign headquarters, manufacturing facilities, and staff housing
- **Special Uses**—American lifestyle/expertise, retail, other services and products
- **Hospitality**—resorts, hotels, and spas
- **Entertainment**—amusement and theme parks, sports venues
- **Technology and science**—laboratories, research, health care, and environmental facilities

American and foreign joint venture developers with American specialties. These building types are quite similar to those mentioned in the American client category. This client type differs only because it is partly foreign and will require marketing efforts to be expended in more than one country. Typical building types include:

- Retail
- Entertainment and sports facilities
- Technology
- Transportation
- Hospitality
- Convention facilities

Institutional and governmental organizations. Various institutions and the U.S. government are good sources for international projects. Among those building projects are:

- Embassies and military installations, including military housing
- Trade and commodities associations
- Educational institutions, from international schools to universities

The foreign individual or company. Citizens of many foreign countries have a special interest in American design. Reasons foreign clients have for hiring American architects vary and frequently depend on the level of development in the client's own country. Many clients are searching for a "signature designer" and are less demanding of specialized knowledge for a particular building type. Others are searching for the design expertise, perhaps for program, function, or feasibility, that they cannot get at home.

Highly industrialized nations, such as Canada, Australia, Japan, and those in the European Union, are likely to be interested in hiring firms with expertise in the following:

- Communications technology
- Retail shops or centers
- Corporate interiors
- Senior and special needs housing
- Sustainable design and resource management
- Universal design

Private and government clients in developing nations are typically searching for designers who can help them build a solid foundation for their country. Some projects they would commission, in addition to those listed for industrialized countries, are:

- Infrastructure—roads, utilities, commercial districts, and the companion buildings for each
- Transportation facilities
- Housing for both urban and rural settings, with special attention to energy conservation
- Medical and health care, including hospitals, clinics, and medical buildings
- Industrial facilities for the manufacture of products from raw materials and from capital resources

Foreign corporations in the United States. International work includes buildings on American soil for clients from other countries. While U.S. law, standards, and contracts will prevail, the architect will encounter foreign cultures."

Williams Meyer 2001, 101–102.

Other questions that should be covered in the marketing plan include:

1. How do we generate leads?
2. How do we qualify leads and determine whether they are worth pursuing?
3. Who is going to follow up and how?
4. What is the normal process? Is it qualifications based, is it fee based, is it a design competition, or is it some other process unique to the country? While U.S. and Canadian clients tend to follow North American practices for their projects overseas, most foreign clients do not. Many foreign clients like to see some work up front before selecting an architect. In some cases, this is in the form of legitimate competitions and (see sidebar "Guidelines for Foreign Competitions"). And, in many other cases, it is just clients looking for free work to help them make a choice. Therefore, it is essential to research how the process works in each country of interest and to determine whether the selection process is acceptable.
5. What are the prevailing fee levels? And how are contracts structured to keep them adequate?
6. Who is going to make the sales presentations, and what are the important issues? Many firms work hard to establish a local network of advisors, associate firms, and friends if they intend to make a major commitment to a particular country. Other firms focus on U.S.

clients and the federal government. These two client groups actually provide the majority of international billings at many firms, according to the 2003 AIA Survey.

7. Are there government resources that can help us with introductions and marketing assistance?
8. What special skills are required to be successful? The marketing skills a firm has acquired in North America are usually relevant to international work, but there are new skills required in almost every foreign country. Many of these are covered in the case studies in Chapter 2 and country write-ups in Chapter 4.

"I would say most smaller or midsize firms that don't have offices overseas don't really have the luxury to have someone go out and start knocking on doors. It's better if the people who have the need identify who you are and then, once you're out there, you can make the most out of those opportunities and start to do business in that region. What has allowed us to do a fair amount of international work is that we have developed a specialty practice. And, through that, we have been able to develop a reputation, to be published, to win awards. This gives us visibility within a specialty...I think there are more complex and interesting projects being done overseas, particularly in the retail industry, because many of these countries are now coming of age. Here we have a well-built-out retail infrastructure."

James Fitzgerald, FAIA, FRCH Worldwide.
(Courtesy of Thomas Vonier.)

Management and Operations

This part of the plan is even more important than the plans for a domestic practice initiative. Working internationally presents new and more complex challenges. Among the most common issues to be addressed include the following:

- Who is going to manage the marketing effort, and who is going to follow through if projects are obtained?
- What will be done in the home office and what will be done in the project country?
- How will projects be done so that travel and other direct costs are minimized?
- What local resources are available to facilitate projects?
- What technology is necessary to facilitate the work?
- What steps (registrations, etc.) have to be taken to operate legally with minimum tax exposure?

It is important to remember that international work requires the commitment of senior people. What is more, when they are 6 to 12 time zones away, the senior people must be able to operate independently. Critical, also, to successful overseas projects is appropriate and skilled local support as well as a reliable technology umbilical cord to the main office.

Many international projects cannot afford large teams traveling to the site. What is more, few firms can afford to have large numbers of senior people away from the office at the same time. Both of these facts make it vital for firms managing the people who do go overseas to have the right people working within a well-thought-out operations plan.

Financial Plan

The final element of a basic plan is a developed financial structure and budget. The financial plan should include answers to such basic questions as:

- What should the budget be for exploratory trips, marketing, and (if part of the process) competitions?
- How much is the maximum that can be invested before project income starts coming in?
- What is the projected cash flow for the first 12 to 24 months of operations?
- What are the accrual-basis projections for revenues and expenses for the first

12 to 24 months? While accurate projections are always difficult to calculate, the effort will clearly bring out serious issues. Most experienced firms will reflect that their initial forays into international practice cost far more than they had expected. Moreover, if they had been working within a carefully constructed budget, they might not have invested so much.

Together, these six basic parts of a plan can set an initial framework for either a first international effort or for the first steps in a new country. Whichever it is, it is worth remembering the advice of Harold Adams, FAIA, former chairman and president of RTKL, who made the following comments at a conference on international practice:

- "Set aside enough seed money to conduct your marketing—you must have a sound financial base.
- Learn the civilities [of the country or countries you are interested in working in] and culture.
- Know what you're getting into—learn about this region before plunging in.
- Have something special to offer.
- Stay legal. [Use experienced attorneys and tax advisors and be conscious of the U.S. Foreign Corrupt Practices Act.]
- Run your own business. [Beware of agents and 'free' design competitions.]
- Use partnerships and joint ventures as a way to get into the market and understand it.
- Watch the political situation closely and always have a strategy for unrest."

FIRST STEPS

So, you have decided you want to have an international practice, and you have the beginnings of the plan. Now what?

Usually, the first step is getting a strong lead or even a project. To paraphrase H. H. Richardson: "Get the job and then get the next job!" As noted earlier, most of us stumbled into our first assignments. A planned approach, however, is a more effective way to build a successful international practice.

What Country Is the Right Place to Start?

The reality is that for most firms the first foreign opportunities are unplanned; but once there is the determination to pursue

---

The U.S. Government's Role

The founder of the American Institute of Architects' Continental Europe chapter, Thomas Vonier, FAIA, RIBA, noted that the U.S. provides far less support than many European and Asian governments. "The U.S. government itself is a major client for overseas work, with ample opportunities for firms of all sizes and backgrounds. The U.S. Department of State, for example, maintains that its overseas building projects are open to all qualified firms. Its Bureau of Overseas Building Operations is responsible for more than 15,000 facilities worldwide. The Bureau adheres to a qualifications-based selection process for hiring design professionals, but many State Department projects require U.S. citizenship for all personnel who work on them, as well as eligibility for security clearances.

Military construction programs of the U.S. Army Corps of Engineers and the Naval Facilities Engineering Command often entail procuring architectural services, usually in accordance with qualifications-based selection processes. Most military projects require that potential awardees register in the Department of Defense Central Contractor Registration database."

(Courtesy of Thomas Vonier.)

work overseas, there are factors that make a country a better or worse choice. Some of the factors should be uncovered by the market analysis discussed earlier in this chapter. Other factors can be judged with less formal analysis. Some of the other factors to consider include whether you want to spend time in the particular country, whether there is a realistic chance of getting work in the country, and whether you have a guide:

- *Do you want to spend time in the country?* I usually rationalized my initial trips to a new country as quasi vacations if the long-term prospects for work did not pan out. Recognizing that I only had the time to focus on one country, I chose China after initial trips and small assignments in a dozen other countries. My enjoyment of China and the fact that the prospect of several dozen trips in the future was something to look forward to were major motivators for my decision to work there.

"In contrast to firms from many other parts of the world, architecture firms in the U.S. must rely mainly on self-funded entrepreneurial ventures, the innate tenacity and acumen of firm principals, and their professional reputations, to sustain concerted pushes into foreign markets. The United States Trade Representative has been active and supportive in matters affecting international trade in professional services, largely through lending support to free trade initiatives under auspices of the World Trade Organization. The U.S. Department of Commerce has also made notable efforts, but it cannot yet be said that the U.S. government has matched its foreign counterparts in promoting the use of national architects worldwide."

(Courtesy of Thomas Vonier.)

- *Do you have a realistic chance of getting work?* Many of us would like to focus on England, France, or Italy; but for a firm to break into these markets, they probably should have started in the 1980s, when Europe was looking for North American experience. When reviewing his own firm's international opportunities, Peter Moriarty of Burt Hill noted that "the economy of Western Europe is stagnant, population growth is negative, and the area is already overserved by existing well-established firms." In 2006 other regions and countries were more open to North American firms, including the United Arab Emirates and other oil-rich countries in the Middle East, Russia, and, of course, China.

In the 1970s, the key question was "Does the country have oil?" Today, one only has to listen to the experience of other firms with international practices. If a country is open to firms with your profile of capabilities, other design professionals are often willing to advise you.

As I noted in a 1990 conference sponsored and covered by *Architectural Record* (January 1991, 37): "A country's dollar volume of construction, taken by itself, is not the only major criterion for deciding whether or not there are opportunities there. One of the major criteria is strong need for American services, even though there may be a relatively smaller dollar volume." Moreover, the fact that there are many projects does not always mean that the market is open to North American design firms. Thomas Vonier explains:

It is not difficult to determine that a given country has launched a massive hospital or school building program, but it may not be quite as easy to determine whether foreign firms are welcome, merely tolerated, or plainly banned. If a U.S. firm's strength lies in designing advanced pharmaceutical laboratories, it may be natural and a matter of relative ease to assess where else in the world such facilities are planned. What is not always clear is how well qualified local firms are to handle such work and how inclined they may be to partner with U.S. firms. Major national investments in infrastructure projects—for tourism and leisure facilities or public transportation systems—often carry with them major opportunities for foreign participation, particularly if they involve international financial support and funding. (Courtesy of Thomas Vonier.)

- *Do you have a guide?* Few firms enter a country without a guide. In some cases, the guide is a native of the country who is a principal or staff member of the firm and who has family or friends available there to help. In other cases, an agent is hired for this specific purpose; in still others, the guide is a professional adviser, joint-venture partner, or other experienced professional.

In booming markets there is no shortage of people claiming to have the ability to get you work. Most of us who have been working overseas for some time have been conned by one or more of these advisers. In my case, I remember one who had used up his retainer and travel advance before he ever left New York. When he came for a second installment, we cut our

"[We] had several clients domestically interested in expanding their building programs to other countries. Initially, we partnered with various professionals in the countries our clients wanted to expand into. We learned as much about the building process in each country as possible through visiting construction sites and meetings in respective offices. Our initial approach was to partner with the professionals to provide our client with the best possible mix of our expertise with their building program, combined with the host country's professional expertise with that country's building process."

Michael D. Gallagher, BSW International, Inc., Tulsa, Oklahoma.

losses. Learning to distinguish the frauds from those who can really help is an acquired skill. In my experience, to glean useful information about a guide's potential, the following evaluative questions are helpful:

- Is the prospective guide from the city, region, or country that is the primary target? In China, for example, you do not usually retain an advisor from Taiwan or Singapore to help seek work in Shanghai or Beijing.
- Is he or she from a well-connected family, and did they go to the right schools?
- Do they speak and write the language fluently?
- Are they willing to make some or most of their compensation contingent on success?
- Do you like and trust them? Remember, you are likely to be spending a lot of time together sharing the stresses of building an international practice.

How to Start

Most of us start with one or more exploratory trips. These trips may or may not

"I was the lead architect who was interested in Japanese culture and convinced my partners to get involved after I was convinced we could be successful. My experience has been very rewarding. Not only have I developed wonderful relationships in Japan, but I have also diversified company investments without compromising our core services. Through personal interest in Japan, hosting exchange students, and volunteering with Sister Cities International, we heard about a technology-based housing system in Japan and invited the company to visit us in Minnesota. They made the visit and in turn invited us to Japan. After many months of dialogue, we were each convinced we could work together toward the mutual goal of transferring their technology to the U.S. and adapting this building system to U.S. codes and standards in exchange for cash and equity. Understanding cultural differences and communication are key factors. If I had not spent several years reading about Japanese culture and business, as well as studying the language, I might have given up after the first couple of trips without a contract."

James Brew, President, LHB Corporation, Duluth, Minnesota

be paid for by some small introductory assignments. The primary objective, however, is to flesh out a plan and to obtain an understanding of the basics of finding and doing work in the country. Among the issues worth studying are those outlined in the country discussions in Chapter 4, as well as those listed here.

Questions to Answer During an Initial Exploration

1. Is there a market for our services, and how long will it last?
2. Are there enough good reasons to make the effort?
3. What are the likely pitfalls, and how can they be avoided?
4. What skills and capabilities are essential for success?
5. What peer firms are operating there now?
6. Who are the clients and what services and building-type expertise are most in demand?
7. What is the process for getting work?
8. How does one deal with the language and communication issues?
9. What are the licensing and other legal requirements?
10. Are the prevailing fee levels, payment terms, and tax structures such that it is possible to make a profit?
11. What are the major contract-negotiation issues?
12. Are there local resources—associate firms, engineers, etc.—who can help?
13. What are the design traditions and client-design preferences?
14. What code and regulatory issues are important, and how do you navigate through them?
15. What is the typical scope of services, and how do projects get done?
16. What are the typical project schedules?
17. What are the construction capabilities, normal construction practices, and sources of construction materials?
18. Is the country safe to work in?
19. What are the most common problems facing design professionals working in the country?
20. What are the most important pieces of advice you need to get during this exploratory phase?

Getting those First Projects

For some firms the first projects come quickly, but for many others they only come after extensive groundwork. In either case, the following normal steps in the marketing process apply.

- *Lay the groundwork:* Many firms will prepare marketing materials in the appropriate language, seek lecture or teaching assignments in the country, get their work published in magazines that will make good third-party references for the firm, and take other preparatory steps.
- *Generate leads:* The first trips—as well as home-office contacts—should begin creating a network that will help identify leads for potential projects. Over time—as this network of friends, clients, consultants, and others expands—it will become relatively easy to have more leads than one can reasonably follow. In some countries, a network can be helped with the aid of an agent, representative, or broker who—for a fee or a percentage—will help find work. As the *AIA Handbook* notes (p. 103), "caution is required…Take care to check references for the past success of an agent." Many cannot really deliver.
- *Qualify leads:* Culling the leads worth pursuing is important due to the cost of pursuing a project overseas, particularly in those countries where competitions are a common method for architect selection. This is where a good agent can find out if the firm "is being invited to compete or invited to win."
- *Courting:* As will be noted again later, the courting stage, where leads are converted into solid opportunities, is particularly important in many foreign countries. As Williams and Meyer note in the *AIA Handbook:* "The biggest challenge designers face…is understanding their clients…[and] getting close to the client—the real decision maker—is far more complicated than with domestic projects" (p. 100). Many international clients are looking for a

personal connection before they hire a firm. My first major project in China materialized after several dinners and meetings with leaders from the Chinese Academy of Sciences. These had been arranged by a Chinese friend and were helped by the presence of my brother, who was then head of the Asia Center at Harvard. Once they were comfortable with me, we were invited to a paid competition for a new information technology campus, which we subsequently won. That project led to a close personal and professional relationship with the leadership that has resulted in a steady stream of projects.

- *Presentation:* As in North America, many projects are won before the final presentation. But as will be discussed again later, the quality of the presentation is critical in many foreign settings. Particularly in less

---

"The most effective method we have found to identify leads for foreign projects is through our strategic partners—local firms with whom we have established relationships. Currently, we have associations throughout the Middle East and in Korea, Vietnam, Cambodia, Italy, and the United Kingdom. In any given month I receive at least a couple of notices of design competitions from local firms looking for an American design partner. We are extremely selective with design competitions—we rarely participate in open, unpaid competitions, and we look very hard before agreeing to proceed with limited, invited ones. Competitions can be a viable way to break into international work, however, provided one is willing to risk making the investment. I have helped teams win several international design competitions in the past; but overall I feel they are a very inefficient and costly way of developing business."

James M. Wright, AIA, PageSoutherlandPage, Washington, D.C.
(Courtesy of Thomas Vonier.)

sophisticated areas, a superior presentation can beat superior substance.

• *Closing:* This is again a time when good agents should earn their keep. This is also where personal relationships matter as well. In many countries, architect selection procedures are often very informal and easily influenced by outside forces. A good agent and a strong personal connection can insulate the firm from these forces and reinforce the strength of your firm's proposal.

No two firms get their first jobs in the same way. While each firm usually has to deal in some way with the steps discussed here, there is a lot of be learned from the stories of other firms. Some of these stories are included in the next chapter.

Contract Issues

Once a first project is secured, the next challenge is to negotiate a contract that minimizes the major risks inherent in many overseas projects. The AIA Documents Committee is developing a set of agreements; but helpful as these will be, they are just the starting point for a full contractual agreement. Among the issues to consider are the following:

• *Does the client have the financing and is the project viable?* This is far harder to determine in most foreign countries than it is in North America.
• *What is the client's reputation?* This, too, can be hard to check. But research through the credit agencies, other firms who have worked with the client, the U.S. Department of Commerce Foreign Commercial Service, and other sources can be helpful.
• *Does the client have assets or operations in the U.S. or Canada?* If so, it

strengthens the firm's legal options if things go wrong. Trying to use legal remedies against a foreign entity in the entity's own country is often fruitless.

• *How will you be sure to get paid?* The *AIA Handbook* chapter on Practicing in a Global Market (Williams and Meyer, 2001, p. 104) on this topic lists four suggested contract provisions:
  • "An irrevocable letter of credit can be conditioned upon the shipment of documents or an agreement with the client that your statement of project completion is acceptable evidence to the bank.
  • An escrow account can be set up that will be drawn from upon evidence of completion of a phase or task.
  • A retainer can be credited to the final invoice that is sufficient to cover all the work being done between regular payments.
  • A fixed schedule of monthly payments for a specified amount can be established, not necessarily related to the work performed."
• *How will you avoid scope creep?* The *AIA Handbook's* "Practicing in a Global Market" (Williams and Meyer 2001, p. 104) offers the following advice: "The rest of the world is not as litigation-prone as the United States. It is, however, aware of how hard it is for U.S. firms to enforce payment provisions offshore and will often take advantage of the situation by requesting more and more work as a basis for payment. The greatest risk in overseas work is in not getting paid. In many countries along the Pacific Rim, a contract is considered a starting place for negotiation, not the final word. Always make sure your expectations align with those of your client before

you begin work, and then hold the client to the letter of the agreement."

- *How do you manage client expectations?* Foreign clients—even more than domestic ones—rarely understand what we do and don't do; what is the proper sequence and scope appropriate for each phase (design development, for example, is often considered unnecessary by foreign clients); how much work the project requires; and many other issues that can be the difference between a successful, profitable project and an unhappy experience for all parties.

- *How do you get the client to accept younger staff when they think they are*

Contract Provisions

Use your contract to minimize the risk of not being paid. Then, be prepared to stand by the provisions it contains to enforce your rights.

- Confirm that all payments are net of taxes. Pass the taxes on to the client through "net of taxes" contract provisions.

- State explicitly the currency to be paid. Payment in U.S. dollars is always the best. If payment is in a foreign currency, address the issue of currency fluctuations. Architects should not be in the business of currency speculation. Consider purchasing a currency insurance policy if payment in dollars is not an option.

- Include "pay when paid" provisions in subcontractor and joint venture agreements

- Assert the right to stop work in case of nonpayment. Contract for the right to withhold deliverables.

- Include ownership of documents and copyright provisions (which is often a sticking point).

- Address dispute resolution. International arbitration is increasingly popular and is institutionalized through the American Arbitration Association.

- Specify the right to bill by fax, which can eliminate one to two weeks on accounts receivable.

- Send two invoices, one for services and one for reimbursable expenses, so that questions about expenses will not delay payment of your fees.

- Specify what materials and services are expected from the client before architectural services can commence.

- Identify the client representative who is authorized to approve your work and payment.

- Provide suspension and termination procedures. Overseas projects have a tendency to be delayed or end abruptly. When they cease, the right to stop work and be paid is critical.

- Define reimbursable expenses explicitly. Many overseas clients are not familiar with the concept.

- Consider requesting a retainer to determine a client's intent and protect you from delayed payment.

- Be aware that foreign capital can be frozen or prohibited from leaving the country.

- It is best to contract with a U.S. entity for international projects.

Williams and Meyer, 2001, p. 104.

retaining the firm's senior leaders? Many foreign clients are seeking gray hair and experience, which can make acceptance of a typical project team an issue.

- *How do you convince the client that it is important to retain experienced international consulting engineers and/or specialty consultants to create the team needed?* Many overseas clients, in particular in countries with lots of engineers, are reluctant to pay a premium for these services. As in North America, however, inexperienced or inadequate consultant support can be the cause of major problems. Thus, it is usually important to insist on the right team.

- *How do you divide the work with the local design team required on most overseas projects?* It is often appropriate to create an elaborate responsibility matrix and then assign lead and support roles for the international and local teams to the list of tasks to be completed. Three-party contracts with detailed descriptions of each party's responsibilities are often appropriate.

- *How do you make sure you are compensated for extra services?* Many foreign clients do not (or choose not to) understand the concept of additional services. Thus, it is often necessary to define in greater detail when something is outside the scope of responsibilities or is an additional expense—more so than in a typical U.S. or Canadian contract. This means contracts may need to detail the number of trips covered in the basic fee (and the cost of additional trips beyond that) as well as detail the hourly cost for rework due to inadequate performance of the local consultant team, etc.

- *How do you make sure that out of pocket expenses are fully reimbursed?* Many overseas clients—particularly in China and some other Asian clients—expect travel and other out of pocket costs (renderings, models, printing, etc.) to be built into the fee. This can be a major issue, since these costs are hard to estimate at the beginning of a project and often require a great deal of effort to manage. In our case, it took us a long time to learn how to minimize the wild fluctuations in airfares and other travel costs and to make cost-effective use of local printing, rendering, model-making, and other resources.

Managing Foreign Client Expectations

- "The level of completeness of each service and product should be specifically described and mutually agreed upon to avoid undefined or misunderstood deliverables.

- The true purpose of a project can be different from how it appears to the U.S. architect.

- Compensation amounts and methods are different. Foreign clients are often unfamiliar with the value of the architectural service being provided. Consequently, they are unwilling or unable to afford the level of service required for the project's success.

- The expectation of "winning" is high in many cultures, and for some foreign clients the ends justify the means.

- Negotiation tactics vary widely.

- Clients often expect "loss leaders." Thorough, uncompensated design solutions are frequently required before the architect or development/construction teams are selected.

- Clients sometimes expect the American architect to bring the money or the tenant to the project.

- Many foreign clients expect the architect to be a true generalist and provide services that in America are specialized or unrelated."

Williams and Meyer 2001, p. 105.

- *How do you make sure that key areas of risk and professional liability are insured?* There is a need to be careful to make sure contracts do not have provisions that are uninsurable or that void coverage. Review of draft contracts with the firm's insurance adviser is often appropriate.

- *How do you resolve disputes?* As noted earlier, most foreign clients are less likely to resort to lawyers. There are international arbitration panels available in some countries as well as other established approaches. In any event, it is an important subject to research and define.

- *How do you get out of a bad project?* Sometimes it is best to just walk away, but most contracts make that difficult. Therefore, termination provisions are as important for the design team as they are for the client.

Once all of these—and the many other technical and administrative issues unique to the contract for each project— are resolved, it is time to start the project.

Now comes what should be the fun part. Designing the first project and later building and running an international practice is the subject of the remaining chapters in this book. First, however, we will review case histories in order to learn from the experiences of others.

GETTING STARTED: CASE STUDIES

Every firm that has worked internationally has a story about its first projects. These stories are unique to each firm, but most provide lessons for other firms. Some of these lessons can guide other firms into a particular country, while others apply to international practice in general.

Case One: A Personal Network—Perkins Eastman

All of Perkins Eastman's initial international projects came as referrals from past clients and friends. In Brazil, the first projects came from a family that had been a client prior to establishment of the firm. As with many international assignments, the client-architect relationship had become a close friendship.

In Spain, a close American friend, who had run an international construction company, recommended us to a large Spanish design-build organization looking for an American firm that would strengthen their planning, programming, and concept-design capabilities.

In China, the first opportunities were brought to us by a Chinese-American friend. Only after we had secured our first projects with his help did we begin investing in a major effort to expand our practice there.

In Israel, we were strongly recommended by the administrator of a major U.S. medical center with a strong link to a proposed cancer center near Tel Aviv.

Only in Japan did a foreign client actually identify us as a potential architect for their work before we had been introduced by a friend. Even in Japan, however, an American working for the Japanese client, who knew us, was the key facilitator of our initial introduction.

Fig. 2–01: *Sun City Takatsuki, Takatsuki, Japan. Architect: Perkins Eastman. Photograph by Chuck Choi.*

Lessons learned

This list of experiences contains several general lessons:

1. The same network of relationships that are the foundation of a successful domestic practice may also be key entrees for an international practice.
2. Many firms—ours included—only begin pursuing work overseas when they have a client or solid lead that justifies the marketing expense. Few firms invest more than one or two exploratory trips without such an introduction.
3. In all five countries, both the introduction and the follow-up required the participation of the firm's senior principals. Closing the first projects in any country also typically requires the participation of senior principals.

Fig. 2–02: *Sun City Takatsuki, Takatsuki, Japan. Architect: Perkins Eastman. Photograph by Chuck Choi.*

Case Two: A Client Who Takes You Overseas—Davis Brody Bond

Alan Schwartzman, a retired partner living in Paris, introduced a French-based auto parts maker, Valeo, to the firm. The projects were office and industrial buildings; but the client was supportive of good design. After a successful first project in the U.S., the same client used Davis Brody Bond for subsequent projects in Mexico, France, and Brazil. Several of these projects have won major design awards that have strengthened the firm's design image.

Lessons learned
1. Sometimes international projects can strengthen a firm's domestic image.
2. Nothing is more effective than doing good work.
3. Some unlikely projects can make international practice worthwhile.

Fig. 2–03: *Valeo Security Systems, São Paulo, Brazil. Architect: Davis Brody Bond. Photograph by Nelson Kon.*

Case Three: Clients Seeking Specific Expertise—KPF

When Kohn Pedersen Fox (KPF) started, it focused almost exclusively on large commercial projects. By the mid 1980s, the firm had become a recognized leader in office-building design throughout the U.S. In spite of the firm's success, Gene Kohn remembers the concern he felt when an economist at a 1985 Urban Land Institute conference predicted that many of the commercial firms in the audience would be out of business within 10 years if they did not begin to work overseas. Based on this concern, he began to look for international opportunities.

The first was an office building for Goldman Sachs in London, which was followed shortly thereafter by a German office building project won in an international competition and as well by work in Japan. The Japan trips gave KPF the opportunity to explore Hong Kong and other Asian markets. As Gene describes it, "one thing led to another," and they soon had a substantial practice in Asia that helped carry them through the deep recession of the late 1980s and early 1990s. "There was not a new office building in New York for 10 years," Gene noted.

In London the need to send over a large team for the construction phase of the Goldman Sachs job as well as other jobs won at Canary Wharf soon made a London office seem like a good idea. This office, now quite successful, took a considerable investment in both time and money. Over time most of the staff and principals in the London office were replaced with Europeans; KPF London is now regarded by many clients as a European firm eligible to compete for work normally restricted to EU firms. Gene Kohn also noted that having an office in Europe has reduced the travel load—to some extent—of the U.S. principals and staff.

Today, KPF has one-third of its staff in its London and Shanghai offices, and half of the firm's work is overseas. The firm has completed projects in 26 countries and has designed projects in 10 others. In 2006 the firm had projects in the Middle East, Western Europe, Russia, Brazil, China, Korea, Singapore, Japan, and India.

Fig. 2–04: *Plaza 66, Shanghai, China. Architects: Kohn Pedersen Fox Associates (KPF) with Mr. Frank C. Y. Feng Architects & Associates Ltd. Photograph by John Butlin.*

Moreover, the international work has helped maintain the firm's international reputation as a design leader.

Lessons learned

1. If a firm wants to be an international design leader in large-scale office buildings and mixed-use development, many of the best opportunities are overseas.
2. International work can be a hedge against the low moments in North American economic cycles.
3. When international work is a significant part of the firm's practice, it has a major impact on how the firm organizes itself to carry out projects. Principals have to be willing to travel frequently; the firm has to be able to cover for traveling staff; the firm will require a major support structure (staff and technology); and the firm has to make a continuous investment in learning how to work in new countries. Having an overseas office, however, can reduce some of the organizational strains inherent in overseas work.
4. It is possible to have a true international practice while maintaining both quality and profitability.

Case Four: Clients Seeking Specific Expertise II— Anthony Belluschi Architects

Anthony (Tony) Belluschi built a firm, ABA, which had at its peak 65 staff members. His firm focused on retail and mixed-use projects. Belluschi's and his firm's expertise created opportunities around the world in a variety of ways.

His first project began when a client (an Iraqi-born Israeli citizen) for a project in New Jersey took Tony to Israel to master plan a new community near Eilat. This project was never built, but it began the firm's international practice.

The second project came after the firm had completed a successful retail project in Cleveland, Ohio, with Turner Construction. Turner asked Tony to come to New York to talk to an Australian client who was seeking someone who could come up with a conceptual solution for an urban office and retail building on a tight site in Melbourne, Australia. Several firms had tried and failed. The client invited Tony to Melbourne, where he worked out of a hotel room for a week and came up with a solution. The building was successfully completed and his international practice had its first real project.

The next project was in Goshono, Japan. Urban, a division of JMB Realty, had been retained to put together a development manual for a mixed-use project that included a hotel, a retail complex, and a civic center. Urban hired ABA to put together a kit of parts as well as a schematic design for the project to be included in the manual. The Japanese liked the solution and implemented it.

The fourth opportunity was in Istanbul, Turkey. Tony gave a lecture at a major real estate conference in Las Vegas, Nevada. The senior architect for a major Turkish development group was in the audience. Several years later he remembered Tony and recommended him as the designer for a major mixed-use development in downtown Istanbul, which is now complete.

A project in Riyadh, Saudi Arabia, was next. A developer for a major shopping center had assembled a list of 25 U.S. firms with relevant experience. The 5 Saudi firms under consideration were told they had to bring in one of the 25. The ultimately successful firm had asked another American architect for a recommendation and, based on the recommendation, ABA was selected and subsequently got the project.

Still another opportunity for ABA came up in Paris. The firm received a late notice that there was an international design competition for a major retail center. Tony was in Paris on vacation, but he called the client, met with him, and bonded. The client also liked one of ABA's recent projects in the U.S. and saw it as a model. ABA was selected for the project. Since these initial experiences, Tony's practice (now a strategic affiliate of Perkins Eastman) has become increasingly international.

Lessons learned
1. Even a medium-sized firm can have a varied international practice.
2. The key here, of course, was marketable expertise in building types relevant to international developments.
3. As is often the case, U.S. clients and friends can provide the key introductions.
4. And, as the Paris project illustrates, one of the keys to success in life is just showing up.

Fig. 2–05: *Les Quatre Temps, Paris, France. Architect: Anthony Belluschi/OWP&P. Courtesy of Anthony Belluschi.*

Case Five: An International Competition

In many very visible cases, a firm's international practice may begin after winning an international competition. My grandfather's cousins, Walter Burley Griffin and Marion Mahony Griffin, won the 1912 competition to plan and design the first phase of Australia's capital Canberra. They moved to Australia and later to India. Almost 70 years later, Romaldo Giurgola (and his firm Mitchell Giurgola) won the international competition for the Australian Parliament House in Canberra in 1980. He, too, chose to move and practice in Australia.

On a much smaller scale, many other firms have built their international practices in part on a successful competition entry. Our firm, for example, got its real start in China by winning a major planning competition for the Chinese Academy of Sciences in Beijing. Other firms, however, have not had positive experiences with international competitions. Too many are very expensive, rigged to favor one or two favorites, and time consuming. Moreover, many competitions do not result in a building for the winner.

Most experienced firms are careful about the criteria they use to judge whether or not it is worth entering. (See Fred W. Clarke's advice in the sidebar on page 16.) As one experienced architect noted, somewhat cynically, "we want to know if we are being invited to win or just invited to participate."

Lessons learned

1. Winning an international competition can lead to an architect's most important work.
2. A successful competition win can also be a life- and career-changing experience.
3. Competitions are a hard way to get work internationally and should be entered with caution.

Case Six: An Agent

Most firms do not like to attribute their international projects to the work of an agent or middleman. Even when these representatives—some of whom work on a commission basis—are fully professional, there is the feeling that they sound slightly shady. There are, however, many firms who have found it necessary or very helpful to use an agent. In some countries, these agents are a normal source of introductions, contract-negotiation advice, local intelligence, and other essential support services.

Case Seven: A Split—Basler Mosa Design Group

Shawn Basler and Ibrahim Mosa were two of the younger partners in a large firm. Among their responsibilities were several projects in the Middle East. When the firm decided that it did not want to continue doing work in the Middle East, the two partners amicably withdrew to establish their own firm with two projects in Egypt as their first assignments.

Basler Mosa set up a small office in New York and a larger office in Cairo to carry out the work. The two partners were stretched thin carrying out the work, and when the first projects began to wind down, there was a crisis in their workload. With the effort required by several international projects, they had had very little time to pursue new work.

They shrank the firm, focused more of the effort back in New York, and began to build a broader practice. They found, however, that as a new firm they could not compete on their own for many projects without more resources and a larger portfolio of completed work. Therefore, they approached a large, national firm that they heard was interested in the Middle East to form a strategic allegiance.

The combination of the two principals' strong connections in the region and the resources of a large firm resulted in new projects almost immediately.

Lessons learned

1. Most importantly, this case illustrates the fact that even young, new firms can compete internationally if they have the skills and contacts.
2. As a small, new firm, however, the strain of doing work overseas can distract one from the essential tasks of building a practice.
3. One of the best ways for a young firm to overcome its lack of resources and a portfolio of completed projects is to leverage effort and relationships to attract a strategic partner with both.

Fig. 2–06: *Golden View Resort, Sharm el Sheikh, Egypt. Architect: Basler Mosa Design Group, Inc. Photograph courtesy of Marriott International.*

Case Eight: A Personal Interest—Liebman Melting Partnership

Ted Liebman, whose 12- to 15-person, New York–based practice is not typical of the firms seeking work in Russia, has nonetheless had one of the most successful experiences in the former Soviet Union. He has been working there for 16 years on a wide variety of projects. Moreover, unlike many of his much larger competitors, most of his projects have been, or are currently being, built. He travels to Russia 6 to 12 times per year and has loved the experience.

Ted's interest in international work was originally stimulated when he won the Rome Prize after graduating from Harvard. His deep interest in housing and neighborhoods and work with Boston's Ed Logue, led him to the New York State Urban Development Corporation (UDC), where he was appointed Chief of Architecture. During his tenure at the UDC, he received the Wheelwright Traveling Fellowship, and with his wife and two young children in tow, he lived in and studied 80 housing projects in 10 countries throughout Europe with a focus on low-rise, high-density housing and

Fig. 2–07: *Ducat One, Moscow, Russia. Architects: The Liebman Melting Partnership with Mosproject1-Studio16. Courtesy of The Liebman Melting Partnership.*

33

neighborhoods. Next, Ted began a two-year assignment with the Harvard Institute for International Development in Tehran, where he developed neighborhood designs and started his private practice.

His first trip to Moscow was in 1975, when he was asked to give a lecture to a group that included the Housing Minister. His return to work in Russia, however, started indirectly in 1989, after the Berlin wall came down, with a call from the U.S. Embassy. A developer was considering building modular housing in East Germany. Ted called and was hired. He invited an American lightweight-steel panel manufacturer to participate in the German work. That led to an invitation to participate in a Moscow development. It was the redevelopment of a factory site that was to be converted into a first-class office space. So, in early 1991, the firm began its Russian experience. After the first building's conversion was underway, Ted pointed out to the owner that 500,000 square feet of office building could be developed on the site. Now that site in the center of Moscow is a three-building complex. The first building is Citibank's headquarters, and the second building, Ducat Two, is for Ted, "perhaps the finest building ever done by our firm."

During his trips there his interest in the people and the culture led to many introductions and friendships with Russian architects and others who have helped him build a continuing practice in Russia as well as two of the former Soviet republics. Today, he has projects in Moscow and in the Black Sea region of Russia, Azerbaijan, and Ukraine. Approximately half of the firm's fees are international.

Because he is known as an architect who can get things done in Russia, his has been one of the most visible North American firms working in the region. Most of his clients are American or Americans in joint venture with Russian companies. He notes that he was lucky to get involved early in an important project that got built. When the market there opened up, people knew him. But, he emphasizes, "a major reason for my success is being there and enjoying it." The Russians want to know the principals of the firms they work with, and they want them to respect and enjoy their culture.

Lessons learned

1. As with several of the other cases, you do not have to be large to have a successful international practice.
2. Success often depends on a major commitment of time and energy by the firm's leaders.
3. Being there and enjoying it are essential ingredients to success.

Case Nine: Acquiring An International Practice

HOK, Perkins & Will, and my firm, Perkins Eastman, all felt it necessary to acquire a local firm in order to practice in Canada. Technically, this was not necessary. All three had opened foreign offices elsewhere with U.S. personnel. The Canadian market, however, has a well-known preference for Canadian firms.

Lessons learned

1. The strategy used to enter any foreign market—even one that is as closely tied to the U.S. as is Canada—must be sensitive to the unique aspects of each country.
2. Entering any foreign market is usually facilitated by employing local expertise early. Even when a foreign client is actively interested in U.S. expertise, local knowledge is also important.
3. Where the image—as well as the substance—of being local is very important, it is often faster and cheaper to acquire a firm rather than to build an office from scratch.

Case Ten: Going Overseas with the Help of Uncle Sam—Belt Collins

Belt Collins—a planning, landscape architecture and engineering firm based in Honolulu, Hawaii—decided by the late 1960s that Hawaii was not a big enough market to support the size and type of firm they wanted. Their first international assignments were tourism studies funded by U.S. AID and the World Bank for Taiwan, Sri Lanka, Malaysia, and other locations. These studies led to a network of relationships with potential clients, which became the foundation for their current international practice. Today, over half the firm's revenues, as well as half of its 450-member staff, are in Asia. The firm has a network of offices in Asia, including a 150-person production office in Manila, Philippines, that acts as an outsource support group for the Asian offices.

Lessons learned

1. Planning skills are often the most effective way to enter a foreign market.
2. There are a variety of projects—funded by public and quasi-public entities in the U.S.—that are available to firms with the right skills.
3. International practice can become the dominant aspect of an overall practice.

Case Eleven: Replicating a Successful U.S. Model—Burt Hill

Burt Hill is a large architectural-engineering firm based in Pennsylvania. It defines itself as a regional firm with a set of offices located close enough to support each other easily. When they decided to go overseas, they sought out a single region where they could build a similar regional practice. As they put it, "Our philosophy both in the U.S. and overseas is to be a local practice wherever we go." Under their own assessment of their strengths and weaknesses, they selected the Persian Gulf states and opened a firm in Dubai in 1998. Peter Moriarty, the President of Burt Hill, said Dubai was a good base to work in the United Arab Emirates, Kuwait, Qatar, Oman, and other nearby countries.

He said the key to success there was to get a principal-level person to move there and make it happen. In 2005 a partner made this commitment, and 12 months later

Burt Hill had 200 people and three additional partners in Dubai. Once they had a real presence in Dubai, they rapidly became a firm of choice in the region. Clients saw they were there with leadership in place. This gave them a major competitive advantage over firms who had to fly in a team. To meet the need for a rapid buildup of staff, they hired from India, Pakistan, Korea, and other sources. It was difficult, but they found them. So, today, Burt Hill is one of the most successful firms in one of the busiest international markets. Pete Moriarty also made a final point about the value of being on the ground. He feels that because they are there and they see the clients regularly, "we get paid first."

Lessons learned

1. Burt Hill started with a realistic self-assessment and selected an international strategy that fit their strengths, weaknesses, and current operating model.
2. As Pete Moriarty noted, focusing on one region—rather than "hop scotching around the world chasing projects"—made it easier on their people. "Our people know where to go, when to go, and how to get there."
3. Success usually requires a leader's commitment and presence.
4. If there is a commitment to and presence in a market, it often makes it easier to overcome typical problems such as collections, client service, and recruitment.

Case Twelve: An Extended Visit—Stephen Forneris

Stephen Forneris received his master's degree in architecture from Syracuse University and then traveled to his then-wife's home country of Ecuador. Although he "could hardly imagine a developing nation would be able to support me," he immediately began making contacts that led to a first building. As he noted, "I returned to the U.S. ten years later having completed more than 35 buildings. I was involved in everything from high-end residential to low-income houses, clinics to hospitals, schools to office buildings, etc. I learned:

- How to look at the U.S. through the eyes of a non-American…
- That design is the smallest portion of the service…contracts, liability, building codes (or lack of them), construction administration, [etc.] all take on much larger weight in Latin America…
- That we may feel it is our design ability they want, but since they have wonderful designers it is design technology they truly want…
- That the most basic difference [from U.S. practice] is language, and I am not referring to Spanish and English. The language difficulties come in the form of building culture. We use the same words, draw plans, and think we understand each other, but we do not.
- That there are no up-to-date architectural texts in Spanish. No Graphic Standards, Time Saver Standards, AIA (equivalent) Contract Forms, Building Codes…
- To question everything."

After returning to the U.S., Forneris joined a large New York firm as a principal, and in 2005 helped the firm open an office in Ecuador, which in 2006 had seven employees.

Lessons learned

1. An entrepreneurial person, with appropriate skills, can often find interesting and challenging opportunities working in a foreign country. Many countries are short of these skills and can provide even a young architect with experience that is often not available in the U.S. or Canada.
2. Experience gained overseas can often be a stepping-stone to an accelerated career back in the U.S. or Canada.

Case Thirteen: Deciding to Stay—Charles Legler

Charles (Chuck) Legler grew up in Boulder City, Nevada; he went to architectural school and played basketball at Louisiana State University; he went to France to play professional basketball in the European leagues. As his basketball career wound down, he realized that he and his American wife wanted to stay. So, he opened a practice that focused on housing and resort design, based in the Provence region of France. The practice has prospered, and he continues to work in France as well as in a number of other countries. He recalled the sense of satisfaction and amazement he felt when he, "a boy from a small Nevada town who went to school in Louisiana—was sitting in Cannes receiving a major design award for a project he had designed in Turkey."

Lessons learned

As in the preceding case, North American training—and the right entrepreneurial skills—can be the formula for a successful practice, even in as unlikely a place as Provence, France.

Case Fourteen: Pursuing a Specific Lead—NBBJ

In a paper presented at a 1994 AIA Southeast Asia: Architectural Markets and Practice conference, three senior members of NBBJ (Daniel C. White, AIA; Neil Anderson, AIA; Ching-Ya Yeh) described their first entry into the Asian market:

> In the late 1980s, the then seven partners met and made a conscious decision to pursue international projects…They spent several months deciding how to divide up the globe into different spheres of responsibility…It was split so the Columbus office would be responsible for the Americas, Europe and the Middle East, while the Seattle office would handle all of the Pacific Rim. Within months, the

Columbus office was negotiating for our first project in Taiwan—so much for our strategic plan!

An architect native born in Taiwan, Ching-Ya Yeh, was employed in our Columbus office. While he had lived in the United States for over a decade, he was still a regular reader of the Taipei newspapers. In 1998, he read an article reporting on the need for a modern cancer hospital in Taiwan. Several points in the news story caught his interest. First, the article referenced a physician, originally from Taiwan, Dr. Andrew Huang, as the major force in promoting this idea on behalf of his homeland's welfare. Dr. Huang was reported to be associated with the Duke University Medical Center. Our firm had prior work experience with Duke University, and that experience provided an avenue to introduce ourselves to Dr. Huang. Additionally, Dr. Huang was interested in introducing and advancing the state-of-the-art for cancer treatment through this proposed facility. Our firm had recently completed a state-of-the-art cancer hospital for Ohio State University. A review of this article by Neil Anderson, the principal in charge of health care for NBBJ, and other related business, social, and cultural factors encouraged our employee to pursue this lead.

We proceeded to send an unsolicited letter to Dr. Huang at Duke University, inviting him to visit and tour this new medical facility in Columbus, Ohio. To our great pleasure, he readily accepted our invitation. His visit became the first in a long series of relationships that were key to the ultimate realization of this project. Personal relationships were vitally important throughout the project. Our offer to Dr. Huang was very low key and a very soft sell approach. We merely attempted to show him what we had done with this project and our areas of architectural specialization. In his trip touring the facility, he received many favorable comments from the staff on our firm's knowledge of this type of cancer facility and our ability to work with the client in developing both the program and the design. As a result of these initial contacts, Dr. Huang made a recommendation of our firm to Dr. C. F. Koo, and Jeffrey Koo. The Koo family was to be the sole sponsor of the new cancer center. It was brought to our attention that the Koo family was consistently ranked on the *Forbes'* list of billionaires. He urged their consideration of our qualifications, credentials and references. Dr. Huang also revealed to us that he was a nephew of Dr. C. F. Koo. This recommendation was key to our being considered as the architect for this project.

Lessons learned

1. A firm's foreign-born staff is often one of the most productive links to overseas opportunities.
2. Demonstrated expertise is often key to a successful project pursuit.

Case Fifteen: Personal Global Practices—Arquitectonica and Rafael Viñoly

Two large U.S.-based firms—Arquitectonica and Rafael Viñoly—have demonstrated that major, global practices can be built to support the design interests of the founders. Arquitectonica is a 400-person practice, based in Miami, with overseas offices in Lima, São Paolo, Buenos Aires, Hong Kong, Shanghai, Manila, Paris, and Madrid. Rafael Viñoly has a New York staff of approximately 150, with overseas offices in England and South America. Both firms have many projects around the world. In most cases, these projects came in because of the founders' design reputation.

What is hard to understand is that both firms are the personal extensions of their founders: the husband and wife team of Peruvian-born Bernardo Fort-Brescia and Laurinda Spear leads Arquitectonica, and Uruguayan-born Rafael Viñoly leads his firm. While both have strong supporting casts, the founders lead virtually all aspects of their practices from business development to design. In both cases, it involves record-setting airline mileage.

Lessons learned

It is possible for a centrally controlled firm to operate globally if the founders have the appetite and stamina required.

Fig. 2–08 (left): *Tokyo International Forum, Tokyo, Japan. Architect: Rafael Viñoly Architects PC. Photograph by Benny Chan/Fotoworks.*

Fig. 2–09 (right): *Le Meridien Cyberport Hotel, Hong Kong, China. Architects: Arquitectonica with Wong Tong & Partners. Photograph by Amral Imran/Arquitectonica.*

Case Sixteen: Been There, Done That—Polshek Partnership

Polshek Partnership Architects is the type of firm that could do work internationally if it wanted. With its high-profile work for a long list of major U.S. clients, it has the reputation and expertise to compete effectively for a wide variety of international projects. But after successful projects in France and Korea, the firm stopped pursuing work overseas. As Managing Partner Joseph Fleischer explained, "We are busy closer to home. In addition, most of the partners have young children, and the required travel would be a hardship."

Lessons learned
1. International practice is neither necessary nor of compelling interest for many firms.
2. For firms that have the option to work internationally, deciding to stay home requires discipline.

Case Seventeen: From Outsource to Full Service—FreemanWhite

FreemanWhite is a 220-person, 115-year-old consulting and design firm that specializes in healthcare. The firm is based in Charlotte, North Carolina, and has offices in Raleigh, North Carolina, San Diego, California, and London. In 2001 the firm set up an office in Trivandrum in southern India. According to FreemanWhite–president Alan Baldwin, the goals were to:

- Increase the talent pool of highly qualified professionals.
- Allow the firm to use the time difference to operate "two shifts."
- Provide support, in the short term, to the other FreemanWhite offices.
- Use the office, after the first few years, "to market the firm to India and the Pacific Rim."
- "Leverage salary differences for increased profitability and more production hours to increase quality of deliverables for our clients."
- Offer staff "the opportunity to experience working in a foreign country."

If they were going to outsource, they felt that it should be to their own staff who are trained to work the way FreemanWhite provides its services. They have worked to overcome the typical start-up problems, and now they have a growing office that is projected to double in size in 2007. In 2006 the firm produced 8 percent of its work product in India; it has been able to attract talented, hardworking professionals; and it has been able to develop a team with excellent production, building-information modeling, presentation, animation, and other services. Moreover, it has provided a base for successful marketing in the Persian Gulf and Pacific Rim.

Lessons learned

1. Building an outsource capability can be a cost-effective way to expand an international practice.
2. Once you are present in a region, other opportunities open up.
3. FreemanWhite's view that it is "one firm with multiple offices" is another indication of what globalization could mean for the North American design profession.

Case Eighteen: Blend Shoring—CAD Force

In 2001 Robert Vanech invested in an outsourcing start-up, CAD Force, based in California. Initially, CAD Force focused on drafting services that picked up red-lined drawings and did paper-to-CAD conversions. The incentive to use CAD Force for clients was that it offered to do the work for approximately 50 percent of the normal budget. The savings came, of course, from using overseas labor. CAD Force tried contracting teams in the Philippines, Sri Lanka, Russia, India, China, and Uruguay. They also considered teams in Argentina and Mexico. Today, in part because of overseas staff fluency in English, they have settled on four teams—totaling 125 people—in India managed by 30 employees in the U.S.

Vanech projects growth by 2007 to result in the staff growing to 70 in the U.S. and 250 to 400 overseas. At the time this book was written, they had 350 clients, including 310 architects, and 9 of the largest home builders. Vanech argues that they are not just an outsource or an offshore team. By combining U.S. and overseas staff, they offer "intelligent draftsmen" or "blend shore," meaning a blend of U.S. and off-shore capabilities according to Vanech. They tell their clients to "focus on the value-added tasks and they will take care of the repetitive ones." As is discussed in more detail on page 52, however, there are a large number of important management lessons to be learned in order to make this service a success. Robert Vanech openly discusses all of the lessons they learned—many by trial and error. As he says, "You can't just send the task off and expect it to be done correctly. Systems, technology, commitment to make it work at both ends, well-trained staff, communications, and many other factors are critical to success."(personal correspondence)

Lessons learned

1. The economics of outsourcing are compelling and will help drive the growth of this approach to construction documents (CDs) production and other tasks.
2. Successful outsourcing requires strong management at both ends.
3. Constant communication is essential.

Chapter 3
Running an International Practice

MANAGING AN INTERNATIONAL PRACTICE

Once a firm is committed to international practice, the principals must recognize that this commitment creates a whole new set of management challenges. Some of the lessons learned from running a multi-office practice, or even from managing projects in other states, are relevant to international practice—but they are not enough. International practice is very different from practice in the U.S. and Canada. Distances, language barriers, cultural issues, overseas practice costs, differing legal systems and tax codes, and dozens of other issues require special management responses. This chapter covers some of the most common issues as well as how firms manage them.

Models for Overseas Practice

One of the first questions facing a firm with a growing practice overseas is what to do in the home office and what should be done overseas. What follows are some of the typical choices.

- *Intermittent presence:* At the beginning of an international practice, most firms try to perform their services with home-office staff supplemented by foreign associate firms. As the firm's involvement in a country or region expands, this limited approach becomes expensive and a strain on home-office resources. Senior home-office personnel have to fly on short notice to cover even minor meetings. Moreover, lack of staff on the ground makes it hard to use inexpensive local resources or to respond in time to new project opportunities. This lack of a continuous local presence can be partially mitigated by having a local agent (who may be only a part-timer) represent the firm when home-office personnel are not in country. The agent typically provides the firm with a local address and help negotiating contracts, collecting bills, and logistical support.

- *Liaison or representative office:* The next step is a representative or liaison office. This limited commitment typically involves one principal or senior staff member transferred from the home office, supplemented by one or several local staff. This arrangement provides a continuous marketing presence and some limited ability to supervise local technical resources and to supplement home office services. For firms with centralized design or production structures, this may be as far as they want to go. Such a small commitment, however, still depends on home-office personnel to provide virtually all services and does not create the presence required for a long-term involvement in the country.

  A variation on this form of office has been referred to as the "fishing hole." The representative office is expected to catch fish to feed the home office(s). If, however, the representative is not seen to be senior enough or able to commit a knowledgeable home-office team with the relevant experience, this approach may have only limited effectiveness.

> **Typical Foreign-Office Models**
>
> - Intermittent presence
> - Liaison or representative office
> - Technical support office
> - Production office
> - Full-service office

- *Technical support office:* The next level of commitment involves hiring or sending enough technical staff to minimize the need for travel by home-office personnel. In China, for example, several firms have created low-cost offices to carry out the competition phase required by most major projects. This approach is dependent on procedures that facilitate multi-office participation in projects.
- *Production office:* Since foreign offices suffer from the same variations in workload that make domestic practice a constant challenge, some firms have started to ship production work to even out the work-load. We have done it with all of our offices, including Toronto. And firms, such as HLW International, have also made it a way to cut the cost of doing U.S. projects. As will be discussed later in this chapter, it is hard to recruit staff for and manage a pure production office. Most design professionals—even overseas—want more than a drafting job.
- *Full-service office:* Over time, many firms with long-term commitments to a country or region convert their foreign presence to full-service offices. This was the case with many of the large firms—SOM, KPF, HOK, RTKL, and others—that opened offices in London and elsewhere in Europe during the 1980s and 1990s. Today, most of the remaining offices are full service or the representative offices of a European regional office. Moreover, most of the staff in these offices are now local or at least European.

> "We have a three-pronged strategy to provide the best quality of service on projects and to clients around the world: First, we centralize talent in one location, Seattle, rather than distribute and dilute it across multiple offices around the world. That provides clients with the very best skill and team, no matter where the location of the projects. However, we do aggressively locate staff with clients and projects, as the specific needs require or economy or efficiency of work dictates. This gives clients access to the relevant skills—design, management, or construction review—as needed and when needed. Second, we are very proactive in building and using relationships with local firms to use their knowledge, talent, and cost-effectiveness in an integrated team for better client service. Because we are not focused on building a network of offices across the globe, we do not have a competitive attitude about local firms. We are able to invest in partnerships with them to increase local insight, improve communication with agencies and entitlement processes, share design knowledge, and improve our cost effectiveness. Finally, we take leading-edge approach to using technology and a 24-hour work schedule."
>
> *Bill Karst, AIA, Chief Executive Officer, Callison, Seattle, Washington*

Ten Home-Office Management Issues

Each of these models has a variety of implications for home office management. Ten of the most important include:

- *The involvement of the firm's senior leadership:* Most successful international practices are a reflection of the interest and involvement of the firm's senior leadership. Not only is their support important in terms of bringing in the first projects but also their protection is often required during the awkward early period when the office may not be profitable. As an international practice matures, a regular presence is still required for major presentations and other events where overseas clients expect to see the firm's leaders. These trips also help communications and the morale of the firm's overseas personnel.

Firms that send staff overseas without this support often have limited success. Therefore, if the senior leadership is not interested in maintaining an involvement with the overseas practice, they should probably rethink making any effort at all to do work overseas.

- *A mobile reserve:* A common issue for many firms is finding principals and senior personnel willing to go overseas. Midcareer professionals with children, and often with a working spouse, have a hard time leaving home and missing school plays, soccer practices, shared parenting duties, etc. Therefore, assembling a group of experienced professionals who are able to operate fairly independently overseas is a basic home-office management task.

Getting people to go to Europe, or even the more attractive parts of Asia, is relatively easy. Finding appropriate staff willing to go to the Middle East in the summer or Moscow in the winter is much more of a challenge. We have had to turn down more than one project because our people just did not want to go. Most firms with major overseas commitments are always looking for and recruiting those personnel who willingly travel on short notice and are able to function effectively in a strange new environment.

- *Language skills:* It is essential that someone in the home office have a good command of the language of any country where the firm is actively building or maintaining a practice. Late night phone calls from overseas, urgent e-mails, Requests for Proposals (RFPs) with short turnaround times and many other aspects of overseas communications must be fielded and managed by someone who reads and writes the language at a high level. Outside translators, which most of us use as well, can supplement this person or persons; but in-house foreign language–speaking staff members are very important.

- *Technology infrastructure:* The home office will find that it has to make a number of new technology investments in addition to the high-speed connections required for overseas communications. There will be new requirements for translation programs, enhanced firewalls to defend against foreign viruses, and software compatible with that of overseas associates, as well as many other new requirements. For example, as of 2006, our technology infrastructure, which supports our international practice, included:

- A wide range of communication devices and systems including international cell phones, video-conferencing equipment, digital cameras, web-conference capabilities, file transfer protocol (FTP) sites, and a reliable e-mail system.
- Access to high-speed Internet connections capable of transmitting large files.
- Portable hardware, including high-speed, fully loaded laptops, portable scanners and printers, memory sticks and flash drives, and other gadgets.
- Compatible software at both ends as well as protocols to manage the transmission of materials.
- Security systems and equipment to create a firewall between the home office and problems overseas.
- Software to facilitate special issues, such as the need to write using foreign alphabets or characters.
- And, most important, a tech-savvy person at both ends who is available

Ten Home-Office Management Issues

1. The involvement of the firm's senior leadership
2. A mobile reserve
3. Language skills
4. Technology infrastructure
5. Technical support
6. Financial management
7. Marketing support
8. Sales
9. Contracts
10. Special issues— travel management and staff health and safety

24/7 and who can make all of this equipment work.

In addition, as our information technology (IT) director noted, the technology support systems must address five key issues:

1. *Collaboration:* The ability to collaborate is "essential" and "crucial" to a successful effort in building an international practice. The technology platform must be planned and scheduled to support overseas locations. It must include "broadband facilities" linked to office VPN (Virtual Private Network) capabilities for full integration into enterprise IT infrastructure. The ability to transfer large data files among offices, "outposts," or an overseas staff member 24/7 is a basic requirement.
2. *Communication:* Communication measures need to be established, especially with staff. Full-time accessibility and support should be provided via remote access and related menus. VPN capabilities, e-mail accessibility, and wireless handles are needed. Communication protocols should be used to facilitate lines of communication.
3. *Homogeneity:* System standards need to be enforced and implemented. Standards should be used for all areas of the facility, from wide-area networking (WAN) to local-area networking (LAN) to desktop equipment. This includes users' desktop applications such as computer-aided design (CAD), graphics, and office software applications. In addition, the LAN environment and project-

data management must be standardized.
4. *Security:* Intrusion measures will also need to meet enterprise standards and be compliant. Intrusion-detection measures and equipment implementation will be required for internal and external threats to the enterprise as a whole. All new locations should be secure and not become a vulnerable opening in the firm's security system.
5. *Local expertise:* Finally, the realities of the local technical expertise and skills must be recognized and factored into the production process.

Since outsourcing is so dependent on reliable electronic communications, the investment also has to include the backup equipment and IT staff to keep the systems operational. Nothing is more frustrating than being unable to download a presentation that is due in 12 hours. Every firm using offshore resources has horror stories. For example, while in China preparing a major presentation, several of us found ourselves locked out of our server for an entire weekend. On Monday we found out that an IT staff member had been terminated, and all passwords had been changed. We were not amused, and the IT staff learned to notify overseas staff when there were potential problems with the technology lifeline.

- *Technical support:* In most parts of the world, the drawings will have to be in metrics, and many places expect all documentation to be in two languages. Over time, most firms find they also need to create a library of the architecture of the country, translations of the relevant codes, information on normal building techniques, information on consultants operating in the country, and sources for key materials. This library is an important asset to a core group of professionals who share their accumulated knowledge of how to do projects in the country. Few firms can afford to start from scratch on every international assignment.

- *Financial management support:* The firm's financial staff must establish banking relationships that facilitate wire transfers, letters of credit, and the other services needed to support overseas operations. In addition, someone will have to become skilled at managing the issues of payments in foreign currency, how to avoid losses due to currency fluctuation, tax minimization strategies, how to use nonconvertible currencies (such as the Chinese Yuan), tax issues facing staff based overseas, and dozens of other financial and accounting issues.

- *Marketing support:* Marketing staff will have to prepare support materials relevant to the sales effort in each country and proposals in two languages, as well as address many other new requirements. Many firms start by using their traditional domestic-marketing materials but soon learn that these have to be adapted for each country. What works in Chicago does not necessarily work in Dubai or Korea.

- *Sales:* Sales in many countries are highly dependent on personal relationships. Qualifications, presentation skills, and other factors are all important as well, but even more than in North America, establishing a personal connection with a client and/or a local associate firm can be the major determinant in the success of your international marketing efforts. This is one of the rea-

sons that the personal involvement of the firm's leadership is so important. Many firms use family connections of their staff, consultants who are already established in the country, friendships, and all of the other normal network-building techniques to start these relationships. In some countries, a local advisor or agent is a key door opener. Once in the door, however, the firm's next steps should be informed by an understanding of local customs and expectations. In China, for example, experienced firms joke that we could get any job we wanted if we could get the client's one child into an Ivy League school. On a more serious note, however, helping the families of clients, hosting them during their trips to the U.S., and presenting thoughtful (not necessarily elaborate) gifts can all be important. So can participation in, and enjoyment of, local customs. In China, and some other countries, many meetings include a meal and some involve drinking contests. After outlasting my Chinese hosts in one of these drinking contests one night, the chairman of the client group leaned over to my adviser and said, "I can work with this man!" Having an advisor who knows local customs is important. So is the adviser's background. An advisor who comes from the region, who has an upper-class background (even in a "classless" society like China), and who went to the right schools is far more likely to be effective. Finally, to compete internationally, a firm should invest in enhanced presentation skills. In many cases—and not just in the places that have a competition system—the visual impact of a good presentation is as important as the substance.

> "Once you've analyzed and targeted an area, send your most senior principal to meet and interview potential local alliance firms. Find firms that need your expertise to advance their business, market them, and have them looking for opportunities that work for the relationship in that country."
>
> *Rick Lincicome, Chief Executive Officer, Ellerbe Becket, Washington, D.C.*

- *Contracts:* International contract issues could fill a book, but experienced firms usually recommend the following 10 points:

  1. Develop standard contract forms in English and the other language to be used. This speeds the negotiation process and reduces the likelihood of differences between the English and the translated version, which is usually the governing version.
  2. Be far more detailed in defining the scope than would be typical in North America. This should include detail on each step of the process, the scale and type of each deliverable, the number of people who will attend each meeting, etc. Scope creep is one of the easiest ways to lose money on overseas projects.
  3. Be equally clear about the schedule assumptions. Again, an extended schedule can run up the cost of providing the service.
  4. Most contracts call for a retainer, and everyone tries to have the progress payments keep them ahead of their work. This is good advice but very hard to achieve.
  5. Be clear about the currency to be used and how it will be paid. More than one firm being paid in foreign currency has seen the fee erode due to currency fluctuations.
  6. Be sure you understand the tax issues. Most of us have had some unpleasant surprises in this area, but careful planning and a good contract can often minimize tax exposure.
  7. Get professional advice on key issues. Sometimes the agent or adviser can provide this; but if not, someone knowledgeable should be retained.
  8. Carefully budget travel and other expenses. In some countries, the clients expect these to be included in the fee.
  9. Carefully spell out the roles and responsibilities of any local firms working on the project. Most contracts should have a clear responsibility matrix that defines the role of each team member on each task.
  10. Build in a dispute-resolution procedure that will help avoid the use of legal remedies. Resorting to the courts in a foreign country is usually a waste of time and money.

- *Special issues:* Finally, the home office needs to deal with a number of other issues related to foreign travel, including:
  - *The management of air travel.* For firms who travel regularly to some countries, it is possible to negotiate favorable corporate rates for air travel, hotels, and other expenses. What is more, careful use of the Internet, consolidators, and special-fare offers can cut some travel costs by 30 to 50 percent.
  - *Having a plan for overseas health care issues,* including a plan for emergency evacuation to a place that can provide appropriate care.
  - *Creating a plan for other emergencies.* Most of us have known people who had to get out of Iran after the Shah fell or out of Kuwait when Iraq invaded. I have had staff jailed by mistake overseas and had to help them obtain their release. These events are hard to plan for; but at very least the firm should monitor events in the more volatile regions and make it clear that staff have the option to

leave by the first available means if they feel in danger.

Key Foreign-Office Responsibilities

The ten management issues defined above are usually the responsibility of the home office, but there are management issues that are common to most overseas offices as well. The ten most common follow:

- *Local staffing:* For most firms, local staffing begins with one or more staff sent out from the home office, supplemented by one or more local staff people. Both the expatriates and the locals need to be people who can operate effectively without a lot of structure and support, who integrate easily, and who help create the appropriate image. The manager of an overseas office has to see each transfer or local hire as an opportunity. There are usually some expats who talk a good game but are ineffective. On the other hand, most of the overseas managers I know have found one or two locals who through their energy, local knowledge, and connections rapidly become indispensable. Moreover, when you find good local knowledge, it is important to listen to it. One such person—hired to help set up a U.S. firm's London office—was ignored when she said that she should order such things as filing cabinets. The U.S. architect in charge wanted a "look" only to find out after installation of the imported files that European paper sizes do not fit in some North American cabinets.
- *Office location:* Another early decision is where to locate. Again, image may be important. In countries where the client is likely to come to the office, it

may be necessary to locate in a good downtown office building. In other countries, where clients are unlikely to visit, an address is all that matters. In our early years in China, we conducted most important client meetings on the concierge floor of our hotel while our local staff shared space with another firm in an inexpensive loft space. In Dubai, on the other hand, our choice was a space in a new development near the city center, because local registration required leasing space in a specified zone.

- *Staff training:* If the office is to become capable of providing production support for the home office or offices, a well-structured training program will be important. HLW International, which has one of the more successful technical support groups, had the advantage of having one of its New York technical partners decide that he wanted to go back home to Shanghai. His knowledge of the firm's procedures and projects as well as his ability to speak Chinese made him an ideal person to build a team in the new office. This team today not only supports projects in the U.S. but also strengthens the firm's ability to carry out major design assignments in China.
- *Quality control:* On many projects, the international design firm's role ends with the completion of schematic design. In others, design development completes the design firm's role. During these initial design phases, code analysis and some other key tasks are typically carried out by the local design firms working with the international design lead. The *AIA Handbook of Professional Practice* chapter on "Practicing in a Global Market" explains that:

Key Foreign-Office Responsibilities

- Local staffing
- Office location
- Staff training
- Quality control
- Building a local network
- Local intelligence
- Identifying local resources
- Managing the effectiveness of home-office staff visits
- Communications
- Staff support

"Basic knowledge of any of the three U.S. building codes will suffice for the design phases of international work…In most countries building codes are best interpreted by the client representative, joint venture architect, or contractor. Usually they are open to wide interpretation and special relationships" (Williams and Meyer 2001, p. 105). While this statement is often true, there are some serious exceptions. If a local firm or firms finish the documentation and oversee the construction, things do not always go right. What emerges often deviates significantly from the international firm's design intent. When the deviations are merely aesthetics, it can be embarrassing and upsetting. When they include serious compromises in building integrity and life safety, they can expose the international firm to significant liability. As architect Stephen Forneris noted:

I would submit that while most developing nations will correctly claim they have and use building codes, it can be clearly established they do not possess a building code culture. On closer examination, we will see that many employ only portions of two elements: a building code and building administration. Unfortunately even these are not sufficiently developed.

In the city of Guayaquil, Ecuador—population three million—where I worked for 10 years as a registered architect, I operated off a building code some 30 years old. This code, poorly translated from English to Spanish, contained only excerpts from just two of the 36 chapters of the complete book it was copied from. While legally constructing dozens of projects during that time, I was never once visited by a building inspector from the city, because there were none as we know them. So minimal was the building department staff that not one plan received a formal review of even the structural design. Obviously, a vigorous upgrade of the building code and the establishment of a rigorous inspection system were actions needed to improve building quality. However, the government's response was to pass a law exacting severe penalties, including prison, on anyone violating the existing building code. It was ironic that you could not obtain a copy of the code book because the government had ceased publishing it! (personal correspondence)

As he went on to comment on a building developed by a local firm from a U.S. firm's concept design that violated basic life safety and egress standards: "Who is to blame when people die—the locals for misusing, or not knowing how to use, [the U.S.] architect's plans, or is it the U.S. firm that gives them what they want and then does not question how it is used?"

Thus, the local office probably has a real obligation to see that the original intent and international best practices are followed.

• *Building a local network:* Once established, another important role for the local office is to build a network of local relationships. There is a tendency among some local managers to gravitate to other expats. Some of these relationships are important—in particular, if they help the new office learn how to operate in the country. Over time, however, local relationships are more important. For firms with a long-term commitment to a foreign location, the sooner the office becomes fully integrated into the country, the more likely it is to have long-term success.

- *Local intelligence:* One of the major benefits of a local office with a good network is the ability to find out information that is hard or impossible to get from a distance. Key marketing decisions—such as whether the competition is open or wired—are best answered locally.
- *Identifying local resources:* A key part of the local network are the local firms—architectural firms, engineers, renderers, printers, travel agents, etc.—who can help a firm carry out its projects. Over time these resources can also become a referral source for project leads and introductions to potential clients. In every country where we have worked, some of our next projects were referred to us by the firms who had been our local associates on initial assignments.
- *Maximizing the effectiveness of home-office staff visits:* The overseas office should also help make trips by home-office personnel efficient and enjoyable. Having someone who takes care of logistical support (e.g., hotel and air reservations, local transportation, clerical support, printing, scheduling of meetings, translation services, etc.) can double the effectiveness of a visitor. In our case, we also encourage local personnel to host meals, make visits to local landmarks, give shopping advice, and offer other things to make visits enjoyable. Overseas travel can be hard,

and we want those who have to do it to view their trip—at least, in part—as an enjoyable privilege.

- *Communications:* The overseas office also should play a strong role in establishing clear communications. As Stephen Kliment noted in his book *Writing for Design Professionals*, "Communications, whether in writing or by voice, are a critical component of success." To aid communications, he suggests the following:[1]

  - "Recruit the ideal employee—a local design professional trained in the United States or other English-speaking nation;
  - Vet all written material for potential misinterpretation of words, phrases and usage;
  - Become familiar with the host nation's culture and values;
  - Keep written material simple: eliminate pages, sections, paragraphs, sentences or words that don't contribute to the message and that could raise the odds on a gaffe finding its way into text;
  - Say it through drawing if possible."

  The overseas office should play a strong role in this by recruiting and managing translators, monitoring translated communications, and developing other quality-control measures.
- *Staff support:* Assisting the expatriate staff in dealing with the many challenges of an overseas assignment: affordable housing, schools for their children, local health care as well as emergency health-care resources, etc.

Firmwide Governance Issues

Opening a foreign office—in particular, a large, permanent one—can change the character of a firm. Peter Moriarty of Burt

Hill makes a point about the importance of the links between the home and overseas offices. He states: "We want them to be intimately tied to our U.S. practice because we want to:

- Use the U.S. for training expatriates and foreign hires so that they pick up the firm's culture and procedures;
- Have a specific place where expatriates can return after working overseas and feel welcome and appreciated with their careers still on track;
- Buffer the offices from peaks and valleys in the workload of offices both in the U.S. and overseas by making it easy to move work to where it is needed" (personal correspondence).

Achieving this requires strong links between the domestic and foreign offices. Peter Moriarty also shared some new firmwide issues raised by large overseas operations, for example:

- How to safely set fees when a "single percentage point on a billion dollar project is 10 million dollars in fee." The financial impact of an inadequately negotiated fee can be very serious.
- How to negotiate contracts that will be accepted by the teams who will have to carry them out, even with the often unreasonable schedule demands of many overseas projects.
- How to create a "one firm" culture.
- How to get the U.S. and foreign offices to work together on jointly staffed projects.
- How to limit the liability that could be incurred on one of the large overseas projects when they are expected to work at "a scale and pace that is unprecedented, with [recently hired staff],

on projects that are being built by contractors who are largely unknown to us, and who are similarly overworked."

- How to attract, hire and train quality staff.
- How to adjust the firmwide ownership and office structure to reflect the leadership of a large overseas office.
- How to create the next generation of homegrown leaders for the overseas office when the first generation wants to return to the U.S.
- How to encourage key U.S. staff to move overseas and when necessary to extend their time in the foreign office.
- How to judge when big is big enough and when another overseas office or a cap on office size is appropriate (personal correspondence).

The full management responsibilities of the home and overseas offices, as well as every possible firmwide issue raised, are beyond the scope of this book. Those listed above, however, are an introduction to some of the important reasons that international practice differs significantly from even a complex, multioffice domestic practice.

OUTSOURCING

Reasons to Consider Outsourcing

The design professions are not immune from globalization. The same economic forces that cause companies in other industries to move jobs overseas are beginning to impact architecture and engineering. At the time this book was written (2005–2007), only a few architects (but a much larger number of engineers) are having some of their domestic work done by foreign offices or services. There are also a growing number of companies offering drafting, performed by teams overseas, as a service. Most large firms, however, believe that this practice will accelerate for at least six reasons:

1. *Reduced cost*: In a field such as architecture, the opportunity to carry out required tasks at 20 to 50 percent of the usual cost is hard to ignore.
2. *Better use of more expensive and better-educated North American personnel:* Firms have come to recognize that using North American architects, with five to seven years of college and training, to do routine drafting is a poor use of such expensive training.
3. *Technology:* It is now possible for people on opposite sides of the world to work on the same drawings.
4. *Speed.* Experienced firms can send off marked-up drawings at the end of the day in New York and expect the corrected documents back on their computers the next morning.
5. *Availability of quality staff overseas:* In the field there is a chronic search for the most elusive of personnel: the trained intermediate architect with excellent drafting skills. Since my first years running an architectural firm, I have echoed my colleagues' common complaint that few, if any, are to be found. In China, India, the Philippines, Latin America, and Eastern Europe, however, there are many well-trained individuals—as well as entire firms—eager to fill this need.
6. *Evening out the domestic workload:* One of the most challenging management tasks of any firm is finding a way to accommodate spikes in the workload without overstaffing.

With all of these compelling reasons, why isn't it a more common practice? The simple answer is that it is not as easy to do as it might seem. In addition, there are a number of, as yet, unresolved issues to be addressed, including:

- Clarification of the licensing requirement that drawings be developed under the "responsible control" of the person sealing the documents.
- Security issues associated with non-citizens working on the development of documents—something prohibited by some clients.
- The impact of Building Information Modeling (BIM) and whether this more sophisticated tool can be successfully outsourced offshore.
- Whether any special insurance issues are raised.

Key Issues in Outsourcing

Many firms have experimented with outsourcing; but, as of 2007, only a few have made it work. As more and more firms focus on this issue, however, the procedures and management for successful outsourcing are being worked out. Among the issues to be dealt with are:

- *Plan:* As with so many aspects of international practice, the first step should be planned. This plan should clearly define the reasons for doing it, recognize the effort and expense that will be required, and address all of the issues raised in this chapter. The plan should also incorporate the advice of other firms who have already been using foreign resources for part of their workload. While most firms that use outsourcing have developed their own unique answers to the major issues, they all can provide advice that will shorten the learning curve.

Key Issues in Outsourcing

- Plan
- Continuity
- Management
- Technology
- Simplicity
- Standards
- Training and incentives for overseas staff
- Communications and face time
- Leadership at home and overseas
- Mitigation of home-office impacts

- *Continuity*: Few, if any, firms have made outsourcing work without a steady, continuous effort. Just finding a reliable source for overseas support can take time as well as trial and error. Once identified, the working relationship with that source—whether it is the firm's own staff in an overseas office or a subcontracting firm—requires time to mature. Outsourcing is not something that can be successfully done as an occasional way to deal with a temporary peak in the domestic workload.
- *Management*: Someone has to take on management of the effort. It is not something that can be done as an afterthought—even after the initial procedures have been worked out.

Robert Vanech, CEO of CAD Force, introduced on page 41, recounted some of the major lessons learned as they built their service: "You cannot just send drafting offshore. It has to go to a team that understands the goals and schedule. This takes committed, trained management and staff both in North America and overseas."

According to Vanech, some of the most important management lessons he has learned include:

1. "Language is a major barrier. This makes it harder to work with teams that are not fluent in English. Even if they speak English, you have to make sure they understand idioms.
2. Ongoing, continuous communications are essential. E-mail, chat rooms, web conferences, and even office visits are important. The overseas staff tend to say yes, because they are not comfortable saying no. Without constant communication, deadlines are missed and work has to be done over.
3. The commitment of the team sending work overseas is critical. If they want it to succeed, they can make it work. If they want it to fail, it will fail."

- *Technology*: Outsourcing typically requires a significant investment in technology. In our case, we have found that it is far more than a hardware and software issue, but the hardware and software are important. Most issues noted in the section on technology infrastructure (page 45) are relevant to outsourcing.
- *Simplicity*: Most firms, our own included, find that keeping it simple is important. For many of us this has meant selecting one building type as the focus of the outsourcing effort. In HLW, corporate interiors make up much of the work shipped to their Shanghai office for drafting support. For Kaplan McLaughlin Diaz (KMD), much of the work shipped to their Mexico City office related to their justice facilities. And for us, we worked out our outsourcing procedures by moving housing projects to our Toronto office.

By concentrating on one building type, we found that hiring and training overseas staff, managing the communications, and overseeing quality control were all easier. In an increasingly specialized world, even drafting support is facilitated by standards and procedures relevant to the requirements of a particular building type.

A growing number of firms also outsource specific tasks to overseas specialists. Those of us who work in China have all come to know the skilled (and inexpensive) companies that do computer renderings and animations. We now use them for U.S. projects as well. We typically provide the wire frame, elevations, and color palette and then edit the progress drawings or animations sent electronically at the end of the Chinese workday.

Still other firms are experimenting with drafting services set up to serve North American and European firms. This has the advantage of shifting much of the management and training burden to another company. Moreover, it is easier to cut off if the firm's domestic workload does not justify subcontracting work overseas. The disadvantages, however, include reduced control and the likelihood that sporadic use of the service will result in inferior communications, quality control, and service.

- *Standards*: Most firms find that standards are even more important for outsourced work than they are for most domestic projects. Layering, symbols, dimensioning, etc., need to be standardized to simplify communication (particularly in countries where English is not the first language) and quality control is uneven.
- *Training*: Again, training is often more important for successful outsourcing than it is in domestic practice. It is one of the ways to overcome the communications and technical barriers inherent in outsourcing. Experienced outsourcing firms and their overseas providers both stress the need to make a major investment in training. With the introduction of Building Information Modeling, this need is only growing.

It is also important to recognize that even overseas staff will rapidly burn out if all they are doing is picking up red-line markups or providing routine drafting. Retaining the best staff usually requires a mix of professional challenge and a sense of growth.

- *Communications and face time:* Electronic communications are rarely enough. For firms making a major commitment to outsourcing, face-to-face communications are often important. Video and web conferencing technologies are improving, but some communications are vastly improved when both parties are in the same place looking at the same drawing, sample, or document.

HLW even maintained an apartment in New York that was used by its Shanghai staff when they were brought over to work and train in the home office. This opportunity to travel to New York was both an incentive for the Chinese staff and a catalyst for improved communication.

Even when English is the common language, differences in training, culture, and vocabulary can cause problems that are more easily resolved in person. Having been in an English firm with partners from seven English-speaking countries, I was constantly reminded of George Bernard Shaw's famous quip: "Two peoples separated by a common language."

Face time also has one other intangible benefit. It can help integrate the overseas staff and make them feel part of a team. Many managers of outsource staff complain of high turnover, because their personnel feel no connection to the project or the North American project leadership. Richard Hayden of Swanke Hayden Connell commented on this issue as it impacted his Istanbul office. The Istanbul office's primary role is production support for the firm's European offices, but it also does some prime work in Turkey. Hayden noted: "We find that it is important for the staff to have a mix. It would be hard to keep them motivated if all they got to do was production for other offices."

- *Leadership at home and overseas:* One of the things we found to be essential was responsible leadership at both ends of the telephone. Someone at each end had to take responsibility for making the outsourced project successful. Moreover, the extent, as well as the limits of the outsourcing team's role, decision making, and design discretion must be clear. It is usually not possible to ship off a task and then forget about it until the overseas office completes it. One firm emphasized the importance of having home-office leadership who carefully package the work being sent and then followed up with careful monitoring of the work as it was being done. As Michael Jansen, president of Satellier, LLC, a leading offshore production firm, noted at the September 2006 AIA Roundtable on Offshore Outsourcing: "The project architect's ability as a design manager is critical. This includes the ability to organize the job, to divide up and assign tasks, and to manage quality control. At the same time, the overseas office has to have someone who takes ownership of the project and is committed to seeing it done right within whatever decision-making framework is set by the home office."

- *Mitigation of home-office impacts:* Outsourcing can have some significant impacts on the home office—some good and some problematic. If outsourcing becomes as widespread as some of us believe it will, there is a concern that many young architects and other design professionals in North America will never get the hands-on training that is a basic part of their apprenticeship today. Personally, I think that if younger staff can spend less time in front of a computer screen and more time doing research, seeing projects under construction and engaging in problem solving, they will learn more and faster. There will probably always be a need to communicate with drawings quickly and clearly, but the profession will not be harmed by a sharp reduction in the percentage of the total effort devoted to production versus design, problem solving, and presentation.

Moreover, in a field as competitive as the design professions, the growing use of outsourcing is likely to change the economics of practice. As was the case with the large productivity gains made possible by the computer, firms that were slow to convert found themselves at a distinct disadvantage.

One final note of caution. Outsourcing is also changing the economics of practice in countries providing the service. Architectural salaries in India have been rising at 18 percent per year due to overseas demand, according to Michael Jansen of Satellier. This means that some firms experimenting with this service have had to be flexible and to follow their providers as they look for new labor pools around the world.

CASE STUDIES

Four case studies will help illustrate how several firms are using outsourcing.

Case One: Perkins Eastman

While we believe that we will eventually outsource work to Asia, our outsourcing to our Shanghai office is limited to renderings, animations, and a few other tasks. Instead, we have been working on the procedures for outsourcing by shifting work between our offices. For us the goal has been to solve two chronic, design-firm, management problems: leveling the workload in each office and maximizing the gross profit margin on low-profit projects. Because our offices do not operate as competing profit centers, busy offices are strongly encouraged to move work to offices with spare capacity rather than hire additional staff. This significantly reduces the peaks and valleys that are a chronic problem in all offices. At the same time, we also try to move projects with tight fees—such as senior living and housing—to our lower-cost offices. For example, the combination of the exchange rate and the difference in salaries make it up to 40 percent less expensive to do part of a project in Toronto than it would be in New York. Together, the lessons we have learned are forming the foundation for more international outsourcing in the future.

Case Two: FreemanWhite (India)

FreemanWhite, a large Charlotte, North Carolina–based architectural firm that specializes in health care, decided to open an office in Trivandrum in southern India in 2001. They spent the next three years ramping up. They brought 20 of the local staff to the U.S. for training and sent U.S. and European-trained staff to the India office.

They established it on the "one-firm" model. In other words, the India office was fully integrated into the firm. As Alan Baldwin, president of FreemanWhite, noted, you can expect serious problems shipping work to a "third party with different values, standards, training, etc." In an AIA Roundtable on Outsourcing, Baldwin also noted that in his personal experience a number of issues that need to be addressed include:

1. "Assimilating the outsourcing entity as a fully integrated member of the project team.
2. Ongoing education of the outsourcing member relative to U.S. codes, building systems, and firm conventions.
3. Communications through a well-delineated protocol for giving directions and managing the outcome.
4. Developing a quality-control plan for the process of sending, producing, and returning work from offshore sites.
5. Meeting licensing requirements for being in "responsible control" for the production of documents" (AIA International Committee Offshore Outsourcing Roundtable Reader, September 15, 2006. Washington D.C.: AIA, 14-15).

FreemanWhite's plan to deal with these issues focused in part on training. Each professional is brought to the U.S. for three months of training, and some are making second trips. In addition, a minimum of two U.S. project managers spend time in the Indian office for three months (or more). All 110 in-house training courses are now offered in the Indian office.

The first five years were not without problems. They worked through some of the typical issues, including unclear communications ("same words, different meanings" and "poor or inadequate instructions from other offices"); learning curves for differences in construction systems, engineering systems, and codes; the education required to overcome cultural traditions ("to take initiative, to ask questions, to be assertive, to feel free to express oneself, etc."); and the initial reluctance of the other offices to use the Indian office.

Today, FreemanWhite's office has grown and matured. It plans to double its staff in India in 2007 and open a second office in Delhi. In addition to providing good, cost-effective production support, it is now a base that has made it possible for the firm to secure major health-care projects in India and the Pacific Rim.

Case Three: Swanke Hayden Connell and Belt Collins

Some firms have international offices that serve primarily as production support for other overseas offices. Belt Collins' Manila, Philippines office supports its Asian offices and Swanke Hayden Connell's Istanbul, Turkey, office supports its European offices.

Case Four: HLW International

HLW, a large New York–based architectural and engineering firm set up its office in China in 1994. It did this to follow up on the perceived opportunity of major projects during a slow period in the U.S. One of the other factors that facilitated this decision, however, was the HLW-partner J. C. Ru's desire to return to his original home, Shanghai. Ru was a partner responsible for technical production in the New York office. His presence in the new Shanghai office gave HLW a person who could communicate with both local staff and the North American offices. It also gave both offices someone with the experience to design and implement an effective outsourcing system. By 2005 the Shanghai office had grown to as many as 60—most of whom were providing production support for the U.S.

Chapter 4

Regional and Country Issues

This chapter introduces the opportunities and issues facing North American design professionals in countries in 10 regions of the world. Where there are special opportunities in individual countries in a region, the regional introduction is followed by expanded country summaries based on input by one or more North American firms active in that country. In a few cases, expanded coverage of countries that are significant markets were not included, since I was unable to find a reliable source on current conditions in those countries.

A cross section of major issues are covered for countries that have real or perceived potential for North American design firms. For the many other countries that are unlikely to offer many opportunities, only a brief summary is provided. In these limited reviews, there is a brief introduction to the country, an overall assessment of its potential as a market, a description of the languages used in the country, and an overview of the information technology and telecommunications infrastructure. These last two issues are included to give interested firms an indication of what it will take to operate effectively in the country.

In the most extensive reviews, some or all of the following twenty issues are covered:

- A review of the country's market: Unless indicated otherwise, the historical, population, and economic data is drawn from *The World Factbook*, an online resource regularly updated by the Central Intelligence Agency

(https://www.cia.gov/cia/publications/factbook/index.html). Most of the commentary, however, is based on my experience and the experiences of many colleagues in other firms.
- Reasons to be there
- Reasons to be cautious or to avoid particular countries
- Skills and capabilities that are important
- Who is operating there now?
- Who are the clients?
- What is the process for getting work?
- Languages and communications: Commentary on the telecommunications infrastructure in each country—an essential element in assessing the ability to work internationally these days—is primarily drawn from *The World Factbook*.
- Licensing and legal issues: The information in these sections was, unless otherwise indicated, initially drawn from the Web site of the National Council of Architectural Registration Boards' (NCARB)—www.ncarb.org—or the Collegi d'Arquitectes de Catalunya (Architects' Association of Catalonia, or COAC)—www.coac.net—in 2006 and 2007. The COAC, while representing architects of the Catalonia region of Spain, has collected information on its Web site related to practicing architecture in many countries. This information tends to change over time, and may not be current or available on the NCARB or COAC Web sites by the time of publication. Contact NCARB or the association of professional architects in a given country

Contents

Countries in bold receive longer descriptive sections.

directly for the latest time-sensitive information.

- Scope of services
- Fee levels, payment terms, and taxes
- Major contract issues
- Local resources
- Design issues
- Code and regulatory issues
- Typical schedules
- Local construction capabilities
- Personal safety and health issues
- Most common problems
- Key pieces of advice
- Sources of information: Architectural associations and other sources of information for each country are generally drawn from the Web sites of the National Council of Architectural Registration Boards, International Union of International Architects, the Collegi d'Arquitectes de Catalunya, and other regional architectural organizations. There is much more information on organizations and associations on these Web sites, but only information that could be independently verified (as of January 2007) is included here. As this information tends to change over time, some of the data may even be obsolete by the time of publication.

Many of these regional and country issues are illustrated with examples of projects designed by North American firms. As these projects demonstrate, some of the most challenging and exciting projects are overseas.

THE AMERICAS

According to the 2003 AIA survey, almost 30 percent of the U.S. firms working outside of the country work in the Americas. Countries in the western hemisphere have been divided into three groups: North America (Canada and Mexico), Latin America, and the Caribbean. Within these three groups are scores of countries and incredible diversity. North American firms have worked in virtually all of them, but only a minority have real potential for the foreseeable future. Thus, most of this chapter is devoted to the countries with significant opportunities for North American design firms.

North America

As the closest neighbors of the United States, Canada and Mexico should, in theory, be primary targets for any American firm considering working in a foreign country. The reality is far more complex. While many American firms are working in both countries, there are considerable barriers. As a result, the effort to be successful in either Canada or Mexico is

Table 4.1 North America Population and Economic Statistics[1]

Country	Population	Population Growth Rate (%)	GDP—Purchasing Power Parity*	GDP—Official Exchange Rate*	GDP—Per Capita ($)
Canada	33,099,000	0.88	1.165 trillion	1.089 trillion	35,200
Mexico	107,449,525	1.16	1.134 trillion	741.5	10,600

In billions of U.S. dollars unless otherwise noted.

comparable to that required in countries far more remote.

Canada

Canada is the United States' closest neighbor and ally, and it is easy to mistake its 10 provinces and three territories as just another set of states. It is, however, a foreign country, and all of the guidelines suggested in this book for approaching international work apply to Canada as well. As almost any Canadian client will tell you, Canada is not just an extension of the U.S.

Many U.S. firms work in Canada, but it is not a large market. Its 10 provinces and three territories can be divided into several distinct areas: the Maritimes (Nova Scotia, Newfoundland, Labrador, and Prince Edward Island, with a combined pop-

ulation of approximately 1,587,000); Quebec, with a population of approximately 7,637,000; Ontario (population approximately 12,631,000); the western provinces of Manitoba, Saskatchewan, Alberta, and British Columbia (with a combined population of approximately 9,793,000); and the lightly inhabited territories of Northwest Territories, Yukon Territory, and Nunavut with a combined population of approximately 103,000.[2] In recent years, most of the work for U.S. firms has been in Ontario and the western provinces; but there are occasional projects in Quebec and other provinces as well. In the 1970s, Montreal was the site of the Olympics and a World Fair, and it was a major destination for international architects.

Fig. 4–01: *Trillium Health Centre— Queensway Site, Betty Wallace Women's Health Center, Mississauga, Ontario, Canada. Architect: Perkins Eastman Black. Photograph by Ben Rahn/ A Frame Studio.*

The market

With a total population of 33,099,000, or about 11 percent of the U.S. population, Canada's architectural market is the equivalent to that of one or two of the larger states in the U.S. While not a large market by U.S. standards, there are many challenging projects that can be obtained by U.S. and other foreign firms. Federal, provincial, and local government play a more direct role in more building programs than is the case in the U.S. This fact, combined with the sharper policy changes inherent in parliamentary governments, often leads to the start or cancellation of large groups of architectural projects, such as hospitals, long-term care facilities and courthouses.

The government's large, direct role has also been a barrier to the involvement of U.S. firms. Many Canadians—and the government in particular—are not enthusiastic about shipping public funds south of the border. Moreover, there is more than enough nationalist sentiment to fuel a strong "buy Canadian" view on the part of many clients, and the exchange rate reinforces this view by making U.S. and other foreign design services relatively expensive.

In our case, we ran into this issue on a regular basis until we demonstrated that the work would be done primarily in our Toronto office by Canadian staff under the direction of Canadian principals. Only key specialists from the U.S. offices come in to reinforce the local teams.

There is also a second set of invisible barriers that impact where projects go. These are the long-standing issues between provinces and regions. The best known is, of course, the one between French Canada (Quebec) and the other, English-speaking provinces. Others relate to the view of some that Ontario plays too dominant a role—not unlike the view in the U.S. about the role of New York. And, of course, there are the Canadian design professionals. There are sophisticated firms with strong backgrounds and proven design talent for virtually every project type. During the 1980s real estate boom in the U.S., major Canadian developers, such as Olympia & York, Cadillac Fairview, and Trizec Hahn, brought many of these firms to the U.S. During that period, it is likely that more Canadians worked on U.S. architectural projects than U.S. architects were working on projects in Canada.

These and many other real issues present significant problems for U.S. firms seeking work in Canada. Nevertheless, many U.S. firms have successfully sought work north of the border, and some of us now have permanent offices there. In this highly developed, sophisticated country there are many interesting projects, and the clients for many of them are willing to cast a broad net when seeking the right design team.

Reasons to be there

There are a number of possible reasons for U.S. firms to seek work in Canada. Among the ones typically cited are the following:

- As with any major North American market, there is always room for another good firm. Moreover, U.S. firms with specialized expertise will find some of their best potential projects north of the border. For example, when Montreal's four major English-speaking medical institutions began planning a new, merged campus, virtually every North American health-care specialist pursued this huge project.
- Some firms have principals with personal ties. In our case, one of our founding principals, Mary-Jean Eastman, grew up and began her career in Montreal, and two of the others had helped lead a Toronto office for another firm early in our careers. Thus, Canada was a familiar and attractive place to work.
- Some firms acquire or build offices to serve particularly important clients.

HOK, for example, acquired a Toronto firm and built a large office around it, in large part to serve the large international building program of Nortel.
- Others, including Perkins & Will, acquired a Canadian firm (Busby in Vancouver and Victoria, British Columbia), both to open up project possibilities in Canada and to add a highly respected designer to the firm's overall leadership. More recently P&W acquired a second firm in Toronto. In an era of globalization, the search for talented leaders cannot be constrained by national boundaries.
- A few—ourselves included—regard Canada as a good place to work out the issues of international practice and cross-border teaming. We have found that we could shorten the learning curve on these common international practice issues by working with teams in a country with the great advantages of proximity, shared experiences, and easy communication.

Reasons to be cautious

The main reason to cautiously approach potential work in Canada is the complexity of working across any national boundary. In spite of the many similarities, Canada is a foreign country with significantly different laws, tax codes, professional procedures, and other complications. Moreover, the U.S.-Canadian exchange rate (in 2007) makes it hard for U.S. firms to be competitive. And, as noted earlier, there is no shortage of strong local competition for most projects. Thus, for most U.S. firms, Canada is a difficult market to penetrate. This tends to narrow the field of interested firms to those who have one or more of the motivations noted above.

Fig. 4–02: *University of Toronto Graduate Student Housing, Toronto, Canada. Architects: Morphosis with Stephen Teeple Architects Inc. Photograph by Tom Arban.*

Skills and capabilities that are important

For the most part, practice in Canada is similar to practice in the U.S. Thus, the same skills and capabilities are required for success in either country. Because of the things that are different, however, the following additional skills and capabilities may be important:

- Access to good legal and tax advice that understands the issues facing a foreign firm practicing in Canada.
- An appreciation of and sensitivity to the many things that are different about the built environment in Canada. The climate, regional factors, health-care delivery, education, justice system, building and other codes, and the importance of hockey. Many other factors are different, too, and these differences have a material impact on who Canadian clients will feel is an appropriate design team for their project.
- The ability to communicate easily in French is essential if one wants to work in Quebec.
- An understanding of the design issues related to the harsh winter climate in many parts of Canada.

Who is operating there now?

Many U.S. firms have done one or more projects in Canada. Moreover, a growing number of U.S. firms have acquired firms or established offices north of the border. As noted earlier, Perkins & Will (Busby Perkins & Will in Canada), HOK, Perkins

Eastman (Perkins Eastman Black in Canada), and Gensler (which maintains a project office in Calgary) are among the firms with established offices on both sides of the border.

Who are the clients?
In theory, U.S. firms should be able to compete for the full range of projects, but in reality firms based south of the border are usually limited to:

- Projects for developers seeking a particular firm's expertise
- Projects for institutions—such as medical centers—where specialized expertise is required
- Projects for international corporations

Most others—for the reasons noted above—are limited to Canadian firms or international firms with Canadian offices.

What is the process for getting work?
In most cases, the process in Canada is similar to that in the U.S. The main difference is the greater government interest in what is referred to there as 3P (Public Private Partnership) or AFP (Alternative Finance Procurement). In Canada this means either design-build-finance or design-build-finance-operate. This approach, which usually requires a very expensive developer or contractor-led proposal, is often subject to provincial governmental preferences and can change as soon as the government changes.

Languages and communications
French and English are the official languages in Canada. English is the primary language in most of Canada, but French is essential in Quebec. The telecommunications system, of course, meets modern standards.

Licensing and legal issues
A National Council of Architectural Registration Boards (NCARB)–certified U.S. architect can receive reciprocal registration in the major Canadian provinces. In addition, the major provinces also have reciprocity for Canadian architects—something that was not true in the past.

An explanation of licensing requirements in Canada can be found on the NCARB and Collegi d'Arquitectes de Catalunya (COAC) Web sites, and the requirements are detailed here:

- *Is a license required?* Yes. Any person, Canadian or foreign, needs to be registered or licensed to practice architecture in Canada. Registration, license, or a temporary license is required to offer or perform any service. In most provinces, a firm must hold a certificate of practice in addition to individual registration and licensing.
- *Licensing requirements:* A Canadian Architectural Certification Board Certificate recognizing a degree from an accredited Canadian university architecture program or approved equivalent education. A compulsory 5600 hours of approved work experience and completion of the Architect Registration Examination. And, in Quebec, licensing requires architects to demonstrate an ability to work in French. This requirement is not imposed by the architectural association but rather by a provincial government code that applies to all professionals employed in the province.
- *What agency licenses?* In each of Canada's 10 provinces, architectural licensing

is self-regulated by professional associations in accordance with legislative statutes enacted by the provincial government. The Northwest Territories and the Yukon Territories accept licensing from other jurisdictions.

- *What is the professional architectural organization?* Each province has a separate professional association. The professional association in each province is the licensing agency for its jurisdiction. Activities are coordinated by the Committee of Canadian Architectural Councils.
- *To practice, is a local representative required?* In order to practice in Canada, a foreign architect must have a license (or temporary license) or be associated with a local architectural practice and have liability insurance. In addition, there are special requirements that may vary by Province for U.S. firms that have an office in Canada.

Scope of services

Many projects follow the same programming—design, documentation, bidding and negotiation, and construction—service steps common to U.S. projects. As noted earlier, however, the major differences are often the result of provincial or national policy in Canada. In recent years, for example, there has been considerable government interest in "design, build, and finance" as well as "design, build, finance, and operate" approaches to major public projects such as hospitals. Changes in government can also result in radical changes in approach. Finally, the greater influence of government policy and/or financing often leads to significant gaps in project schedules. It is common for such projects to stop for a year or more, more than once, while waiting for government approvals.

Fee levels, payment terms, and taxes

One of the major barriers to entry in Canada is the exchange rate. At the end of 2006, the Canadian dollar stood at 0.8586 to the U.S. dollar. As a result, even though Canadian fees would be comparable to U.S. fees if the two dollars were of equal value, the exchange rate makes it hard for U.S. firms to be cost competitive.

Fig. 4–03: *Lester B. Pearson International Airport, Toronto, Canada. Architects: Joint venture with Moshe Safdie & Associates and Skidmore, Owings & Merrill. Photograph by Timothy Hursley.*

If this major issue can be overcome, fees, contracts and payment terms are similar to those in the U.S. Taxes, however, vary considerably from the U.S. approach. The differences are far too complex to cover here, and any firm considering working in Canada should get good, professional tax advice.

Major contract issues

Other than coverage of responsibility for any additional tax liabilities, most of the contract negotiation issues are the same as those in the U.S.

Local resources

The major cities of Canada have virtually the same technical resources that can be found in the U.S. One major difference is that Canada has architectural technologists in addition to architects. The technologists provide a pool of technically competent staff.

Design issues

Again—although many Canadians might want to disagree—it is hard to find a real difference in design traditions or preferences between the northern U.S. and Canada. One area where there is some difference, however, is in a greater recognition of the severity of winter weather in most provinces.

Code and regulatory issues

There is a national building code, but some codes vary by province, and even from city to city. Most, however, are comparable to U.S. codes. There are some subtle differences though—accessibility standards, for example, can be more stringent than U.S. codes in some areas but

Fig. 4–04: *Toronto 2015 World Exposition, Toronto, Canada. Architect: Perkins Eastman Black. Courtesy of Perkins Eastman.*

less so in others. In housing, some issues—such as a kitchen exhaust—also differ from U.S. practice. The differences, therefore, make it important for any work in Canada by a U.S. firm to be preceded by a careful code analysis.

Typical schedules

As noted above, privately sponsored projects are likely to follow schedules similar to their U.S. counterparts. Government financed or sponsored projects, however, are likely to take far longer.

Local construction capabilities

Canada has sophisticated construction capabilities and, therefore, it is possible to build virtually any building type.

Personal safety and health issues

Other than the increased likelihood of frostbite, Canada is one of the safest places to live and work in the world.

Sources of information

U.S. Embassy, Canada
Telephone: 1-613-238-5335
E-mail: web@usembassycanada.gov
Web site: http://ottawa.usembassy.gov

Alberta Association of Architects
Telephone: 1-780-432-0224
E-mail: info@aaa.ab.ca
Web site: www.aaa.ab.ca

Architects Association of
 Prince Edward Island
Telephone: 1-902-566-3699
E-mail: info@aapei.com
Web site: www.aapei.com

Architects' Association of New
Brunswick
Telephone: 1-506-433-5811
E-mail: inquiries@aanb.org
Web site: www.aanb.org

Architectural Institute of
 British Columbia
Telephone: 1-604-683-8588
E-mail: info@aibc.ca
Web site: www.aibc.ca

Canadian Architectural Certification
Board (CACB)
Telephone: 1-613-241-8399
E-mail: info@cacb.ca
Web site: www.cacb.ca

Manitoba Association of Architects
Telephone: 1-204-925-4620
E-mail: info@mbarchitects.com
Web site: www.mbarchitects.org

Newfoundland Association of Architects
Telephone: 1-709-726-8550
E-mail: naa@warp.nfld.net
Web site:
 www.newfoundlandarchitects.com

Nova Scotia Association of Architects
Telephone: 1-902-423-7607
E-mail: info@nsaa.ns.ca
Web site: www.nsaa.ns.ca

Ontario Association of Architects
Telephone: 1-416-449-6898
E-mail: oaamail@oaa.on.ca
Web site: www.oaa.on.ca

Ordre des Architectes du Quebec
Telephone: 1-514-937-6168
E-mail: info@oaq.com
Web site: www.oaq.com

Royal Architectural Institute of Canada
Telephone: 1-613-241-3600
E-mail: info@raic.org
Web site: www.raic.org

Saskatchewan Association of Architects
Telephone: 1-306-242-0733
E-mail: saa@link.ca
Web site: www.saskarchitects.com

Mexico

Mexico and the United States have a complex relationship. The implementation of the North American Free Trade Agreement (NAFTA) in 1994 has accelerated the economic interrelationships between the three North American economies, and millions of Mexican citizens work in the U.S. Nevertheless, there have been over 160 years of periodic conflict—including the United States' annexation of northern Mexico to create Arizona, New Mexico, Nevada, Utah, part of Colorado and California, and indirectly Texas. More recently much of the friction is related to Mexico's continuing efforts to avoid domination by its large neighbor.

Mexico is a large country with a population of over 106 million and an economy with a gross domestic product (GDP) that now exceeds $1 trillion. Per capita income is now one-fourth that of the U.S., but income distribution is highly unequal. It suffered through a severe economic crisis in 1994 but has recovered and is growing steadily again.

As in many developing countries, there has been a rapid shift of population from rural areas into the major cities. The metropolitan area around Mexico City, the capital, has grown from 3,145,000 in 1950[3] to over 19,230,000 in 2005.[4] While Mexico has large numbers of both rural and urban poor, it also has large numbers of highly educated professionals. Mexico also has a rich culture, which regularly produces world leaders in architecture and the arts. Many have worked both in Mexico and internationally.

At the same time, design professionals from the U.S. and Canada regularly work in Mexico, and a growing number of firms have established offices there. Most of those who have worked in Mexico believe that the cross-border involvement of design professions will grow in the future.

The market

Mexico is a large market for U.S.-design firms, if they can overcome the relatively high cost of services from north of the border. Some firms (Kaplan McLaughlin Diaz, HKS, HOK, and others) have dealt with this issue by opening offices in Mexico City. Others—our firm included—have dealt with it by limiting our services

Fig. 4–05: *W Hotel, Mexico City, Mexico. Architect: Kaplan McLaughlin Diaz (KMD). Photograph by Gordoa Photography.*

to planning and schematic design. In any event, Mexico is a large nearby country with clients that regularly commission major projects in a wide variety of building types. There can be many frustrations working in Mexico, but it will continue to be an important market for North American architects.

The government and the economy are stable. Tourism is strong and foreign companies are establishing operations in Mexico. High-end residential and Class A–office demand has been strong as well. Thus, the outlook in 2007, to quote the head of one of the U.S. firms based in Mexico, "is good."

Reasons to be there
Among the many reasons to consider Mexico are the following:

1. It is nearby and shares time zones with the rest of North America.
2. It is a large economy, and clients (including many clients based in the U.S. and Canada) want U.S. expertise and regularly commission major projects.
3. It is an excellent location to experiment with outsourcing through a local subsidiary.
4. There are large numbers of talented design professionals available as local associates or staff.
5. It is a beautiful and culturally rich country with a fascinating history.
6. In spite of the long, difficult relationship between the U.S. and Mexico, the two countries are closely linked. NAFTA has made it somewhat easier for Americans and Canadians to work there.
7. It is a country where design excellence is possible.
8. As noted by Federico Bernal of AKF's Mexico City office, "a presence in

Mexico is beneficial for work in Latin America."

Reasons to be cautious
1. It is a low-cost country, where it is hard to be competitive using U.S. or Canadian staff.
2. Sending profits North is usually not a productive strategy, due to the exchange rate.
3. Government policies—including tax policy—have often been hard to understand and manage.
4. Crime, particularly in Mexico City, has become a serious personal safety issue.
5. Corruption can also be a problem for firms trying to operate in the country.
6. Federico Bernal notes that: "The Mexican market generally mirrors the U.S. market but is not as strong. When the U.S. economy is down, it seems to hit Mexico a little bit harder." (personal correspondence)

Skills and capabilities that are important
Among the important skills and capabilities are:

1. The ability to conduct business in Spanish. The educated classes often speak English, but fluency in Spanish is essential for many project and business operations.
2. Staff and/or local associates and advisers who understand how to do business in Mexico.
3. Skills and experience that are demonstrably different than those offered by Mexican professionals.
4. The ability to invest the time and resources to build productive relationships in Mexico—although Mexico is close enough to do only an occasional project.

Who is operating there now?

As noted earlier, a number of major firms have established offices in Mexico. In addition, many others are doing one or more projects.

Who are the clients?

U.S. and Canadian architects have designed a wide variety of projects in Mexico. While I was in college in the 1960s, my father's firm, Perkins & Will, was designing one of its most successful projects—a major expansion of the agriculture university at Chapingo, near Mexico City. Currently, U.S. and Canadian firms are engaged in projects ranging from major beach resort developments to office interiors for international corporations. There is a lot of international investment in Mexico. Most international financial institutions, for example, have operations in Mexico and many like to use U.S. firms for their design needs. The same is true of many of the international hotel chains. And U.S. expertise is often in demand for high-end residential, health-care, and technically complex projects. As noted earlier, if a firm has good local contacts and the ability to be cost competitive, a wide range of projects are potential commissions.

What is the process for getting work?

For some U.S. and Canadian firms, the selection process is likely to be qualifications-based and similar to the selection process in their home markets. For others, however, the process is less formal. As one principal stated: "Work is obtained by cultivating personal relationships. This is very important in Mexico. The introduction meetings are primarily social and a trust needs to be developed before you start working together."

Languages and communications

Spanish is the national language, but various Mayan and other Amerindian languages are spoken by parts of the population. English is widely spoken or understood by the educated classes, but according to Federico Bernal, "to be successful the principals and senior staff in Mexico should be bilingual." The telecommunications infrastructure is adequate for business, but overall it still needs extensive expansion and modernization.

Licensing and legal issues

Foreign firms working in Mexico must hire a local, licensed professional firm to file design documents. Licensing requirements are as follows:

- *Is a license required?* Yes.
- *Licensing requirements:* A degree and both a written and oral examination are required.
- *What agency licenses:* Secretariat for Public Education Direccion General de Profesiones.
- *What is the professional architectural organization?* Colegio de Arquitectos de la Ciudad de Mexico, A.C.
- *To practice, is a local representative required?* A foreign architect may practice independently if an accord of mutual recognition is signed between Mexico and the country of origin— e.g., NAFTA.

Scope of services

As noted earlier, many firms only provide planning and design, leaving documentation, local approvals, and construction phase services to local associates. Firms with offices in Mexico, however, do provide full services.

Fig. 4–06: *Villa de Macharro,
Baja, Mexico. Architect: Perkins
Eastman. Courtesy of Perkins
Eastman.*

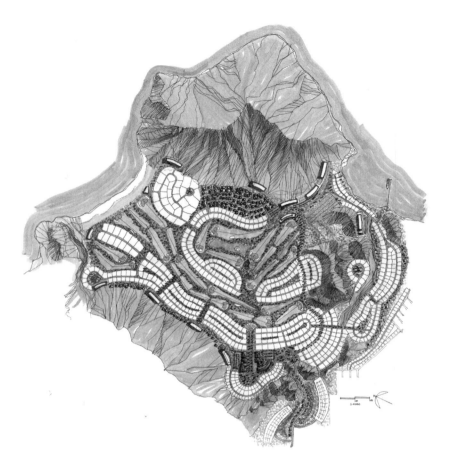

Fee levels, payment terms, and taxes

Each Colegio de Arquitectos has specific fees for the services offered by architects, but fee levels are often only 50 to 70 percent of U.S. norms. Except in the early phases, it is hard to compete for work using U.S. or Canadian staff. There is a value-added tax (VAT) of 15 percent on fees, which is typically passed on to clients. Corporate profits are taxed at 40 percent, and there is a 36 percent social-security tax on labor.

Major contract issues

All of the recommendations in Chapter 2 apply if the client is a Mexican national. If the client is from the U.S. or is Canadian, the contract issues are the same as in the U.S. and Canada. Again, as reported by AKF's Federico Bernal, "other than price, scope of work, and reimbursable expenses, contracts are fairly straightforward."

Local resources

Capable local associates, consultants, and support resources exist in the major cities; but care should be taken in their selection. The quality is uneven.

Design issues

Mexico has strong design traditions (often forgotten) that have been shaped by the

Fig. 4–07: *Valeo Electrical Systems, San Luis Potosí, Mexico. Architects: Davis Brody Bond with Aedas. Photograph by Héctor Velasco Facio.*

hot, dry climate, and local construction capabilities. Most, major buildings are concrete or steel structures. Much of this country's best design work is based on modern adaptations of its rich architectural heritage.

Code and regulatory issues

A uniform, countrywide building code does not exist. Each city has its own code and regulations. Many of the higher profile projects will voluntarily follow the IBC (International Building Code), NFPA (National Fire Protection Association), NEC (National Electric Code), and ASHRAE (American Society of Heating, Refrigerating, and Air-Conditioning Engineers)—all of which tend to be more stringent than the local codes.

Typical schedules

Project schedules are roughly comparable to those north of the border.

Local construction capabilities

There is a large construction industry, but much of it is less sophisticated than U.S. firms. As a result, it is often necessary for design teams to show much more detail if they want to get the intended result in the field. Some U.S. construction managers are now operating in Mexico.

Personal safety and health issues

Normal dietary precautions (e.g., bottled water, etc.) need to be observed. In addition, Mexico City's high altitude bothers many. And, as noted earlier, violent crime is a serious issue in Mexico City and some other parts of the country.

Sources of information

U.S. Embassy, Mexico
Telephone: 52-55-5080-2000
E-mail: embeuamx@state.gov
Web site: www.usembassy-
    mexico.gov/emenu.html

Colegio de Arquitectos de la Ciudad
    de Mexico, A.C.
Telephone: 52-55-700-007
E-mail: contacto@arquired.com.mx
Web site: www.arquired.com.mx

Dirección General de Profesiones
    en Mexico, D.F.
Telephone: 52-55-509-000
Web site:
www.sep.gob.mx/wb2/sep/sep_3766_
    direccion_general_de

La Federacion de Colegios de
    Arquitectos de la Republica Mexicana
Telephone: 52-55-550-6049
E-mail: presidencia@fcarm.org.mx
Web site: www.fcarm.org.mx

The Caribbean and Island Nations of the Western Atlantic

The AIA firm surveys in 2000 and 2006 noted that the many countries in the Caribbean were one of the major markets for U.S. architects in spite of this regions' small population and limited economies.

The island nations and territories that lie south and east of the United States include:

- Bermuda
- The Bahamas and Turks and Caicos Islands
- The Greater Antilles:
  - Cuba, Jamaica, Haiti, Dominican Republic, Puerto Rico, and Cayman Islands
- The Lesser Antilles:
  - The Leeward Islands: The Virgin Islands, Netherland Antilles, Anguilla, St. Maarten, Antigua and Barbuda, Saint Kitts-Nevis, Montserrat, Guadeloupe, and Dominica
  - The Windward Islands: Martinique, Barbados, Saint Lucia, Saint Vincent and the Grenadines, Grenada, Trinidad and Tobago
- Aruba and the Netherland Antilles

Most are former (and a few remain) British, French, Spanish, or Dutch colonies. However, there are strong U.S. and Canadian ties to most of these countries. Because of their proximity to North America, American and Canadian design firms have a long involvement in this region. A large part of the islands' extensive tourism facilities, as well as many of the airports, hospitals, and other major buildings, were planned and designed in North America.

Puerto Rico and the U.S. Virgin Islands, both self-governing Caribbean states, are not covered, since they are U.S. territories. They have special economic conditions and local regulations that put some limits on the use of outside design professionals, but, in general, the differences do not justify covering them in this book.

Many of these islands are very small and relatively poor. There are occasional tourism developments and other projects funded by offshore investors or international aid organizations. Other islands are substantial and have diverse economies that can generate demand for North American design services. Therefore, this section provides only brief introductions to the smaller and poorer countries and colonies but provides expanded coverage of the more important potential markets for North American design services.

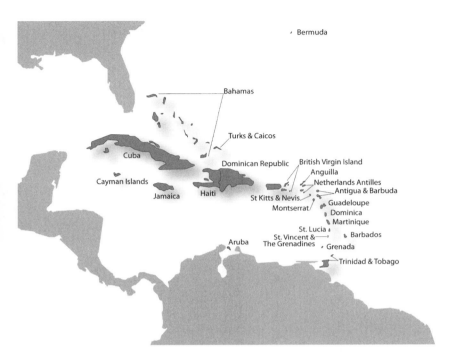

Map labels: Bermuda, Bahamas, Turks & Caicos, Cuba, Cayman Islands, Jamaica, Haiti, Dominican Republic, British Virgin Island, Anguilla, Netherlands Antilles, Antigua & Barbuda, St Kitts & Nevis, Montserrat, Guadeloupe, Dominica, Martinique, St. Lucia, St. Vincent & The Grenadines, Barbados, Grenada, Aruba, Trinidad & Tobago

Anguilla

Following a revolt in the 1960s, Anguilla separated from Saint Kitts-Nevis and became a separate British dependency in 1980. This tiny (population 13,500) territory is heavily dependent on tourism and a small but growing offshore-banking sector.

The market

There are occasional tourism-related projects.

Languages and communications

English is the official language.

Antigua and Barbuda

These islands became an independent state within the British Commonwealth in 1981. Tourism accounts for more than half of the GDP, but this sector has slowed in recent years.

The market

There are occasional projects in the tourism sector.

Languages and communications

English is the official language.

Aruba

Aruba seceded from the Netherland Antilles in 1986 and became a separate autonomous member of the Kingdom of the Netherlands. The economy is stable and relatively prosperous. Tourism is the main economic sector but offshore banking and oil refining and storage are also important. Most of the growing tourism comes from the U.S.

The market

The main design opportunities are in hotel design and related tourism projects.

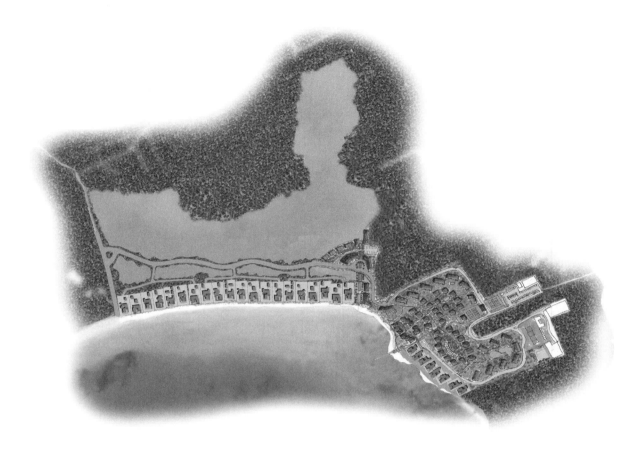

Fig. 4–08: *Rendezvous Bay, Anguilla, British West Indies. Architect: Perkins Eastman. Courtesy of Perkins Eastman.*

Languages and communications

Dutch is the official language, but English and the dialect Papiamento are widely spoken.

Bahamas

The Bahamas became a British colony in 1783 and independent in 1973. The country has prospered through tourism, international banking, and investment management. The Commonwealth of the Bahamas is an archipelago of 700 islands and cays with a population of about 310,000; over half its population is concentrated on the island of New Providence, where Nassau, the capital, is located. Most of the 700 islands have little or no habitation. Population settlements, in addition to those in New Providence and Grand Bahama, where Freeport (the second largest city) is located, are concentrated in Eleuthera, Andros, Abaco, Bimini, Cat Island, San Salvador, Acklins, Exuma, Crooked Island, Long Island, and Mayaguana. The population is 85 percent black, 12 percent Caucasian, and 3 percent Asian and Hispanic. The climate is subtropical, which is significantly moderated by the waters of the Gulf Stream, particularly in winter.

The Bahamas, as a former British crown colony, remains a member of the Com-

Table 4.2 Caribbean Population and Economic Statistics[5]

Country	Population	Population Growth Rate (%)	GDP—Purchasing Power Parity*	GDP—Official Exchange Rate*	GDP— Per Capita ($)
Anguilla	13,000	1.57	0.1	0.1	8,800
Antigua and Barbuda	69,000	0.55	0.8	0.9	11,000
Aruba	72,000	0.44	2.2	2.2	21,800
The Bahamas	304,000	0.64	6.4	6.1	21,300
Barbados	280,000	0.37	5.1	3.1	18,200
Bermuda	66,000	0.61	4.5	N/A	70,000
British Virgin Islands	23,000	1.97	0.9	0.8	38,500
Cayman Islands	45,000	2.56	1.9	N/A	43,800
Cuba	11,383,000	0.31	44.5	40	3,900
Dominica	69,000	-0.08	0.4	0.2	3,800
Dominican Republic	9,184,000	1.47	73.7	19.9	8,000
Grenada	90,000	0.26	0.4	0.4	3,900
Guadeloupe	453,000	0.88	3.5	N/A	7,900
Haiti	8,309,000	2.3	14.5	5.9	1,800
Jamaica	2,758,000	0.8	12.7	8.5	4,600
Martinique	436,000	0.72	6.1	N/A	14,400
Montserrat	9,000	1.05	N/A	N/A	3,400
Netherlands Antilles	222,000	0.79	2.8	N/A	16,000
Saint Kitts-Nevis	39,000	0.5	0.3	0.4	8,200
Saint Lucia	168,000	1.29	0.8	0.8	4,800
Saint Vincent and the Grenadines	118,000	0.26	0.3	0.4	3,600
Trinidad and Tobago	1,066,000	-0.87	21	15	19,700
Turks and Caicos Islands	21,000	2.82	0.2	N/A	11,500

monwealth of Nations. The government is a multiparty, constitutional democracy, and it has a parliament with an elected assembly and an appointed senate. The country is governed by a cabinet headed by a prime minister; elections are held every five years.

The market

The country is a stable, developing nation with an economy heavily dependent on tourism and offshore banking and insurance. Tourism accounts for more than 60 percent of the GDP of $6.4 billion, with about 80 percent of the visitors coming from the United States. Directly or indirectly, tourism employs almost half of the labor force. Steady growth in tourism, strongly endorsed by the government, has led to a boom in the development of new hotels, resorts, and residences in recent years.

Reasons to be there

In addition to being able to design in the Caribbean, which has a charm of its own, most of the work that attracts foreign architects is either private residences for very well-off clients or large hospitality-centered developments. In both instances, commissions are often for repeat clients with whom the architect has an established relationship. Or the commission is for a major project within an area of market specialty of the architect, and it is important to secure the job to enhance or maintain the architect's reputation in that market sector.

Reasons to be cautious

Before starting a project, it is good to check that there are no major political or approval obstacles that will prevent the project from being implemented and that, if the approvals are in hand, adequate financing is available to execute the project. Financing mechanisms in the Bahamas tend to be less formal than those in North America, and it is often difficult to determine whether a project is real. The risks of working in the Bahama are comparable to the risks in North America. If the client is an international hotel developer, contractual and other issues generally do not change just because the project is located in the Bahamas. If the client is a Bahamian development group, issues of timely payment can become a problem. Lawsuits for payment filed in Bahamian courts tend to favor Bahamians, thus making collections difficult to enforce.

In selecting a local associate architect, care needs to be taken to ensure that real value will be received for the fee and that the contract documents are not just rubber stamped. It is important to develop a scope of work that corresponds to a level of effort justified by the local architect's fee.

Skills and capabilities that are important

For large hospitality-related projects, knowledge of the issues related to design for that market sector are the same as elsewhere. The main local ingredient is sensitivity to infrastructure requirements that are often scarce or unavailable—particularly water supply and sanitary waste-disposal facilities. For large projects, the selection of a Bahamian architect who can review and certify that the contract documents comply with Bahamian codes is important. In addition to the professional skills of the local architect selected, it is helpful if that person or firm has a positive relationship with the government.

For private residences, it is important to establish a relationship with a Bahamian architect who can assist with securing local approvals, selecting a contractor, and assisting during construction administration.

Who is operating there now?

Alexiou and Associates, a Bahamian firm, has an association with OBM, a Bermuda-based architectural practice located with offices in the Caribbean and Florida. There are no North American firms with offices located in the Bahamas, but among the firms that have done work in the Bahamas are Wimberly, Allison, Tong & Goo (WATG) on the Atlantis Hotel and Casino; MHA Studio for the new BahaMar hotel and casino resort being developed at Cable Beach in New Providence; Stantec, who have designed an airport; and Hillier, who are currently working on another large resort.

Who are the clients?

There are several market areas for which foreign firms might be considered; however, most firms are exclusively retained for hospitality-related developments, including hotels and resorts, casinos, and associated uses. Since the Bahamas is also a place of residence for the rich and famous, partly because it levies no personal income tax or estate tax, there are opportunities to design private residences, usually located in gated communities such as Lyford Cay on New Providence or as private estates on the various islands that make up the country.

Other projects, while appropriate for foreign architects, such as buildings to house offshore insurance and banking facilities, airport terminals and government buildings, are usually designed by local architects. Should a major replacement for the Princess Margaret Hospital in Nassau ever proceed, this specialist facility would most likely need to be designed by a foreign architect contracted by the government.

Among the major hotel developers or operators currently in the Bahamas or planning resorts in the near future are Wyndham, Club Med, Kerzner International (operating the 2,300-room Atlantis hotel and casino), Hilton, Radisson, Comfort Suites, Best Western, Sandals, Amanresorts, and Starwood. In addition to the large resorts in New Providence and Paradise Island, smaller, more exclusive developments are now taking place in Exuma, Eleuthera, the Abacos and Bimini.

What is the process for getting work?
Generally, most developer clients that hire foreign architects are non-Bahamians, though Bahamians may have a financial interest. A limited number of projects, however, are exclusively developed by Bahamians. For those projects that are Bahamian developed, by either the private or public sector, advance knowledge

of the project and local contacts can be critically important. For projects developed by international entities, either a prior contact with the entity or an established reputation in the market sector is essential to receive a request for proposal.

Languages and communications
English is the official language and is spoken by all. Internet capabilities are improving, making electronic communication and transmittal of drawings and other documents comparable to, though not as seamless as, North America.

Licensing and legal issues
Architects are now required to be locally licensed in order to practice. However, if not licensed, a locally licensed architect must endorse the plans and ensure that they comply with Bahamian codes. At this writing, there is no such requirement for engineering services. The Professional Architects Act (1994) created and empowered the Professional Architects Board to issue licenses to persons qualified to practice as professional architects in the Commonwealth of the Bahamas. Among the requirements for licensure is being recognized by an approved board such as the AIA (American Institute of Architects), RIBA (Royal Institute of British Architects), etc., to provide evidence of satisfactory training in architecture. In addition, the applicant must be a citizen of the Bahamas or a permanent resident of the Bahamas with a permanent residence certificate permitting engagement in gainful employment and have worked in the Bahamas in architectural practices for not less than six months. Overall, the requirements discourage licensing foreign individuals that intend to work only on a limited number of projects

and are not fully committed to living and working solely in the country.

Fee levels, payment terms, and taxes

Fee levels are basically the same as those in the U.S., and they are subject to the usual points of negotiation. There are no income taxes levied by the government of the Bahamas on professional fees earned in connection with work in the Bahamas. However, certain situations require obtaining a local business license with fees levied based on a percentage of gross income.

Most Bahamian clients are accustomed to using AIA Owner/Architect agreements, though they tend to prefer to utilize the 1987 editions rather than more recent versions. It can be assumed that international entities who are clients will either use the latest AIA or equivalent contracts or have developed their own Owner/Architect agreements.

Local resources

There are currently approximately 110 architects licensed by the Professional Architects Board. Most of these either operate as sole practitioners or have small firms capable of designing and overseeing the construction of small- to medium-sized projects. Since there are few large projects developed at any one time, and since the developers of most large projects retain foreign-based design firms, the ability of local firms to assist in the design of large, complex projects is somewhat limited.

There are likewise a number of local mechanical, electrical, and plumbing engineers and structural and civil engineers. Of these, the structural engineering firms are the most qualified to assist in projects that are medium to large in scale. There are qualified engineers to assist in all facets of small- to medium-sized projects. Several local engineering firms are accustomed to associating with foreign firms on larger projects.

Specialists, such as renderers, low voltage and security, elevator, lighting, food service, and environmental consultants are generally not available. There are some qualified landscape design firms that can handle larger projects.

Design issues

The Bahamas have an interesting historical, architectural vernacular of clapboard structures with wood-shingled roofs that date back to the loyalist settlements in Harbour Island, Spanish Wells, Green Turtle Cay, and New Plymouth. These were developed by former residents of New York, Virginia, and the Carolinas after the American Revolutionary War. There are also some handsome British colonial structures. In spite of these historic traditions, the current stylistic preference for new buildings is Spanish colonial. Regardless, the most successful projects are those that respond to, and take advantage of, local climatic conditions.

Code and regulatory issues

Development and building construction is under the jurisdiction of the Ministry of Works and Utilities. Large-scale development planning is reviewed by the Department of Physical Planning, and building permits and inspections are administered by the office of the Building Control Officer within the Ministry. The Bahamas Building Code, amended most recently in 2005, is largely based on the BOCA (Building Officials and Code Administrators) building code, though caution is required, as there are Bahamian modifications to that code.

There is a trend requiring more environmental assessments and reviews, particularly for large-scale developments and projects. While there are currently no specific legal requirements, governmental consent for large projects to proceed often includes an environmental review process.

Typical schedules

As far as professional architectural services are concerned, the process is very similar to that in the U.S. and Canada. What is different from North American practice is the approval process, particularly for large projects that may require special permits for the use of large numbers of foreign construction workers, relief from import duties, land purchase agreements, and the like. While most of these issues are not the direct responsibility of the architect, they can affect the project schedule and project feasibility.

Local construction capabilities

There are a number of construction companies that do excellent work for small- to medium-sized projects with a number of these specializing in upscale, private residences. In addition, there are some larger firms that are very capable constructors of medium to larger projects. Some firms have formed conglomerates that are 60 percent Bahamian and 40 percent foreign controlled in order to compete with foreign entities for large projects. Since the numbers of skilled and specialist workers, such as steel erectors, is limited, most large projects require the importation of foreign workers. Work permits for foreign construction workers are always a source of political controversy and are, therefore, carefully monitored.

Personal safety and health issues

Since the Bahamas is a major international tourist destination, health issues are carefully monitored by the government, and no serious issues exist. Likewise, because of the importance of the tourist industry, personal safety is generally not an issue as long as usual precautions are observed, as they would need to be anywhere in the developed world.

Most common problems

For smaller projects, and especially private residences, attention and constant monitoring needs to be done during construction to ensure that construction schedules are met. Entrepreneurial drive and worker dedication are not comparable to that in North America, and unless there is a good construction supervision, work progress and quality can fall short of expectation.

Large projects, for which foreign workers are almost always required, need good construction coordination to ensure that workers are available for the various project stages. Contracted arrangements with management companies are necessary to facilitate customs-clearance procedures and paperwork for the importation of construction materials in a timely manner.

Maintenance of buildings, particularly mechanical and electrical equipment, is a major issue. Care needs to be exercised in selecting appropriate systems as well as manufacturers so that replacement parts and service are locally available. Most construction materials and equipment are imported, with the exception of sand and concrete block, which is manufactured locally with imported cement. This makes the specification of products that are locally represented very important.

Key pieces of advice

Bahamians have a great deal of national pride. When foreign firms do work in their country, respect for their culture and traditions goes a long way in establishing meaningful relationships. Foreign firms are often viewed as stealing work from locals, work that could have been performed by Bahamian professionals. Whenever possible, teaming with local professional firms to perform appropriate services is important.

Sources of information

U.S. Embassy, Bahamas
Telephone: 1-242-322-1181
E-mail: embnas@state.gov
Web site: http://nassau.usembassy.gov

Bahamian Society of Engineers
Telephone: 1-242-328-1858
E-mail: jamielms@batelnet.bs
Web site: www.bahamasengineers.org

Institute of Bahamian Architects and
  the Professional Architects Board
Telephone: 1-242-326-3114
E-mail: iba@bahamas.net.bs
Web site:
  www.pab-iba.org/association.lasso

Barbados

Barbados is a small island near the southern end of the Lesser Antilles. It became independent from the United Kingdom in 1966. It has a population of 280,000 and an economy heavily dependent on tourism and sugar, rum, and molasses. It has been a popular tourism destination—particularly for the British and Irish—for decades.

The market

Its tourism infrastructure is relatively mature, and few major projects are underway at any one time. As this book was being written, one of the few big projects in

Fig. 4–09: *Grantley Adams International Airport, Christ Church, Barbados. Architect: Queen's Quay Architects International Inc. Courtesy of Queen's Quay Architects International Inc*

planning was being done by BTA in Cambridge, Massachusetts.

Languages and communications
English is the official language.

Bermuda
This island was first settled in 1609 by shipwrecked English colonists headed for Virginia. Today Bermuda is one of the smaller but also one of the most developed island countries. It has a population of 66,000 and a per capita income that by some measures is greater than that of the U.S. It remains a dependent territory of Britain, although independence comes up occasionally for debate. It is very close to the U.S. and Canada and a popular tourism destination.

Bermuda is also the reinsurance capital of the world, as well as home to many other "foreign, offshore" financial companies. Approximately 10,000 international companies, including 750 of the Fortune 1000, have incorporated or have subsidiaries in Bermuda. The significant tax incentives offered by Bermuda encourage businesses to base their operations there. There are many U.S. owned and operated companies with "headquarters" (albeit a satellite) office in Bermuda. Thus, if a design firm does work for XL Capital in the U.S., they may also be asked to work on the Bermuda office as well.

Bermuda is a very developed and technically advanced island due to the demand for the complex infrastructure required by the many offshore companies. While the island has its own unique architectural style, it could be seen as an opportunity for North American architects to create a synergy between local traditions and international experience. For example, since Bermuda is very small and essentially has no natural resources, the need for conservation of things like fresh water, electricity, etc., is of great importance, and there are opportunities to introduce sustainable-design concepts. The greatest hurdle that Bermuda's planners now have is how to save open spaces and curtail a boom in residential construction. Perhaps of equal or even greater significance is the trend by local developers in the city of Hamilton to push for taller office buildings. Until now, the building code only allowed for six stories above grade, but due to the need for larger buildings and the lack of large sites, several proposals now include eight-story buildings.

The market
The island has a GDP of $4.5 billion and a per capita GDP of almost $70,000. Bermuda is not a large market, but there are frequent opportunities for international firms.

Nevertheless, one Bermudan architect cites general reasons to be cautious:

1. Bermudans are very proud of their native abilities and whenever an offshore entity comes to the island to provide services and expertise deemed available on the island, the situation can turn political. Essentially, it is viewed as taking away money from local pockets and the local economy.
2. Construction practices and means and methods are quite different from those in the U.S., both in design and materials. A firm must make a significant investment in learning how projects are done there.
3. It is an expensive place to operate.

Skills and capabilities that are important
Managing political and labor issues is very important. It would be almost imperative

that an international firm partner in some way with a local architectural firm or developer. Knowledge of the Bermudan work culture is also key, as is understanding and respecting the local building codes, which are very strict and vigilantly enforced.

Who is operating there now?

Both U.S. and Canadian firms, including my firm, have had occasional projects. BTA Architects, of Cambridge, Massachusets, for example, recently worked on a master plan for the redevelopment of King's Point, a former U.S. Naval Annex, into a resort-based, mixed-use development. Cannon Design, in partnership with a local firm, provided strategic and master planning of the entire Bermudan hospital system.

Who are the clients?

Typically, only very large projects for an international client—such as a new hotel, hospital, infrastructure, plant, etc.—generate the need for a North American design firm. In recent years, however, several local firms have designed the newer hotels.

What is the process for getting work?

The process of getting work in Bermuda is similar to the methods used in the U.S. If a client wants a firm to get an RFP (Request for Proposal), the U.S. firm simply submits in a similar manner as one would on a U.S. project. It is helpful, however, if the firm has a contact or prior experience with the local government.

Languages and communications

Bermuda's native language is English, and there is a small population of Portuguese and various Asian nationalities. English, however, is spoken by all. Both the English and metric systems of weights and measures are used.

Licensing and legal issues

Architects are not required to be licensed in order to practice. Drawings are not "signed and sealed" prior to submission to the Planning Authority. They are reviewed by government-appointed planning inspectors (who are also not required to be licensed) and are rejected or approved on content and/or design. However, if you wish to own and operate a firm, and be a major stakeholder in that firm, then you must be recognized by an approved board—e.g., AIA, RIBA, etc.

Non-Bermudan workers, whether they are employed by a local firm or a U.S. firm, need to apply for work permits (visas), and these are not easily obtained. There is a long advertisement process and then a thorough review of the applicant's credentials as compared to local talent in the same position.

Following a U.S. Supreme Court ruling, Bermuda-based but U.S.-owned or U.S.-operated companies can sue or be sued in the U.S.

Licensing requirements are as follows:

- *Is a license required?* At the time the NCARB information was collected, no license was required, just proof of registration in U.S., Canada, Britain, or countries where recognized registration procedures exist.
- *Licensing requirements:* See above.
- *What agency licenses:* Bermuda Government Registrar General, advised by the Architects Registration Council.
- *What is the professional architectural organization?* The Institute of Bermuda Architects.
- *To practice, is a local representative re-*

quired? Yes. While a license may not be required, other online resources at the time this book was written indicate that architects must be Bermudan or working for a Bermudan firm. Any local practice must be directed by a Bermudan national and so firms cannot operate independently if they are not Bermudan and registered under the Architects Registration Act of 1969.

Fee levels, payment terms, and taxes

Below are the 2006 rates of a typical firm in Bermuda. Some other firm rates are higher and some lower:

Senior architect or partner	$135–$145
Architects	$125
Interior design director	$135
Senior interior designer	$120
Architectural technologists	$105–$115
Architectural graduates	$85–$105
Administrative staff	$65–$85

Local resources

Bermuda has a wealth of foreign and local architects and designers, but the majority of the architects and designers are non-Bermudan, and many come from the U.S. and Canada. There are several Bermudans who are established and own local firms. There are several exceptional residential designers who do the Bermuda house well. Most of the new buildings going up in Hamilton, as well as the larger residential buildings that are currently under development, are designed by non-Bermudans. Engineers are much the same as above. There are some Bermudans, but it appears that most are non-Bermudan. Renderers are less available. A firm might have someone on staff that can render; but for large and complex renderings, one local firm brings in a person from Canada, who then renders for two weeks at a time.

Design issues

Bermuda has its own vernacular that is quite unique. Any U.S. firm wanting to do projects in Bermuda will want to pick up a Bermuda design handbook. The Planning and Approvals Board is very much in favor of keeping the island's traditional look. For example, the "Glass Box" building is not allowed. In the city of Hamilton, no building shall rise taller than the 250-year-old Hamilton Anglican Cathedral.

Code and regulatory issues

Bermuda has adopted the BOCA code, but it also has many traditional code requirements related to hurricane issues and building integrity. Essentially, if any concrete structure is "inserted into the ground," it requires review from the Planning Board.

Typical schedules

The process is similar to that in the U.S., but it also uses the English quantity survey approach for some projects.

Local construction capabilities

There are several general contractors who do the majority of the larger projects. There are lots of smaller companies that do most of the housing projects. The industry is, and has been, booming in recent years. There is major renovation work on houses, development of unused land, subdivisions, and converting of old hotel properties into mixed condo-hotel residence units.

Personal safety and health issues

Bermuda is free from major health issues such as cholera, malaria, etc., and it has a low crime rate.

Most common problems

The Department of Immigration for work visas and the labor industry related to construction are both problems. The island mentality and work ethic is seen as slow-paced, and things generally take longer to get done.

There are also many problems with building supplies. Bermuda makes some concrete block and has a lot of sand. All other supplies are imported, and this can obviously cause lead-time issues, particularly when it comes to commercial projects.

Key pieces of advice

If nothing else, foreign firms doing work in Bermuda need to show the locals that they are concerned about Bermuda's traditions, ideals, and cultures. A firm would be ill-advised to attempt to change the way things are done. Bermudans are very proud of what they have achieved and are resistant to the pressures for change.

Sources of information

U.S. Embassy, Bermuda
Telephone: 1-441-295-1342
E-mail: HmlAmConGen@state.gov
Web site: http://hamilton.usconsulate.
  gov/index.html

Institute of Bermuda Architects
Telephone: 1-441-296-2253
E-mail: info@dl.bm
Web site: www.iba.bm

British Virgin Islands

These islands are a self-governing overseas territory of the United Kingdom. The economy is one of the most stable and prosperous in the Caribbean. Tourism accounts for approximately 80 percent of GDP and employment, but legislation offering incorporation and confidentiality in offshore companies has resulted in over 400,000 company registrations by 2000.

The market

The robust tourism sector and offshore companies generate some projects, but this is still a very small place.

Languages and communications

English is the official language. And due to the close economic ties with the U.S., the U.S. dollar is the official currency.

Cayman Islands

This small, three-island grouping remains a British Crown colony. It has no direct taxation and is a booming offshore financial center. Over 40,000 companies, including 600 banks and trust companies, are registered there. Tourism accounts for 70 percent of GDP and 75 percent of foreign exchange. Approximately 50 percent of the tourists come from the U.S.

The market

Both the financial sector and the tourism industry provide some design opportunities.

Languages and communications

The official language is English.

Cuba

Cuba was a Spanish colony until it achieved independence during the Spanish-American war in 1898. For the next 60 years Cuba was closely tied to both the U.S. and the U.S. economy—for better and often for worse. In 1959 Fidel Castro overthrew the government and eventually allied with the Soviet Union. In 1990 the Soviet Union withdrew its subsidies and caused a severe economic recession.

Cuba's future is probably linked to normalization of its relations with the U.S.—a difficult prospect while the Castros remain in power. This island nation of over 11.3 million people is only 90 miles from the U.S., and it has some of the greatest tourism assets in the Caribbean. While Canadians, Europeans, and others are free to visit and invest in Cuba, American governmental policies prohibit U.S. firms from being involved. Many people believe that Cuba will one day be a major development opportunity for U.S. corporations and tourism companies.

The market
There will be a big opportunity for U.S. firms once the U.S. normalizes relations with Cuba; but until then, it is only a limited market for a few American firms.

Languages and communications
Spanish is the primary language.

Dominica
This former British colony achieved independence in 1978. The economy is based on agriculture, in particular bananas. Efforts to build tourism are hampered by the lack of beaches and an international airport.

The market
The market for North American design firms is very limited, but there are a few tourism projects.

Languages and communications
English is the official language.

Dominican Republic
The Dominican Republic shares the island of Hispaniola with Haiti. The country finally achieved independence from Spain in 1865. Since that date it has had a difficult political history, but it has moved to become a representative democracy in recent years. It is a major exporter of sugar, coffee, and tobacco; but the service sector (tourism and free-trade zones) is now the largest employer. This country has managed to avoid many of the problems of its neighbor on the western third of the island, but it still faces significant challenges. Among these are high unemployment, significant income inequality, and a 25 percent poverty rate.

It is closely tied to the U.S. economy, which accounts for approximately 80 percent of the country's export revenues, and its future should be strengthened by the ratification of the Central America-Dominican Republic Free Trade Agreement (CAFTA-DR) in 2005.

The market
The tourism sector has produced a steady stream of design commissions for North American architects, landscape architects, planners, and interior designers. CAFTA-DR could produce other commissions if foreign investment increases.

Languages and communications
Spanish is the primary language, but English is widely understood.

Grenada
Grenada became autonomous in 1967 and independent from Britain in 1974. Grenada was seized by a Marxist military council with some Cuban advisors in 1983. Six days later the U.S. (as creatively reenacted by Clint Eastwood in *Heartbreak Ridge*) and six Caribbean allies invaded, and the bad guys were rounded up. Free elections were reinstituted and have continued since.

Tourism and a developing offshore financial industry account for most of the recent development. The island, however, remains small and relatively poor.

The market
Except for the occasional tourism project, the market for design services is small.

Guadeloupe
Guadeloupe is an overseas department of France. Tourism—primarily from the U.S.—is a key industry as is agriculture (sugarcane, bananas, etc.). The economy is dependent on large subsidies and imports from France.

The market
The market for North American design sources—except for tourism-related projects—is limited.

Languages and communications
French is the official language

Haiti
Following a slave revolt, Haiti became the first independent black republic in 1804. Political violence and mismanagement have plagued much of the country's history. Today, Haiti is the poorest country in the western hemisphere, and over 80 percent of the population lives in poverty. Widespread crime, a high AIDS mortality rate, political instability, rampant inflation, and other problems make it hard to be optimistic about this country's future.

The market
The very limited demand for design services is likely to come from the small number of projects funded by foreign aid.

Languages and communications
French and Creole are the official languages.

Jamaica
Jamaica gained independence within the British Commonwealth in 1962. It is one of the largest and most beautiful of the Caribbean islands, and it has been a major tourist destination for decades. The economy, however, faces serious long-term problems, including a large public debt, inflation, increasing competition, large-scale unemployment, and a significant trade deficit. These problems—combined with chronic unrest and a growing crime problem—cloud the island's future.

The market
The major market for foreign design professionals has been the tourism sector. Resorts and vacation homes are typical commissions. As in the other larger islands, however, local design professionals do not like seeing too much of this work go offshore.

Languages and communications
English is the primary language.

Licensing and legal issues
Licensing requirements are as follows :

- *Is a license required?* Yes. Temporary registration is available for foreign architects.
- *What agency licenses?* The Architects Registrations Board.
- *What is the professional architectural organization?* The Jamaican Institute of Architects.
- *To practice, is a local representative required?* Yes. The representative must be either a citizen or a resident in Jamaica.

Sources of information
U.S. Embassy, Jamaica
Telephone: 1-876-929-4850
E-mail: opakgn@pd.state.gov
Web site:
  www.usembassy.state.gov/Kingston

Jamaican Institute of Architects
Telephone: 1-876-926-8020
E-mail: jia@cwjamaica.com
Web site: www.jiarch.org

Martinique
Martinique is an overseas department of France. The economy is based on sugarcane, bananas, tourism, and a small manufacturing sector. The economy also depends on a large annual aid transfer from France.

The market
The market for North American design professionals is limited. There are occasional tourism assignments.

Languages and communications
The official language is French.

Montserrat
This tiny overseas territory of the United Kingdom was devastated by volcanic eruptions that began in 1995. Two-thirds of the small population left, and the capital was abandoned. Half of the island is expected to remain uninhabitable for another decade.

The market
Other than a few projects funded by aid from the U.K., there is no real market for foreign design services.

Languages and communications
English is the official language

Netherlands Antilles
This autonomous country within the Kingdom of the Netherlands is made up of two island groupings: Curaçao and Bonaire, near the coast of Venezuela and St. Martin, Saba, and Saint Eustatius (Statia), which are east of the U.S. Virgin Islands. The islands' economy is based on tourism, petroleum refining, and offshore finance. Agriculture is very limited, due to poor soils and water supplies. The islands are relatively well developed and more prosperous than most of their neighbors.

The market
There are some design opportunities in tourism and other development projects.

Languages and communications
Dutch is the official language, but English is widely spoken, as is Papiamento (a Spanish-based Creole language).

Saint Kitts-Nevis
This two-island nation of Saint Kitts and Nevis (which continues to try to separate into two countries) achieved independence from the U.K. in 1983. Sugar is the major agricultural crop, but tourism, offshore banking, and some manufacturing are growing. Tourism is the chief source of the country's foreign exchange.

The market
The tourism sector continues to provide a number of opportunities for North American design professionals

Languages and communications
English is the official language.

Saint Lucia
Saint Lucia became independent from the U.K. in 1979. It is another island that used

to be dependent on bananas but now has growing offshore banking, tourism, and manufacturing sectors. It remains, however, relatively poor.

The market
Saint Lucia is another island where most of the design opportunities for North American design professionals are in tourism.

Languages and communications
English is the official language, but a French patois is also spoken.

Saint Vincent and the Grenadines
These small, relatively poor islands are dependent on agriculture and tourism, both of which are seasonal and often impacted by tropical storms. They became independent from the U.K. in 1979.

The market
The market for design services is very limited. As with many of the other islands, the major opportunities are in tourism.

Languages and communications
English is the official language, and a French patois is also spoken.

Trinidad and Tobago
This two-island country became independent from the U.K. in 1962. Shortly thereafter the U.S. abandoned its large lend-lease naval base on the island. The island's oil (approximately 1-billion-barrel reserve) and natural gas have helped support one of the Caribbean's more prosperous economies. Its government, a parliamentary democracy, has been relatively stable. It continues to attract foreign investment.

Tourism is also important but less so than in other parts of the Caribbean. The beaches of Trinidad are impacted by silt from the Orinoco River. Tobago is the main resort destination.

The market
With a growing trade surplus and a growing economy, Trinidad and Tobago are generating some opportunities for foreign design professionals.

Languages and communications
English is the official language; but due to a very diverse population, Hindi, French, Spanish, and Chinese are also spoken.

Sources of information
Ministry of Housing
Telephone: 1-868-623-4663
E-mail: info@housing.gov.tt
Web site: www.housing.gov.tt

Trinidad and Tobago Institute
  of Architects
Telephone: 1-868-624-8842
E-mail: administration@ttiarch.com
Web site: www.architecture.co.tt/

Turks and Caicos Islands
The Turks and Caicos almost became independent in 1982, but the islands remain a British overseas territory today. The small economy is based on tourism, fishing, and offshore financial services. Together they make these islands relatively stable and prosperous.

The market
The major opportunities are in the growing tourism sector.

Languages and communications
The official language is English.

Latin America

Latin America, as the region is defined in this book, is made up of the six countries of Central America and the seven Spanish-speaking countries and one Portuguese-speaking country of South America. Guyana, Suriname, and French Guiana are not covered in this section, because they are insignificant markets for North American architects. The region obviously could also include several of the Caribbean countries as well as Mexico, but they are covered in other regional summaries.

Most of the countries in this region are former colonies of Spain that achieved independence early in the nineteenth century. The largest country in the region is Brazil, a former Portuguese colony. Ever since the U.S. established the Monroe Doctrine in 1823, this region has had a special relationship with the United States, although not necessarily one that many in the region wanted. The region has a diverse population of over 415 million. Most of the countries have rich and varied cultural and economic histories. Today the countries range from advanced societies with diverse economies (Chile, Argentina, and Brazil) to countries with limited resources and very poor economies, such as Bolivia, Paraguay, Honduras, and El Salvador. And most, unfortunately, have long, chaotic political histories.

Because of the diversity, it is impossible to generalize about the countries in the region. Instead, the countries need to be examined on a case-by-case basis. This chapter goes into more detail about the countries that have the most potential for North American design firms. The other countries in the region are, as noted earlier, covered by brief summaries. The po-

tential of a country as a market for design services can change quickly. Economies and currency collapse overnight—as happened in Argentina in the first quarter of 2000—and political instability can be very disruptive. A hotel and casino project we were planning in Paraguay ended abruptly when the minister responsible for issuing the required permits machine-gunned a rival and had to quickly leave the country.

Many of the countries have rapidly growing cities, most have important tourism destinations, and virtually all have need of the specialized design resources available in North America. There are hundreds of skilled design firms in Latin America, but there is always some need for North American design skills.

Central America

The seven countries of Central America: Guatemala, Belize, Honduras, El Salvador, Nicaragua, Costa Rica, and Panama are all relatively small and poor. Specifically, the approximate population and GDP in 2007 is summarized in Table 4.3.

All of the Central American countries have important economic ties to the U.S. and Canada. "El Norte" is a major market for the region's exports, a major source of tourists, and a work place for hundreds of thousands of the region's citizens (both legal and illegal).

The region, however, has a very ambivalent relationship with the U.S. in particular. Historically, the U.S. has, at times, played a very mixed role in several of the countries. The U.S. engineered a coup in Guatemala in 1954, and U.S. corporations have played a less than benign role in the economy of the country. U.S. Marines were sent into Nicaragua from 1912 to 1925. As recently as President Ronald W. Reagan's administration, the

Contents

Countries in bold receive longer descriptive sections.

Table 4.3 Central America Population and Economic Statistics[6]

Country	Population	Population Growth Rate (%)	GDP—Purchasing Power Parity*	GDP—Official Exchange Rate*	GDP—Per Capita ($)
Belize	288,000	2.31	2.3	1.1	8,400
Costa Rica	4,075,000	1.45	48.7	20.77	12,000
El Salvador	6,822,000	1.72	33.2	15.14	4,900
Guatemala	12,293,000	2.27	60.5	28.84	4,900
Honduras	7,326,000	2.16	22.1	8.41	3,000
Nicaragua	5,570,000	1.89	16.8	4.81	3,000
Panama	3,191,000	1.6	25.2	16.2	7,900

In billions of U.S. dollars unless otherwise noted.

U.S. was actively involved in El Salvador's internal conflicts. And the U.S. actively helped engineer the separation of Panama from Colombia in 1903 to help pave the way for the U.S. plans to build the Panama Canal. Following construction of the canal, the U.S. stayed actively involved (both publicly and covertly) in Panamanian politics, and in 1989 the U.S. even invaded the country to oust Panamanian general Manuel Noriega. It is little wonder that the region has mixed feelings about the U.S.

The region is also not homogeneous. Each country has a distinct history and character. In brief:

- *Belize* (formerly British Honduras, until 1981) is a small country where the official language is English. It has a very limited economy and relies heavily on tourism for foreign exchange.
- *Costa Rica* is unique in Central America. For more than 100 years, its democratic development has been marred by only two periods of violence. Its econo-

my has strong tourism and technology sectors, and the standard of living is relatively high for the region. As this book was being written, Costa Rica's tourism industry was stimulating some of the more interesting design opportunities, and a growing number of North American firms are involved. Gensler, for example, has an office there. It was initially set up to provide production support for other Gensler offices, but it is now getting local hospitality and residential projects.

- *El Salvador* is also a small, poor country with a struggling economy. A twelve-year civil war ended in 1992, and the economy has been improving since then.
- *Guatemala* is a beautiful country with a complex history. It has a rich Amerindian (Maya and others) and Spanish colonial heritage and a tragic recent history. In 1996 the government signed a peace agreement to end a 36-year civil war that left more than 100,000 dead and created over one million refugees. It is the largest and most populous country in Central America, but corruption, civil war, and other problems have hampered economic development. Seventy-five percent of the population (which is 60 percent mixed or European and 40 percent Amerindian) lives below the poverty line.
- *Honduras* is one of the poorest countries in the Americas. Moreover, it does not have the tourism assets of either Guatemala or Belize.
- *Nicaragua* is another small, very poor country that suffered from corruption, civil war, and international (mostly U.S.) interference. Since 1990, however, the country has been slowly rebuilding.

- The U.S. helped engineer *Panama's* secession from Colombia in 1903, as part of the plan to build the canal. Until 1977, the canal was under U.S. sovereignty. The 1977 agreement started a transfer of control that was completed in 1999. Its economy has a well-developed service sector based on the Panama Canal Zone, banking and insurance, and tourism.

Reasons to be there

Most of the limited opportunities in Central America for North American architects are in tourism projects. This is not a region that justifies a sustained involvement by North American firms. Instead, it is a region where the occasional opportunities are likely to come from personal relationships or a strong reputation for a building type needed in one of the countries. It is, however, a diverse, interesting and, in some areas, very beautiful region.

Reasons to be cautious

In addition to the problem of the limited opportunities, there are other reasons to be cautious. One of them is the high crime rate in all of the countries except Costa Rica.

Skills and capabilities that are important

The main issue is having the specialized skills (resort planning and design, for example) which are needed, an understanding of what local resources and firms are available to assist in getting and carrying out a project and fluency in Spanish (except in English-speaking Belize).

Who is operating there now?

Many North American firms have had an occasional project in the region.

Who are the clients?

As noted above, resort and hotel developers are one of the few client types that might require foreign design skills. Other clients could include North American corporations building facilities in the region and local developers looking for more design ability or prestige than local architects can provide. At this time, the latter client type is most likely to be in Panama and Costa Rica.

What is the process for getting work?

It is hard to generalize about the process. It varies widely from project to project.

Languages and communications

While many people speak English, Spanish is the required language skill (except, as noted above, in Belize).

Licensing and legal issues

- *Costa Rica:* Licensing requirements are as follows:
  - *Is a license required?* Yes. The architect must register at the Costa Rican Association of Engineers and Architects. *Note:* The license is constituted by the act of being registered in the Engineers and Architects Federated Association.
  - *What agency licenses?* The Costa Rican Federated Association of Engineers and Architects (Colegio Federado de Ingenieros y Arquitectos de Costa Rica).
  - *What is the professional architectural organization?* Colegio Federado de Ingenieros y Arquitectos de Costa Rica.
  - *To practice, is a local representative required?* Yes, a U.S. architectural firm must have a local representative who has a minimum of five years residence in Costa Rica and is registered with the Engineers and Architects Association. *Note:* A foreign architectural firm must have at least one Costa Rican licensed on its staff in order to practice in Costa Rica. A foreign architect can obtain a temporary membership at the Association (one year, extendable) if his or her specialty is needed in Costa Rica or a permanent membership if residing in Costa Rica for five years or more.

- *Guatemala:* Licensing requirements are as follows:
  - *Is a license required?* Yes.
  - *Licensing requirements?* Foreign architects must pass a written exam at the University of San Carlos and hold a current degree in architecture recognized by the licensing authority.
  - *What agency licenses?* Colegio de Arquitectos de Guatemala.
  - *What is the professional architectural organization?* Colegio de Arquitectos de Guatemala. The architecture school provides the proper legal exams to become a registered architect. The board provides legal registration based upon results from the University's School of Architects.
  - *To practice, is a local representative required?* While a U.S. firm may provide consulting services to locally registered architects, once a project reaches the construction phase at least one local licensed professional must be directly involved in the project. A U.S. firm may apply for local registration, or they may look for a locally registered architecture firm.

- *Honduras:* Licensing requirements are as follows:

- *Is a license required?* Yes.
- *Licensing requirements?* For foreign architects, a degree is required from a five-year program from a recognized university. An internship and written examination is also required for foreign architects.
- *What agency licenses?* National Autonomous University of Honduras (UNAH) and Honduras Association of Architects (Colegio de Arquitectos de Honduras).
- *What is the professional architectural organization?* Honduras Association of Architects (Colegio de Arquitectos de Honduras).
- *To practice, is a local representative required?* An architect must be registered by the Committee Intercolegial de Registro y Clasificacion de Empresas Constructoras y Consultoras en Ingenieria y Arquitectura (CIRCE).
- *Nicaragua*: Licensing requirements are as follows:
  - *What agency licenses?* An operating license (licencia de operacion) is issued by the Ministry of Construction and Transportation.
  - *What is the professional architectural organization?* There are two associations. However, only one of them has a significant number of associates: Asociación Nicaraguense de Ingenieros y Arquitectos (ANIA).
- *Panama*: Licensing requirements are as follows:
  - *Is a license required?* Yes. A license is required for foreign persons only under special conditions. Persons are not allowed to advertise themselves publicly without having first registered.
  - *Licensing requirements:* A degree in architecture from a recognized authori-

ty. Written examinations for graduates of some foreign universities.
  - *What agency licenses?* Junta Técnica de Ingeníeria y Arquitectura.
  - *What is the professional architectural organization?* Sociedad Panameña de Ingenieros y Arquitectos (SPIA).
  - *To practice, is a local representative required?* Yes. A firm must establish a society for specific purposes, then register the society before the Junta Técnica with a suitable professional as its technical representative.

Fee levels, payment terms, and taxes

Except for projects sponsored by international clients, prevailing fees are significantly lower than those in the U.S. and Canada. This tends to restrict most foreign design firms to the planning and design phases. Costa Rica has a compulsory fee scale published by the Colegio de Arquitectos (Architects' Association of Costa Rica). Fees are based upon a percentage of the value of the project.

Personal safety and health issues

Except in Costa Rica, personal safety is a significant issue in many parts of the region. There are also occasional outbreaks of a number of tropical diseases. It is important to research these issues before working in most Central American countries.

Sources of information

U.S. Embassy, Costa Rica
Telephone: 506-519-2000
E-mail: hdssjo@pd.state.gov
Web site: www.usembassy.or.cr

Colegio de Arquitectos de Costa Rica
(College of Architects of Costa Rica)
Telephone: 506-202-3974

E-mail:
info@colegiodearquitectoscostarica.com
Web site:
www.colegiodearquitectoscostarica.com

U.S. Embassy, El Salvador
Telephone: 503-278-4444
Web site: www.usinfo.org.sv

Oficina de Planificación del Área Metro-
politana de San Salvador (OPAMSS)
Telephone: 503-223-4060
E-mail: direccion@opamss.org.sv
Web site: www.opamss.org.sv

Colegio de Arquitectos de El Salvador
(Cades)
Telephone: 503-262-3872
Web site: www.cades.org.sv

Registro Nacional de Arquitectos e
Ingenieros (National Registrar of
Architects and Engineers)
Viceministerio de Vivienda y Desarrollo
Urbano, El Salvador
U.S. Embassy, Guatemala
Telephone: 502-2326-4000
E-mail: AmCitsGuatemala@state.gov
Web site: http://guatemala.usembassy.gov

Colegio de Arquitectos de Guatemala
Telephone: 502-369-2911
Web site: www.colegiodearquitectos
deguatemala.org

U.S. Embassy, Honduras
Telephone: 504-236-9320
Web site: http://honduras.usembassy.gov/
english/index_e1.htm

Committee Intercolegial de Registro
y Clasificacion de Empresas Construc-
toras y Consultoras en Ingenieria y
Arquitectura (CIRCE), Honduras
Colegio de Arquitectos de Honduras
U.S. Embassy, Nicaragua
Telephone: 505-266-6010

E-mail:
ManaguaPASWebmaster@state.gov
Web site: http://managua.usembassy.gov

U.S. Embassy, Panama
Telephone: 507-207-7030
E-mail: usembconsulate@cwp.net.pa
Web site: http://panama.usembassy.gov

Panameña de Ingenieros y Arquitectos
(SPIA), Colegio de Arquitectos
Telephone: 507-269-7734
E-mail: spiawebmaster@spia-pma.org
Web site: www.spia-pma.org/spia/spia.htm

South America

There are 13 countries in South America.
As noted above, French Guiana, Guyana,
and Suriname are not covered, because
they represent minimal market opportunities. The remaining countries are former
Spanish colonies, except for Brazil, which
was part of the Portuguese Empire. Most
are complex countries with rich cultures
and histories. Most have suffered from a
variety of major problems.

At the time this book was written, the
basic population and GDP statistics for the
countries under discussion were summarized in Table 4.4.

Argentina, Chile, and Uruguay

These three nations at the southern tip of
South America are all relatively sophisticated countries, with literate populations
and often violent histories. During the
periodic good economic times, these
countries are among the most prosperous
in the western hemisphere. Political tur-
moil and economic mismanagement,
however, have caused periods of severe
economic adversity. At the time this book
was written, all three were doing relatively well. As a result, they offer an occasional market for international design firms.

Argentina

Argentina is a sophisticated country that has suffered from tragically misguided political leadership throughout its history. It has rich natural resources, a highly literate population, and a diversified agricultural and industrial base. The greater metropolitan area of the capital, Buenos Aires, has a population over 13 million and an architectural character similar to some of the more attractive European cities.

With a population approaching 40 million and a GDP of almost $600 billion, Argentina is an important player in Latin America. Its educational system regularly produces leading architects and other professionals, and its sophisticated economy generates opportunity for both domestic and international design professionals.

The country's tragic political history, however, often intrudes. Periods of prosperity are regularly interrupted by periods of chaos—both political and economic. Any design professional who has worked there has had to deal with periods where all opportunities dry up.

Table 4.4 South America Population and Economic Statistics[7]

Country	Population	Population Growth Rate (%)	GDP—Purchasing Power Parity*	GDP—Official Exchange Rate*	GDP—Per Capita ($)
Argentina	39,922,000	0.96	599.1	210	15,000
Bolivia	8,989,000	1.45	27.21	10.22	3,000
Brazil	188,078,000	1.04	1.62	620.7	8,600
Chile	16,134,000	0.94	203	100.3	12,600
Colombia	43,593,000	1.46	366.7	105.5	8,400
Ecuador	13,548,000	1.5	60.48	32.57	4,500
Paraguay	6,506,000	2.45	30.64	7.70	4,700
Peru	28,303,000	1.32	181.8	76.09	6,400
Suriname	439,000	0.2	3.10	1.4	10,700
Uruguay	3,432,000	0.46	36.56	14.3	6,900
Venezuela	25,730,000	1.38	176.4	147.9	6,100

* In billions of U.S. dollars unless otherwise noted.

Chile

Chile is a relatively small country with a population of 16 million and a GDP of approximately $203 billion. Its relatively sophisticated and stable population, government, and economy, however, have made it a leader in the region.

In 2004 a free-trade agreement with the U.S. went into effect. Even with this agreement, however, the opportunities for North American design professionals in Chile are limited.

Uruguay

Uruguay is the smallest of the three countries, and it is heavily dependent on the economies of its larger neighbors—Argentina and Brazil. It has a population of approximately 3,432,000. Its GDP was $36 billion in 2006 and is closely linked to international commodity prices and its export-oriented agricultural sector. It is also a tourism destination—particularly its eastern town, Punta del Este—for its two larger neighbors.

The market

These three countries are not a steady market for any North American firm—except, as noted below, for firms with strong personal ties to the region. Due to the sophistication and relative wealth of this region, there are occasional opportunities for firms with specialized skills and/or international design reputations.

In addition, in 2000, after years of limited construction in Argentina, growing tax revenues, increases in investments by local companies, and the renegotiation of foreign debt have created an opportunity for the federal government and some provinces to start funding architectural and engineering projects again. Roads, bridges, social housing, and schools will

Fig. 4–10: *Telecom Headquarters, Buenos Aires, Argentina. Architects: Kohn Pedersen Fox Associates (KPF) with Hampton/Rivoira y Asociados. Photograph by Facundo de Zuviria.*

probably be among the projects to be developed by the government in the next few years.

Reasons to be there

Due to the cost and distance, this region should be of interest to those firms with strong interest in or ties to one or more of the three countries. While there are very good local architects operating in each country, there is a lack of local experience in many of the larger and more complex building types. Most firms have fewer than 10 to 15 architects, and specialized con-

sultants are rare. Thus, there is a need for foreign expertise. But, while all three of these nations are interesting and often beautiful countries with sophisticated societies, this region cannot yet support a continuous presence by any North American architectural firm.

Reasons to be cautious

Developing and doing work in the region can be very time consuming and expensive. The region (Argentina in particular) has had periods of severe economic and political instability, and the execution of

Fig. 4–11: *Las Casas Farm, Jose Ignacio, Uruguay. Architect: Agrest and Gandelsonas Architects. Courtesy of Agrest and Gandelsonas Architects.*

architectural projects can be affected by politics and corruption.

Skills and capabilities that are important

Among the basic skills and capabilities important to work in the country include the following:

- Access to a network of local, well-connected relationships that can facilitate working in the region.
- Capabilities in and a reputation for the services needed.
- The ability to communicate fluently in Spanish.

Who is operating there now?

At this time, the most visible North American architects operating there are Cesar Pelli and Rafael Viñoly, both of whom came to the U.S. from Argentina (although Rafael Viñoly is Uruguayan by birth). In recent years, however, a number of firms have worked there, primarily in Argentina, for example:

- Cesar Pelli designed three buildings: Edificio Republica, an office building; Bank Boston Argentina headquarters; and the Argentinean headquarters of the oil company Repsol.
- Rafael Viñoly designed the Museum for the Fortabat Collection, as well as a residential building at Casares and Gelly in Argentina, and he is currently designing the Carrasco International Airport and the Edificio Acqua in Punta del Este—both in Uruguay.
- KPF designed the local telecom building.

- SOM designed an office tower for Citibank in Santiago, Chile.
- HOK designed an office building, El Malecon, and an addition to offices of the newspaper *La Nació*.
- Agrest & Gandelsonas have designed high-end residences in Uruguay.
- A number of North American firms have designed corporate interiors.
- And my firm worked briefly on a hotel and casino project in Uruguay for a North American developer.

Who are the clients?

As is illustrated by the examples listed above, most clients are major corporations or developers (both domestic and international) seeking international expertise in a particular building type or a "high profile building." There are undoubtedly future opportunities for firms with other areas of expertise, including research facilities, health care, and other programmatically complex building types.

What is the process for getting work?

In Argentina all public work is required by law to go through open competition. The government of Buenos Aires recently held an international competition for the renovation of the original post office building. This competition format usually requires a team of developers, financiers, architects, and engineers, where the first stage is a demonstration of the team's capabilities (in financial and experiential terms). This is followed by a conceptual stage, in which the building's use is outlined, and a third stage, in which a financial offer is made for the project. Political connections always increase a firm's chances in being awarded the project. Some private clients use invited competitions. And, as in most of the world, many

projects come from the architects' relationships and networking. Requests for Proposals and formal qualifications-based selection procedures are far less common than in North America.

Languages and communications

Fluency in Spanish is essential. While many people speak English, technical communication has to be done in Spanish. All three countries have relatively up-to-date telecommunications and computer infrastructures.

Licensing and legal issues

Graduate architects are automatically eligible for a license without further exams. The Architects' Association of Catalonia, or Collegi d'Arquitectes de Catalunya (COAC) Web site states that architects can work independently in both Argentina and Chile, but a joint venture with a local architect is recommended. In Argentina foreign architects must have their qualifications validated by the national university, and they must register with the Consejo Profesional de Arquitectura y Urbanismo (CPAU) or their local professional association.

Scope of services

The scope of service for an architect is roughly the same as in the U.S. A project is divided into schematic design, design development, construction documents, and construction administration, and the fees are divided accordingly.

Fee levels, payment terms, and taxes

In general the compensation for architectural professional services is based on an agreed lump sum between the client and the architect or a percentage of the construction cost. In Argentina there is a recommended fee scale approved by national law that varies within the different provinces. Some provinces require a percentage of the fee to be paid to the provincial retirement fund, regardless of what is the fee value. Foreign firms are allowed to be paid in dollars. The professional services of a foreign firm for work performed within the country are bound to a tax that could reach 35 percent. Chile also has a recommended fee scale published by the Colegio de Arquitectos de Chile (Architects Association of Chile).

Major contract issues

The exchange rate, and a reasonable cost of living that keeps down local salaries, make it very hard for foreign architectural firms to compete with local architectural and engineering companies. Being hired by an American corporation is probably the best option to do nongovernmental work in this region. When this book was written, Argentinean provinces and municipalities were awarding contracts to architects but limiting them to local firms.

Local resources

As noted earlier, there are good local architects available to work in association with North American firms. Argentinean firm Antonioni Schön Zemborain (ASZ) worked together with SOM on the competition organized by the federal government for the relocation of the Supreme Court. The project never came to realization, but Mr. Schön felt the experience was very rewarding, specifically for the local firm, because it gave them exposure to such a large and complex project. The local firm was involved during the design process and helped with the local regulations, available construction systems, and coordination with the local engineers. SOM provided the ex-

pertise on the type of project, the technological backup, and the renown of a large U.S. firm. The same firm has also worked with Arrowstreet Inc. of Boston for the Hoyts' movie theaters, and currently they are working with firms from Chile on projects located in Chile and Argentina. There are many other local firms with experience working with foreign firms. Understanding the language, metric system, and local regulations were key components of the successful relationships. The firms are, however, typically small and have limited experience with large, complex projects. They grow as needed per project, mostly by using the help of students. The engineering and other consultant disciplines are all represented, but again the firms are limited in terms of size and experience.

The other resources—printers, model builders, renderers, etc.—all exist in the major cities but are also limited in capacity and sophistication.

Design issues

The major cities of the region have drawn heavily on European design traditions. New buildings tend to be modern, but the historic fabric of Buenos Aires and other cities looks more like Paris than the more Mediterranean design traditions found in the typical buildings built in the other Latin American countries. In addition, due to the relatively low cost of labor, some important architectural trades, such as masonry and stonework, are affordable. And—as is the case in most low labor-cost areas—structures are typically cast-in-place concrete, and the quality control still exists to use concrete as an exterior finish.

Code and regulatory issues

Buenos Aires has a zoning and a building code, and each province (state) also has its own zoning and building codes. Planning and zoning reviews are administered by the municipalities. Code consultants or expeditors are most commonly used to review the project for code compliance and filing for permit with the local municipalities. The typical approval process is based on the review of the construction documents by the local building department, the reviewer looks at the fire-protection systems, elevators, structure, and code compliance.

Typical schedules
Both design and construction typically take longer than for comparable projects in North America.

Local construction capabilities
There are good contractors and skilled craftsmen available for most projects.

Personal safety and health issues
Argentina, Chile, and Uruguay are all relatively safe places to visit, live, and work.

Sources of information
U.S. Embassy, Argentina
Telephone: 54-11-5777-4533
E-mail:
    Buenos.Aires.Office.Box@mail.doc.gov
Web site: www.buenosaires.usembassy.gov

Consejo Profesional de Arquitectura
    y Urbanismo
Telephone: 54-11-5-238-1068
E-mail: servicios@cpau.org
Web site: www.cpau.org

Asociación Mutual de la Sociedad
    Central de Arquitectos
Telephone: 54-11-4812-48722
E-mail: infoamsca@amsca.com.ar
Web site: www.amsca.com.ar

Federación Argentina de Entidades
    de Arquitectos
Telephone: 54-221-4218032/4
Web site: www.fadea.org.ar

Sociedad Central de Arquitectos
Telephone: 54-11-4813-2375
Web site: www.socearq.org

Colegio de Arquitectos de la
    Provincia de Buenos Aires
Telephone: 54-0221-421-8032
E-mail: info@capba.org.ar
Web site: www.capba.org.ar

Buenos Aires Herald:
    www.buenosairesherald.com
Fundacion Invertir Argentina—
    The Complete Guide to Business with
    Argentina: www.invertir.com

U.S. Embassy, Chile
Telephone: 56-2-232-2600
E-mail: SantiagoAmCit@state.gov
Web site: www.santiago.usembassy.gov

Colegio de Arquitectos de Chile
Telephone: 56-2-353-2300
Web site: www.colegioarquitectos.com

U.S. Embassy, Uruguay
Telephone: 598-2-418-7777
E-mail: webmastermvd@state.gov
Web site: www.uruguay.usembassy.gov

Brazil
Brazil is the largest country in Latin America, with a population of approximately 186 million and a land area comparable to the lower 48 of the United States. It is a country of extreme economic contrasts. It has large, prosperous economic sectors and many sophisticated, educated leaders. On the other hand, it has

massive urban slums as well as large areas of rural poverty.

The population is heavily concentrated along the coast—much of it in large cities such as São Paulo (urban population around 18 million), Rio de Janeiro (population eight million), and Salvador (population over two million). The south, and in particular São Paulo, generate a disproportionate share of the GDP, and the country is, on average, poorer as one goes north toward the Amazon River. In an effort to stimulate development of the interior, the capital was moved to the new city of Brasília in 1960. Today, Brasília is a sprawling city with a population of around 2.2 million.[8]

For a large country, it has a remarkably peaceful history. Even independence was achieved peacefully. In my view, when someone suggested a revolution, someone else suggested going to the beach, and the latter always prevailed. Brazil is a spectacularly beautiful country with many large, underdeveloped tourism assets. The food is good, the people are friendly, and it can be an extremely enjoyable place to work. It can also be a very frustrating place to work. The economy varies from stable prosperity one minute to hyperinflation and recession the next. Corruption is endemic in some sectors, and many things do not go quite as planned. For this and many other reasons, many people refer to Brazil as "the land of the future and it always will be."

The market

Brazil has offered North American design firms a wide variety of opportunities. My

Fig. 4–12: *Praia do Forte Resort, Bahia, Brazil. Architect: Perkins Eastman. Courtesy of Perkins Eastman.*

experience there included several large resort master plans and an office building for a major bank. Other firms have designed office buildings, hotels, and a wide variety of other building types.

Reasons to be there

- First of all, Brazil is the largest economy in South America, and there is a potential growth in many sectors. The great majority of multinational American and European companies operate in Brazil and can demand the service of architectural firms that work with the head offices.
- The the scale of the country is vast—Brazilians claim they live on a continent rather than in a country.
- The economy is slowly improving due to increases in exports as well as controls on inflation and energy imports.
- Urban design and planning are not generally taught in Brazil's architectural schools; this means there is scope for outside expertise.

Reasons to be cautious

- There are the usual risks of flaky clients and the costs of navigating a new, complex regulatory environment.
- Brazilian firms and architects have been short of work for several years: too few good commissions and too many practices. Thus, there is the potential for resentment of "outside" firms taking over the few good design opportunities.

Skills and capabilities that are important

- The best Brazilian firms have the same technical ability as American firms. The key differences include the North American firms more extensive experience. There are areas like resorts, big residential projects, theme parks, and high-end offices where American firms generally have more experience.
- "Smart" and "green" technology is taught at some schools but not widely put in practice. An opportunity exists to provide this expertise.
- Most Brazilian practices focus only on traditional architectural services, and the low fees often result in little experimentation.
- Few large firms exist. Larger practices are 30 to 40 architects.
- Among the larger Brazilian practices are the following:
  - Botti Rubin: One of the country's largest firms, with 20 architects.
  - ETJN: High quality design practice; collaborated with SOM on Bank Boston headquarters in São Paulo.
  - Aflalo & Gosperini: Residential, institutional, and commercial buildings, including World Trade Center, São Paulo; firm founded in 1962.

Who is operating there now?

SOM, KPF, and many others that operate in market niches or provide the head offices of multinational corporations have done projects in association with Brazilian architectural practices in Brazil.

Who are the clients?

The multinational corporations, big national companies, and private developers.

What is the process for getting work?

In general, the big clients search for leading firms in each market; but project awards are often due to personal or social relations, as everywhere else.

Licensing and legal issues

Licensing requirements are as follows:

Fig. 4–13: *Torre Almirante, Rio de Janeiro, Brazil. Architects: Robert A.M. Stern Architects with Pontual Arquitetura. Photograph by Joe Aker of Aker/Zvonkovic Photography.*

- *What agency licenses?* Each state has its Regional Council of Engineering, Architecture, and Agronomy, which is responsible for issuing the registration to practice in that state.
- *What is the professional architectural organization?* The Instituto de Arquitetos do Brasil.
- *To practice, is a local representative required?* No local representation is required, but a member of the U.S. firm must be registered (licensed) in Brazil. If the U.S. firm has a local representative, he or she may be a U.S. citizen but must be registered in Brazil. The representative has to be registered at the Regional Council of Engineering, Architecture, and Agronomy. A foreign citizen from a country without a bilateral agreement for recognition of qualifications must have their diploma revalidated.

Fee levels, payment terms, and taxes

The Institute of Architects of Brazil publishes a fee schedule, but the fees on many projects are below the recommended levels. Currently, most architectural firms work on fees based on 1.5 percent of total construction cost. Some manage to get 2 percent or even 2.5 percent, but this is not the norm. This low fee structure has limited the interest of outside firms, especially given that average construction costs are much lower than in the U.S.

Local resources

There are few problems in this area, since the Brazilian engineering professionals are well advanced and responsive to the technology available in the country. Three-dimensional modeling is available at the best level and costs far less than North American services.

- *Is a license required?* In order for both Brazilians and foreign persons to practice architecture in Brazil, architects must graduate from a school of architecture and register at the Regional Council of Engineering, Architecture, and Agronomy.
- *Licensing requirements:* A degree in architecture from an institution recognized by the state where the architect is to practice. Practical training is not legally required for the initial licensing.

Languages and communications

Portuguese is Brazil's official language but some Spanish, English and French are also spoken. The country has a good working telecommunications system.

Sources of information

U.S. Embassy, Brazil
Telephone: 55-61-3312-7000
Web site:
www.embaixadaamericana.org.br

Instituto de Arquitetos do Brasil (IAB)
Telephone: 55-11-3151-4672
E-mail: iabsp@iabsp.org.br
Web site: www.iab.org.br

Federacoa Nacional dos Arquitetos
e Urbanisatas
Telephone: 55-61-3347-8889
E-mail: fna@fna.org.br
Web site: www.fna.org.br

Conselho Federal de Engenharia,
Arquitetura e Agronomia
Telephone: 55-61-348-3700
e-mail: sege@confea.org.br
Web site: www.confea.org.br

Bolivia, Paraguay, Peru, and Ecuador

These four countries of Spanish-speaking South America are all relatively poor. While interesting to visit, none offer more than an occasional opportunity for North American firms. The four countries can be summarized as follows:

Bolivia

Bolivia has a long history of political instability combined with poverty, social unrest, and a major drug problem. It has a population of approximately 8,989,000, and its GDP is estimated to be $27.2 billion. On a per capita basis, it is one of the poorest countries in Latin America.

Ecuador

Ecuador is another country with major tourism assets; however, it has an economy that performs poorly, political instability, and poverty. It has a population of approximately 13,548,000 and a GDP of only $60.5 billion. The economy is overly dependent on the country's substantial petroleum reserves, which account for 40 percent of its export earnings.

Paraguay

Paraguay is a landlocked country with a long, tragic history and a poorly performing economy. Its population is estimated at 6,506,000 and its GDP at $31 billion. Corruption, inadequate infrastructure, lack of structural reform, and other factors have made this one of South America's poorest performing economies.

Peru

This beautiful country is the historic home of the Incan civilization. It has an extremely varied geography, ranging from an arid coastal plain to high mountains and tropical areas adjacent to Brazil and Colombia. The economy is overly dependent on minerals and metals and has a primitive infrastructure. Its significant tourism assets are relatively undeveloped. It has a population over 28 million but a GDP of only $181.1 billion. Economic performance has improved somewhat in recent years, but there is widespread corruption, unemployment, and poverty.

The market

While each of these four countries has assets that could provide a foundation for future growth, they are all weak performers

Fig. 4–14: *Lima Marriott, Lima, Peru. Architect: Arquitectonica. Courtesy of Lima Marriott.*

they must have a diploma in architecture, be inscribed in the register, contract for services, and be residents of Bolivia.

For Ecuador the licensing requirements are as follows:

- *Is a license required?* Yes, from the Colegio Nacional de Arquitectos del Ecuador, which is the same agency that acts as the professional architectural organization.
- *To practice, is a local representative required?* No, but it is encouraged that architects enter into an agreement with a local architect or firm. A local representative must be living in Ecuador with at least a resident visa. The requirements for establishing local representation include being a legally established company in the home country, having a permanent local representative, and having capital in the activity.

For Peru the licensing requirements are as follows:

- *Is a license required?* In order to practice architecture in Peru, a license is not required. Indigenous and foreign persons alike, however, are required by law to be active members of the Colegio de Arquitectos del Perú (CAP), the College of Peruvian Architects, which is a professional architects' society.
- *Licensing requirements:* A license is not required but a degree in architecture from a legally recognized institution that meets the national standards is required by law. An indigenous or foreign person who has acquired a degree in Peru, or in a university of a foreign country that has a bilateral agreement with a Peruvian university, is automati-

economically speaking and provide minimal potential for North American design firms. Chapter 2 includes a case study of a young American, Stephen Forneris, who practiced successfully in Ecuador; but he was pretty sure he was the only North American practicing there full time (see section pages 33–34).

I worked briefly on a resort and gaming project in Paraguay—where a casino license can be obtained—but even that experience merely confirmed how little potential there is in Paraguay at this time. Nevertheless, KPF and other major international firms are occasionally brought in for major projects.

Licensing and legal issues

According to the COAC Web site, architects can practice independently in Bolivia if they meet certain requirements;

cally legally qualified to apply for membership in CAP. Persons, either indigenous or foreign, who have not acquired their degree in the universities mentioned above must have their degree revalidated in accordance with the law of the country and the regulations of CAP. In order to become a member of CAP, a U.S. architect would have to have his or her degree revalidated in Peru to meet the standards required by law and by CAP. The following is a pro forma description of some steps that have to be taken to have a degree in architecture revalidated: Have all pertinent documents (e.g., diplomas, degrees, transcripts, and complete course content descriptions) notarized locally in a Peruvian consulate or embassy so that these documents will be accepted by Peru. Have all pertinent documents translated officially by either the Ministry of Foreign Affairs in Lima or the U.S. Embassy in Lima. The Comisión Nacional Interuniversitaria then interviews the applicant and evaluates the courses taken to see whether or not the degree meets the legal standards of the country. If the degree does not meet these requirements, the person will have to study the courses stipulated by the commission to be eligible to apply for membership in CAP.

- *What agency licenses?* The Colegio de Arquitectos del Perú is established as a legal entity by public law and is responsible for carrying out a function comparable to that of a licensing agency.
- *What is the professional architectural organization?* Colegio de Arquitectos del Perú.
- *To practice, is a local representative required?* Yes, a local representative is needed in order for a U.S. architectural firm to practice in Peru. The local representative does not have to be a Peruvian and could be a U.S. citizen. In order to establish local representation, one can either form a partnership with an architect who is an active member of CAP or become an active member of CAP.

Fee levels, payment terms, and taxes
Bolivia and Ecuador both have compulsory fee scales. In Ecuador the fees are based on the building type and the construction cost.

Sources of information
U.S. Embassy, Bolivia
Telephone: 591-2-216-8000
E-mail: lpzirc@state.gov
Web site: www.lapaz.usembassy.gov

Colegio de Arquitectos de La Paz
E-mail: colegioarquitectoslp@cdalp.net
Web site: www.cdalp.net

U.S. Embassy, Ecuador
Telephone: 593-2-256-2890
Web site: www.usembassy.org.ec

El Colegio Nacional de Arquitectos
    del Ecuador
Telephone: 593-2-583-938
E-mail: cae-sen@pi.pro.ec
Web site: www.cae.org.ec/default.html

U.S. Embassy, Paraguay
Telephone: 595-21-213-715
E-mail: paraguayusembassy@state.gov
Web site: http://paraguay.usembassy.gov

U.S. Embassy, Peru
Telephone: 51-1-434-3000
E-mail: lima.office.box@mail.doc.gov
Web site: http://lima.usembassy.gov

Colegio de Arquitectos Del Perú
Telephone: 51-1-265-4098
Web site: www.cap.org.pe

Colombia

Colombia is one of the larger countries in Latin America, with a population of approximately 43 million. Its economy has had chronic difficulties, but the GDP approaches $300 billion.

As with most of Latin America, Colombia has sophisticated business and professional sectors, as well as large numbers of rural and urban poor. The major cities, Bogotá (2005 census population: 6,776,000), Cali (2005 census population: 2,068,386),[9] and Cartagena (2005 census population: 846,801)[10] continue to attract immigration from rural areas.

There has been a chronic insurgency for over 40 years, as well as a large drug trade, which have been major problems. Nevertheless, Colombia has important economic ties to the U.S. and North American design professionals have occasional assignments in Colombia.

Licensing and legal issues

Licensing requirements are as follows:

- *Is a license required?* Yes. A license and registration is required of national and foreign professionals who wish to practice architecture in Colombia.
- *Licensing requirements:* Architects domiciled in a foreign country who wish to undertake a contract with a Colombian public or private entity may request authorization to work in Colombia directly from the National Professional Council for Engineering and Architecture. This authorization is valid for one year only, but it may be renewed.
- *What agency licenses?* Licenses are approved by the Consejo Profesional Nacional de Arquitectura y sus Profesiones Auxiliares (National Professional Council for Architecture and its Auxiliary Professions).

- *What is the professional architectural organization?* Sociedad Colombiana de Arquitectos (Colombian Society of Architects).
- *To practice, is a local representative required?* According to Decree 222 of February 12, 1983 (Title 11, Article 7), foreign firms executing contracts with the government of Colombia or government-controlled entities:

must establish a branch having its domicile in the national territory if the purpose of the contract is of a permanent nature; if the purpose of the contract is of an occasional nature, they must appoint an agent, domiciled in Colombia, duly empowered to present the bid, execute and perform the contract, and represent the entity in or out of the court. The regulation (in each case) shall define, for the purposes of this article, what is meant by an object of a permanent or of an occasional nature. In the case of contracts of a permanent nature, the foreign entity must present the bid through a duly appointed agent, unless it is presented personally by a legal representative thereof.

Colombia has bilateral agreements with a number of countries for recognition of qualifications but the architect's academic record still must be submitted for recognition.

Sources of information

U.S. Embassy, Colombia
Telephone: 57-1-285-1300
Web site:
http://usembassy.state.gov/posts/co1/wwwhmain.html

Sociedad Colombiana de Arquitectos
Web site: www.sociedadcolombian
adearquitectos.org/menu.html

Consejo Profesional Nacional de
Arquitectura y Sus Profesiones
Auxiliares
Telephone: 57-1-350-2700
Fax: 57-1-380-4201
Web site: www.cpnaa.gov.co

Venezuela

At the time this book was written, Venezuela and the U.S. were in the midst of strained relations. Since Venezuela does not provide many opportunities for North American design professionals, this has not helped things very much.

Venezuela is a relatively small country. Over 4.7 million of the country's 25 million people live in the capital region around Caracas. The economy is heavily dependent on oil, which makes up one-third of its $176.4 billion GDP, 80 percent of the export revenues, and over half of the government's operating revenues.

Licensing and legal issues

Licensing requirements are as follows:

- *Is a license required?* Yes.
- *Licensing requirements:* If the architecture degree is from a foreign university, a written and oral examination and thesis will be required. Thesis requirement must be a complete architectural project.
- *What agency licenses?* Colegio de Ingenieros, Arquitectos y Profesiones Afines de Venezuela (CIV).
- *What is the professional architectural organization?* Colegio de Arquitectos de Venezuela has close ties to CIV, and ar-

chitects are normally associated with Colegio de Ingenieros de Venezuela.
- *To practice, is a local representative required?* Yes.

Sources of information

U.S. Embassy, Venezuela
Telephone: 58-212-975-6411
E-mail: embajada@state.gov
Web site: http://caracas.usembassy.gov

U. S. Embassy, The Commercial Service
Telephone: 58-212-907-8689
E-mail: caracas.office.box@mail.doc.gov
Web site: www.buyusa.gov/venezuela/en

Colegio de Ingenieros Arquitectos y
Profesiones Afines (Association of
Engineers, Architects and Related
Professions)
Colegio de Arquitectos de Venezuela

WESTERN EUROPE

Western Europe—a geographic designation with less relevance each year—is made up of 23 countries; all, except Andorra and San Marino, are discussed here, even if briefly.

Most of these countries (with the exception of Switzerland and Norway) are now part of the European Union (EU), and 12 share a common currency—the euro. For all of the talk of a united Europe, however, national boundaries still matter. Moreover, opportunities for North American design professionals vary significantly from country to country. While many opportunities remain for North American design firms, most of them go to firms that established themselves in Europe in the 1980s and early 1990s. Twenty years ago, Europe started building projects—offices, shopping centers, laboratories, hospitals, airports, corporate interiors, etc.—based on North American models. Because of their greater

Contents

*Countries in bold receive
longer descriptive sections.*

experience—as well as the North American corporations and developers who brought many of them—a significant number of the U.S. and Canadian firms that came over at that time and established offices are still there and, in most cases, prospering. Over the twenty years since the North American invasion, the Europeans have learned how to compete. Now they are exporting their skills to North America.

For the most part, these countries are prosperous and have sophisticated economies. They are not without serious problems, however. Many of them have high unemployment, an aging work force, and very small population growth. Competition from Eastern Europe and Asia is also a problem. As a result, real growth in the region has been slow.

In spite of increased competition from European architects, North American firms remain very active in Western Europe. In the larger countries, there are still many opportunities for firms that bring

Table 4.5 Western Europe Population and Economic Statistics[11]

Country	Population	Population Growth Rate (%)	GDP—Purchasing Power Parity*	GDP—Official Exchange Rate*	GDP— Per Capita ($)
Austria	8,193,000	0.09	279.5	309.3	34,100
Belgium	10,379,000	0.13	330.4	367.8	31,800
Cyprus	784,000	0.53	17.79	16.35	22,700
Denmark	5,451,000	0.33	198.5	256.3	37,000
Finland	5,231,000	0.14	171.7	196.2	32,800
France	60,876,000	0.35	1.871 trillion	2.154 trillion	30,100
Germany	82,422,000	-0.02	2.585 trillion	2.858 trillion	31,400
Greece	10,688,000	0.18	251.7	222.5	23,500
Iceland	299,000	0.87	11.04	13.85	38,100
Ireland	4,062,000	1.15	177.2	202.4	43,600
Italy	58,134,000	0.04	1.727 trillion	1.78 trillion	29,700
Liechtenstein	34,000	0.78	1.786	2.487	25,000
Luxembourg	474,000	1.23	32.6	34.37	68,800
Monaco	32,000	0.41	0.870	N/A	27,000
Netherlands	16,491,000	0.49	512	612.7	31,700
Norway	4,611,000	0.38	207.3	261.7	47,800
Portugal	10,606,000	0.36	203.1	176.6	19,100
San Marino	29,000	1.26	0.940	0.880	34,600
Spain	40,398,000	0.13	1.027 trillion	1.081 trillion	27,000
Sweden	9,017,000	0.16	285.1	371.5	31,600
Switzerland	7,524,000	0.43	252.9	386.8	33,600
United Kingdom	60,609,000	0.28	1.903 trillion	2.341 trillion	31,400

* In billions of U.S. dollars unless otherwise noted.

special skills, experience, or design ability. Nevertheless, it has become more difficult for firms—who were not there before the mid-1990s—to break in. Thus, while Europe is a huge potential market, it is a hard one to penetrate.

Austria

Austria was once the center of a large empire, but today it is a small, landlocked republic in the center of Europe. It became a member of the European Common Mar-ket in 1995 and the euro zone in 1999.

Today it is a prosperous, democratic nation that is well positioned as a bridge to the emerging EU economies to the east. Its economy is also closely tied to Germany's. The economy has strong financial, industrial, agricultural, and services sectors. As with many of its neighbors, it has very slow population growth, an aging population, and constant need for actions to help keep the economy competitive.

Fig. 4–15: *Hypo Alpe-Adria Center, Klagenfurt, Austria. Architect: Morphosis. Photograph by Ernst Peter Prokop.*

The market

The market for North American design services is limited.

Languages and communications

German is the national language; but Slovene, Croatian, and Hungarian are the first languages in a few regions. The telecommunications and IT infrastructure is sophisticated.

Sources of information

U.S. Embassy, Austria
Telephone: 43-1-313-390
E-mail: embassy@usembassy.at
Web site: www.vienna.usembassy.gov

Bundesministerium fur Bildung,
    Wissenschaft und Kultur
Telephone: 43-1-53-1200
Fax: 43-1-53-120-3099
E-mail: ministerium@bmbwk.gv.at
Web site: www.bmbwk.gv.at

Architekturzentrum Wien
Telephone: 43-1-522-31-15
Fax: 43-1-522-31-17
E-mail: office@azw.at
Web site: www.azw.at

Architekturstifftung Österreich
Telephone: 43-1-513-08-95
Fax: 43-1-513-08-95-4
E-mail: aaf@aaf.or.at
Web site: www.aneta.at

Bundesministerium fur Wirtschaft
    und Arbeit
Telephone: 43-1-711-000
E-mail: service@bmwa.gv.at
Web site:
www.bmwa.gv.at/EN/Contact/default.htm

Bundeskammer der Architekten und
    Ingenieurkonsulenten
Telephone: 43-1-505-58-07
Fax: 43-1-505-32-11
E-mail: office@arching.at
Web site: www.arching.at

Belgium

After invasion and occupation during the two world wars, the Kingdom of Belgium has emerged as a modern, technologically advanced country. The country is a parliamentary democracy with a constitutional monarchy, and it is a member of the EU and the euro zone.

Even as a small, sophisticated country, it still has its ethnic tensions. These tensions—between the Dutch-speaking Flemings in the north and the French-speaking Walloons in the south—has led to increased autonomy for the two regions.

Belgium has a modern economy with a diversified industrial and commercial base. Its economy is highly sensitive to external economic influence, and roughly 75 percent of its trade is within the EU.

The market

Belgium is a limited market for North American design professionals, except for those with existing European offices and relevant expertise.

Languages and communications

The official languages are Dutch, French, and German with the vast majority speaking Dutch or French. The telecommunications and IT infrastructure is sophisticated.

Licensing and legal issues

Licensing requirements are as follows:

- *Is a license required?* Yes. A license is required by law to practice architecture for both indigenous and foreign persons. An architect licensed in any European Union member state is entitled to practice in all other EU member states.
- *Licensing requirements:* A degree in architecture, issued by an architectural school (approved by the Belgian Department of Education or other accredited authority) and two years practical training (exemptions from this are pos-

sible if there is an equivalent in practical training and experience).
- *What agency licenses?* The organization issuing the license to practice is the Orde Van Architecten, Nationale Raad (National Order of Architects). The organization also has a disciplinary responsibility. Actual registration is done by one of the 10 regional branches, each one located in one of the nine provinces, with the province of Brabant having two branches. Geographical location of the architect's office determines the Order's branch that will register the individual architect's license. Title and license only are granted to an individual person, never to a firm. The architect remains personally liable for his or her work during a 10-year period after the construction has been completed (Decennial Liability). Belgian law specifies that the architect has to remain totally independent from the contractor. Under no circumstances may an architect act as a contractor or be paid by one.
- *What is the professional architectural organization?* The National Order of Architects is an independent organization established by law as the sole agency entitled to issue architecture licenses.
- *To practice, is a local representative required?* A non-Belgian may act as an architect in Belgium, provided he or she is an EU-member-state citizen and has graduated from an EU architectural school. All architects who sign the plans, control construction, and personally bear decennial liability have to be registered with the Order. Several architects may jointly perform the same assignment. Persons who are not members of the European Union may obtain a Belgian license for a single or permanent

assignment. The process involves a Royal Decree, or law drawn from the Secretary of Education, and usually takes from a few months to one year. Retaining a local law firm, consultant, or lobbyist may considerably accelerate the process. Decisive factors are reciprocity agreement and degree equivalence. Holding a degree from an internationally known U.S. architecture school or an institution from which graduates have in the past obtained a Belgian architecture license makes the process much easier; graduates from lesser-known schools may be required to take additional examinations in Belgium. There are no legal requirements regarding the establishment of local representation of local participation. Non-EU persons must obtain a local work permit.

Sources of information
U.S. Embassy, Belgium
Telephone: 32-2-508-2111
Web site: www.usembassy.be/main.html

Federation Royale des Societes
  d'Architectes de Belgique
Telephone: 32-2-512-34-52
Fax: 32-2-502-82-04
E-mail: info@fab-arch.be
Web site: www.fab-arch.be

Orde Des Architectes / Orde Van
  Architecten (The National Order of
  Architects)
Telephone: 32-2-647-06-69
E-mail:
  conseil.national@ordredesarchitectes.be
Web site: www.ordredesarchitectes.be

Cyprus
The Republic of Cyprus is an island nation and former British colony. It achieved independence in 1960. It suffers from long running tensions between the Greek and Turkish Cypriot minorities, and in 1974 Turkey intervened leading to the northern third of the island declaring itself the Turkish Republic of Northern Cyprus—an entity only recognized by Turkey. The entire island became part of the European Union in 2004, but EU rights only apply to the Republic of Cyprus–controlled areas.

The economy is primarily service based, and tourism and financial services are the most important sectors. The Turkish north is far poorer than the rest of the island.

The market
The small size of the country and economic fluctuations exacerbated by ethnic tensions make this a very small potential market for design services. Tourism is probably the most likely sector to generate opportunities, but Stantec is designing two airports.

Languages and communications
Greek, Turkish, and English are all spoken. It has a relatively modern telecommunications system.

Sources of information
U.S. Embassy, Cyprus
Telephone: 357-22-393-939
E-mail: info@americanembassy.org.cy
Web site: http://nicosia.usembassy.gov

Denmark
The Kingdom of Denmark has grown into a modern, prosperous country with a constitutional monarchy. It is a member of the EU but not part of the euro zone. It has a modern, market economy that supports high living standards for most of its population. As with many of the neighbors, an aging population will pose increasing challenges.

The market

As with the other small, highly developed western European countries, the opportunities for North American design services are limited.

Languages and communications

Danish is the national language, but English is the predominant second language. The telecommunications and IT infrastructure is sophisticated.

Licensing and legal issues

Licensing requirements are as follows:

- *Is a license required?* No
- *Licensing requirements:* Not applicable.
- *What agency licenses?* Not applicable.
- *What is the professional architectural organization?* The Federation of Danish Architects.
- *To practice, is a local representative required?* No.

Sources of information

U.S. Embassy, Denmark
Telephone: 45-33-41-7100
E-mail: CopenhagenACS@state.gov
Web site: www.usembassy.dk

Danske Arkitekters Landsforbund/
Akademisk Arkitektforening
(The Federation of Danish Architects)
Telephone: 45-30-85-9000
E-mail: aa@aa-dk.dk
Web site: www.dal-aa.dk/aa

Finland

The Republic of Finland became completely independent in 1917, after centuries of rule by Sweden and Russia. Following World War II, it has made a rapid transformation from an agricultural and forest-product economy to a highly indus-

Fig. 4–16: *Danish Jewish Museum, Copenhagen, Denmark. Architects: Studio Daniel Libeskind with Susanne Milne. Photograph by Bitter Bredt Photographie.*

trialized, largely free-market economy. Its per capita GDP is now equivalent to that of the major western European economies. Trade—ranging from high-tech cell phones to timber—accounts for 40 percent of GDP. Finland is now a member of the EU and the euro zone. It has a small, aging population and a slow population-growth rate.

The market

The home of Alvar Aalto is a tiny market for North American design professionals. Steven Holl designed the Museum of

Fig. 4–17: *Kiasma, Museum of Contemporary Art, Helsinki, Finland. Architect: Steven Holl Architects. Photograph by Paul Warchol.*

Contemporary Art in Helsinki, but very few others have had opportunities there.

Languages and communications

Finnish is the national language. As one of the home countries of high-tech cell phones, the IT and telecommunications infrastructure is advanced.

Licensing and legal issues

Licensing requirements are as follows:

- *Is a license required?* No
- *Licensing requirements:* A recognized degree in architecture is required for practice. In Finland, such degrees are granted by the following: Helsinki University of Technology, Tampere University of Technology, and University of Oulu. A foreign degree in architecture is subject to recognition by one of the above-mentioned universities.
- *What agency licenses?* Not applicable.
- *What is the professional architectural organization?* The Finnish Association of Architects.
- *To practice, is a local representative required?* No, but the requirements are undergoing changes. Information is given by the Ministry of Trade and Industry.

Sources of information

U.S. Embassy, Finland
Telephone: 358-9-616-250

E-mail: HelsinkiACS@state.gov
Web site: www.usembassy.fi

Suomen Arkkitehtiliitto / Finlands
    Arkitektforbund (SAFA), Finnish
    Association of Architects
Telephone: 358-9-584-480
Fax: 358-9-544-4222
E-mail: safa@safa.fi
Web site: www.safa.fi

Arkkitehtitoimistojen Liitto (ATL)
    The Association of Finnish Architects
    Offices
Telephone: 358-9-5844-4218
Fax: 358-9-176-950
Web site: www.atl.fi

France

France is one of the three most influential
countries in Europe. Its 61 million population, two-trillion-dollar economy, and
sophisticated population have maintained France's position as an important
world leader in many fields. It has always
had a complicated relationship with the
United States (key ally during the Revolutionary War, World War I, and World
War II and frequent critic much of the
rest of the time) and was the original col-
onizer of Canada until supplanted by the
British in the middle of the eighteenth
century.

At the time this book was written,
American-French relations were in one of
its frequent low periods. In spite of the
popularity of anti-American sentiments,
France has been important for North
American architects. Its École des Beaux-
Arts was a popular training ground for
many architects in the nineteenth century. Today it continues to be influential as
well as an occasional market for North
American architects.

The market

As is the case with other wealthy sophisticated countries, French clients often seek
out "the best" irrespective of nationality.
In some cases, such as I. M. Pei's commission for the Louvre and Richard Meier's
building for Canal Plus, it was a direct
qualification-based selection. In other cases, North American firms have won projects via France's frequent competitions,
such as Canadian Carlos Ott's winning
entry for the new Paris Opera House. In
addition, some international clients—

Fig. 4–18: *Rouen Concert Hall
and Exhibition Center, Rouen,
France. Architect: Bernard Tschumi Architects. Photograph by Peter Mauss/Esto.*

such as Disney—bring their own architects with them. Thus, while it has not been a large market for U.S. and Canadian firms, it has provided some high-profile projects for architects able to compete in a very competitive market.

When considering France as a place to seek work, it should be remembered that France has a large, sophisticated design community. As Thomas Vonier notes, France "has long invested in architecture as a national enterprise closely linked to the country's self-avowed *mission civilisatrice*...Quasi-public design organizations, such as *Aéroports de Paris*, offer a wide range of design, construction and management services...In the 1990s a group of French firms established *Architectes Français à l'Export* (AFEX), an association whose aim is to promote use of

French architects by foreign clients...They have focused on such specialty areas as restoration of historic properties, urban design and museum and cultural tourism—not coincidentally, areas in which French architects have distinguished themselves at home" (courtesy of Thomas Vonier). Thus, one should assume that domestic competition from local French firms will be strong both in France and abroad.

Reasons to be there

France's overall attractions are well known. In addition, there are several relevant business reasons to be interested:

1. It has project opportunities (particularly in the public sector) with high potential for design excellence.

Fig. 4–19: *Grand Hotel du Cap Ferrat, Cap Ferrat, France. Architects: Voorsanger & Mills Architects with Michel Mosser. Courtesy of Grand Hotel du Cap Ferrat.*

2. For firms with an interest in practicing in Europe, work in France can be both visible and influential.

Reasons to be cautious

France is very bureaucratic; anti-Americanism is very fashionable; and there is a great deal of competition for most significant projects.

Skills and capabilities that are important

As the examples listed above illustrate, it helps to have a reputation for design excellence as well as relevant building-type expertise. Fluency in French or a French partner is usually important as well.

Who is operating there now?

To date, no North American firm has been able to obtain more than an occasional commission; but the ones who have obtained projects there include many of the best-known firms, including: Frank Gehry, Richard Meier, Pei Cobb Freed, and Robert A. M. Stern. More recently, Anthony Belluschi designed a major shopping center in Paris; Davis Brody Bond designed a project for Valeo, an auto parts supplier; Edward I. Mills designed an addition to the Grand Hotel du Cap Ferrat; Thom Mayne is designing an office tower in Paris, and Studios Architecture maintains an office for interior design clients in Paris.

Who are the clients?

Most of the projects awarded to North American firms have come from:

- The government (the Louvre, Paris Opera House, etc.)
- Major French corporations (Canal Plus)
- International corporations (Disney, etc.)
- Real estate development companies
- Organizations with strong ties to the U.S.

What is the process for getting work?

As noted above, competitions are frequently used along with the elaborate process reserved for high-profile commissions such as the Louvre. For most firms interested in working in France, a more productive process will involve focusing on specific clients or team members (contractors, local architects, consultants) with connections to upcoming projects.

Languages and communications

Fluency in French is very important.

Licensing and legal issues

Licensing requirements are as follows:

- *Is a license required?* Yes, for any project over 170 square meters. Sixty-eight percent of construction in France is done without an architect—although most of this is private housing.
- *Licensing requirements:* Though no architecture license is required by law in France, each practicing architect has to hold a government-approved diploma. European Community or U.S. architectural schools have to be recognized by the Ministere de l'Équipement (French Ministry of Equipment). Architectural studies must last five years. A final exam is required. This applies to French and foreign nationals. Practicing architects are registered at the Conseil Regional de l'Ordre des Architectes (Regional Council of Architects). In the case of a foreign architect, an oral

121

examination may be required; but most may be approved on the base of professional references examined by a special commission.

- *What agency licenses?* The French government agency responsible for regulations regarding architectural activities and validation of diplomas is the French Ministry of Culture.
- *What is the professional architectural organization?* Ordre des Architectes. For practicing architects, membership of the Conseil National de l'Ordre is mandatory.
- *To practice, is a local representative required?* There is no legal requirement for a U.S. architectural firm to have a local representative. However, suppliers of architectural services in France have to cope with a host of rules, standards, and legal requirements. Therefore, it is often advantageous for a U.S. architectural company to work with local representation or acquire an existing French company. Experience has shown that successful U.S. architectural firms either have made substantial investments before market entry or have worked through a local partner.

Fee levels, payment terms, and taxes

Fees for private sector projects are freely negotiated between the architect and client. For public sector projects, the architect's fee depends on the type of project, as well as the complexity and scale of the project. The French government has issued a "guide" that is used as a base for fee negotiations in the following ways: evaluating project complexity, agreeing on a "complexity coefficient" and "reference coefficient," and calculating fees for each stage of a project. The fee can be cal-

culated in three different ways: a percentage of total construction costs pretax, an hourly base, or a mix of the above. Payments of 5 to 8 percent are generally made at the permit phase and 2 to 3 percent at the construction stage.

Insurance need not be French, as long as it is valid in France. Contact the Ministère des Finances for a list of insurance companies.

Local resources

The major cities of France—and many of the smaller cities as well—have sophisticated architects, engineers, and other consultant disciplines. In addition, the necessary support services—printers, model shops, etc.—exist as well.

Design issues

As one French architect friend of mine noted, "There are traditions to be aware of so you know how to ignore them when necessary."

Code and regulatory issues

The codes and regulatory issues are, in outline, similar to those in much of North America. Some of the differences, however, in codes and regulatory issues are as follows:

- The code is national and applies statewide.
- A different underlying legal code.
- An extra step in the approval process is required for some projects to obtain Local Association Approval.
- The architect has less control of the schedule during the construction administration phase than in the U.S.

Local construction capabilities

French contractors, as well as the international contractors operating in France, are sophisticated and capable of building virtually any project.

Personal safety and health issues

France is, of course, one of the safer places to visit, live, and work.

Sources of information

U.S. Embassy, France
Telephone: 33-1-43-122-222
Web site: www.amb-usa.fr

Organisation for Economic Co-operation
and Development
Web site: www.oecd.org/country/
0,3021,en_33873108_33873376_
1_1_1_1_1,00.html

Conseil National de l'Ordre
des Architectes
Telephone: 33-1-56-58-67-00
Fax: 33-1-56-58-67-01
Web site: www.architectes.org

Société Française des Architectes (SFA)
Telephone: 33-1-56-81-10-25
Fax: 33-1-56-81-10-26
E-mail: contact@sfarchi.org
Web site: www.sfarchi.org

Mutuelle des Architectes Français (MAF)
Telephone: 33-1-53-70-30-00
Fax: 33-1-53-70-32-10
Web site: www.maf.fr

Union Nationale des Syndicats Français
d'Architectes
Web site: www.archilink.com

Germany

The Federal Republic of Germany (FRG) has been suffering from a long period of economic stagnation but remains the world's third-largest economy. As with all major economies, there are many projects requiring sophisticated design services. Germany is no exception and has offered a large number of project opportunities to international firms.

Reasons to be there

As noted above, architecture and the other design professions are respected, and this respect extends to foreign firms. As a result, Germany is one of the more receptive countries in the EU to international firms. In addition, it:

- Is politically and economically stable
- Has a sophisticated legal system
- Has a relatively "fair and sophisticated," government-sponsored fee structure
- Has a construction industry capable of performing at a high-quality level
- Has a regular flow of challenging projects
- Is a reasonable base for doing work elsewhere in Europe
- Can be an enjoyable place to visit, live, and work

Reasons to be cautious

As with all sophisticated countries, it is complex. Thus, it is a country requiring considerable research and assistance before a firm can expect to be successful. Moreover, it is—as is most of Europe—a very expensive country in which to pursue work, to live, or to work. At the time this book was written, Germany was suffering from a period of relative economic stagnation, which has sharply slowed the design and construction industry.

Skills and capabilities that are important

Among the many skills, capabilities, and qualities cited by firms with experience in Germany as important include:

> "I think there is a general attitude in Europe that technology and advancement in construction lead to a betterment of life and society."
>
> *Helmut Jahn, FAIA, Murphy/Jahn*

Fig. 4–20: *Jewish Museum Berlin, Berlin, Germany. Architect: Studio Daniel Libeskind. Photograph by Bitter Bredt Photographie.*

- A German-speaking staff
- A marketable reputation for design excellence or expertise in a particular building type
- Technological sophistication

Who is operating there now?

Many U.S. and Canadian firms have designed projects in Germany: Murphy/Jahn, KPF, Libeskind, Eisenman, HOK, Richard Meier, Gehry, and many others. A few have even established offices or maintained a long-term presence; although more recently some, such as HOK, have closed offices in Germany.

Who are the clients?

As elsewhere in Europe, some North American design firms are brought by North American clients, such as the major U.S. developer Tishman Speyer. German clients, however, also hire international firms. Major corporations, government agencies, developers, and cultural institutions have all hired U.S. and other international firms for high-profile projects.

As these examples illustrate, many of the most visible commissions go to firms with demonstrated international expertise in a particular building type and/or a high-profile design reputation.

What is the process for getting work?

Many of the examples quoted above were selected in qualifications-based processes, but Germany also has a very sophisticated system of public competitions. The "bible" of German architects wishing to enter competitions is the *Wettbewerbe Aktuell*. It lists all currently running competitions. Many are limited to German architects, and often to architects in only a limited number of German states. Others are open to the EU, and some are open to a wide range of international competitors.

Languages and communications

Many people in Germany speak English, but foreign architects still need to have staff fluent in German. Drawings, specifications, and official communications are all in German. Germany, of course, has a sophisticated telecommunications infrastructure.

Licensing and legal issues

Germany does not have licensing exams. Germans can obtain a license three years after graduating from architecture school. Most foreign firms rely on local-partner firms for tasks requiring a license. However, if a firm works regularly in Germany, a regional license can be obtained.

Licensing requirements are are as follows:

- *Is a license required?* Yes.
- *Licensing requirements:* Architects from European Community (EC) countries are entitled to work in the FRG; but other foreigners, including U.S. architects, have to apply for acknowledgement through the Minister of Science of the appropriate state. Foreign applicants who wish to be licensed in the FRG must satisfy the same requirements as German citizens. If the foreigner has studied abroad, his or her educational background must be equivalent to a German architectural education. To determine whether the foreign architect's

qualifications meet German standards, the State Chamber of the state where the foreign architect will reside will consult with the German Central Office for Foreign Educational Affairs (Zentralstelle für ausländisches Bildungswesen). Licensed, but otherwise inexperienced, foreign architects may be required to serve an appropriate internship before a German license is granted.

- *What agency licenses?* The license is issued by the appropriate chamber of architects in the state (land) where the applicant has residence. At present, 11 chambers of architects cover the whole Federal Republic of Germany. The umbrella organization for the state chambers of architects is the Bundesarchitektenkammer (Federal Chamber of Architects), which represents the interests of the 11 state chambers, particularly as they relate to professional education. In addition to the licensing requirement, self-employed architects must also be members of their appropriate state chamber. In some states the membership of civil service and employed architects is compulsory as well, while in other states, membership in the state chamber of architects in these categories is voluntary.
- *To practice, is a local representative required?* No local representative is required if the foreign architectural firm can deliver proof of meeting Chamber of Architects' requirements. However, all customary requirements for operating any type of business in Germany (e.g., registering in the trade register at the local district court) do apply.

Scope of services

As in North America, project managers and construction managers have taken an

Fig. 4–21: *Westendstrasse 1/DZ Bank Headquarters, Frankfurt, Germany. Architects: Kohn Pedersen Fox Associates (KPF) with Nägele Hofmann Tiedemann & Partner. Photograph by Dennis Gilbert.*

increasing role in project direction, supplanting—in many cases—the architect's primary position.

Fee levels, payment terms, and taxes

Architectural fees are typically set in accordance with the Honorarordnung für Architetekten und Ingenieure (HOAI) fee structure. It is becoming common, however, for architects to quote fees below these standards when competing for a project.

Local resources

Excellent local architectural associates, engineers, specialist consultants, renderers, etc., exist throughout Germany.

Design issues

German clients are typically seeking technologically sophisticated modern design solutions when they hire international architects.

Code and regulatory issues

Code requirements are typically regulated by the German states, and the approval processes are managed by local public authorities. In general, code requirements and approval processes are similar to those in North America.

Local construction capabilities

Construction quality standards and capabilities are among the best in the world. Quality, however, has eroded somewhat due to the growing use of foreign subcontractors.

Personal safety and health issues

Germany is a very safe place to live and work as long as one does not try to compete with the faster drivers on the autobahn.

Sources of information

U.S. Embassy, Germany
Telephone: 49-30-238-5174
Web site: www.usembassy.de

Vereinigung Freischaffender Architekten Deutschlands (VFA), or the Association of Independent Architects
Telephone: 49-30-3949-4019
E-mail: info@vfa-architekten.de
Web site: www.vfa-architekten.de

Forum für Architektur
Telephone: 49-30-615-0820
E-mail: bdia@architekt.de
Web site: www.architekt.de

Bund Deutscher Baumeister, Architekten
  und Ingenieure e. V. (BDB), or The
  Union of German Architects
Telephone: 49-30-841-8970
E-mail: infor@baumeister-online.de
Web site: www.baumeister-online.de

Bund Deutscher Architekten (BDA), or
  The Federation of German Architects
Telephone: 49-228-635-964
E-mail: kontakt@bda-bonn-rhein-sieg.de
Web site: www.bda-architekten.de

Bundesarchitektenkammer, or Federal
  Chamber of Architects
Telephone: 49-30-263-9440
E-mail: info@bak.de
Web site: www.bak.de

Greece

After 150 years of efforts to free itself
from the Ottoman Empire, to reunify
the Greek-speaking islands of the
Aegean, and to endure German occupation during World War II, a protracted
civil war, and a military dictatorship,
Greece finally emerged as a parliamentary republic in 1974. It became part of
the EU in 1981 and a member of the euro
zone in 2001.

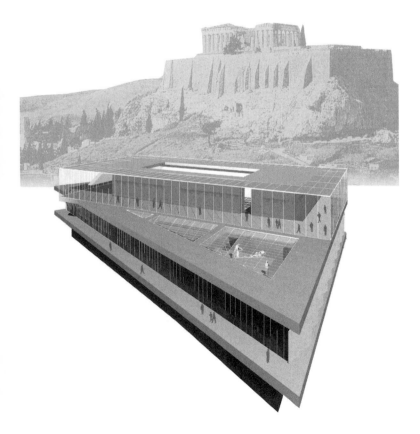

Fig. 4–22: *New Acropolis Muse-
um, Athens, Greece. Architect:
Bernard Tschumi Architects.
Courtesy of Bernard Tschumi
Architects.*

It is one of the poorer members of the EU and is a major beneficiary of EU aid. The Greek government continues its struggle to cut government spending and reduce the size of the large public sector, amongst other reforms. Tourism is a major sector of the economy, accounting for about 15 percent of the GDP. The economy went through a brief boom from 2003 through 2005 due to the investments and upgrades made to host the 2004 Olympic Games but then settled back into a slower growth period.

The market

Greece is another limited market for North American design professionals. There are occasional opportunities in tourism and with some building types where specialized expertise is important. Sasaki Associates, for example, was at work on a resort project as this book was being written.

Languages and communications

Greek is the national language. The IT and telecommunications infrastructure is adequate with modern networks and good mobile phone coverage.

Licensing and legal issues

Licensing requirements are as follows:

- *Is a license required?* Yes.
- *Licensing requirements:* To practice architecture in Greece, one must, by law, possess a license. The person must be licensed in Greece or in another European Union (EU) country. Companies and/or individuals registered in any EU country can practice architecture in Greece. A recognized university degree in architecture is required. If the degree is not from a Greek university, the architect must have his or her degree officially recognized by an interuniversity body located in Athens called Dikatsa. The procedure is cumbersome. Foreign architects who live and work in Greece for at least 10 years and are closely related to a Greek citizen have the right to be registered in Greece after recognition of their studies and passing an examination (in Greek) to be registered as a local architect.
- *What agency licenses?* The Technical Chamber of Greece (TEE).
- *What is the professional architectural organization?* Athens, Thessaloniki, and a dozen other cities have associations of architects. The largest association in Greece is the Athens Association of Architects.
- *To practice, is a local representative required?* Architectural partnership firms, individual firms, and corporations must have a local representative and/or employ architects or architectural firms licensed to practice in Greece (Greek or from EU countries). It is recommended that U.S. firms form a joint venture with a Greek or other EU-country registered firm. Appointing a U.S. citizen as a representative is not useful, unless he or she is licensed in an EU country.

Fee levels, payment terms, and taxes

The COAC Web site states that there is a compulsory fee scale that is published by the government. On projects that obtain official permission, the fees are compulsory.

Sources of information

U.S. Embassy, Greece
Telephone: 30-210-721-2951
E-mail: AthensAmEmb@state.gov
Web site: www.usembassy.gr

The Athens Association of Architects
Syllogos Architektonon Diplomatouchon
Anotaton Scholon—Panellinia Enosi
  Architektonon (SADAS-PEA),
  Association of Greek Architects
Telephone: 30-2-10-321-51-46
Fax: 30-2-10-321-51-47
Web site: www.sadas-pea.gr

Iceland

This island nation achieved full independence from Denmark in 1944. It is a small (population approximately 300,000), prosperous country that is heavily dependent on fishing. To date, Iceland has refused to join the European Union.

The market

Due to its small size, this is not a significant market opportunity. A growing tourism sector, however, could generate a few opportunities in the future.

Languages and communications

Icelandic, English, German, and Nordic languages are all spoken. It has a relatively modern communication infrastructure.

Licensing and legal issues

Licensing requirements are as follows:

- *Is a license required?* Yes
- *Licensing requirements:* A license is required by law for indigenous and foreign persons to practice architecture in Iceland (e.g., to submit architectural construction documents to building authorities). The initial licensing of indigenous and foreign architects requires a degree approved by the Association of Icelandic Architects, an examination, and a minimum of two years on-the-job experience as an architect.

- *What agency licenses?* A license is granted by the Ministry of Industry upon the recommendation of the Association of Icelandic Architects.
- *What is the professional architectural organization?* The Association of Icelandic Architects.
- *To practice, is a local representative required?* A U.S. architect can be a representative if he or she has a work permit and an architecture license.

Fee levels, payment terms, and taxes

The Architects' Association of Iceland publishes a recommended fee scale.

Sources of information

U.S. Embassy, Iceland
Telephone: 354-562-9100
Web site: http://reykjavik.usembassy.gov

Arkitektafélag Islands—
  Association of Icelandic Architects
Telephone: 354-551-1465
Fax: 354-562-0465
E-mail: ai@ai.is
Web site: www.ai.is

Ireland

Ireland is a small island country with strong cultural links to the United States. The island is divided between the Republic of Ireland, with a population of about 4.2 million on five-sixths of the land area, and Northern Ireland, part of the United Kingdom, with 1.7 million on the northeastern one-sixth of the landmass. Ireland was merged into the United Kingdom in 1801. The census in 1841 counted a population of over eight million; but during the Great Famine of that decade, over one million died and another million emigrated—many to the U.S. Emigration has continued until recently.

The Republic of Ireland emerged after a long struggle in 1921. The struggle between the Catholic and Protestant portions of Northern Ireland continues—although violence has been on the decline since 1998, and in 2005 the Provisional IRA (Irish Republican Army) announced the end of its armed campaign.

There was a long recession in the 1970s and 1980s, but in the 1990s a major economic boom began. This boom has made Ireland one of the most successful countries in Western Europe.

The market

Ireland—although relatively wealthy—is a small country. It is a market primarily for firms based in Europe or for North American firms with strong links to the country. Some North American corporations have invested in Ireland and brought their own architects.

Languages and communications

English is generally used, and the Irish have produced many of the greatest writers of English. Moreover, English is the language of business. Gaelic, however, is the other official language and technically the native tongue. The telecommunications infrastructure is modern.

Licensing and legal issues

Licensing requirements are as follows:

- *Is a license required?* No.
- *Licensing requirements:* There is a European directive on architectural qualifications—EC Directive 85/384/EEC, also called *The Architects' Directive.* Holding a degree recognized under the directive entitles you to practice as an architect in any EU member state.
- *What is the professional architectural organization?* The Royal Institute of the Architects of Ireland.
- *To practice, is a local representative required?* There are no Irish laws requiring U.S. architectural firms to have local representatives if the firms wish to practice in Ireland. However, any national of a non-European Union (EU) country (such as the U.S.) must obtain a work permit from the Department of Enterprise and Employment, and, before accepting employment in Ireland, permission from Ireland's Department of Justice must be obtained. Foreign corporations are required to register with the Department of Enterprise and Employment before establishing a business in Ireland.

Sources of information

U.S. Embassy, Ireland
Telephone: 353-1-668-8777
E-mail: acs_dublin@state.gov
Web site: http://dublin.usembassy.gov

The Royal Institute of the Architects
of Ireland
Telephone: 353-1-676-1703
E-mail: info@riai.ie
Web site: www.riai.ie

Italy

If given a choice, most North American design professionals would rank Italy as their first choice when it comes to places to work internationally. This country of 58 million people has everything that makes working internationally desirable—a beautiful country; a sophisticated, friendly people; memorable food and wine; and many other assets. Unfortunately, it has many talented architects and

Fig. 4–23: *Chapel of the Holy Spirit, Vatican City, Italy. Architect: Astorino. Photograph by Louis Astorino.*

very little work open to international firms. There are, however, a few commissions, such as Richard Meier's Chapel of the Holy Sprit, Astorino's chapel at the Vatican as well as for one of the Italian hospitals, and a land-planning assignment in Milan that our firm, jointly with others, worked on several years ago.

Giancarlo Alhadeff, speaking at an AIA conference on practice in Europe, talked about his experience practicing in Milan: "Italy does have a great many talented designers, but as a country it is unable to produce the kind of public work one finds in much of the rest of Europe." He also noted that "practicing in Italy [is]

Fig. 4–24: *Memoria e Luce,
9/11 Memorial, Padua, Italy.
Architect: Studio Daniel Libeskind.
Photograph by Bitter Bredt
Photographie.*

the growing economic competition from China, India, and other developing countries; and other current economic problems; it is not surprising that major new projects are limited. Thus, while Italy remains prosperous, it is not likely to generate more than the occasional opportunity for North American firms.

The market

As noted above, there are occasional opportunities, but Italy is a limited market even for Italian architects.

Licensing and legal issues

Licensing requirements are as follows:

- *Is a license required?* Yes. A license is required to practice architecture in Italy, which includes planning, designing, and supervising projects for any kind of structural work for which a building license has been granted.
- *Licensing requirements:* To call oneself an architect and to be legally recognized as such by the Italian authorities, the following requirements must be met: European Union (EU) citizenship and possession of a university degree obtained from an Italian government-approved university after a five-year course and final thesis. The controlling government body is the Italian Ministry of Public Education. Passage of the government qualifying exams consists of an eight-hour written and graphic test and an additional oral test to be taken approximately five months later. There is no training period, but at the time a graduate takes the written test (not before six months after the degree), it is assumed that the recently graduated architect has already had a period of

very difficult and often frustrating…Most architects in Milan seem to make a living designing furniture rather than buildings."[12]

This problem has been exacerbated by an aging population and almost nonexistent population growth. When combined with the economic malaise that accompanied the shock of joining the euro zone;

Fig. 4–25: *Elementary and high school, Italy. Architect: Mitchell/Giurgola Architects, LLP. Photograph by Elio Ciol.*

training with senior architect(s) and/or legally established Italian architectural firms(s), as well as membership on the provincial roll of architects. Please note that to become a member, an architect must comply with qualifications set forth above. Non-EU persons who have graduated from Italian universities have the same rights and obligations as Italian-born architects. Non-EU persons who have graduated abroad cannot officially practice architecture in Italy until the equivalence of their studies and degrees has been approved by government authorities. U.S. architects enjoy a privileged position as a result of the U.S.-Italy Friendship, Navigation and Commerce Agreement signed on February 2, 1948 (Law No. 385 of June 18, 1949, published on the Official Gazette No. 157 of July 12, 1949) and integrated on September 26, 1951 (Law No. 910 of May 1, 1960, published on the Official Gazette No. 213 of September 1, 1960).

- *What agency licenses?* The 90 provincial rolls of architects who register according to their official residence are under the jurisdiction of the Consiglio Nazionale Architetti (National Council of Architects). The controlling government body is the Italian Ministry of Justice and Pardon.
- *What is the professional architectural organization?* The Consiglio Nazionale Architetti.

- *To practice, is a local representative required?* Any U.S. architectural firm can operate in Italy provided a member or partner of the firm is a professional EU architect. This EU architect is the only legal representative of the U.S. firm before Italian authorities such as municipalities (building licenses) and central government entities (taxes, legal matters, etc.).

Fee levels, payment terms, and taxes

According to the COAC Web site, obligatory minimums and a compulsory fee scale are published by the Ministry of Justice. They may be followed for public procurement projects but not for private sector projects. Contact the Ministry for Ministerial Decree 44/2001 "Update of the fee scales for Engineers and Architects."

Sources of information

U.S. Embassy, Italy
Telephone: 39-6-467-410
E-mail: uscitizensrome@state.gov
Web site: rome.usembassy.gov

Consiglio Nazionale degli Architetti, Pianificatori, Paesaggisti e Conservatori (CNAPPC), or The National Council of Architects
Telephone: 39-6-688-9901
E-mail: esteri.can@awn.it
Web site: www.ace-italia.archiworld.it or www.archiworld.it

Associazione Nazionale Ingegneri Architetti Italiani (The National Association of Italian Engineers and Architects)
Telephone: 39-6-442-31170
E-mail: info@aniai.org
Web site: www.aniai.org

Liechtenstein

The tiny, landlocked Principality of Liechtenstein became a sovereign state in 1806 and was closely tied to Austria. After World War I, it shifted its economic ties to neighboring Switzerland. Its low taxes, diversified economy, and banking sector have supported economic growth and prosperity.

The market

With a population of only 34,000, Liechtenstein is not a significant market for design services in spite of its relative prosperity.

Languages and communications

The national language is German. The country has a modern telecommunications infrastructure.

Luxembourg

The Grand Duchy of Luxembourg is a constitutional democracy. It is a small, landlocked country with a very high standard of living. Its economy used to be based on heavy industry but is now 85 percent services based. Financial services are a particularly important part of the service sector.

Luxembourg has the highest per capita income in the world ($68,800). The country has a relatively low national debt. The Luxembourg government plays an active role in the national economy. Multinational corporations (e.g., Goodyear, DuPont, Guardian Glass, AOL, Amazon.com) have large operations there. The European Court of Justice and the European Bank for Investments are also located in Luxembourg. Americans are generally welcome, largely due to fond memories related to World War II.

The market

In spite of the small size of the country, Luxembourg has provided occasional opportunities for North American architects, including Arquitectonica (Banque du Luxembourg), Pei Cobb Freed (Museum of Modern Art Grand Duc Jean), and Richard Meier (German HypoVereinsbank). Most large projects, however, are awarded to firms with local contacts or representation. Nevertheless, the Luxembourg national government, the larger municipalities, European Union institutions, international banks and corporations, and others are willing, at times, to hire international architects. Competitions are often used for major public projects, and they are open to European offices. Again, however, teams with Luxembourg representation are usually preferred.

Architectural fees are, on average, lower than in some other developed countries, but services are different as well—fewer services during the construction documents phase and more services during construction administration phase. The architect has more responsibility for coordinating the trades, although clients have also started using specialized consultants and construction managers for those tasks.

Languages and communications
Luxembourgish is the national language, but French and German are official administrative languages. Even English is common for meetings and contracts. The telecommunications system is highly developed.

Sources of information
U.S. Embassy, Luxembourg
Telephone: 352-46-01-23
Web site:
   http://luxembourg.usembassy.gov

Ordre des Architectes et des
   Ingénieurs-Conseils

Telephone: 352-42-23-06
E-mail: oai@oai.lu
Web site: www.oai.lu

Monaco
The principality of Monaco is a constitutional monarchy on the southern coast of France. It has fewer than 32,000 residents, but it is a popular tourism destination (in large part due to its casino) and its status as a tax haven. It is the second smallest independent state (after Vatican City).

The market
Monaco is a relatively prosperous country; but it is far too small to be a real market

Fig. 4–26: *Banque de Luxembourg, Luxembourg. Architect: Arquitectonica. Photography by Richard Bryant.*

for North American design firms, beyond an occasional tourism-related project.

Languages and communications

French is the official language, but English and Italian are also commonly used—after all, the U.S.-born Grace Kelly was the wife of the late Prince Rainier and mother of Prince Albert II. It has a modern telecommunications system.

Fig. 4–27: *Mahler 4, Amsterdam, The Netherlands. Architect: Rafael Viñoly Architects PC. Photograph by Raoul Suermondt.*

Netherlands

The Kingdom of the Netherlands is a constitutional monarchy with a prosperous economy. Unlike most of its neighbors, the Netherlands avoided most wars (except World War II) of the last three centuries and have, in general, experienced a "long holiday from history." The famous German poet Heinrich Heine quipped: "When the world ends I'll go to Holland because there everything happens 50 years later." It was a founding member of the EU and the euro zone.

For centuries, its economy has relied heavily on foreign trade. It also plays a major role in international finance and attracts considerable foreign investment.

The market

Gensler had an office in Amsterdam until recently, and other North American firms have found occasional projects there. It remains, however, a relatively small market for North Americans. It is currently one of the most creative design communities in the world and is more likely to export design skills than to import them.

Languages and communications

Dutch and Gisian are the official languages, but the Dutch often speak two or more languages, including English. The IT and telecommunications infrastructure is sophisticated.

Licensing and legal issues

Licensing requirements are as follows:

• *Is a license required?* There is no license required to practice architecture in the Netherlands, but any service designated as architectural given by a foreign or indigenous person or company established in the Netherlands requires registration.

- *Licensing requirements:* For foreign architects, the Dutch government uses the European Union (EU) Architects Directive, which means that architectural educations from all EU countries are recognized. Architectural educations from non-EU countries will be judged by the Dutch government on a case-by-case basis.
- *What agency licenses?* Stichting Bureau Architectenregister.
- *What is the professional architectural organization?* Koninklijke maatschappij tot Bevordering der Bouwkunst Bond van Nederlandse Architecten (BNA).
- *To practice, is a local representative required?* U.S. architectural firms do not need a local representative to practice in the Netherlands. However, in view of local regulations and norms, it is recommended to work with local firms. The establishment of local representation requires procedures applicable for operating any type of business activity in the Netherlands.

Sources of information

U.S. Embassy, The Netherlands
Telephone: 31-70-310-2209
Web site: http://thehague.usembassy.gov

Stichting Bureau Architectenregister
Telephone: 31-70-346-70-20
Fax: 31-70-360-30-28
E-mail: info@architectenregister.nl
Web site: www.architectenregister.nl

Bond van Nederlandse Architekten—
Royal Institute of Dutch Architects
Telephone: 31-20-555-36-66

Fig. 4–28: *Provinciehuis, The Hague, The Netherlands. Architects: Kohn Pedersen Fox Associates (KPF) with Liag Architekten en Bouwadviseurs. Photograph by H.G. Esch.*

Fax: 31-20-555-36-99
E-mail: bna@bna.nl
Web site: www.bna.nl

Nederlands Architektuurinstitut
   (Netherlands Architecture Institute)
Telephone: 31-10-440-12-00
Fax: 31-10-436-69-75
E-mail: info@nai.nl
Web site: www.nai.nl

Norway

The Kingdom of Norway is a constitutional monarchy that gained independence from Sweden in 1905. Although closely linked to the rest of Europe, Norway has not joined the EU.

The country has extensive natural resources: e.g., oil, hydropower, fish, forest products, and minerals. Oil accounts for one-third of exports and provides a major underpinning of the economy. Since oil reserves are expected to begin running out in about 20 years, the country has been investing its surplus abroad.

The market

Norway is a small country with capable local design resources. As a result, the opportunities for foreign firms are limited. Nevertheless, NBBJ and a few others have had projects there over the last two decades.

Languages and communications

Norwegian is the official language. The country's IT and telecommunications infrastructure is sophisticated.

Sources of information

U.S. Embassy, Norway
Telephone: 47-2-44-8550
E-mail: oslovisa@state.gov
Web site: http://norway.usembassy.gov

Norske Arkitekters Landsforbund
   (The National Association of Norwegian Architects)
Telephone: 47-23-33-2500
E-mail: nal@arkitektur.no
Web site: www.arkitektur.no

Portugal

After a series of repressive governments in the first seven decades of the twentieth century, a coup finally installed a democratic government in 1974. Portugal gave up its colonies in 1975. It is now a parliamentary democracy and a member of the EU and euro zone.

It is one of the poorest countries in Western Europe. Due to a poor educational system, competition from Asia and Eastern Europe, and other problems, Portugal faces some significant economic challenges.

The market

Portugal is a limited market for North American design firms, but a few firms have obtained occasional projects. If the economy ever starts to grow rapidly, there will be a need for international design firms, since the local professionals are relatively unsophisticated compared to their European neighbors.

Languages and communications

Portuguese is the national language, although Mirandese is also used locally. The IT and telecommunications infrastructure is modern.

Licensing and legal issues

Licensing requirements are as follows:

- *Is a license required?* There is no license as such; however, one has to be a member of or registered at the Associação dos Arquitectos Portugueses (Portuguese Association of Architects, PAA).

- *Licensing requirements:* One has to have a degree in architecture or, in the case of a foreigner, one has to have a certificate of equivalency approved by the Ministry of Education and be a resident to become a member of or to be registered at PAA, with the exception of those with EU diplomas.
- *What agency licenses?* Ordem dos Arquitectos.
- *What is the professional architectural organization?* Associação dos Arquitectos Portugueses.
- *To practice, is a local representative required?* No, as long as all submitted architectural plans are submitted by a registered member.

Sources of information
U.S. Embassy, Portugal
Telephone: 351-21-727-3300
E-mail: reflisbon@state.gov
Web site: http://lisbon.usembassy.gov

Ordem dos Arquitectos
   (Portugese Order of Architects)
Telephone: 351-21-324-11-00
Fax: 351-21-324-11-01
E-mail: cdm@ordemdosarquitectos.pt
Web site: www.arquitectos.pt

Spain
With a population of over 40 million, Spain is the fifth largest country in Western Europe. Since the death of the dictator-general Francisco Franco in 1975, Spain has rapidly emerged as an increasingly prosperous, constitutional monar-

Fig. 4–29: *Endesa Headquarters, Madrid, Spain. Architects: Kohn Pedersen Fox Associates (KPF) with Rafael de la Hoz. Photograph by H. G. Esch.*

chy. Following its bloody civil war, which preceded World War II, and during Franco's long rule, Spain was one of the poorest countries in Europe. Now it has a diverse economy, with a GDP that is, according to *The World Factbook*, on a per capita basis about 80 percent of the four leading European economies.

The market

Spain's modernization started after that of many of its European neighbors, but it has been accelerating. Some of it has been stimulated by the major investments associated with the Olympics in Barcelona in 1992 and the World Expo in Seville in the same year. In addition, Spain has been supportive of major—often avant garde—architecture. Some of these projects—most notably Frank Gehry's Guggenheim Museum in Bilbao—have been designed by North American architects.

When we were a young firm, we had some of our first international opportunities in Spain. A large Spanish design and construction organization felt their clients wanted "American expertise" during the planning, programming, and conceptual design phase of their projects. They were right, and we enjoyed a variety of interesting—albeit relatively brief—assignments.

Many other firms have also found Spain to be a receptive and enjoyable place to work. As a result, it continues to be one of the best potential markets for North American design firms.

Reasons to be there

As noted above, U.S. firms have been successful in Spain for the last 20 years. In addition, Spain:

- Is stable both politically and economically

- Is an interesting and attractive place to work
- Has a regular flow of challenging projects
- Has less anti-Americanism than some other parts of Europe
- Has supportive clients for innovative modern architecture

Reasons to be cautious

As with all sophisticated countries, Spain is complex. Moreover, it is an expensive place to pursue and do work, due to the relative state of the dollar and the euro.

There is a regular stream of interesting projects, but there is also a lot of competition. Most firms who have worked there have not felt that there was enough work there to justify an office, and it is not a logical base for a North American firm's European practice.

Skills and capabilities that are important

Among the skills a firm needs according to firms with experience in Spain are:

- A Spanish (preferably Castillian Spanish) speaking staff, since business is not conducted in English.
- A marketable reputation for design excellence and/or for a particular building type.

Who is operating there now?

A long list of North American firms have worked in Spain over the last 20 years: Frank Gehry, Richard Meier, Robert A. M. Stern, de Stefano, John Burgee, Perkins Eastman, Leo Daly, KPF, Pei Cobb Freed, HOK, KMD, Cooper Robertson, Morphosis, Arquitectonica, and others. Moreover, these firms have worked on a wide variety of the building types on

which North Americans have traditionally been leaders: e.g., museums, office buildings, shopping centers, laboratories and mixed-use developments. Only Arquitectonica and Leo Daly have claimed to have offices there. Most others focus on individual projects.

Who are the clients?

As the above list of architects and projects implies, a variety of clients have hired North American firms:

- North American developers, such as the Prime Group and Gerald Hines
- Spanish and other European developers
- Cultural institutions (both Spanish and international)
- Major international corporations

In most cases the major commissions go to firms with demonstrated international expertise in a particular building type and/or a high profile design reputation.

What is the process for getting work?

Many of the examples quoted above were selected in qualifications-based processes.

Languages and communications

According to the NCARB Web site: "Spanish is the official language throughout Spain. In the autonomous communities of Catalan, the Basque Country, Galicia, and Valencia, their native languages (Catalan, Vascuence, Gallego, and Valenciano) are also official. All other communities have only Spanish as their official language. English is fairly well known, especially among the younger generation, as well as the real estate and architectural communities."

The telecommunications infrastructure is modern with adequate density.

Fig. 4–30: *Entertainment and retail center at Diagonal Mar, Barcelona, Spain. Architects: Robert A.M. Stern Architects with Kendall/Heaton Associates. Photograph by Hines.*

Fig. 4–31: *Elementary school, Spain. Architect: Mitchell/Giurgola Architects, LLP. Photograph by Jeff Goldberg/Esto.*

his or her signature registered in order to authorize and/or sign blueprints.

- *Licensing requirements:* For EU citizens, an architecture diploma as listed in Directive 85/384/CE. For other foreign architects, an architecture diploma must be recognized or validated by the Ministry of Education and Culture.
- *What agency licenses?* Colegios de Arquitectos in each of the autonomous regions.
- *What is the professional architectural organization?* There are 18 Colegios de Arquitectos in Spain, each one acting in a different territory, which usually corresponds to the Autonomous Communities. There are exceptions, though, such as Andalucia and Castilla-Leon, where there are two colleges in each territory.
- *To practice, is a local representative required?* If the foreign architect is a member of the College of Architects, it is not necessary for him or her to have a local representative. Otherwise he or she could practice in an unofficial status only, and all work would have to be signed by an authorized architect. In such cases, a local representative or an association with a Spanish firm would be necessary. The local representative need not be a Spanish citizen, but he or she would need to have a degree validated and would have to be properly registered at the corresponding College of Architects.

Licensing and legal issues

Licensing requirements are as follows:

- *Is a license required?* Yes. Nonregistered architects are allowed to participate in all aspects of a project, except for those aspects in which they need to use their signature. An architect needs to have

Fee levels, payment terms, and taxes

Since 1997 the application of mandatory fees has not been allowed by law, but there are recommended scales published by the Colegios de Arquitectos (Associations of Architects) based on the type of building,

Fig. 4–32: *Studio Weil, Mallorca, Spain. Architect: Studio Daniel Libeskind. Photograph by Bitter Bredt Photographie.*

the level of quality to be achieved in construction, and the degree of complexity of the project. It is against the law to fail to pay your architect.

Local resources

Excellent consultants, renderers, associate architects, etc., exist in the major cities.

Design issues

As a 2006 exhibit at New York's Museum of Modern Art illustrated—and as can be confirmed by a visit to many locations in Spain—there is wide acceptance of very modern architecture in spite of the country's rich architectural heritage.

Local construction capabilities

Spain has large, sophisticated construction companies capable of building complex, high-quality projects.

Personal safety and health issues

Spain is a safe place to live and work.

Sources of information

U.S. Embassy, Spain
Telephone: 34-91-587-2200
Web site: www.embusa.es

Portal de Arquitectura y Construcción
   Arquitectos de España
Telephone: 34-91-426-21-67
Fax: 34-91-575-38-39
E-mail: admonarquinex@arquinex.es
Web site: www.arquinex.es

Consejo Superior de los Colegios de
   Arquitectos de España (Superior
   Council of Spanish Architects)
Telephone: 34-91-4352-200
E-mail: cscae@arquinex.es
Web site: www.cscae.com

Asociación de Seguros Mutuos de
Arquitectos Superiores
E-mail: info@asemas.es
Web site: www.asemas.es

Hermandad Nacional de Arquitectos
(HNA)
Web site: www.hna.es/web/hna.html

Caja de Arquitectos
Telephone: 34-934-826-800
Fax: 34-934-826-863
E-mail: info@arquia.es
Web site: www.arquia.es

Sweden

The Kingdom of Sweden has managed to
avoid the European wars of the last two
centuries. During that period, this constitutional monarchy has built a successful,
high-tech capitalist economy that is able
to support extensive welfare benefits.

Sweden was a late entry into the EU and
has not jointed the euro zone. The economy is heavily focused on foreign trade.

The market

Sweden has occasional opportunities for
North American firms, primarily those already established in Europe, but it is a
small market.

Languages and communications

Swedish is the national language. The
country has a sophisticated IT and telecommunications infrastructure.

Licensing and legal issues

Licensing requirements are as follows:

- *Is a license required?* No license or certification is necessary to practice architecture in Sweden for either indigenous
  or foreign persons.

- *What is the professional architectural organization?* Arkitektforbundet (AF),
  the Swedish Union of Architects, is a
  professional organization for architects,
  interior designers, and landscape designers. The organization numbers
  7,000 members. (Svenska Arkitekters
  Riksförbund, or SAR).
- *To practice, is a local representative required?* No, although it is recommended.

Sources of information

U.S. Embassy, Sweden
Telephone: 46-8-783-5300
E-mail:
  stockholm.office.box@mail.doc.gov
Web site: http://stockholm.usembassy.gov

Svensk Teknik och Design (The
  Swedish Federation of Architects and
  Consulting Engineers)
Telephone: 46-8-762-6700
E-mail: std@std.se
Web site: www.std.se/english/index.htm

Sveriges Arkitekter—
  Swedish Association of Architects
Telephone: 46-8-5055-7700
E-mail: kansli@arkitekt.se
Web site: www.arkitekt.se

Arkitekforbundet
  (The Swedish Union of Architects)

Switzerland

The Swiss Confederation was formed in
1291 and secured its independence from
the Holy Roman Empire in 1499. The
country has a strong commitment to neu-
trality and has managed to avoid direct
involvement with its neighbors' many
wars. It only recently joined the United
Nations and still remains outside the European Union. As a result of both its po-

litical and economic policies, the country has long been a peaceful, prosperous, and stable market economy with a per capita GDP greater than that of its larger neighbors. It also remains a preferred location for international investors because of its stable currency and strict bank-secrecy laws.

The market
The country's small size, mature economy, and sophisticated local design resources make this a very limited market for North American design professionals. As Werner K. Ruegger, a Swiss-American architect based in Zurich, said at an AIA conference: "Some would say there is nothing more to build in Switzerland since it has all been built." (Werner K. Ruegger, "Teaming with U.S.-Based Firms: A Key to Success in Switzerland?", 1997. *Europe: Architectural Markets and Practice April 25-28, 1996 Paris.* Washington, D.C.: American Institute of Architects. 24)

In reality there are occasional commissions of international interest, but many are heavily (if informally) restricted to Swiss and/or European firms. There are, however, many U.S corporations and international agencies based in Switzerland who sometimes use North American design firms on some of their projects.

Languages and communications
German, French, and Italian are all official languages, but Swiss German is spoken as the first language by a majority of the population. Needless to say, the country's telecommunications and IT infrastructure is very sophisticated.

Licensing and legal issues
Licensing requirements are as follows:

- *Is a license required?* Yes, although this may differ in the various cantons.
- *What agency licenses?* Schweizerisches Register der Ingenieure, Architekten und Techniker.
- *What is the professional architectural organization?* Schweizerischer Ingenieur und Architekten Verein (SAI); Schweizerischer Technischer Verband (STV).
- *To practice, is a local representative required?* In the cantons, where registration is not compulsory, local participation is not required by law. It may be wise, however, to cooperate with a local firm that is familiar with the myriad regulations in the building industry. These regulations can be quite different from canton to canton and even from city to city. Cooperation with a local firm may also facilitate negotiations with the local building commission by which each project must be approved.

Sources of information
U.S. Embassy, Switzerland
Telephone: 41-31-357-7011
Web site: http://bern.usembassy.gov

Société Suisse des Ingenieures
  et des Architectes (SIA)
Telephone: 41-44-283-1515
E-mail: contact@sia.ch
Web site: www.sia.ch/f/index.cfm

Schweiz Register der Ingenieure,
  Architekten und Techniker
Telephone: 41-1-252-3222
E-Mail: info@schweiz-reg.ch
Web site: www.schweiz-reg.ch/
  reg_d1.htm

Bund Schweizer Architekten
Telephone: 41-61-262-10-10

Fax: 41-61-262-10-09
Web site: www.architekten-bsa.ch

Verband Freienwerbender Schweizer
  Architekten / Fédération Suisse des
  Architectes Indépendants
Telephone: 41-44-772-83-03
Fax: 41-44-772-83-90
E-mail: wethli@wethli.com
Web site:
  www.architecte-fsai.ch/index.html

Conférence Suisse des Architectes
  (CSA)
Telephone: 41-32-729-82-88
Fax: 41-32-729-82-89
E-mail: csa-archi@vtx.ch
Web site: www.csa-archi.ch

Union Technique Suisse (UTS)
Telephone: 41-21-617-7979
E-mail:info.sr@swissengineering.ch
Web site: www.uts.ch

United Kingdom

The United Kingdom (U.K.) has been very important in the evolution of international practice. As the dominant colonial power in the nineteenth century and first half of the twentieth century, its professionals demonstrated how services could be exported internationally. My own architectural career included four years as a principal of a London-based firm working on projects around the world. This was in the 1970s, when North American firms were just beginning to expand overseas. Today, firms based in the U.K. remain among the most influential in international practice, and many hundreds of the Royal Institute of British Architects (including two of my partners) reside outside the U.K.

The U.K., however, has also been important in helping North American firms expand internationally. In the 1980s and 1990s, many firms were able to get projects there as major corporations, developers, and institutions sought out North American experience and expertise. As Thomas Fridstein, who served as the managing director of SOM's London office from 1988 to 1992, recounted:

In 1986 American firms offered services and specializations that were greatly needed and did not much exist in London. After the "Big Bang," which liberalized the banking and finance regulations, large U.S. financial institutions rushed to set up large offices in London; but there was very little modern office space available to accommodate their requirements for large floor plates and the infrastructure for information technology. Also, most British architecture firms and building contractors did not have the methodologies for designing and building large and complex buildings in short time frames. This was a unique opportunity for American architects to come to London, because they understood how to design modern office buildings and to work in a fast-track, construction management methodology for construction. A similar condition existed in the late 1990s when there was a major drive to modernize and expand the hospital systems in England. American firms again had an opportunity to bring a much-needed expertise that was in short supply. There are also a few examples of American firms in London that have succeeded in competing with the top British firms on a pure high

Fig. 4–33: *Metropolitian University Graduate Centre, London, England. Architect: Studio Daniel Libeskind. Photograph by Bitter Bredt Photographie.*

design impact basis by just being really great designer (private correspondence, 2007).

These projects made it possible for a number of firms to establish offices—usually in London—that became platforms for working in Europe and the Middle East.

Today, the U.K. remains an important center for international architectural practice. Its $1.9 trillion economy generates many opportunities for a wide variety of firms. Of equal importance, however, a U.K. base has made it far easier for North American firms to operate in Europe and elsewhere overseas.

It should not be overlooked, however, that the U.K. has a large, sophisticated planning and design community, with a long tradition of competing internationally against the best firms in the world. ARUP, Sir Norman Foster, Lord Richard Rogers, Sir Nicholas Grimshaw, and others are formidable competition in the U.S. as well as the U.K. and many other countries around the world. In addition, the British government actively supports U.K. firms seeking work overseas. As Thomas Vonier FAIA, RIBA, notes: "Architecture and architectural design are explicit elements of the U.K.'s national export strategy."

The market

As noted above, the U.K. is not only a good base for firms working in Europe but it has also been a good market for North American architects. Architects from the U.S. and Canada have designed many of the major new office buildings, shopping centers, museums, hospitals, and other buildings of the last 25 years. Projects such as Canary Wharf and the National Gallery have, for better or for worse, left a distinctly North American mark on the country.

Today, most of the many commissions that still go to North American architects are won by firms with an established presence in the country. Ironically, in the 20 plus years since most of the local UK offices were founded, the original North American staffing has been replaced by British and European architects.

Reasons to be there

There are many reasons to be there:
1. It is a large market and provides challenging opportunities for architects.
2. It is one of the most interesting places to live and work.
3. Practices in the U.K. can be quite profitable.
4. It is an excellent English-speaking base for working in Europe, Africa, and the Middle East.
5. There is a large pool of well-trained staff.
6. It is a nation of laws, and it has a comprehensible business environment.
7. There is a demand and respect for quality design and service.

Reasons to be cautious

Today, however, the U.K. is a difficult place to break into for the following reasons.

1. It is a very expensive place to pursue work and an even more expensive place to open an office. Assume that one British pound (with an exchange rate as of January 2007 of almost two dollars) only buys in the U.K. what one dollar buys in the U.S. Gene Kohn of KPF is just one of the firm's leaders who has commented on the large investment required to open an office there.
2. The large competitive edge that North American firms had in the 1980s has eroded, and today the U.K. has many homegrown firms that can compete in the same terms both in the U.K. and overseas.
3. In spite of the cordial relations between the U.K. and the U.S., many British still resent 1776, as well as later being supplanted by the U.S. as the world power. The World War II British view of Americans as "overpaid, oversexed, and over here" still applies.

Skills and capabilities that are important

For firms that are not already established in the U.K., some of the key capabilities often required include:

1. A service or unique design reputation or specialty clearly different from and/or superior to that offered by existing firms in the country. As Tom Fridstein of Hillier stated: "For an American architecture firm to successfully enter the London market, they must offer a specialization or service that does not already exist in the market or is in high demand and short supply. The London architectural community is highly skilled, and the clients are quite sophisticated so there are significant hurdles to entry for a foreign firm" (personal correspondence, 2007).
2. A network of local relationships that can support both marketing and carrying out projects.

Who is operating there now?

Many of the largest North American firms maintain offices in London, including:

HOK, KPF, Rafael Viñoly, Gensler, SOM, Perkins & Will, NBBJ, EDAW, RTKL, HLW, Anshen + Allen, Swanke Hayden, and others. Some smaller firms have also had offices—some of these to service specific projects or clients.

Who are the clients?

Established firms with local offices are able to compete for the full range of private, institutional, and public projects—although most find the private sector the most receptive. New firms in the market are most likely to be hired by international developers or corporations interested in their particular skills and capabilities. There are occasional projects, such as some of the major museums and major hospitals, which will do an international architectural search.

Moreover, as Tom Fridstein noted:

The climate for architectural services in London is very demanding. The clients are generally very sophisticated and are exacting in their requirements. The public and press demand high-quality design and building. There is much focus on the quality of details and the artistic quality of the design. In London, most major projects go through an exacting review process by the authorities, which demands design excellence. As a result, clients will favor architects that they believe will be more acceptable to the authorities and facilitate the approvals. (personal correspondence, 2007)

What is the process for getting work?

For most projects the process for getting new work is both similar—and as varied—as in North America. One of the major differences, however, is the much greater reliance on 3P (public private partnership), design/build/develop or design/build/finance/operate approaches. These approaches can be a very expensive way to get work.

Languages and communications

The language is English. However, as Tom Fridstein noted:

As George Bernard Shaw said, the U.S. and Britain are two great nations separated by a common language. This affects architectural services in two ways. First, the British have different meanings for many terms American architects commonly use. For example, what Americans call a Program, the British call a Brief; what the British call a Program, Americans call a Schedule; what Americans call a Schedule, the British call a List. Conversations can be confusing and misunderstood until this is clarified. More importantly, Americans tend to assume that the scope of services in standard British contracts is identical to U.S. scope of services because the names of the phases are similar: British Scheme Design v. U.S. Schematic Design and British Detailed Design v. U.S. Design Development. This is a serious mistake, as Scheme Design typically requires a level of detail of approximately 30 percent [whereas]U.S. Design Development and Detailed Design typically include… preliminary construction documents. (personal correspondence, 2007)

The telecommunications infrastructure in the U.K. is modern.

Fig. 4–34: *Thames Court,
Rabobank Headquarters, London,
England. Architect: Kohn
Pedersen Fox Associates (KPF).
Photograph by Paul Tyagi.*

- *Licensing requirements:* Architects recognized by the professional bodies, the Royal institute of British Architects (RIBA) and the Architects and Surveyors Institute (ASI), must have followed a three-year-degree course at a recognized college or university, followed by a two-year diploma in architectural studies and two years of work experience.
- *What agency licenses?* Registration (the only form of licensing that is in effect) is done by the Architects Registration Board, a government appointed body.
- *What is the professional architectural organization?* The Royal Institute of British Architects.
- *To practice, is a local representative required?* No.

Scope of Services

Tom Fridstein of Hillier explains how the scope of services in the U.K. differs from the scope outlined in the AIA standard contract forms familiar to U.S. or Canadian architects:

> Until about 1990 the prevalent form of contract for architectural services was the JCT 80, which held the architect to a high level of responsibility for all details of the design and aspects of the construction. Construction documents were expected to be fully detailed such that there was to be no ambiguity or choices for the builder. Tendering was done based on a Bill of Quantities prepared by a Quantity Surveyor, and the final cost was established upon measurement of the final building and analysis of quantities of materials. This methodology encouraged claims for additional time

Licensing and legal issues

Many North American architects have been able to get licensed in the U.K. Licensing requirements are as follows:

- *Is a license required?* No. No license is required by indigenous persons or foreign persons to practice architecture in the United Kingdom. However, in order to call oneself an architect, membership with a professional body and registration with the Architects Registration Board (ARB) of the U.K. is required.

and payment from contractors and did not encourage speedy construction. Partly due to this, American architects and construction managers were welcomed in London in the early 1990s, as they introduced American-style fast-track design and construction methodologies. In the late 1990 and early 2000s, various forms of design-build were introduced to further remove conflict between the architects and builders and to reduce cost overruns for architectural services and each form of contract has differing scopes of service and responsibilities for the architect. An American architect is well advised to completely understand the form of contract being suggested for a particular project and not assume it is similar to AIA forms of contract. (personal correspondence, 2007)

Fee levels, payment terms, and taxes

The U.K. still has a fee schedule, but it is no longer compulsory or recommended. Thus, there is more fee competition. The fees on large projects can be better than on comparable projects in North America. Nevertheless, working within the available fees is still an issue. As Tom Fridstein noted: "Fees for architectural services in the U.K. are generally higher than in the U.S., but the architect's costs are also higher. Salaries and rent are higher in the U.K. Some firms have been able to secure work in the U.K. at U.K. fees and perform much of the work in their U.S. offices, taking advantage of the lower costs in the U.S. One of the challenges of a London-based architectural office is doing work for projects located in conti-nental Europe, where fees are lower but the architect's cost are high due to the London location. Relative foreign-exchange rates between the pound, euro, and dollar are also major contributors to the level of profitability" (personal correspondence 2007).

Payment terms vary as widely as they do in North America, but professionals are somewhat better protected by the law in the U.K. than in other countries. Tax issues are too complex to be adequately covered in this book and usually require professional advice.

Major contract issues

For the most part, contracts in the U.K. can resemble their North American equivalents.

Local resources

Very competent associate firms, consultants, and support resources exist—primarily in and around London.

Design issues

There is a strong new urbanism-type movement led by Prince Charles, among others, but most of the U.K.'s design leaders have fully embraced modernism. Some of them (Rogers, Grimshaw and others) have also been international leaders in sustainable design.

Code and regulatory issues

The U.K. has its own set of codes and regulations that require expert advice to navigate.

Typical schedules

Because of the complex planning approvals as well as many other factors, projects can take far longer than their North American counterparts. For projects requiring

Fig. 4–35: *Imperial War Museum North, Manchester, England, U.K. Architect: Studio Daniel Libeskind. Photograph by Bitter Bredt Photographie.*

government financing, the time required can be even longer. Some private sector projects, which do not require complex planning approvals, the schedules can be comparable to similar projects in North America.

Personal safety and health issues

The U.K. is an extremely safe place to visit and work. There are no significant health issues if one is careful with unrefrigerated pub food and the local warm beer.

Sources of information

U.S. Embassy, United Kingdom
Telephone: 44-20-7499-9000

E-mail: london.office.box@mail.doc.gov
Web site: www.usembassy.org.uk

Architects Registration Board (ARB)
Telephone: 44-20-7580-5861
E-mail: info@arb.org.uk
Web site: www.arb.org.uk

The Royal Institute of British Architects
Telephone: 44-207-580-5533
E-mail info@inst.riba.org
Web site: www.riba.org

The Architectural Association and AA School of Architecture
Telephone: 44-20-7887-4000
E-mail: development1@aaschool.ac.uk
Web site: www.aaschool.ac.uk

EASTERN EUROPE, RUSSIA, AND THE STATES OF THE FORMER SOVIET UNION

The 28 countries covered here made up the Soviet Empire, until it imploded at the end of the twentieth century. It also includes the several states that were once forced together to form Yugoslavia.

Central and Eastern Europe

The countries that were part of the Soviet Bloc after World War II, along with those that used to make up Yugoslavia, have regained full independence and for the most part are joining the European Union.

As the GDP statistics in Table 4.6 illustrate, these countries have fallen behind their western neighbors. Other indications, however, show that some of these countries are beginning to catch up. As they catch up, both public and private clients have been commissioning the building types that usually come with rapid

Contents

Countries in bold receive longer descriptive sections.

modernization: office buildings, hotels, shopping centers, airports, etc. As in Western Europe in the 1980s, many of these projects are being done by North American design teams or teams drawn from the European offices of U.S. and Canadian firms.

Albania

Between 1990 and 1992, Albania finally ended 46 years of communist rule. Today it is the Republic of Albania with a government committed to economic reform and a reduction in the widespread crime and corruption. The road to democracy and reform for this predominantly Muslim country has been rocky. It is one of the poorest countries in Europe and economic progress has been hampered by many problems. Nevertheless, it is now growing and working toward joining NATO and the EU.

The market

Albania is a small country (population approximately 3.6 million) and poor. It is unlikely to be a significant market opportunity for North American design firms.

Languages and communications

Albanian is the official language, although parts of the population speak the languages of neighboring countries. The telecommunications systems are very limited but improving.

Bosnia and Herzegovina

Bosnia and Herzegovina declared independence from Yugoslavia in 1992. The Serbian minority, supported by neighboring Serbia and Montenegro, started an armed effort to partition the country along ethnic lines. The fighting was bloody and brutal.

Table 4.6 Central Europe, Population and Economic Statistics[13]

Country	Population	Population Growth Rate (%)	GDP—Purchasing Power Parity*	GDP—Official Exchange Rate*	GDP— Per Capita ($)
Albania	3,582,000	0.52	20.21	9.31	5,600
Bosnia and Herzegovina	4,499,000	1.35	24.8	9.16	5,500
Bulgaria	7,385,000	-0.86	77.13	27.85	10,400
Croatia	4,495,000	-0.03	59.41	37.35	13,200
Czech Republic	10,235,000	-0.06	221.4	118.9	21,600
Hungary	9,981,000	-0.25	172.7	113.1	17,300
Macedonia	2,051,000	0.26	16.91	5.65	8,200
Moldova	4,467,000	0.28	8.971	2.59	2,000
Montenegro	630,000	3.5	3.394	4.74	3,800
Poland	38,537,000	-0.05	542.6	265.4	14,100
Romania	22,304,000	-0.12	197.3	79.17	8,800
Serbia	9,396,000	NA	44.83	19.19	4,400
Slovakia	5,439,000	0.15	95.35	46.9	17,700
Slovenia	2,010,000	-0.05	46.08	37.64	22,900

* In billions of U.S. dollars unless otherwise noted.

Sarajevo, once the site of the Winter Olympics (1984), and many other areas were devastated. The fighting was largely ended by the Dayton Peace Accords in 1995; but NATO troops, and later European Union troops, have been needed to oversee the truce and the fragile movement toward a democratic republic.

The economy suffers from the impact of the past conflict and continuing tensions as well as the residual problems of Yugoslavia's inefficient, socialist economy. Unemployment is over 45 percent, according to official statistics.

The market
This is an unlikely market for North American design services until the country can focus on rebuilding its economy.

Languages and communications
Bosnian, Croatian, and Serbian are the main languages. The telecommunications system needs modernization.

Bulgaria
The Republic of Bulgaria became independent from the Ottoman Empire in 1908 but came under Soviet control after World War II. Communist domination ended in 1990, and the country is now moving toward EU membership. It joined NATO (North Atlantic Treaty Organization) in 2004. The government has been committed to economic reform. The result has been reasonable growth and considerable foreign investment in spite of significant problems with public corruption and organized crime.

The market
This is still a limited market for foreign design services.

Languages and communications
Bulgarian is the dominant language. The telecommunications system is antiquated.

Croatia
The Republic of Croatia was part of Yugoslavia until it declared its independence in 1991. It took four more years of fighting with Serbia (the major remaining part of Yugoslavia) before Croatia gained control of most of its territory. The last Serb-controlled area was returned in 1998.

Since the struggle for independence and control was concluded, Croatia has stabilized its economy and begun growing. Tourism, banking, and public investment have all stimulated this growth.

The Dalmatian coast, with assets like Dubrovnik, gives the country considerable tourism potential.

The market
While small and still poor, Croatia could be an occasional market for North American firms—particularly for firms or individuals with ethnic ties. Our firm, working in association with Charles Legler, is one example of a North American team working in Croatia's expanding tourism sector.

Languages and communications
The population speaks Croatian. The telecommunications systems need modernization.

Sources of information
U.S. Embassy, Croatia
Web site: http://zagreb.usembassy.gov

Udruzenje Hrvatskih Arhitekata (UHA)
Croatian Architects Association (CAA)
Telephone: 385-1-48-16-140
Fax: 385-1-48-16-197

E-mail: uha@uha.hr
Web site: www.uha.hr

Hrvatska Komora Arhitekata I Inzinjera
U Gradjevinarstvu
Telephone: 385-1-4854-411
Fax: 385-1-4855-668
E-mail: hkaig@hkaig.hr
Web site: www.hkaig.hr

Czech Republic

Czechoslovakia emerged as a country following World War I. Issues with ethnic minorities (German and Ukranian, in particular) were a significant problem for Czechoslovakia between the wars. Following World War II, Czechoslovakia came under Soviet control. The country regained independence in 1989 and, in a

Fig. 4–36: *Danube House, River City, Prague, Czech Republic. Architects: Kohn Pedersen Fox Associates (KPF) with ADNS, S.R.O. Photograph by H.G. Esch.*

"velvet divorce," separated from Slovakia in 1993.

The country is one of the most stable and prosperous of the Eastern European states. The economy is helped by a strong trading relationship with Germany and some of the other Western European countries.

The market
Working in the Czech Republic, as elsewhere in Eastern Europe, is complicated by the relatively high cost of Western European and North American firms.

Languages and communications
The official language is Czech. The IT and telecommunications infrastructure is quickly being modernized after a slow start.

Licensing and legal issues
Licensing requirements are as follows:

- *Is a license required?* Yes.
- *Licensing requirements:* Degree in architecture recognized by a recognizing authority. Three years of on-the-job experience in architecture. Written and oral examination, oral presentation of previous practice, written examination of knowledge of legal regulations.
- *What agency licenses?* Czech Chamber of Architects—Commission for Authorization.
- *What is the professional architectural organization?* Czech Chamber of Architects.
- *To practice, is a local representative required?* U.S. architectural firms must cooperate with an architect authorized by the Czech Chamber of Architects in any establishment governed by the Czech commercial law.

Sources of information
U.S. Embassy, Czech Republic
Telephone: 420-257-02200
E-mail: consprague@state.gov
Web site: www.usembassy.cz

Ceska Komora Architektu
    (Czech Chamber of Architects)
Telephone: 420-2-575-35034
Fax: 420.257.532.285
E-mail: cka@cka.cc
Web site: www.cka.cc/en

Hungary
Hungary is another country that came out of the collapse of the Austro-Hungarian Empire after World War I. Hungary came under Russian domination after World War II. The Republic of Hungary had its first democratic elections in 1990 and has subsequently joined NATO and the EU.

Hungary began to liberalize in 1968 and has now made the transition to a market economy. The economy has been growing and attracting significant foreign investment. Germany is, by far, Hungary's major trading partner.

The market
There have been a number of opportunities for North American firms in Hungary, but it is not currently a significant market for U.S. and Canadian firms.

Languages and communications
Hungarian is the national language. The IT and telecommunications infrastructure has been modernized.

Licensing and legal issues
Licensing requirements are as follows:

- *Is a license required?* Yes.

- *Licensing requirements:* Licensing requirements for practice in Hungary should be reviewed, as the information on the NCARB Web site was collected before Hungary was admitted to the European Union. At that time, licensing required a degree in architecture, two to five years practical training, no examination, and that an application form and a portfolio of the applicant's works be submitted to the registration board.
- *What agency licenses?* Registration Board of the Chamber of Hungarian Architects.
- *What is the professional architectural organization?* The Chamber of Hungarian Architects.
- *To practice, is a local representative required?* Yes, unless there is a convention of reciprocity between Hungary and the architect's country of origin.

Fee levels, payment terms, and taxes
The Chamber of Hungarian Architects publishes a recommended fee scale.

Sources of information
U.S. Embassy, Hungary
Telephone: 36-1-475-4400
E-mail: acs.budapest@state.gov
Web site: http://budapest.usembassy.gov

Chamber of Hungarian Architects
Telephone: 36-1-318-2444
E-mail: teampannon@teampannon.hu
Web site: www.mek.hu

Association of Hungarian Architects
(MESZ)
Telephone: 36-1-318-2444
E-mail : meszorg@t-online.hu
Web site: www.meszorg.hu/info_en.htm

Macedonia
Unlike other parts of the former Yugoslavia, the Republic of Macedonia gained independence peacefully in 1991. Since it is not really the home of Alexander the Great, Greece has objected to its name and imposed a 20-month embargo. It also suffered from an Albanian insurgency in 2001.

It was the least developed of the Yugoslav republics. It remains poor and has not attracted much outside investment. Economic growth has resumed but from a very low base.

The market
This is a small, poor, landlocked country that is unlikely to be a significant market for foreign design firms, unless they come attached to outside investment funds.

Languages and communications
Macedonian is the major language, but a quarter of the population speaks Albanian. The telecommunications system needs modernization.

Moldova
The Republic of Moldova is a landlocked country between Romania and Ukraine. It was formerly part of Romania but was incorporated into the USSR (Union of Soviet Socialist Republics) at the end of World War II. Although independent since 1991, Russian troops remain in the eastern part of the country. It is the poorest country in Europe, with a per capita GDP of only $1,800. The economy is growing but still needs major reforms.

The market
This country is too small and poor to be of interest to international design firms.

Languages and communications

Moldovan (Romanian) is the official language, but Russian and a Turkish dialect (Gagauz) are also spoken. The telecommunications system is outmoded.

Poland

Although it has been a nation since the tenth century, in the eighteenth and nineteenth centuries the country was partitioned by Russia, Prussia, and Austria. It regained independence in 1918, only to be overrun by Germany and Russia in 1939. Following World War II, it came under Soviet domination.

In 1980 the formation of the independent trade union, Solidarity, began its move away from Soviet control. In 1990 Solidarity took control of parliament and the presidency. Economic reforms were introduced, and after an initial painful period, it has become one of the most robust economies in Central Europe.

Its economy is still challenged by high unemployment (one of the highest in the EU), outmoded infrastructure, a rural underclass, money losing state-owned enterprises, and other problems. It joined NATO in 1999 and the EU in 2004, and it has benefited from EU subsidies and surging exports.

The market

Poland has attracted considerable outside investment as well as many western design firms. Some of these have come from North America and include HOK, A. Epstein and Sons International, William McDonough + Partners, and many others. If the economy continues to develop, it could become a regular market for U.S. and Canadian firms with the right capabilities and local contacts.

Languages and communications

The population speaks Polish. The telecommunications system is underdeveloped and outmoded, but some modernization is underway.

Licensing and legal issues

Licensing requirements are as follows:

- *Is a license required?* Yes, although preliminary design and/or interior design can be done by an unlicensed person. When construction elements are designed and/or there is electrical, gas, or water installation, then the project is valid only if signed by a licensed architect.
- *Licensing requirements:* To be able to practice architecture, an individual must practice designing under the supervision of a licensed architect for three years and pass a compulsory examination.
- *What agency licenses?* Examination boards appointed by the Regional Chamber of Architects.
- *What is the professional architectural organization?* The Association of Polish Architects, or Stowarzyszenie Architektow Polskich (SARP).
- *To practice, is a local representative required?* Yes. In order for a project to be valid, a licensed Polish architect must participate and must sign off on the plans. To establish a local representative, permission from the Ministry of Foreign Economic Relations is required.

Fee levels, payment terms, and taxes

The Association of Polish Architects (SARP) publishes a recommended fee scale based on estimated construction costs, degree of complexity, and size. Usually the architect's design fee (including other engineers and consultants) varies from 3 to 8 percent of construction costs.

Sources of information
U.S. Embassy, Poland
Telephone: 48-22-504-2000
Web site: http://warsaw.usembassy.gov

Stowarzyszenie Architektow Polskich
(Association of Polish Architects)
Telephone: 48-22-827-8712
E-mail: zg@sarp.org.pl
Web site: www.sarp.org.pl

Izba Architektow
Telephone: 48-22-827-85-14
E-mail: izba@izbaarchitektow.pl
Web site: www.izbaarchitektow.pl

Romania
Romania became independent from the Ottoman Empire in the mid-nineteenth century. It joined the Allies in World War I and was rewarded with new territories, including Transylvania. During World War II, however, it allied with Germany and was rewarded with Soviet occupation and control after the war.

For much of the period of Soviet control, the country was run by a dictator, Nikolai Ceausescu, who was overthrown and executed in 1989. The Communists were finally pushed from power in 1996. Romania joined NATO in 2004, and if it can achieve overdue reforms, it will join the EU in 2007 or 2008.

It is a relatively large country, with a population of over 22 million, but its economic infrastructure is obsolete. Corruption and the lingering impact of communist-era bureaucracy still plague the economy. Nevertheless, reforms and some economic progress has begun.

The market
Romanian schools have produced many talented design professionals—many of whom have emigrated. The ones who remain work at such low fees that it is hard for international firms to compete. This may be a market in the future, but it is very limited right now.

Languages and communications
Romanian is the official language, but Hungarian and German are also spoken. The telecommunications infrastructure is undergoing rapid modernization.

Licensing and legal issues
Licensing requirements are as follows:

- *Is a license required?* Yes.
- *Licensing requirements:* A degree in architecture, experience in architecture, and an examination are required for registration.
- *What agency licenses?* Ordinul Arhitectilor din Romania (Architects' Order of Romania).
- *What is the professional architectural organization?* The Union of Romanian Architects (UAR).
- *To practice, is a local representative required?* Yes.

Fee levels, payment terms, and taxes
A compulsory fee scale exists and is published by the Union of Architects of Romania with the agreement of various government ministries.

Sources of information
U.S. Embassy, Romania
Telephone: 40-21-200-3300
E-mail: infobuch@state.gov
Web site: www.usembassy.ro

Union of Romanian Architects (UAR)
E-mail: rna@com.pcnet.ro
Web site: http://uar.ong.ro

Ordinul Arhitectilor din Romania
Telephone: 40-21-317-26-34
Web site: http://www.oar.org.ro

Asociatia Arhitectilor de Interior
  din Romania
Societatea Arhitectilor Romani
Asociatia Profesionala a Urbanistilor
  din Romania
Uniunea Nationala a Restauratorilor
  Monumente Istorice
Uniunea Femeilor Arhitekt din Romania

Serbia and Montenegro

The remaining two parts of Yugoslavia separated as this book was being written. Serbia was the largest of the Yugoslav republics, and it came under the disastrous rule of President Slobodan Milosević, who led them into a costly effort to unite the ethnic Serbs in neighboring republics into a "greater" Serbia. His policies brought on international sanctions and intervention, leading to a series of costly defeats. He was transferred to stand trial for war crimes, but he died during his trial. As a result of the Milosević period, Serbia and Montenegro are just beginning to recover and remain very poor.

The market

Serbia is a proud, literate country that could grow into a market—particularly for design professionals with ethnic ties or who are linked to international investment. At this time, however, it is a very limited market. Montenegro is quite small and an even more limited market.

Languages and communications

The population speaks Serbian except for a small Albanian minority. Its telecommunication infrastructure is badly in need of investment and modernization.

Licensing and legal issues

According to the COAC Web site, foreign architects cannot work independently. They must work with a local company or in a joint venture.

Slovakia

Following World War I, until their peaceful separation in 1993, the Slovaks and the Czechs were joined as Czechoslovakia. Following World War II, Czechoslovakia was under Russian control, until 1989. Slovakia joined both NATO and the EU in 2004.

The country is making the transition from a centrally planned, communist economy to a modern, market economy. The country's reforms and business friendly policies seem to be generating reasonable GDP growth.

The market

This is a small country that is not likely to have many opportunities for North American firms, unless they have personal ties to the country.

Languages and communications

Slovak is spoken by the vast majority, but a few other languages are spoken. *The World Factbook* states that their IT and telecommunications infrastructure is improving with a modernization and privatization program in place to increase service.

Sources of information
U.S. Embassy, Slovakia
Web site: http://bratislava.usembassy.gov/

Slovenská Komora Architektov
  (Slovak Chamber of Architects)
Telephone: 421-2-5443-1080
Fax: 421-2-5443-0863
E-mail: komarch@komarch.sk
Web site: www.komarch.sk

Slovenia

Slovenia was part of the Austro-Hungarian Empire until the conclusion of World War I. In 1918, it joined with several other Balkan countries to form Yugoslavia. By 1991 Slovenia was fed up with Serbian domination and after a brief war became independent. Since independence, the Republic of Slovenia has tied itself to Western Europe (becoming a member of NATO and the EU in 2004) and has been building a stable and increasingly strong economy.

The economy, however, faces some serious challenges: the need to privatize much of the economy; compete with China, India, and other low cost competitors; and remove the rest of the Yugoslavian economic legacy.

The market

Slovenia is a very small country with a declining population. It provides a limited number of opportunities for North American design firms.

Languages and communications

Slovene is spoken by 90 percent of the country, but the remainder use Croatian, among others, as a first language.

Sources of information
U.S. Embassy, Slovenia
Web site: http://ljubljana.usembassy.gov/

Zbornica Za Arhitekturo I Prostor
  Slovenije (Chamber of Architecture
  and Spatial Planning of Slovenia),
  ZAPS
Telephone: 386-1-24-20-670
Fax: 386-1-24-20-680
E-mail: zaps@zaps.si
Web site: www.arhiforum.si

Zveza Drustev Arhitektov Slovenije
Telephone: 386-1-252-79-30
Fax: 386-1-252-79-31
E-mail: drustvo.arhitektov.lj@siol.net
Web site: www.drustvo-arhitektov-lj.si

Russia and the States of the Former Soviet Union

After almost 75 years of communist rule, the modernization policies introduced by Mikhail Gorbachev led to changes that splintered the Soviet Union. A much smaller Russia and 14 independent republics emerged in 1991–92. Since then these 15 countries have taken their separate paths. Most of them are struggling, but Russia and a few others are becoming significant markets (or potential markets) for North American design firms.

Armenia

The Republic of Armenia has a long history of invasion and control by the adjacent empires: Roman, Byzantine, Arab, Persian, and Ottoman. Part of Armenia was ceded to Russia in the early nineteenth century. Although Armenia tried to assert its independence after World War I, Soviet Russia conquered it and incorporated it into the USSR.

Table 4.7 Russia's and Former Soviet Union States' Population and Economic Statistics[14]

Country	Population	Population Growth Rate (%)	GDP—Purchasing Power Parity*	GDP—Official Exchange Rate*	GDP— Per Capita ($)
Armenia	2,976,000	-0.19	15.99	$6.6	5,400
Azerbaijan	7,962,000	.66	58.1	$14.05	7,300
Belarus	10,293,000	-0.06	80.74	$28.56	7,800
Estonia	1,324,000	-0.64	26	$13.62	19,600
Georgia	4,661,000	-.34	17.79	$5.27	3,800
Kazakhstan	15,233,000	.33	138.7	$52.6	9,100
Kyrgyzstan	5,214,000	1.32	10.49	$2.24	2,000
Latvia	2,275,000	-0.67	35.08	$16.13	15,400
Lithuania	3,585,000	-0.3	54.03	$25.78	15,100
Russia	142,894,000	-.37	1.72	$733	11,100
Tajikistan	7,321,000	2.19	9.45	$2.07	1,300
Turkmenistan	5,043,000	1.83	45.11	$16.16	8,900
Ukraine	46,711,000	0.06	355.8	$81.53	7,600
Uzbekistan	27,307,000	1.7	54.81	$10.78	2,000

* In billions of U.S. dollars unless otherwise noted.

A conflict with neighboring Azerbaijan broke out in 1988 over control of the Armenian part of Azerbaijan. The fighting escalated after both of the Soviet republics achieved independence in 1991, and a cease fire was put in place in 1994. Needless to say, this conflict and the residual impact of Soviet rule have hurt the economy. The economy is now growing (from a very small base), but it is hampered by a wide variety of problems.

The market
At this time, Armenia is a very small potential market for North American firms. Architects of Armenian ancestry are the most likely to be interested and involved.

Languages and communications
Armenian is the predominant language used. The telecommunications infrastructure is inadequate but undergoing modernization.

Azerbaijan
This Muslim nation gained its independence in 1991, after the collapse of the Soviet Union. It soon entered into a conflict with neighboring Armenia, which has cost it 16 percent of its territory and forced it to care for over 500,000 displaced persons. It has large, undeveloped petroleum reserves, and some economists estimate the GDP could double by 2010. Nevertheless, it needs significant economic reform, resolution of the conflict with Armenia, and a reduction in the endemic corruption for real progress to be made.

The market
Because of the growing oil wealth, there will undoubtedly be some projects for the adventurous. It is, however, a small, poor country and thus not a major market.

Languages and communications
Azerbaijani (Azeri) is the dominant language. The telecommunications infrastructure is in need of major expansion and modernization.

Belarus
The Republic of Belarus achieved independence in 1991 but has retained extremely close ties with Russia. Under its current government, it retains a number of the less desirable government policies of the former USSR. The economy is growing but from a very low base. Government policies have discouraged foreign investment.

The market
Although one of the larger countries in the region, this is a very limited market for North American design firms.

Languages and communications
Belarusian and Russian are the major languages. Its telecommunications infrastructure is inadequate.

Estonia
The Republic of Estonia has been ruled by the Danes, Swedes, Germans, and Russians. After a brief period of independence from 1918 to 1940, it was forcibly incorporated into the Soviet Union. It regained independence in 1991 and joined NATO and the EU in 2004.

The economy has made most of the transition to a modern market economy. It has strong electronics and telecommunications sectors and close ties to Finland, Sweden, and Germany.

The market
Estonia is a very small country with limited opportunities for North American firms.

Languages and communications

The majority of the people speak the official language, Estonian. Approximately 30 percent, however, use Russian as their first language. Thanks in part to foreign investment, the IT and telecommunications infrastructure is relatively modern.

Georgia

Georgia was absorbed by Russia in the nineteenth century, but it had three years of independence (1918–1921) following the Russian Revolution. It was then forcibly incorporated into the USSR and—along with the other states—regained its independence in 1991. Some progress on economic and democratic reform has been made since independence, but there have been many problems. Two regions—Abkhazia and South Ossetia—have broken away and are ruled by unrecognized, Russian-supported governments. The economy—which is based on agriculture, mining, and a limited industrial sector—is growing but from a very small base. Georgia is a very poor, small country.

The market

Georgia is unlikely to be a significant market for North American design services.

Languages and communications

Georgian is the official language, but Russian, Armenian, and other languages are spoken in some regions. The telecommunications infrastructure is very limited.

Sources of information

Association of Town Planners of Georgia
National Union of Architects of Georgia
Telephone: 32-995-22-74-02
Web site: http://arcunion.iatp.org.ge/
    index_ge.html

Kazakhstan

Kazakhstan is the largest of the former Soviet republics in terms of territory. It was conquered by Russia in the eighteenth century and became a Soviet republic in 1936. Russia encouraged the influx of immigrants that now outnumber the native Kazakhs. Kazakhstan today has a booming economy due in part to economic reform, foreign investment, and good harvests. The main source of growth, however, has been the continuing development of the country's vast fossil fuel reserves.

Fig. 4–37: Tengizchevroil Headquarters, Atyrau, Kazakhstan. Architects: Yost Grube Hall Architecture with Design Academy Kazgor. Photograph by Joachim C. Grube.

The market

Due to the wealth generated by the country's oil, there has been a growing real estate boom. Foreign investment has also been growing. These factors have made Kazakhstan a small—but growing—market for foreign design professionals.

Languages and communications

Kazakh is the state language, but Russian is the official language used in everyday business. The telecommunications infrastructure is antiquated.

Kyrgyzstan

Kyrgyzstan is a Central Asian country annexed by Russia in 1864. It achieved independence in 1991 but remained under the rule of a Soviet-era strong man until public protest forced his ouster in 2005. The country is poor and mountainous, and its economy is predominantly agricultural. It has been liberalizing its economy and has been growing slowly, but the growth is from a very small base.

The market

This country is too small, poor, and far away to be a significant market for North American design services.

Languages and communications

Kyrgyz and Russian are the official languages. The telecommunications infrastructure is primitive.

Latvia

Latvia was annexed by the Soviet Union in 1940 but regained independence in 1991. The large Russian minority (30 percent) remains a concern to Moscow. Latvia, however, joined NATO and the EU in 2004.

The economy is in a period of transition from Russian dominated and centrally planned to market and EU oriented. There has been progress, but many challenges remain.

The market

Latvia is still a small, relatively poor country with a shrinking population. There may be occasional opportunities for North American firms, but this will remain a small market.

Languages and communications

Latvian is the official language, but Russian is spoken by almost 40 percent of the population. The IT and telecommunications infrastructure is in need of significant modernization, but is improving.

Sources of information

U.S. Embassy, Latvia
Web site: http://riga.usembassy.gov/

Latvijas Arhitektu Savieniba
Telephone: 371-721-2802
Fax: 371-722-3902
E-mail: latarch@latnet.lv
Web site: www.architektura.lv

Lithuania

The Republic of Lithuania was independent between the World Wars but was annexed by Russia in 1940. In 1990, it was the first of the Soviet republics to declare independence, which Moscow finally recognized in 1991. In 2004 it became part of NATO and the EU.

The economy was closely linked to Russia's, but it is now more oriented to the West. It has also made the most of the shift away from a command (state-controlled) economy to a market economy. It is still one of the poorest countries in the EU, but it is growing.

The market

It is a small country, but its economic growth could generate occasional opportunities.

Languages and communications

Lithuanian is the primary language, but Russian and Polish are spoken by parts of the population. The telecommunications infrastructure is in need of considerable modernization.

Sources of information

U.S. Embassy, Lithuania
Telephone: 370-5-266-5500
E-mail: WebEmailVilnius@state.gov
Web site: http://vilnius.usembassy.gov

Lietuvos Architektu Sajunga
   (Architects Association of Lithuania)
Telephone: 370-2-755-948
E-mail: architektu.sajunga@takas.lt
Web site: www.alas-architektai.lt

Russia

Following 200 years of Mongol domination, the Principality of Muscovy emerged and began conquering and absorbing its neighbors. In the seventeenth, eighteenth, and nineteenth centuries, expansion of what was renamed the Russian Empire extended from the Baltic Sea to the Pacific Ocean. Following major defeats in World War I, widespread unrest in the major cities in 1917 led to the overthrow of the ruling family, the Romanovs. Following a long, bloody civil war, the Communists under Lenin gained control over most of the former Russian Empire. Josef Stalin's brutal rule from 1928 to 1953 and World War II cost the country tens of millions of lives. Following World War II, however, the Union of Soviet Socialist Republics (USSR) was—by some measures—the second most powerful country in the world.

Its economy and society stagnated during the postwar period. When Mikhail Gorbachev introduced liberalizing policies between 1985–1991, he unintentionally let loose forces that led to the breakaway of the satellite states (such as Poland, Czechoslovakia, and Hungary) and 14 of the USSR's republics. Even though much diminished, Russia still has a population of approximately 143 million. Russia went through a difficult transition to a market economy, which was punctuated by a severe financial crisis in 1998. Since then the economy has had strong economic growth, averaging 6.4 percent per year.

Fig. 4–38: *Ducat Two, Moscow, Russia. Architects: The Liebman Melting Partnership with Too Diar—Archady M. Polovnikov. Courtesy of The Liebman Melting Partnership.*

When this book was written, Russia's GDP was estimated to be almost $1.6 trillion (purchasing power parity) and had a GDP per capita in excess of $11,000. There is significant income disparity in the country, however, and this gap was widened by the rampant corruption that accompanied the sell-off of state-owned assets and the shift to a market economy. Nevertheless, there has been a decline in poverty and an expansion of the middle class.

Oil, natural gas, metals, and timber account for 80 percent of the exports, making the economy vulnerable to fluctuations in world commodity prices. Internally, however, Russia is a large market that is seeking to modernize. If its major weaknesses (obsolete infrastructure, need for more structural economic reform, a weak banking sector, corruption, etc.) do not derail the current economic expansion, modernization will inevitably lead to a demand for more modern buildings.

The market

Foreign architects have had a long involvement in Russia's built environment. Even St. Petersburg's Hermitage Museum and parts of the Kremlin were designed by European architects. Moreover, during the early years of Soviet rule, foreign architects did significant work; but by the middle of the Soviet period, foreigners had little involvement in the design of buildings in Russia. In the last 15 to 20 years, however, the market began to open up and a number of U.S. and European firms began to work there.

The initial years have been full of frustrations for many of the firms that have tested this market. Many firms have stories of projects that never happened, clients who disappeared, fees unpaid, bureaucratic twilight zone, and serious tax problems. Paul Abelsky's 2005 article in *Russia Profile* argues that more than a decade after "The Americans Are Coming" appeared in *Progressive Architecture* "not a single important project by a foreigner has been completed as few outsiders have shown much ability or willingness to navigate the labyrinth that is Russia's construction market." (Abelsky 2005, p. 26). While this is not a completely accurate picture of the Russian experience, it is true enough to be a warning.

Patricia S. Kuehn, an American architect who worked in Russia in the 1990s, was even more negative. Her experience there encountered: bureaucratic intransigence; resistance to foreign methods and materials; shoddy Russian products; arbitrary tax rulings; an uncooperative local partner; and even a mafia hit on one of her clients. She summarized her experience in this way: "My...recommendations to anyone considering doing business in Russia are: first, don't."[15]

Nevertheless, there are a growing number of North American architects who find working in Russia both enjoyable and rewarding. One of those is Ted Liebman, whose experience there was introduced in Chapter 2. In summary, Russia is a difficult market but one with a great deal of potential. North American design skills are needed, and there are clients who can afford them.

Reasons to be there

Ted Liebman's story (see Chapter 2) summarizes the main reasons to be in Russia:

- There are a growing number of major design opportunities.
- Russia has a rich history and culture.

- Russians often like North Americans and will enter into close friendships that make travel there enjoyable.

Reasons to be cautious

As noted above, Russia has been a difficult place for many North American firms for several reasons.

- The bureaucracy can be arbitrary, rigid, and stifling.
- Policies, including such important issues as taxation of foreign entities, can change quickly.
- Russian clients can be even more elusive than clients in other countries. (Our first three clients in Russia all disappeared at some point, and the projects died.)
- There is little legal recourse if things go wrong.

- It can be an expensive place to market and do business.

Skills and capabilities that are important

Ted Liebman feels that "being there and enjoying it" has been an essential ingredient of his success. That is, of course, also true in most other countries. In addition, other important issues include:

- *Spending the time necessary.* It is not a country where the senior principal can fly in for just 24–36 hours and expect to be successful.
- *Creating a network of local relationships and resources.* As Ted Liebman noted, for example, "Every city has a Chief Architect and knowing them and having a good relationship with them can be very helpful" (personal correspondence).

Fig. 4–39: *Riverstones, Moscow, Russia. Architects: The Liebman Melting Partnership with ABD Limited. Rendering by ABD Limited.*

- *Learning how to get things done and buildings built.* Part of Ted Liebman's success was getting some visible, successful projects built early.

Who is operating there now?

Many firms have worked in Russia. Among the more active at the time this book was written include SOM, NBBJ, Swanke Hayden Connell, and many other large firms. Smaller firms, such as Liebman-Melting, are also active.

Who are the clients?

A significant number of projects in Russia have American or European investors. As a result, many of the projects are office buildings, hotels, shopping centers, condominium developments, and other income-producing properties.

What is the process for getting work?

Most North American firms working in Russia are coming in as design consultants. As consultants, they are usually selected on the basis of contacts and qualifications.

Languages and communications

Russian is the dominant language, but many minority languages are also spoken. The telephone and other telecommunications systems are improving; but Russia still has a ways to go if it is to effectively serve a market economy.

Licensing and legal issues

This is a somewhat murky subject. Most firms work as design consultants and face few legal issues. Swanke Hayden Connell reportedly has registered as a Russian firm.

Licensing requirements are as follows:

- *Is a license required?* Yes.
- *Licensing requirements:* Foreign citizens may practice in Russia if that is provided for by an international agreement with the Russian Federation. If there is no international agreement with the Russian Federation, foreign citizens and persons without citizenship can take part in architectural activities only in collaboration with an architect-citizen of the Russian Federation.
- *What agency licenses?* Russian License Architectural Centre (state institution).
- *What is the professional architectural organization?* The Union of Architects of Russia (UAR).
- *To practice, is a local representative required?* Yes, a local licensed representative must be involved from the beginning of the project. At this time, there are no international or bilateral agreements permitting independent practice for foreign architects.

Scope of services

Most foreign firms only provide planning and design services. The later phases are provided by Russian firms, many of which were formerly state-owned design organizations.

Fee levels, payment terms, and taxes

Fee levels are negotiated and should be set high enough so that a client's failure to make the final payment will not eliminate the likelihood of a profit. An 18 percent value-added tax (VAT) is added to all design contracts; but if the work is done offshore, the tax can be avoided. Nevertheless, it is advisable to have all contracts define fees as net of Russian taxes.

Fig. 4–40: *Moscow International Business Center, Moscow, Russia. Architect: Swanke Hayden Connell Architects. Rendering by PMB Design NY.*

Major contract issues

Contracts in Russia are of questionable value. Thus, having advanced payments that keep you ahead of your client is a good idea.

Local resources

Russia does have skilled architects, engineers, renderers, and other local resources in the major cities, but the quality is uneven.

Design issues

Ted Liebman believes Russian architects "have a better sense of scale and respect for such issues as preservation of vistas. There is still a socialistic sense of the community good." In addition, many of the projects include the adaptive reuse of projects in sensitive urban settings. The climate is also a factor. Russia's long, hard winters in most of the country need to be recognized.

Typical schedules

Russian schedules are typically longer; this is due in part to the difficult approval process faced by most projects.

Code and regulatory issues

Russian codes and other regulations are complicated and evolving.

Local construction capabilities

Russia has extensive construction capabilities, but quality construction requires continuous supervision. Some foreign firms, with more experience in quality construction, are active in Russia as well.

Personal safety and health issues

The usual cautions about unpeeled or uncooked food as well as the water apply in Russia. There is also a significant crime problem, but this does not affect most foreigners directly. Finally, all experienced firms warn about the heavy drinking that accompanies many business and social activities.

Sources of information

U.S. Embassy, Russia
Telephone: 7-495-728-5000
E-mail: consulMo@state.gov
Web site: http://moscow.usembassy.gov

Union of Architects of Russia (UAR)
E-mail: avtograf_sar@mail.ru
Web site: www.uar.ru

Russian Academy of Architecture and Construction Sciences (RÄÄëS)
E-mail: raasn@edunet.ru
Web site: www.raasn.ru

Union of Russian Designers (URD)
Telephone: 7-495-995-05-95
E-mail: info@mvk.ru

Web site: www.mvk.ru/eng/partners/partner_81.shtm

Moscow Committee for Architecture and Urban Planning (Moskomarchitectura)
Telephone: 7-095-250-55-20
Web site: www.mka.mos.ru

Associate Board of Architecture, Construction, Development, and Reconstruction of Moscow
E-mail: webmaster@stroi.ru
Web site: www.stroi.ru/eng

Moscow Architectural Institute (MARCHI)
Web site: www.miarch.ru/eng

Moscow Architecture and Preservation Society
E-mail: info@maps-moscow.com
Web site: www.maps-moscow.com/?chapter_id=228

Russia Profile, an English-language information service offering expert analysis of Russian politics, economics, society and culture, www.russiaprofile.org. (Abelsky 2005, p. 26).

Tajikistan

The Tajiks, a largely Muslim people, came under Russian rule in the second half of the nineteenth century and became independent in 1991. A civil war lasted from 1992 to 1997. Since then the country has been relatively stable and has moved toward democracy and a free market economy. Tajikistan is one of the poorest countries of the former USSR. Only 6 percent of the land is arable, viable industry is almost nonexistent, natural resources are limited, and the civil war weakened an already weak economy. There has been some increase in international economic assistance in the wake of the war in Afghanistan.

The market

Except, possibly, for projects funded with international aid, this is not a market for North American design services.

Languages and communications

Tajik is the official language, but Russian is widely used in government and business. The telecommunications infrastructure is primitive.

Turkmenistan

This region was annexed by Russia in the second half of the nineteenth century and became independent in 1991. Although nominally a republic, it was ruled by an authoritarian ex-communist president, Saparmurat Niyazov, until his sudden death in December 2006. It is largely a desert country, almost half of its irrigated land was used to grow cotton. Today, its main economic assets are its large oil and gas reserves. In spite of its oil and gas, there is widespread internal poverty and poor economic management.

The market

If a more enlightened leadership emerges someday, more positive development might begin to occur. Until then, it is likely to be a very small market for international building design services.

Languages and communications

Turkmen is the dominant language, but Russian, Uzbek, and other languages are

spoken. The telecommunications infrastructure is poorly developed.

Ukraine

During the tenth and eleventh centuries, Ukrain was the center of the first Slavic

Fig. 4–41: *Univermag Ukraina, Kiev, Ukraine. Architects: The Liebman Melting Partnership with RTKL. Courtesy of The Liebman Melting Partnership.*

state, Kievan Rus. This powerful state was eventually overrun and ruled by a succession of neighboring countries, but the legacy of Kievan Rus formed the basis of Ukraine's nationalism through the centuries. In the eighteenth century, it was conquered by Russia and except for a brief period after World War I, it was controlled by Moscow—often brutally—until the dissolution of the USSR in 1991.

The legacy of state control and widespread corruption stalled much progress in the first post-Soviet decade. The Orange Revolution, at the end of 2004, however, brought in a reformist party led by Victor Yushchenko, who finally gives Ukraine some hope of political and economic progress.

Except for Russia, the Ukraine was the most important economy of the former USSR. It has a large agricultural sector and a major industrial base. Lack of reform stalled most progress after 1991, but the new government is beginning to make progress.

The market

Ukraine is a very limited market for North American design services today, but it is large enough to be a significant market in the future when it begins to see the need for the modern building types we design.

Languages and communications

Ukrainian is the official and dominant language, but Russian and a number of other languages are spoken as well. Ukraine's telecommunications infrastructure is "antiquated, inefficient and in disrepair" but is beginning to be modernized, according to *The World Factbook*.

Uzbekistan

Russia conquered Uzbekistan in the late nineteenth century, and it became independent in 1991. It is a dry, landlocked country that relies on the intense cultivation of its limited, irrigated river valleys. It is the world's second-largest cotton exporter and also has oil and gas reserves. Its economy, however, has sputtered since independence due to poor government policies. Outside investment in its gas and oil industry could improve growth prospects.

The market

This is a very poor country with little potential for North American design firms.

Languages and communications

Uzbek is the predominant language but Russian, Tajik, and other languages are also spoken. *The World Factbook* reports that the telecommunications infrastructure is "antiquated and inadequate."

AFRICA AND THE MIDDLE EAST

This is a very diverse region. It includes countries as different as Egypt, South Africa, Iran, and Saudi Arabia. Many of the countries have Islamic majorities, but there is great cultural, economic, and ethnic diversity. Therefore, it is very hard to generalize.

In this chapter, for the purposes of discussion, the region has been divided into four subregions:

- *Northern Africa:* The largely Muslim countries stretching from Morocco to the Horn of Africa.
- *Northwestern Africa:* The 20 countries that stretch along the western side of the continent south of Morocco to Cameroon. All but Cape Verde and Western Sahara are covered.
- *Southern Africa:* The 24 countries that make up the southern tip of the continent.

- *The Middle East:* The Muslim (and single Jewish) countries that extend from along the Levant to Iran.

A growing number of these countries are—or are becoming—major markets for design services.

Northern Africa

There are 10 countries located at the northern end of the African continent. Most have suffered, or are currently suffering, from periods of brutal violence, but several of these countries are now very stable and others are returning to normalcy. Nevertheless, this region's close ties and physical proximity to Europe, its physical assets, and the presence of some highly educated and sophisticated leadership in most countries make this an area of potential interest to North American design firms.

Some of the countries—Egypt, in particular—have spectacular cultural and touristic assets. Others have oil, gas, or other natural resources that support the economy. Most are Muslim, but they all have colonial histories that tie them to one or more countries in Europe. All together, the 10 countries have a total population of over 291 million as well as aspirations to create cities, communities, and economies that will require new buildings. Some of the key population and economic statistics are summarized in Table 4.8.

In spite of the combined size and aspirations of these countries, only Egypt offers significant opportunities for North American firms at the time this book was written. Therefore, only Egypt is covered in detail. Other countries may offer occasional project opportunities but not enough yet to warrant a major marketing effort by North American firms.

Contents

Countries in bold receive longer descriptive sections.

Algeria

After 100 years of French rule and years of armed conflict, Algeria achieved independence in 1962. The National Liberation Front (FLN) has dominated the country's politics. The government is a republic, but the army plays a major role at times. In the 1990s, an Islamic insurgency, and government efforts to suppress it, led to over 100,000 deaths. Since then, the insurgency has been significantly reduced, but it continues.

The population is almost 33 million and predominantly Muslim. The economy has a GDP of $253 billion (purchasing power parity) or $92 billion (official exchange rate) and is highly dependent on petroleum. Petroleum accounts for 60 percent of the government's revenues, 30 percent of GDP, and 95 percent of export earnings. In spite of the oil and gas revenues, the economy has struggled with corruption, high unemployment, low living standards, lack of infrastructure, and other problems.

Table 4.8 North Africa Population and Economic Statistics[16]

Country	Population	Population Growth Rate (%)	GDP—Purchasing Power Parity*	GDP—Official Exchange Rate*	GDP—Per Capita ($)
Algeria	32,930,000	1.22	253.4	92.22	7,700
Djibouti	487,000	2.02	0.62	0.70	1,000
Egypt	78,887,000	1.75	328.1	84.51	4,200
Eritrea	4,787,000	2.47	4.47	1.24	1,000
Ethiopia	74,778,000	2.31	71.63	9.79	1,000
Libya	5,901,000	2.3	74.97	34.83	12,700
Morocco	33,241,000	1.55	147	56.72	4,400
Somalia	8,863,000	2.85	5.02	2.48	600
Sudan	41,236,000	2.55	96.01	25.5	2,300
Tunisia	10,175,000	0.99	87.88	32.95	8,600

* In billions of U.S. dollars unless otherwise noted.

The market
Until Algeria improves its economy and government, it will remain a very limited market for North American design firms.

Languages and communications
Arabic is the official language, but French and Berber dialects are also used. The telecommunications infrastructure is out of date and inefficient, according to *The World Factbook*.

Djibouti
This former French territory became Djibouti in 1977. It was a one-party state until 1999, when it had its first multiparty election. It endured a civil war until 2001, but it is now relatively calm.

It has close ties to France, and its ties to the U.S. are strengthening. France maintains a military presence, and the U.S. has its only military base in sub-Saharan Africa there.

It has a population of approximately 407,000, some two-thirds of whom live in the capital, while the rest are nomadic herders.

The country has limited natural resources and little industry. Its GDP, which is estimated to be only $619 million, makes it a very poor country. There is 50 percent unemployment. The government is virtually bankrupt, and the country survives on foreign aid. Its limited economy is largely focused on services related to the country's free-trade zone and its strategic location at the mouth of the Red Sea.

The market
Unless there is a project commissioned by the U. S. military, this is an unlikely market for North American design firms.

Languages and communication
Both French and Arabic are official languages, but Somali and Afar are also spoken. The telecommunications infrastructure is adequate.

Egypt

Egypt has been an important country since 3200 BCE, the time of the first unifying dynasty. The fertile Nile River valley has supported a series of rich societies and attracted a long succession of conquerors. Because of its location astride the short cut to Asia, in 1869 it also became the site of one of the most important engineering feats—the creation of the Suez Canal. Egypt achieved partial independence in 1922 and full independence from the last of its foreign overseers, Great Britain, after World War II.

Following independence, Egypt became a republic under the first of a series of military leaders, Gamal Abdul Nasser, from 1952 to 1970. Nasser centralized the economy, aligned the country with Russia, and led a group of Arab allies in three unsuccessful wars with Israel in 1948, 1956 (with Britain and France as well in a last ill-advised attempt by the two European countries to keep control of the Suez Canal), and 1967. In this third war, Egypt lost control of the Sinai Peninsula, which was occupied by Israel. Nasser's successor, Anwar el-Sadat, led Egypt and its allies in a fourth war in 1973. A truce following the war lasted until Sadat decided to seek peace with Israel in 1978, and the treaty was officially signed in 1979. Though this peace effort cost him his life, in 1981, when he was assassinated, his courageous act allowed Egypt to regain control of the Sinai and made it possible for Egypt to focus on its internal needs rather than its external ambitions. This peace also realigned Egypt with the U.S. and made it a major recipient of U.S. aid.

Today Egypt is ruled by a third strong man, Hosni Mubarak, and he is struggling to improve the economy. Egypt has a population of approximately 79 million, which is the largest in the Arab world. Its GDP, however, is only about $328 billion (purchasing power parity) and $84 billion at the official exchange rate. In spite of economic reforms, the public sector operates at a substantial deficit, foreign direct investment is low, and living standards for the average Egyptian are stuck at a low level. Moreover, there are some concerns about Egypt's future, as it moves slowly toward a more democratic government while countering a growing problem with Islamic fundamentalists.

Egypt, however, does have many assets. Its natural gas reserves are being developed; it has a significant number of skilled and educated professionals; it has spectacular cultural and touristic assets; and it is the center of gravity in the Arab Middle East.

Egypt is also a culturally rewarding and diverse experience for an international architect. Very few countries offer a market that is as layered with history and culture, yet possesses a vision for growth into the future. From the new cities surrounding Cairo to the Red Sea resorts, the Egyptian market is diverse and expanding. The terrain of Egypt varies from the shores of the Mediterranean, to the deserts of the west, to the Red Sea, and upper Egypt. Considered the "melting pot" of the Middle East, this distinct population holds a common spirit, which makes them uniquely Egyptian.

Over the past 10 to 15 years, Egypt has seen a renaissance in development and significant increase in projects in both the touristic and private sectors. Most of this has been helped by the efforts of the government in privatizing land, assigning properties to successful business leaders, and encouraging development. This has led to growth in the country's GDP and established a growing middle class.

Fig. 4–42: *Alexandria Marriott Renaissance, Alexandria, Egypt. Architect: Basler Mosa Deign Group, Inc. Courtesy Marriott International.*

One of the most significant developments in Egypt over the past 10 to 15 years has been transformation of Egypt's coastline into world-class resort destinations. With tourism representing almost 12 percent of the GDP, Egypt takes in about $35 billion each year from about 6 million tourists. By transforming the sleepy fishing villages of Sharm el-Sheikh, Hurghada, and Marsa Alam into resort towns, Egypt has increased the total number of guestrooms significantly. Airports have been transformed to receive international flights, allowing direct charter connections for international travelers, and town centers that once had 4 to 5 buildings now are thriving centers of culture and entertainment, supporting the tourism industry.

The development of the tourism sector has stimulated substantial growth in the private sector. With the creation of new jobs come more planned communities and supporting infrastructure. Areas in the desert have been transformed into thriving villages, new cities, and areas for second homes for those seeking reprieve from the bustling streets of Cairo. An increase in goods and services has also been stimulated by the increase in Egypt's GDP, as well as the nearly $2 billion of U.S. aid given each year to the country.

While Egypt has experienced rapid growth, as with all developing countries, it has incurred its setbacks. In early 2002, the Egyptian pound was significantly devalued. Development projects slowed, and many were put on hold. The devaluation of the pound eventually led to a market correction. A considerable number of developers who had overextended themselves, and others who were found corrupt, were flushed from the market in one way or another. This allowed for a market correction and thus a more stable development arena.

The past couple of years have once again seen a resurgence in development. There are fewer inexperienced or speculative developers. In addition, an influx of foreign investment is helping Egypt. With ambitious infrastructure projects either complete or underway, the Egyptian market has a promising future.

The market
Egypt has been a significant market for a number of North American firms.

Reasons to be there
1. The scale of the projects is greater than many in North America.
2. Each project involves a different history, culture, and location.
3. Big projects get built.
4. Large completed projects in Egypt can significantly help in showing experience while firms pursue jobs in North America.
5. Egypt has a rich culture and history.
6. Traveling within Egypt can be a very interesting and diverse experience.
7. Many projects developed in Egypt will be recognized throughout the Middle East and develop strong credibility for firms wanting to expand in the region.
8. Client relationships can be built that last a lifetime.

Reasons to be cautious
1. A considerable amount of commitment and time is required to get the first job in Egypt.
2. As one is always reminded, Egyptians have been professionals at business and negotiations for thousands of years. Securing a contract is nothing like doing business in North America.
3. The fee structure is considerably less than that in North America, and there is very little legal recourse if things go wrong.
4. New project development and ongoing projects can take enormous amounts of principal time. Moreover, many projects remain a mystery as to when and where they start.
5. Owners want to see principals and work directly with them, as most of them are involved in their projects on a day-to-day basis. Therefore, principals must be willing to spend considerable time on their projects in Egypt.
6. Many projects begin with a piece of land and no program. Owners look to the architects to help them develop a program, which can lead to internal confusion as well as considerable redrawing.
7. A considerable number of owners have never developed before and now find themselves in unfamiliar territory on very large projects. They place a lot of trust in the architects to help guide them through the program and process.
8. There are some physical health and safety issues.

Skills and capabilities that are important
The two biggest skills that are important for success in Egypt are patience and perseverance. Without knowledge of the local business customs and strategies, a firm could spend endless efforts chasing projects that never come to fruition. Very lit-

tle goes as planned, so firms must have the ability to rebound and change their approach if necessary. The following are other capabilities that are required for successful practice:

- An Arabic-speaking principal or senior staff member.
- A support staff that can deal with the owner's in-house team on a day-to-day basis and can support ongoing projects.
- An understanding of local customs and traditions.
- Appreciation for the history and various cultures of Egypt.
- Ability to know when to decline an opportunity.
- A calendar showing all the Egyptian holidays, so you don't get stuck in Cairo waiting for the big meeting when everyone else takes a three-day holiday.

Who is operating there now?

Over the years, most of the large firms have worked in Egypt. Yet Egypt is a place that offers equal opportunities for both large and small firms. Many clients may decide to work with a small firm because of the amount of time and dedication they will receive from the principals and senior staff. Smaller firms may also have the ability to work on more constrained budgets, which give them the flexibility when starting on new jobs while giving them exposure to much larger projects than they could secure in North America. The successful firms in Egypt include both small and large firms, but all have made a commitment to the region and have a continuous presence.

Who are the clients?

There are a multitude of clients in Egypt, and each offers its own risks and rewards.

The following are clients who would most likely hire an international consultant:

- *Government agencies:* The government typically will work with a reputable local firm, unless it is a project that is funded by foreign investment such as U.S. Agency for International Development (USAID).
- *New private developers:* One thing to understand is that while the government has tried to privatize most of the country, many developers have never built more than the garage on their house. Now these would-be developers find themselves with a considerable parcel of land. In some cases, the government assigns land, while in others, a successful businessman in a completely different sector may seek to invest some of his earnings in real estate or to use it for political advancement. The inexperience should not deter a firm in working with a particular client, yet the amount of additional time and effort involved should be considered.
- *Existing developers:* These are current developers who have completed projects before. It should be recognized that it is likely that not so long ago, these people were new developers as described above.
- *Foreign developers:* With the boom in the Gulf region, many successful developers or investors from other countries are now involved in projects in Egypt.
- *Private institutions:* There are projects for such institutions as universities and hospitals that are developing projects or expanding their existing facilities.

These clients are all developing projects in a number of building sectors: mixed-use, hotels and resorts, universities, hospitals, museums, residential planning, and regional master planning.

Most of the work commissioned in Egypt involves architecture, planning, landscape architecture, and interior design. All projects are commissioned through either concepts or design development, and a local architect is associated with the project for construction documentation. The local Egyptian engineering expertise is extremely high and should be utilized on projects.

What is the process for getting work?

The process of getting work in Egypt may appear at first to be similar to North America, but quickly one realizes it is really very different. The most important advice when networking and negotiating with clients is to understand that they have you there because they want to hire an international consultant. Agents can help make introductions and facilitate negotiations, but some can be a barrier to a successful conclusion. Principals or senior management of the firm should be networking and following up with clients. There is considerable social separation in Egypt, and clients want to deal with the principals or decision makers of those firms they hire, at least when negotiating contracts or developing new work.

Languages and communications

Arabic is the official language of Egypt. In fact, the Arabic spoken in Egypt is considered the most pure or beautiful dialect. Most of this stems from the fact that almost all the famous actors as well as singers from the mid-twentieth century were Egyptian and were heard in every Arabic-speaking house in all other countries in the Middle East.

Almost all business is done in English, and most clients as well as their senior staff will speak English. Many of them, also, will have been educated in North America. Even with this, it is extremely important to have Arabic-speaking senior staff. If possible, an Arabic-speaking principal can also add tremendous credibility and allow relationships with clients to be more personal.

The IT and telecommunications infrastructure is relatively modern after a major upgrade in the 1990s.

Licensing and legal issues

Setting up a corporation in Egypt involves dealing with a lot of red tape. There are plenty of local attorneys who can assist you in wading through the bureaucracy. Firms wanting to establish an entity in Egypt must be prepared for a lengthy process but with an eventual end.

Firms wanting to set up an office in Egypt should recognize first that the reason clients hire international firms is because of their experience. There is a considerable fee difference between international and local firms. If an international firm is established in Egypt, then clients may have a different expectation with regard to performance and fees. In addition, clients may want to pay in local currency, which is subject to fluctuation. Most firms opt to open a small liaison office for administrative purposes only. This can be done by setting up a branch office or simply by utilizing an existing company and their facilities. Not having a registered office in Egypt would only limit projects in working with the government or other agencies. Most such projects, however, are typically awarded to large local consultants.

Licensing requirements are as follows:

• *Is a license required?* Yes.

- *Licensing requirements:* BSC Architecture or BA in Architecture obtained from an Egyptian University or an approved equivalent.
- *What agency licenses?* The Architecture Branch of the Society of Egyptian Architects (SE ARE).
- *To practice, is a local representative required?* Yes. A local architect must be not only a representative but also a partner or associate and must be an Egyptian-registered architect in Egypt. The SE ARE must authorize any joint ventures. The local partner is responsible for applying for building permits and signing all the required documents and must be involved in the construction phase.

Scope of Services

As one architect put it, "If you have ever seen an Arabic orchestra play, you may have a sense of the 'organized chaos' which could very well be a good analogy for any project in Egypt. There are a lot of moving parts, not necessarily all in rhythm, but somehow the product is beautiful" (personal correspondence). The initial planning stage of the process is typically the most difficult, time consuming, and confusing. Many projects may not have a well-defined program, if they even have one. The design firm must have the ability and flexibility to work quickly with the owner to flesh out various ideas and define a program. The planning phase is usually limited to a maximum of two to three months.

An international firm usually provides services through either schematic design or design development, although it is very common for clients to request interior-design services through construction documents and, in some cases, in the construction phase as well. Almost all projects include some sort of review process with the local consultants during the construction documents and construction phases.

Quality control can become a major factor on projects due to the lack of control over CDs (construction documents). Some international firms are requested to extend services through the construction phase or provide more frequent review. In these cases, a local liaison office can go a long way toward offering this service at a reasonable rate, while assuring quality control.

Fee levels, payment terms, and taxes

Fee levels are not at the same level as in North America, but they are much higher for international consultants than for local consultants. A recommended fee scale does exist. All fees for American consultants in Egypt should be paid in U.S. dollars to a U.S. account. Unless required for a certain project, payments should be avoided in local currency. The currency is not stable.

The biggest challenge, as with any job, is getting paid on time. If a project is paid on time, it goes a long way toward establishing a good relationship throughout the project. Typically, a client will request that all out-of-pocket expenses, such as travel, printing, telephone, etc., be included in the overall fee. This will take planning and management of these costs to achieve a profit.

Major contract issues

Typically, the major contract negotiations center on fees. Once fees are established, clients may want to negotiate schedules, reimbursable expenses, or additional services. The scope of services

> "When the full power of a human imagination is backed by the weight of a living tradition, the resulting work is far greater than any that an artist can achieve when he has no tradition to work in or when he willfully abandons its tradition."
>
> —Hassan Fathy

should be extremely clear in the contract with a specific set of deliverables. This will minimize confusion with regard to the scope of what you are expected to produce.

Schedules are always made shorter. Clients will pressure endlessly to make them even shorter, but it is important to argue for a realistic schedule. Schedules should never be linked to payment requests or penalties, since many delays are out of the control of the consultant.

Payment schedules typically create a problem, as they are always loaded in the back rather than the front. The majority of all fees should be in the front of the project, as many projects tend to get put on hold or go through radical changes at the end.

Once a client agrees to a fee, most things like schedules can be worked out to a mutual understanding. What are typically never agreed to are reimbursable expenses such as travel, printing, telephone, etc. The clients usually want them included in the fee. If this is the case, the contract should be specific about how many trips are included and/or who prints the drawings. Typically, drawings can be sent digitally for printing in the client office or local consultant office.

Local resources

Egypt has great local resources with regard to local architects and engineers. A strong local consultant makes every job much easier. Local offices work closely with the construction site, since many items are not well documented in the CDs (construction documents). Many principals have been educated abroad, as have some of the senior staff members. In addition, most firms, at least the large ones, have worked with international consultants and know the process.

Some clients have a strong internal team established as well. This typically consists of architects and engineers for review and advisory purposes. Having this expertise at a client's disposal can help facilitate the process if they are well trained and have experience. In other cases, it can create chaos and confusion among everyone if there are too many opinions trying to influence the client.

Design issues

There are plenty of inspirations in Egypt for an architect, whether it is from the ancient civilizations, the desert architecture, the splendors of the Red Sea and the Mediterranean, the wonders of Old Cairo, or the architectural glamour of the now-passed heyday of downtown Cairo.

The work of Hassan Fathy stood as a recent reminder that architecture in its harmony and proportions can be an inspired form for all social levels. Unfortunately, much of the recent development in Egypt has strayed from this premise and has no cultural or traditional design value. As with most development, in third-world societies, when growth happens at such a rapid rate, architecture often becomes an imported status symbol that has no direct relationship to the local vernacular. Spanish villas line the roads of the new planned communities outside of Cairo, which are owned by the upper middle-class or upper-class citizens. When the local vernacular is interpreted, it has in some cases become a cheap rendition. This is apparent in the endless Pharaonic-style government buildings peppered throughout the urban landscape.

Although it may be difficult to persuade an entire social class not to develop Spanish villas for their second homes, the most successful cultural, commercial, and tourism projects have been inspired from their surroundings and place. Tourists who visit Egypt are not looking for a theme park, but prefer to feel as if they are staying in part of history and tradition. The successful hotels in Sharm el-Sheikh, Hurghada, and the other Red Sea resorts have captured this experience in their architecture and planning. This involves a contemporary interpretation of the vernacular as well as planning of spaces and events, giving the guests a sampling of authenticity to remember for a lifetime.

Commercial and mixed-use buildings being developed along the banks of the Nile in downtown Cairo have a more difficult challenge. Sitting on the Nile and observing the surroundings, one would quickly recognize the significance of this place and the diversity of the skyline, which is distinctly Cairo. Cairo is not Dubai or Singapore, and the sense of place of each building is extremely important when defining the architecture.

The following practical considerations should also be made when working in Egypt:

- Many cultural or commercial developments will require a prayer room for both men and women. In most cases, this is an area for the workers to pray during the day.
- The plumbing is not very reliable; therefore, in smaller developments, placing the kitchens and bathrooms along the exterior wall or along the wall of a common light shaft is required. In most residential developments, as well, kitchen and bathrooms should have operable windows for proper ventilation.

Typical schedules

While most project schedules will follow a normal routine once they reach the con-

struction phase, Egyptian developers are always eager to reach the construction phase. A project may not have a well-defined program and, in most cases, may not have been tested via market research, but clients will want to get out of the gate quickly and into construction. This can create a compromised design process as well as setting up the project for significant changes later. For instance, a client developing a hotel wants to start construction before a hotel operator is on board. When a hotel operator joins the team later, it is assured that changes will need to take place on the project. In other cases, a project may have started construction already, before either the operator or the international design firm is brought into the project.

Code and regulatory issues

Egypt has its own codes and regulations, but it primarily follows the International Building Code (IBC). Local consultants will advise western firms on the specific rules and regulations of each city. The amended codes typically deal with fires and earthquakes and can be easily navigated with an experienced local consultant.

The zoning requirements for each area vary and are constantly changing. The Ministry of Housing has the final say on zoning issues in Cairo, and it can easily amend existing zoning—unfortunately in any direction. In other cities, zoning is typically established by the local municipality and determined by the mayor or governor. A client with strong political connections will have significantly more success.

Local construction capabilities

The local construction companies have considerable experience and capabilities.

Quality control becomes an issue and can be controlled with proper planning and good management. Much of the historic craftsmanship has become a lost art. Again, with proper management and research, construction companies can deliver incredible detailing at very good prices.

Most construction is poured-in-place concrete with stucco walls. Large buildings may use precast panels or simple curtain walls.

Personal safety and health issues

Egypt is a relatively safe country, with the exception of the highway traffic. As an ally in the war on terrorism, the government of Egypt goes to great lengths to ensure the stability and safety of each of its regions. Travelers, as well as foreign workers, are advised to stay abreast of the U.S. State Department's publications regarding traveling in Egypt, as well as register with the U.S. Embassy in Cairo prior to arrival.

The most dangerous part of Egypt is driving on the highways. Typically, in Cairo the traffic moves so slowly the worst you face is a fender bender. When traveling on any of the highways or other high-speed roads, make sure you are buckled up well and don't hesitate to tell your driver to slow down.

There are very few major health risks in Egypt, unless traveling in remote agricultural areas. Normal dietary precautions should be taken with regard to water and food. Bottled water is always a must, and food should be well prepared and cooked thoroughly. Fresh fruits and vegetables can cause certain risks if not washed properly or prepared by a person with good hygiene.

There are occasional terrorist incidents, but these seem more significant in the western press than they do in Egypt.

Key pieces of advice

- Have patience and perseverance.
- Be committed to the market and be prepared to spend considerable time there.
- Recognize the long-term commitment required.
- Develop strong social relationships with clients.
- Realize when to walk away from a project or when the path is a dead end.
- Avoid work that is unpaid.
- Negotiate contracts that are clear.
- Make sure all agreements are signed before getting too far into the project.
- Understand the history and culture of Egypt.
- Only work in Egypt if you thoroughly enjoy the Middle East and the Egyptians.

Sources of information

Very little has been written on doing business in Egypt. Most information comes with understanding the territory and spending a considerable amount of time there. Other resources include:

American Chamber of Commerce in Egypt
Telephone: 20-2-338-1050
Web site: http://www.amcham.org.eg/

See Hassan Fathy's *Architecture for the Poor: An Experiment in Rural Egypt* (Chicago: University of Chicago Press, 2000).

Business Today Egypt
http://www.businesstodayegypt.com/

U.S. Embassy, Egypt
Telephone: 202-797-3300
E-mail: consularcairo@state.gov
Web site: http://cairo.usembassy.gov

Society of Egyptian Architects (SE ARE)
Telephone: 202-419-89-54
Fax: 202-575-75-15
Web site: www.sea1917.org

Egyptian Engineering Society

Egyptian Engineering Syndicate

Eritrea

Eritrea was awarded as a federated state to Ethiopia in 1952 and was annexed by Ethiopia 10 years later. This led to a 30-year armed struggle that ended in 1991, and Eritrea was finally independent in 1993. A border war with Ethiopia continued into the late 1990s.

It is a small (population approximately 4,787,000) and desperately poor (GDP: $4.5 billion at purchasing power parity and $1.24 billion at the official exchange rate) country with an economy based primarily on subsistence agriculture.

The market

This is a very unlikely market for any services other than those financed by international aid.

Languages and communications

Arabic and a number of African languages are spoken. The telecommunications infrastructure is in poor shape.

Ethiopia

Except for a brief period of Italian occupation (1936–41), Ethiopia was never a colony of a European country. The ancient Ethiopian monarchy, who mismanaged the country, were ousted by the military 1991. Multiparty elections were finally held in 1995.

Ethiopia has a large population of almost 75 million, and most are Muslim or Ethiopian Orthodox. Almost 80 percent are employed in agriculture, which is the primary economic sector. The county's economy is poverty-stricken. The GDP is only $71 billion (purchasing power parity) and a little under $10 billion at the official exchange rate.

The market

Unless working for an international aid organization, it is unlikely to be a market for North American design firms.

Languages and communications

English is the major foreign language taught in the schools. But Somali, Arabic, and a variety of African languages are spoken by different groups in the country. *The World Factbook* describes the telecommunications infrastructure as "adequate for government use."

Libya

Italy invaded and made Libya a colony in 1911. With United Nations (UN) support, Libya became independent at the end of 1951. The discovery of oil in 1959 began the transformation of a very poor country into one of the wealthiest states in Africa.

The country was a monarchy until a 1969 military coup led by a young officer named Muammar al-Qaddafi. Since then he has led the military dictatorship of Libya. His support of terrorism resulted in UN sanctions, which were finally lifted in 2003. In recent years, Qaddafi and Libya have made strides to normalize relations with Europe and the U.S.

This rapprochement with the rest of the world has reopened Libya to development. The country of 5.9 million people has one of the highest per capita GDPs,

Fig. 4–43: Concept design for a residential tower for DAMAC Properties, Tripoli, Libya. Architect: Basler Mosa Design Group, Inc. Courtesy of Basler Mosa Design Group.

due to its large petroleum revenues. Petroleum accounts for 95 percent of export earnings, 25 percent of the GDP, and 60 percent of the public sector's payroll. The economy has a GDP of almost $75 billion (purchasing power parity) and $34.8 billion (official exchange), but this relatively high per capita income does not flow down to the majority of the population.

The market
Normalization and high oil revenues should help stimulate development, and this could make Libya of considerable interest to some international design firms. The UN-sanctions period stalled most development, and now both Libyan and foreign groups are initiating new projects. Both American and European firms are getting major projects and believe there are many more to come.

Languages and communications
Arabic is the official language but Italian and English are widely used as well. The telecommunications system is being modernized. A mobile cellular telephone system has been in place for over 10 years.

Morocco
Morocco is a constitutional monarchy that regained full sovereignty in 1956 after a long period of French (and in some areas Spanish) rule. It has a population of 33,241,000 and is 99 percent Muslim. The GDP is estimated at $147 billion (based on purchasing power parity) and almost $57 billion at the official exchange rate. There is high unemployment, but the economy is relatively stable. Tourism is an important economic sector.

The market
Morocco signed a free-trade agreement with the U.S. that took effect in 2006. This could help stimulate Moroccan-U.S. economic ties. At this time, however, the most likely market for U.S. design firm services are tourism-related projects and projects for multinational corporations.

Languages and communications

The official language is Arabic; but French is often used in business, diplomacy, and government. Some parts of the country also use Berber dialects. The telecommunications infrastructure is modern with both telephone and Internet service in place but of low density.

Licensing and legal issues

Licensing requirements are as follows:

- *Is a license required?* An architect will need to be registered. Foreigners may not be registered, however.
- *Licensing requirements:* To be registered as an architect, the individual needs (1) to have a Master's degree from a recognized school of architecture and (2) must be registered with the National Association of Architects. Foreigners are not permitted to register. The only registered foreigners remain a small number of French architects who were born, lived, or practiced in Morocco during the French Protectorate. As far as the latter are concerned, each case is considered individually by the National Association of Architects (l'Ordre National des Architectes).
- *What agency licenses?* National Association of Architects.
- *What is the professional architectural organization?* l'Ordre National des Architectes.
- *To practice, is a local representative required?* Yes. The representative needs to be a citizen of the country. A local representative cannot be a U.S. citizen. In exceptional circumstances, the local partner can be a foreigner only if he or she has been granted special permission, as explained above. Participation of a local representative can be limited to application for the building permit, which can only be obtained through a local partner who will be legally and professionally responsible for the project in Morocco and who will file for the occupancy permit once the project is completed.

Sources of information

U. S. Embassy, Morocco
Telephone: 212-37-762-265
E-mail: ircrabat@usembassy.ma
Web site: www.usembassy.ma

Conseil National de l'Ordre National
   des Architectes

Direction de l'Architecture

Somalia

Rent a copy of the movie *Black Hawk Down*, and then decide if you think it is worth trying to work there.

Sudan

Sudan has been dominated by its military and the Islamic northern part of the country since independence from Britain in 1956. A two-decade conflict with the non-Muslim south left over 2 million people dead. While this conflict has receded, a new one in the western Darfur region had claimed over 200,000 lives by 2007.

Not surprisingly, the economy has struggled, and most of the population of 41,236,000 people live at or below the poverty line. In 2007 the GDP was estimated to be $96 billion (purchasing power parity), or a little over $25 billion at the official exchange rate.

The market

As a very poor, badly governed, and occasionally dangerous place, Sudan is an unlikely market for North American architects and most other design disciplines.

Languages and communications

Arabic is the official language; but English, Nubian, and a number of other African languages and dialects are used. The telecommunications infrastructure was recently updated and is reasonably modern.

Tunisia

Tunisia is a moderate, nonaligned republic with a historical tie to France. It has a relatively small population of 10,175,000. Its economy is diverse and growing. In 2007 its GDP was estimated to be almost $87 billion (purchasing power parity) and almost $33 billion at official exchange rates. Mining, tourism, agriculture, manufacturing, and other sectors support the economy.

The market

Tunisia is likely to provide only occasional opportunities for North American design professionals.

Languages and communications

Arabic is the official language, but French is used as well in business. The telecommunications infrastructure is above average for Africa but still needs significant modernization.

Table 4.9 North Africa Population and Economic Statistics[17]

Country	Population	Population Growth Rate (%)	GDP—Purchasing Power Parity*	GDP—Official Exchange Rate*	GDP— Per Capita ($)
Benin	7,863,000	2.73	8.931	4.62	1,100
Burkina Faso	13,903,000	3	17.87	5.82	1,300
Cameroon	17,341,000	2.04	42.2	16.37	2,400
Cape Verde	421,000	0.64	3.13	1.138	6,000
Central African Republic	4,303,000	1.53	4.91	1.54	1,100
Chad	9,944,000	2.93	15.26	5.26	1,500
Côte d'Ivoire	17,655,000	2.03	28.47	17.19	1,600
Gambia	1,642,000	2.84	3.25	0.46	2,000
Ghana	22,410,000	2.07	59.15	10.18	2,600
Guinea	9,690,000	2.63	19.04	3.74	2,000
Guinea-Bissau	1,442,000	2.07	1.24	0.30	900
Liberia	3,042,000	4.91	2.91	0.90	1,000
Mali	11,717,000	2.63	14.59	5.85	1,200
Mauritania	3,177,000	2.88	8.40	1.64	2,600
Niger	12,525,000	2.92	12.23	3.64	900
Nigeria	132,000,000	2.38	188.5	83.36	1,400
Senegal	11,987,000	2.34	22.01	8.56	1,800
Sierra Leone	6,005,000	2.3	5.38	1.23	900
Togo	5,549,000	2.72	9.25	2.11	1,700
Western Sahara	273,000	NA	NA	NA	NA

* In billions of U.S. dollars unless otherwise noted.

Sources of information

Ordre des Architectes de Tunisie (OAT)
Telephone: 216-71-753-391
Fax: 216-71-231-299
E-mail: Ordre.architectes@planet.tn
Web site: www.oat.org.tn

Northwestern Africa

The northwestern sub-Saharan region includes a number of very poor countries as well as a few of potential interest to international design firms. A first indication of the most promising markets can be deduced from the statistical data in Table 4.9. Most have minimal potential as markets as they are too small and poor to afford international design services—unless the projects come with foreign investment or aid. A few, including Ghana and Nigeria, have occasional projects that employ international architects.

Benin

Benin (formerly Dahomey) received independence from France in 1960. It had a chaotic political history during its first 30 years, but it appears to have moved to democracy over the last 15 years. Again, this is a poor, agriculture-based economy that is struggling.

French is the official language of Benin, but a number of different African languages are widely used.

Burkina Faso

Burkina Faso (formerly Upper Volta) achieved independence from France in 1960. The early years were marked by repeated coups. It is another of the poorest countries in the world. Almost 90 percent of the population is engaged in subsistence agriculture.

French is the official language, but most people speak one of a number of African languages.

Cameroon

French Cameroon and part of British Cameroon merged in 1961 to form the new Cameroon. An ethnic oligarchy controls the government; but the country has, in general, been stable. Because of its oil resources and good agricultural conditions, it is better off than many of its neighbors. Nevertheless, it remains poor and in need of economic reform.

English and French are the official languages, but the population speaks more than two dozen African languages.

Central African Republic

This is another former French colony (previously known as Ubangi-Shari) that became independent in 1960. Its entire post-independence history has been tumultuous and plagued by unrest and frequent misrule. This, too, is one of the poorest countries in the world.

French is the official language, but Sangho is the national language used by most of the population.

Chad

Chad is still another French colony that achieved independence in 1960. Three decades of civil war and invasion by Libya followed. During the last 15 years, the country has moved toward democracy, but this has been marred by a series of rebellions. The majority of the population is Muslim, but there are large Christian and animist minorities. Eighty percent of the population relies on subsistence farming. A consortium—led by two U.S. companies—has invested heavily to develop the country's large oil reserves. Oil exports started in 2004. In spite of oil, Chad is an unstable, very poor country.

French and Arabic are the official languages, but the population speaks 120 different African languages and dialects.

Côte d'Ivoire (Ivory Coast)

A former French colony that, since independence in 1960, has been one of Africa's more prosperous countries. This prosperity has been seriously hurt by a 1999 military coup and subsequent instability. In spite of rising oil production, the country is predominantly agricultural. It is a poor country and unlikely to improve until stability is reestablished.

French is the official language but most of the population speaks one or more of 60 dialects.

Gambia

Gambia was a British colony until 1965. It is a very poor, small, and agriculture-based country. English is the official language, but several African languages are also spoken.

Ghana

Ghana achieved independence in 1957 from Great Britain. It was formed from a merger of the Gold Coast and the Togoland trust territory. It suffered through a series of coups during the first three decades of independence; but for the last 15 years, Ghana has moved toward a functioning democracy. Its economy is somewhat more productive than many of its neighbors, but it is still a very poor country.

English is the official language, but most people speak one of several different African languages.

Guinea

Guinea is a predominantly Muslim country that was a French colony until 1958. It has a long, unstable history, occasionally made worse when unrest in neighboring Sierra Leone and Liberia spills over. It is very poor and underdeveloped, even though it has some significant natural resources.

French is the official language, but major ethnic groups each have their own language.

Guinea-Bissau

Guinea-Bissau was a Portuguese colony until 1974. It has suffered through a number of coups, making this a periodically unstable country. It is ranked as one of the 10 poorest countries in the world. Portuguese is the official language, but several African languages are also spoken.

Liberia

A 14-year civil war ended in 2003. While the country is making some progress toward stability, it has a ways to go. The war left the economy in a shambles. A minor-

ity speak English, the official language, while the rest of the country speaks about 20 different ethnic languages.

Mali

Mali (formerly the Sudanese Republic) obtained independence from France. After initial rule by a dictatorship and several coups, it has had about 15 years of democracy. It is one of the poorest countries in the world, with almost 80 percent of its labor force engaged in farming and fishing.

French is the official language, but most Malians speak Bambara or one of the large number of other African languages.

Mauritania

Mauritania was a former French colony until 1960. It is completely Muslim, but suffers tensions between its black and Berber ethnic groups. Oil production has started, but the country remains very poor. Arabic is the official language, but several others are spoken.

Niger

Niger is another former French colony that achieved independence in 1960. It has been ruled by the military for most of its history but has been functioning as a democracy since 1999. The country ranks last on the U.N. Development Fund index of human development and is one the world's poorest countries. Again, French is the official language, but most people speak one or two African languages.

Nigeria

Britain gradually—and somewhat reluctantly—took control of Nigeria during the nineteenth century. Britain gave Nigeria its independence in 1960. The country fought a bitter civil war in the late 1960s that left one to three million dead from hostilities, disease, and starvation. After the civil war and 16 years of military rule, a peaceful transition to civilian government was achieved in 1999. There were outbreaks of violence as this book was written, but most of the country is relatively peaceful. Nigeria is the one country in Western North Africa that is a substantial potential market for international design services.

The economy is largely petroleum-based, but to date much of this country's large oil revenues have been squandered through corruption and mismanagement. Oil provides 20 percent of Nigeria's $188.5 billion purchasing power parity GDP ($83.4 billion in 2006 at the official exchange rate). It also provides 95 percent of the country's foreign-exchange earnings and 65 percent of its budgetary revenue. The largely subsistence agriculture sector has not kept up with population growth, and the country has shifted from a net exporter to a net importer of food. Overall, its per capita GDP of approximately $1,400 makes it a very poor country.

Its population of approximately 132 million makes it the most populous country in Africa. This population is approximately 50 percent Muslim and 40 percent Christian while 10 percent practice indigenous beliefs. There are more than 250 ethnic groups, but the largest and most influential are the Housa and Fulani (approximately 29 percent), Yoruba (21 percent), Ibo (18 percent), and Ijaw (10 percent). As the *New York Times* (December 13, 2006, A4) noted: "But these days the deepest cleavage in Nigerian society [is]…the chasm between the tiny, rich and powerful elite and the vast, impoverished majority."

The market

Because of oil revenues, however, Nigeria has had the money to develop or import some of the trappings of a modern country. North American design professionals helped plan and design a new capital, Abuja, starting in the 1970, which became the official capital at the end of 1991. Oil has made possible other major projects as well: e.g., hospitals, universities, office buildings, and other projects requiring sophisticated design services. Occasionally, North American firms are given opportunities to work on these projects. Most firms who do work there, including my firm, find it a very difficult place to work. For those with an interest in Africa, the relevant skills, and the patience to deal with the challenge of working there, Nigeria could be an occasional market. For most, however, there are probably more attractive opportunities elsewhere.

Languages and communications

English is the official language, but the major tribal groups have their own languages as well. The telecommunications infrastructure is weak, and modernization has been slow.

Personal safety and health issues

Crime is a major problem, and the risk of infectious disease (malaria, typhoid, etc.) is rated by *The World Factbook* as "very high."

Sources of information

Nigerian Institute of Architects
Telephone: 234-1-470-6003;
    234-803-304-7217
Fax: 234-1-263-7843
E-mail: niarc@beta_linkserve.com
Web site: www.architectsnigeria.org

Senegal

Another French colony that became independent in 1960. One of Africa's most stable countries. Its economy has been growing in recent years, but it remains a very poor country. French is the official language.

Sierra Leone

This country is slowly recovering from a 1991–2002 civil war that killed tens of thousands and caused the displacement of one-third of the population, but it continues to suffer from periods of unrest. It is an extremely poor country. English is the official language, but it is only used by a small, literate minority. Several other languages are used by the rest of the population.

Togo

Togo received independence from France in 1960. It has been a military dictator-ship for most of the years since independence. Its small economy is largely based on agriculture, and the country remains very poor. French is the official language, but several African languages are widely used.

Southern Africa

This region, Southern Africa, includes 24 countries. As in the other parts of the African continent, most of the countries are so poor—or their economies are in such poor shape—that the opportunities for international architects are limited. A few of these countries, however, have some potential for successful projects if firms are willing to invest the time and effort to explore this region.

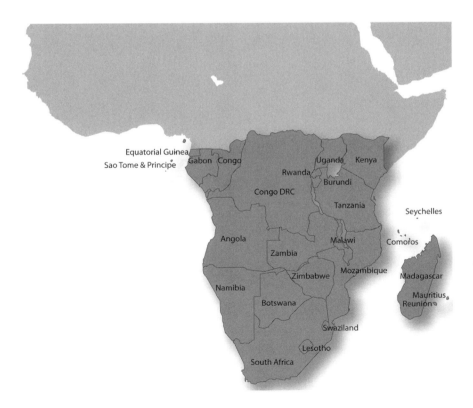

Table 4.10 Southern Africa Population and Economic Statistics[8]

Country	Population	Population Growth Rate (%)	GDP—Purchasing Power Parity*	GDP—Official Exchange Rate*	GDP— Per Capita ($)
Angola	12,127,000	2.45	51.95	28.37	4,300
Botswana	1,640,000	-0.04	18.72	9.70	11,400
Burundi	8,090,000	3.71	57.44	0.78	700
Comoros	691,000	2.87	0.44	0.40	600
Congo, Democratic Republic of the	62,660,000	3.07	44.6	8.06	700
Congo, Republic of the	3,702,000	2.6	4.96	5.09	1,300
Equatorial Guinea	540,000	2.05	25.7	7.64	50,200
Gabon	1,425,000	2.13	10.21	7.05	7,200
Kenya	34,708,000	2.57	40.77	17.39	1,200
Lesotho	2,022,000	-0.46	5.20	1.42	2,600
Madagascar	18,595,000	3.03	17.27	5.10	900
Malawi	13,014,000	2.38	8.04	2.17	600
Mauritius	1,241,000	0.82	16.72	7.14	13,500
Mozambique	19,686,000	1.38	29.32	6.43	1,500
Namibia	2,044,000	0.59	15.04	5.30	7,400
Rwanda	8,648,000	2.43	13.54	1.97	1,600
São Tomé and Príncipe	193,000	3.15	0.21	0.07	1,200
Seychelles	81,000	0.43	0.63	0.71	7,800
South Africa	44,187,000	-0.4	576.4	200.5	13,000
Swaziland	1,136,000	-0.23	5.91	2.21	5,200
Tanzania	37,445,000	1.83	29.25	13.13	800
Uganda	28,196,000	3.37	51.89	8.50	1,800
Zambia	11,502,000	2.11	11.51	5.81	1000
Zimbabwe	12,237,000	0.62	25.05	3.15	2,000

* In billions of U.S. dollars unless otherwise noted.

Angola

The Republic of Angola became independent from Portugal in 1975, but then a 27-year civil war broke out. Up to 1.5 million lives were lost and 4 million people displaced. The economy is heavily dependent on oil, which contributes about half of the GDP and 90 percent of the country's exports. Half the population still survives on subsistence agriculture. While the country has the resources to support a growing economy, major reforms and continued stability are essential. As with most other oil-rich countries, petroleum revenues help fund occasional projects. Perkins & Will, for example, is working on a major expansion of the University of Angola. Portuguese is the official language, but Bantu and other languages are widely used.

Botswana

The Republic of Botswana (formerly the British protectorate of Bechuanaland) achieved independence in 1966. A relatively stable civilian leadership, progressive policies, and capital investment have made it one of Africa's more prosperous countries. Diamond mining has been a major factor in the economy, accounting for about a one-third of GDP and over 70 percent of its export earnings. Diamond production is projected to level off, though. Tourism is growing and financial services and agriculture are also important.

Nevertheless, the country has many serious problems. Unemployment is somewhere between 24 and 40 percent, according to different estimates. The country has the second-highest HIV/AIDS rate in the world (estimated at 37 percent of the adult population).

English is the official language, but most speak Setswana or other African languages.

Burundi

Burundi became independent in 1962 and recently ended (in most of the country) 12 years of horrific ethnic violence in 2005. During the fighting between Hutu and Tutsi factions, approximately 200,000 people died and hundreds of thousands were displaced. Needless to say, the economy stalled at a very low level during these years. Approximately 90 percent of the population depends upon subsistence agriculture. Foreign exchange comes primarily from coffee and tea exports. French and Kirundi are official languages, but Swahili is also spoken.

Comoros

This is a small island nation in the Indian Ocean that gained independence from France in 1975. It is politically unstable and far too small and poor to be a market for international design services.

Democratic Republic of the Congo

The Democratic Republic of the Congo (formerly Zaire and the Belgian Congo) is one of Africa's largest countries. In spite of the country's vast potential wealth (in its natural resources), its economy has been in decline for decades due to war, economic mismanagement, lack of infrastructure, and corruption. Conditions have begun to improve, but the country remains extremely poor.

French is the official language, but a number of African languages and dialects are spoken.

Republic of the Congo

The Republic of the Congo is another French colony that became independent in 1960. It has had a chaotic political and economic history. It once was a major oil producer, but production is declining. Much of the country's revenues have been used to back international borrowing, but the country remains very poor and underdeveloped. French is the official language, but several African languages and many local dialects are spoken.

Equatorial Guinea

This is the only Spanish-speaking country in Africa. It achieved independence from Spain in 1968. Following a coup in 1979, the country has been ruled by President Teodoro Obian Nguema Mbasogo, in spite of legislation that theoretically made the country a multiparty democracy. Historically, the economy was based on agriculture, but significant oil discoveries (with estimated reserves of 1.28 billion barrels) in 1995 set off rapid GDP growth. Oil has attracted significant U.S. investment but has not resulted in much other development in the country. Allegations of corruption and misappropriation of oil revenues are widespread. The country has the second highest GDP per capita in the world, but most of the population—other than the government officials and their families—has not benefited from the surge in revenues. Because of its oil wealth—and the related U.S. investment—there may be opportunities here if either the government or the international investors decide to use their money for projects benefiting the wider population.

Spanish and French are the official languages, but pidgin English and several African languages are also spoken.

Gabon

Gabon is another former French colony that achieved independence in 1960. The country has had just one autocratic leader, El Jadj Omar Bongo Ondima, for the last four decades. Despite the political conditions, abundant natural resources have made the country relatively prosperous. Oil, for example, accounts for 50 percent of GDP. However, weak economic management and severe income inequality have left a larger portion of the small population poor. French is the official language, but several African languages are also spoken.

Kenya

Kenya achieved independence from the United Kingdom in 1963 and was ruled by

Fig. 4–44: *Jomo Kenyatta International Airport, Nairobi, Kenya. Architect: Queen's Quay Architects International Inc. Photograph by Michel Boucher Photography.*

two men (Jomo Kenyatta and Daniel arap Moi) until 2002. Although it is a regional center for trade and finance in East Africa, the country's many problems have hampered economic growth. Major problems include: periodic drought, endemic corruption, weak commodity prices, low investor confidence, political infighting, and weak foreign aid support. The current government is trying to tackle some of these issues, but it is too early to judge its effectiveness.

English and Kiswahili (Swahili) are the official languages, but many other African languages are also spoken.

Licensing and legal issues
Licensing requirements are as follows:

- *Is a license required?* Yes.
- *Licensing requirements:* A recognized degree in architecture, two years of practical work experience, and examinations are part of the licensing requirements.
- *What agency licenses?* The Board of Registration of Architects and Quantity Surveyors (BORAQS) in Kenya.
- *What is the professional architectural organization?* Architectural Association of Kenya (AAK).
- *To practice, is a local representative required?* Yes. The local representative need not be a citizen but must at least obtain a work permit from the principal immigration officer. The foreign firm must be registered as a company with the Attorney Generals chambers.

Fee levels, payment terms, and taxes
The government does have a recommended fee scale, according to the COAC Web site.

Sources of information
U.S. Embassy, Kenya
Telephone: 254-363-6000
E-mail: ircnairobi@state.gov
Web site: http://nairobi.usembassy.gov

Architectural Association of Kenya (AAK)

Board of Registration of Architects

Lesotho
Lesotho is a small landlocked, mountainous nation that is surrounded on all sides by South Africa. Its economy is based on subsistence agriculture. The official language is English, but Sesotho, Zulu, and Xhosa are also spoken. The telecommunications infrastructure is rudimentary.

Madagascar
An island in the Indian Ocean, Madagascar is another former French colony; it gained independence in 1960. The country has been on a bumpy road to democracy, and in 2002 a large part of the country threatened secession. The country is very poor, and 80 percent of the population is employed in agriculture. The official languages are French and Malagasy.

Malawi
The British protectorate of Nyasaland became Malawi when independence was achieved in 1964. Since then it has been ruled by one man for most of its history, but it is now moving toward a multiparty democracy. It is one of the world's least developed and poorest countries. Tobacco accounts for 60 percent of exports. The country faces many problems: e.g., lack of infrastructure, heavy dependence on foreign aid, corruption, environmental issues,

a growing HIV/AIDS infection rate, and a large number of other challenges. Chichewa is spoken by a majority of the population and is the official language.

Mauritius

Mauritius is an island nation that achieved independence from Britain in 1968. It has a stable democracy and attracts some foreign investment. It has a diversified economy but only the tourism sector is likely to use North American design firms.

English is the official language, but it is not widely spoken. Most of the population speaks Creole. The telecommunications system is more modern than most African countries.

Licensing and legal issues

Licensing requirements are as follows:

- *Is a license required?* Yes.
- *Licensing requirements:* Requirements for foreign architects: Qualification in architecture from an educational center that is (a) recognized by the Commonwealth Association of Architects; (b) recognized by the European Union (diplomas listed in the Directive 85/384); or (c) approved by the Minister and the Architects' Council. Also, foreign architects must have proof of (1) at least one year of experience in architectural practice and (2) honorability and good behavior.
- *What agency licenses?* Professional Architects' Council.
- *What is the professional architectural organization?* Professional Architects' Council and the Mauritius Association of Architects.
- *To practice, is a local representative required?* Yes. Any joint venture with a local architect must be approved by the

Architects' Council at the draft stage and prior to the formalization of the contract. Foreign architects may work independently on government-building projects.

Fee levels, payment terms, and taxes

The Mauritius Association of Architects does have a recommended fee scale, according to the COAC Web site.

Sources of information

U.S. Embassy, Mauritius
Telephone: 230-202-4400
E-mail: usembass@intnet.mu
Web site: http://mauritius.usembassy.gov

Mauritius Association of Architects

Mozambique

Five centuries as a Portuguese colony ended in 1975 with independence. Civil war, emigration by many of the white minority, drought, and other problems hindered development. The fighting ended in 1992, and the country has been relatively stable since. The country is very poor and dependent on foreign aid. Most of the population of almost 20 million survives on subsistence agriculture and lives below the poverty line.

Portuguese is the official language, but it is spoken by only about a quarter of the population. The remainder of the population speaks one or more of a large number of African languages, such as Emakhuwa and Xichangana.

Namibia

South Africa only agreed to end its control of this former German colony in 1988, and Namibia became independent in 1990. However, Namibia remains closely tied to South Africa. Half the population survives on subsistence agriculture, but mining is the main source of the country's income. Gem-quality diamonds, uranium, and several metals are all extracted in large quantities. The relatively high GDP per capita disguises extreme income inequality. English is the official language, but Afrikaans and German are widely used, as are a number of African languages.

Licensing and legal issues
Licensing requirements are as follows:

- *Is a license required?* Yes.
- *What agency licenses?* Namibia Council for Architects and Quantity Surveyors.
- *What is the professional architectural organization?* Namibia Institute of Architects (NIA).
- *To practice, is a local representative required?* Yes. Local representatives must be resident in Namibia, in possession of a work permit, and be registered with the Council.

Sources of information
Namibia Institute of Architects
Web site: www.nia.org.na

Rwanda
Rwanda became independent from Belgium in 1962, and it has suffered from terrible ethnic violence between the Hutu and Tutsi for most of its history. In 1994 there was a genocidal slaughter of 800,000 Tutsis and moderate Hutus. When the Tutsi fought back and defeated the Hutu, approximately two million Hutus fled to neighboring countries. Since then the country has struggled to achieve stability. The economy, of course, has been disrupted. About 90 percent of the population is engaged in agriculture—most of it at the subsistence level. Kinyarwanda is the official language, as are French and English. Swahili is also used in commercial centers.

São Tomé and Príncipe
A Portuguese colony until 1975, this island nation had an agriculture-based (mostly cocoa) economy until the recent offshore oil discoveries. The country has been politically unstable for most of its history. Oil revenues have not yet begun to flow, and the country remains very poor. Portuguese is the official language.

Seychelles
This small, island nation achieved independence from Great Britain in 1976. The economy is heavily dependent on tourism. There are occasional opportunities for firms specializing in tourism facilities. English is the official language, but over 90 percent speak Creole. The telecommunications infrastructure is adequate.

South Africa
The British took control of the Cape of Good Hope in 1806, and many of the existing Dutch settlers moved north. The British won the Boer War (1899–1902) against the descendants of the early Dutch settlers, and the Union of South Africa resulted. Independence from Great Britain came in 1910. For most of the twentieth century, the country was dominated by the small (approximately 10 percent) white minority. Beginning in 1948, the country operated under a policy of apartheid, which classified and separated people into racial groups (White, Coloured, Black, and Indian). Apartheid allowed the white minority population to dominate, segregate, exile (to homelands), and subjugate the other races. Apartheid came to an end in the 1990s,

and the country's black majority (approximately 80 percent of the population) now has full voting rights and dominates the political life of the republic.

The country has a large population of over 44 million; a big, growing economy with a GDP of $576 billion ($200.5 billion at the official exchange rate); and lots of serious problems. Over half the population lives below the poverty line, the unemployment rate runs at about 25 percent, and over 5 million of the adult population are estimated to be living with HIV/AIDS.

The market

South Africa is still two countries. It has cities, universities, and other elements that are on a par with the most-developed countries. At the same time, large parts of the population are unemployed and living in abject poverty. The developed part of the country regularly commissions major buildings programs—most by South Africa's own, able design communities. Some, however, could go to overseas firms. South Africa is very far away, so it is probably of most interest to design professionals with family or other ties to the country.

Languages and communications

The educated classes often speak English, but large parts of the population speak Isi Zuli, Isi Xhosa, and other African languages. Many white South Africans still speak Afrikaans. The telecommunications infrastructure is the most modern in Africa.

Licensing and legal issues

Licensing requirements are as follows:

- *Is a license required?* Yes. Only registered architects may design, plan, or supervise the creation of buildings in excess of 500 square meters in architectural area.
- *What agency licenses?* South African Council for the Architectural Profession (SACAP).
- *What is the professional architectural organization?* South African Institute for Architects (SAIA).
- *To practice, is a local representative required?* Local participation is not necessary if the U.S. firm opens an office in South Africa and the person in charge is registered as an architect in South Africa.

Sources of information

U.S. Embassy, South Africa
Telephone: 27-12-431-4000
E-mail: consularjohannesburg@state.gov
Web site: http://pretoria.usembassy.gov

South African Council for the Architectural Profession (SACAP)
Telephone: 27-11-794-8333
E-mail: admin@sacapsa.com
Web site: www.sacapsa.com

South African Institute for Architects (SAIA)
Telephone: 27-11-782-1315
E-mail: admin@saia.org.za
Web site: www.saia.org.za

Swaziland

This is a small, landlocked country that is heavily dependent, economically, on its neighbor South Africa. It is ruled by the world's last absolute monarch. Over 80 percent of the population is engaged in subsistence agriculture, and in the years 2004–05, 25 percent needed emergency food aid. Swaziland recently achieved the tragic distinction of having the world's highest known rate of

HIV/AIDS infection. Approximately 40 percent of the adult population is living with HIV/AIDS.

The market
This is not a market for North American design firms.

Languages and communications
English is the official language, as is Siswati. It has a limited telecommunications system.

Tanzania
Tanzania was formed by a postindependence (from Britain) merger of Tanganyika and Zanzibar. One-party rule ended in 1995, but the subsequent elections have been contentious. It remains one of the world's poorest countries. Agriculture employs about 80 percent of the work force. Kiswahili and Swahili are the official languages, but English is the official language of commerce and higher education. Arabic, along with several other languages, is widely used as well.

Licensing and legal issues
Licensing requirements are as follows:

- *Is a license required?* Yes.
- *Licensing requirements:* Requirements include a degree or diploma from a recognized authority. As well, architects should have two years of work experience and the completion of a written examination.
- *What agency licenses?* National Board of Architects and Quantity Surveyors.
- *What is the professional architectural organization?* Architects Association of Tanzania.
- *To practice, is a local representative required?* There must be a registered office, which may be run by a national, a foreigner, or both.

Sources of information
Architects Association of Tanzania
  Architects and Quantity Surveyors
  Registration Board Tanzania

Uganda
Uganda became independent from the United Kingdom in 1962. Its early history was dominated by two terrible leaders—Idi Amin and Milton Obote. Things have improved somewhat since the 1990s. The country, however, does have natural resources including fertile soils and large copper and cobalt deposits. Agriculture employs 80 percent of the workforce. Coffee is the principal export. Overall, the country has seen steady economic growth since 1990.

English is the official language, but many African languages are also spoken.

Zambia
This former British colony (once known as Northern Rhodesia) gained independence in 1964. As with many of its neighbors, it has had a hard time becoming a democracy. The economy is largely dependent on copper mining and agriculture. In spite of modest economic growth in recent years, it remains very poor.

English is the official language, but most people speak one or more of approximately 80 different African languages.

Zimbabwe
Zimbabwe (formerly Rhodesia and Southern Rhodesia) became a British colony in 1923, and its white-dominated government declared independence in 1965. United Nations sanctions, a guerrilla war, and other factors forced free elections in

1979 and full independence in 1980. Since then the country has been ruled by Robert Mugabe, who has badly mismanaged the country. The economy is in chaos, and the country has experienced high inflation, a decline in the commercial farming sector (the main source of exports and foreign exchange), and a decline in GDP. Thus, it is an unlikely market for international design expertise.

English is the official language, but several African languages and many local dialects are also spoken.

The Middle East

As defined in this book, the Middle East extends east-west from Turkey to Iran and north-south, from Turkey to Yemen. The population and GDP data of the 15 countries constituting this region are summarized in Table 4.11.

With the exception of Israel, the predominant religion in all of these countries is Islam, although as recent history has demonstrated, this has not always been a unifying influence. Many of these countries have significant oil and gas reserves and, as a result, considerable wealth.

Since the first big Organization of Petroleum Exporting Countries (OPEC)–inspired jump in oil prices, this wealth helped fund a major building program in many countries. While the boom has waxed and waned in individual countries for a variety of reasons (war, oil prices, etc.), the region has been a major employer of international architects for over 30 years. Many of us have made multiple visits to the region and have learned first-hand the many rewards as well as the many frustrations of working in the Middle East.

Longer sections have been included on the United Arab Emirates (UAE), because it has been the hottest market in the region recently. It is also a good introduction to the issues of working in some of its oil-rich neighbors. A second extended section on Israel is also included. Israel has been a small but important market for a number of North American firms. Working there is quite different than working in one of Israel's Arab neighbors.

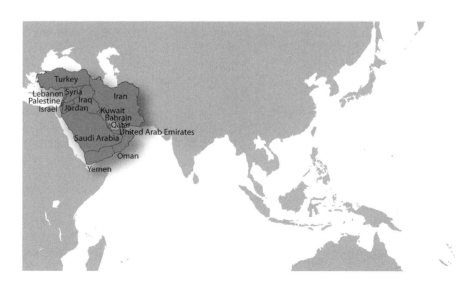

Table 4.11 Middle East Population and Economic Statistics[19]

Country	Population	Population Growth Rate (%)	GDP—Purchasing Power Parity*	GDP—Official Exchange Rate*	GDP— Per Capita ($)
Bahrain	699,000	1.45	17.7	12.12	25,300
Iran	68,688,000	1.1	610.4	194.8	8,900
Iraq	26,783,000	2.66	94.1	46.5	1,900
Israel	6,352,000	1.18	166.03	121.6	26,200
Jordan	5,907,000	2.49	28.89	12.32	4,900
Kuwait	2,418,000	3.52	52.17	58.3	21,600
Lebanon	3,874,000	1.23	21.45	19.62	5,500
Oman	3,102,000	3.28	43.88	27.23	14,100
Palestinian Authority[20]	3,889,000	Gaza 3.71 West Bank 3.06	5.33	3.45	1,500
Qatar	885,000	2.5	26.05	30.76	29,400
Syria	18,881,000	2.3	75.1	27.23	4,000
Saudi Arabia	27,020,000	2.18	374	286.2	13,800
Turkey	70,414,000	1.06	627.2	358.2	8,900
United Arab Emirates	2,603,000	1.52	129.4	110.6	49,700
Yemen	21,456,000	3.46	20.38	15.16	900

* In billions of U.S. dollars unless otherwise noted.

Bahrain

The island kingdom of Bahrain is a small (population almost 700,000) constitutional monarchy with relatively progressive leadership. Faced with declining oil revenues, it has been transforming itself into a petroleum-processing and international banking center. Due to its well-developed communication and transport facilities, many multinational firms with business in the Persian Gulf are based there. Nevertheless, petroleum production and refining still account for 60 percent of both export and government revenues as well as 30 percent of GDP. Non-nationals account for over 40 percent of the labor force.

The market

Due to its relatively small size and declining oil-production revenues, Bahrain is not one of the major markets in the Gulf. Its relatively liberal government, however, has made it one of the easier places for Western firms to do business. Moreover, in 2005, it became the first Gulf state to ratify a free-trade agreement with the U.S. Therefore, while not a prime market target, it should be considered in a firm's overall strategy for working in the region.

Languages and communications

Arabic is the primary language, but English, Farsi, and Urdu are also spoken. Its telecommunications infrastructure is modern.

Iran

In the early to mid-1970s, Iran was a magnet for western architects. Many firms—including the one I was with at the time—opened offices there to carry out a wide variety of major projects: new towns, hospitals, universities, hotels, large housing developments, and many others. The Shah's efforts to modernize—and OPEC's oil prices—stimulated this vast building boom. In spite of the poor quality of some of the projects, a stay at the Teheran Intercontinental or Hilton was like attending an international architectural convention.

Since the fall of the Shah in 1979, Iran has been largely closed to North American architects. In spite of record oil prices and the needs of a population of 68 million, the country's economy has stagnated under the Ayatollahs' rule. As this book was being written, Iran's nuclear ambitions, as well as its foreign policy, had returned U.S.-Iranian relations to the deep freeze.

If and when Iran chooses to take the actions necessary to normalize relations with the West and reinvigorate its economy, it could once again become a destination for Western architects. Until then, stay away.

Iraq

Iraq is a relatively large Arab nation sitting on large oil and gas reserves. For reasons that have been headline news for years—the rule of Saddam Hussein, the wars with the U.S. and previously with Iran, etc.—the country's potential is being dissipated.

The market

Historically (prior to 1990), Iraq was a market for U.S. firms. Since the first Gulf War (1991), this market closed. By 2005, it has become a market again, and there is work there for the very brave (or foolhardy). For the rest of us, it is not a very inviting place.

Languages and communications

Arabic (and Kurdish in the Kurdish regions) are the dominant languages. The telecommunications infrastructure has been severely battered.

Israel

With a population of little more than six million and an economy that is often strained by the needs of the military as well as those of new immigrants, Israel presents limited opportunities for North American architects. Nevertheless, there are occasional projects that are very worthwhile. Moreover, many of these special projects go to North American architects and other design professionals.

Israel has a sophisticated design community, but most firms do not have the experience to lead a design team for some of the larger and more complex projects. In addition, the selection of the design team is often influenced by the philanthropists (many of whom are from North America) who help finance these projects.

If and when peace comes to the region, and the Israeli economy improves, the number of project opportunities will probably increase. Presently, however, most projects go to international design stars, internationally known specialists in specific building types, or firms with proven ties to Israel.

Reasons to be there

Most of the well-known North American firms who have worked in Israel have some tie to the country. In many cases, the lead

Fig. 4–45: *Davidoff Comprehensive Cancer Center Rabin Medical Center, Petach Tikva, Israel. Architects: Perkins Eastman with KMD, A. Spector M Amisar Planners Ltd. and Lerman Architects. Photograph by Ran Erde.*

Fig. 4–46: *Davidoff Comprehensive Cancer Center Rabin Medical Center, Petach Tikva, Israel. Architects: Perkins Eastman with KMD, A. Spector M Amisar Planners Ltd. and Lerman Architects. Photograph by Ran Erde.*

principal is Jewish, and there is a strong emotional or family tie to the country.

There are, however, other reasons to want to work there. Some of the most commonly cited reasons include the following:

• The opportunity to work on challenging projects for clients with high aspirations. Many of the projects that use foreign architects aspire to world-class status. Some of the recent cultural projects—such as Moshe Safdie's Holocaust History Museum at Yad Vashem—achieve this status. Our firm's first project was the first comprehensive cancer center in the Middle East. It was done for a client group who wanted both a good building and an international standard cancer center.

- The opportunity to work in one of the most interesting and beautiful countries in the world.
- To gain a credential of interest to potential clients; for example, working in Israel may provide credibility for the firm when seeking work for many Jewish sponsors in North America.
- Working in Israel might help connections with the Israeli developers active in North America as well as some major Israeli investors in the real estate marketplace.
- Israel is becoming quite influential in the Eastern European construction market. Many construction companies, developers, and Israeli architects are involved in projects in Romania, Bulgaria, and other developing Eastern European countries. Working in Israel might be a stepping-stone to this market.

Reasons to be cautious

There are many reasons to approach work in Israel with caution.

- Except for a few firms, there are not enough projects to support a continuous presence. Even if a firm wants to work in Israel, most only get one or two opportunities to work there. Moreover, most of these opportunities attract a number of highly qualified competitors.
- Partially because of the competition and because the projects are often relatively (to other international projects) modest in size, it is not easy to make money on projects in Israel.
- The security situation is well known; but, in reality, if one uses common sense, it is a relatively safe place to work.

- Working in Israel complicates—but does not preclude—working elsewhere in the Middle East.
- Travel to and from Israel is difficult. It is farther enough from Western Europe to be noticeable, and the working pace in Israel is intense.

Skills and capabilities that are important

Most of the projects that use foreign architects are looking for an international design star and/or a proven expert in the building type. Therefore, unless one has special ties to the client, one or the other of these basic qualifications are important.

A knowledge of and links to some of the leading design firms in Israel can also be important. If you are brought into a project opportunity by a well-connected Israeli firm, this introduction is very helpful. Having a Hebrew-speaking team member is also an advantage. Most people speak some English, but the ability to communicate in Hebrew is important.

Who is operating there now?

Moshe Safdie has maintained an office in Israel, but most firms have only one assignment at a time. Some of the other well-known North American architects who have recently or are currently working in Israel include Frank Gehry, KMD, Eli Attia, Diamond and Schmidt, and SOM.

Who are the clients?

As noted above, the clients are typically individuals, companies, or institutions looking for a design star and/or a building-type expert. Theoretically, this could cover any building type, but in reality most of the projects using foreign architects are:

- High-profile cultural facilities
- Large, complex development projects
- Complex public and institutional projects such as specialized hospitals, research facilities, and airports

What is the process for getting work?

The process for getting work in Israel is similar to that in North America. Most selections are at least partially qualifications-based. Some are awarded after an invited competition. And most require the careful courting and good presentations typical of major project pursuits in North America. In most cases, association with a strong Israeli associate firm (or firms) is important. Since it is a small country, most leading firms have connections to some or all of the client decision makers.

Languages and communications

As noted above, the predominant language is Hebrew, but most educated people speak some English. Knowledge of Hebrew, however, is important. The country has a relatively sophisticated computer infrastructure, as well as an annoyingly omnipresent cell phone system.

Licensing and legal issues

Most North American firms work with an Israeli firm that acts as the architect of record. By serving as a consultant, the North American architect can avoid licensing. If, however, the firm wants to provide full service, the greatest difficulty would be the requirement to prove three years of experience in an Israeli-licensed office. However, most Israeli architects are licensed, and thus hiring a local architect for representation might be the best way forward.

Licensing requirements are as follows:

- *Is a license required?* Yes. Foreign architects are required to obtain a license. For simple structures (up to 2 floors), no license is required for a local resident. However, municipal bylaws differ and may require signatures on plans by licensed architects only. For all other projects, a license is required.
- *Licensing requirements:* A recognized degree and three years of work experience.
- *What agency licenses?* Ministry of Labor, Registration Board for Engineers and Architects.
- *What is the professional architectural organization?* Israel Society of Architects and Town Planners, Association of Engineers, Architects and Graduates of the Technological Sciences in Israel.
- *To practice, is a local representative required?* Yes. The representative must be a local resident (although there are no citizenship requirements) as well as an authorized architect.

Scope of services
Design assignments in Israel are similar in terms of scope of services to comparable projects in North America.

Fee levels, payment terms, and taxes
The COAC Web site states that the Association of Engineers and Architects did have fee scales, but by law it is now prohibited from publishing them. Some government offices do offer fee scales.

Again, if the firm is acting as a consultant, payments can be in U.S. dollars, and these payments are not taxed. The levels and payment terms can be similar to those in a typical North American contract. Getting a premium fee or significant advance payment is unusual. The trick, however, is getting paid on schedule. Many firms complain about slow payment. As always, competent tax advice is essential; but there is a bilateral agreement between Israel and the U.S. allowing for income from both countries to be declared and paid in only one, that is, a firm could choose to declare income from Israel in the U.S., which would satisfy the local authorities.

Major contract issues
For most firms, the major contract issues are:

- A clear definition of the scope and schedule
- The normal protections against scope creep
- A clear payment schedule and the normal protections against late payment
- A definition of the roles and responsibilities of the firm and any associate firms

Local resources
Israel has many talented architects, engineers, and other design professionals. While most firms are small and have limited experience with large, complex projects, it is not hard to assemble a very competent team for most projects. In addition, Israel has the full range of other support services—e.g., computers, printers, etc.—required to support a team working in the country. Salaries are much lower in Israel.

Design issues
As both a very new and a very old country, Israel has some very interesting design

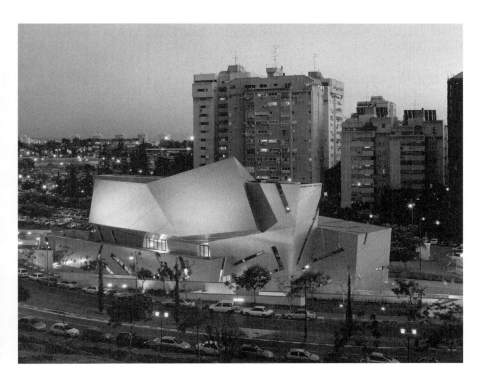

Fig. 4–48: *The Wohl Centre, Ramat-Gan, Israel. Architect: Studio Daniel Libeskind. Photograph by Bitter Bredt Photographie.*

traditions. Most of the major buildings strive to be very modern—some in truly bizarre ways. Many of the best buildings, including those of leading North American architects, are modern. What is more, Tel Aviv has one of the largest collections of Bauhaus-style buildings in some of its older neighborhoods. Jerusalem, however, is influenced by other factors. By code, most new buildings in the central part of the city must be clad with Jerusalem stone, a golden-colored limestone, and are subject to other design controls as well. Many of the new buildings are still very modern, but they are more evocative of their historic setting. As a Middle Eastern country with a hot, arid climate, Israel observes many of the design traditions and practices of the region. Most buildings are built with concrete frames;

clad with stone, masonry, or tile; and designed with sun control and solar heat gain in mind.

Code and regulatory issues

As a relatively sophisticated country, Israel has the full range of codes and regulations one would expect in any developed country. There are, however, some aspects of the code that firms working there must learn. Among these, some of the most important include the provision of a place of refuge from terrorist attack on each floor of a major building.

Typical schedules

Projects in Israel have schedules comparable to those of similar projects in North America. Security incidents, local code reviews, and other factors can, however, introduce disconcerting and unpredictable gaps into a project schedule.

Local construction capabilities

The local construction industry is capable of building sophisticated buildings. There are some problems, however:

- During periods of heightened security controls, the supply of labor is seriously curtailed. Many construction laborers are from the occupied territories and are not able to get to the job site.
- Quality control is often very uneven.
- Projects requiring importation or use of imported systems can cause significant cost and installation issues. A major task for some design teams is finding local substitutes.

Personal safety and health issues

Israel's security issues are well known; but for an experienced business traveler the news stories are more ominous than the reality. Moreover, normal dietary cautions make the likelihood of getting ill comparable to that in other developed countries.

Most common problems

Firms that have worked in Israel cite the following as the most common problems:

- Slow payment.
- Disruptions in project schedules due to external events.
- Most of the projects are built using a construction manager, and it is common to have many changes (normally driven by the client) during construction. It is very hard to control quality and monitor changes that are done on the fly. Experienced architects recommend that design firms should pin this down in their contract with the client,

specifying that changes may not be made without the architect's consent.

Key pieces of advice

Firms who have worked in Israel have several pieces of advice:

- While some projects in Israel can be professionally and financially rewarding, it is not easy. Other countries have more and larger projects with better fees and less demanding clients. For this reason, most firms that pursue work in Israel do so for more than purely business reasons. In other words, a commitment and connection to Israel should be part of the reason for working there.
- Try to negotiate a very clear scope of work and schedule, as well as a clear linkage between changes and additional service fees.
- Develop a professional relationship with one or more of the stronger firms based in Israel. Local knowledge and advice are very important.
- Expect the unexpected during construction.

Sources of information

U.S. Embassy, Israel
Telephone: 972-3-519-7575
E-mail: ac5@bezeqint.net
Web site: http://telaviv.usembassy.gov

Israeli Association of United Architects (IAUA)
Telephone: 972-3-518-82-34
Fax: 972-3-518-82-35
E-mail: architects@newmail.net

Technion—Israel Institute of Technology—Faculty of Architects and Town Planning

E-mail: arcweb@tx.technion.ac.il

Website: http://architecture.technion.ac.
il/index.php

Association of Engineers, Architects and
Graduates in Technological Sciences
in Israel (AEAI)

Telephone: 972-3-524-0274

E-mail: news@aeai.org.il

Web site: www.engineers.org.il/Index.asp?
CategoryID=1427&ArticleID=3450

Jordan

Jordan was created, in large part, by the
United Kingdom when it separated Trans-
jordan from Palestine in the 1920s. Jordan
gained its independence in 1946, and for
most of the rest of the twentieth century, it
was ruled by King Hussein I. King Hussein
I navigated between many internal and external forces and gradually moved the
country toward a relatively stable future.
Since his death in 1999, the country has

been ruled by his son Abdullah II, who has
instituted economic and political reforms.
The two kings have been U.S. allies and
have relatively normal relations with their
neighbors, including Israel.

Jordan is a small country with limited
natural resources and water. It has relied
on Iraq for oil and trade, and these ties
have been severely disrupted due to the
war in Iraq. Nevertheless, the economy is
growing.

The market

Jordan receives U.S. aid, and some of the
projects supported with this assistance use
U.S. design teams. In addition, there are
some other areas where international design services are used. Of these, tourism is
one of the most promising. With major
sites such as Petra and the Wadi Ram
(where *Lawrence of Arabia* was filmed),
Jordan has tourism assets that should attract a growing number of visitors.

Fig. 4–49: *Jordan Valley Marriott
Dead Sea Resort and Spa, Am-
man, Jordan. Architect: Hellmuth,
Obata + Kassabaum, Inc. (HOK).
Photograph courtesy of Hellmuth,
Obata + Kassabaum, Inc. (HOK).*

Languages and communications

Arabic is the official language, although many of the educated classes understand English. The telecommunications infrastructure needs improvement, but it is modernizing.

Licensing and legal issues

Licensing requirements are as follows:

- *Is a license required?* Yes.
- *Licensing requirements:* Licensing requires a combination of a degree in architecture and a practical work experience.
- *What agency licenses?* The Jordan Engineers Association is responsible for licensing.
- *What is the professional architectural organization?* Jordan Architectures Society; all communication is done through the Jordan Engineering Association.
- *To practice, is a local representative required?* Yes, and the local representative can be set up by government or private contract with registration in the Ministry of Industry and Trade and the Jordan Engineering Association.

Sources of information

U.S. Embassy, Jordan
Telephone: 962-6-590-6000
E-mail: amman.office.box@mail.doc.gov
Web site: www.usembassy-amman.org.jo

Jordan Engineering Association
Telephone: 962-6-7616-560
E-mail: info@jea.org.jo
Web site: www.jea.org.jo

Kuwait

Kuwait is a small (population 2,418,000), rich, relatively open country ruled by the Al-Sabah family. It controls about 10 percent of the known world oil reserves, and petroleum accounts for about 50 percent of GDP, 95 percent of export revenues, and 80 percent of the government's income.

Fig. 4–50: *360° Kuwait, Kuwait City, Kuwait. Architect: RTKL. Courtesy of Chris Edgcombe.*

Until 1961, Great Britain oversaw its defense and foreign relations. Following independence, it prospered until the 1990 invasion by Iraq. Since liberation it has returned to prosperity.

The market

Due to its immense oil reserves and the high price of oil in the world market, Kuwait is awash in cash. Its liberation by the U.S.-led coalition reinforced what was already a good relationship. Because of these and other factors, Kuwait is a major market for North American firms. Any firm interested in working in the region should consider Kuwait as part of a regional marketing strategy.

As in the United Arab Emirates, Qatar, Saudi Arabia, and other oil-rich economies, Kuwait-based clients regularly commission a wide variety of building designs (both in Kuwait and in other countries) by North American architects.

Languages and communications

Arabic is the official language, but English is widely spoken. Kuwait has an excellent telecommunications infrastructure.

Lebanon

Lebanon used to be called the Paris of the Middle East. (On a personal note, it was one of the countries that I always enjoyed and looked forward to visiting.) It was the regional playground for its stricter Muslim neighbors. Then, in 1975, its complex balance of Muslim, Christian, Druze, and Palestinian refugee factions erupted in a 16-year civil war that devastated the country and brought in extensive outside (Syrian, Israeli, and other) interference.

Syria was finally forced to withdraw its troops in 2005, and the reduced role of the many factional militias began the process of restoring Lebanon. The country still has a long way to go. The economy is still recovering from the civil war, and—of course—in the summer of 2006 things again deteriorated. The growing role of Hezbollah and its aggression toward Israel unleashed a major military confrontation that required evacuation of foreign nationals and resulted in massive destruction of Lebanon's infrastructure.

The market

Until Lebanon works through its remaining issues (high public debt, limited tourism due to the perception of danger, lack of economic reform, the disruptive influence of Hezbollah, etc.), it will continue to struggle. Thus, it will be a very limited market for North American firms, but, hopefully it will someday recover its status as one of the most attractive places in the Middle East to work or visit.

Languages and communications

The official language is Arabic, but Lebanon is an international crossroads where other languages are spoken.

The telecommunications infrastructure was badly damaged during the civil war, but it was repaired and is relatively modern. As the conflict with Israel that began in the summer of 2006 is still ongoing, it is unclear what the repercussions for the country's infrastructure will be.

Licensing and legal issues

Licensing requirements are as follows:

- *Is a license required?* Yes.
- *Licensing requirements:* No specifics are given on the NCARB Web site.
- *What agency licenses?* Department of Public Works and Order of Engineers and Architects.

Fig. 4–51: *Kamal Mixed-Use, Doha, Qatar. Architects: Perkins Eastman with Diwan Al Emara Architects, Engineers, Planners. Courtesy of Perkins Eastman.*

- *What is the professional architectural organization?* The Order of Engineers and Architects.
- *To practice, is a local representative required?* Yes.

Sources of information
U.S. Embassy, Lebanon
Telephone: 961-4-542-600
E-mail: BeirutACS@State.Gov
Web site: http://beirut.usembassy.gov

Order of Engineers and Architects
of Beirut (Ordre des Ingénieurs et
Architectes de Beyrouth)
Telephone: 961-1-850-111
Web site: www.ordre-ing-bey.org.lb

Oman
In 1970 Qaboos bin Said deposed his father and became the sultan of Oman; the sultanate is an hereditary monarchy. The sultan has opened the country to the outside world and maintained a moderate policy toward its neighbors. It also maintains strong ties to the United Kingdom. It has significant oil and gas resources, but it is not one of the rich petroleum economies. Moreover, it is seeking to diversify the economy. Among other assets, it is quite beautiful and has significant potential for tourism.

The market
Oman is a small country (a population of about 3.1 million), but its relatively progressive, stable government is attracting investment and development. Therefore, for firms already active in the Persian Gulf region, it is a potential market for a variety of projects.

Languages and communications
Arabic is the official language. The telecommunications infrastructure is relatively modern.

Palestine
Palestine (the West Bank and Gaza Strip) is not yet a state, and at the time this book

was written, it was going through another crisis. Due to the Islamist political organization Hamas's role in the government (the Palestinian National Authority), foreign aid is being withheld, and the two major Palestinian factions are engaged in sporadic conflict. Until some degree of normalcy is restored and relations with Israel and its major aid donors are improved, this is not a significant market for U.S. firms.

Qatar

Qatar is a peninsula that borders Saudi Arabia in the south. It has been ruled by the al-Thani family since the mid-1800s. Oil and gas have transformed it from a poor British protectorate into one of the highest-per-capita GDPs in the world. Oil and gas account for 60 percent of exports and 70 percent of government revenues. Much of its wealth was siphoned off by the Emir Khalifa bin Hamad Al Thani until his son Hamad bin Khalifa Al Thani overthrew him in a bloodless coup in 1995. Since he assumed power, the economy has been improving.

The market

Qatar has been a major market for western firms for many years, but the new Emir's policies and high oil and gas prices have made it even more important. Among the many government-sponsored projects are major health-care projects, including a new branch of Cornell's Medical College (which used Perkins & Will, among other architectural firms) and the 1,000-bed Hamad Medical City (which has used NBBJ and Granary Associates, among other firms). Both are intended to make Qatar a regional destination for health care. At the same time, the private sector is also investing in a wide variety of projects, from hotels and apartment buildings

to mixed-use complexes. The design of many of the projects is being done by North American firms. Any plan for work in the Middle East should consider Qatar as a significant potential market.

Fig. 4–52: *Ritz-Carlton Hotel and Resort, Doha, Qatar. Architect: Queen's Quay Architects International Inc. Photograph by Gerd Spans.*

Languages and communications

Arabic is the official language, but English is commonly used as a second language. The telecommunications infrastructure is modern.

Saudi Arabia

Beginning in 1902, Abd Al-Aziz bin al-Rahman Al Saud began a 30-year campaign to unify the Arabian Peninsula. His sons succeeded him, and his family rules to this day. Saudi Arabia is the religious center of the Muslim world. This government takes very seriously its role as the protector of the holy sites—in particular Mecca, which is the pilgrimage destination of every devout Muslim.

The kingdom has a relatively large population of over 27 million (5.5 million of which are non-nationals). It also has over 25 percent of the world's proven oil reserves, and it is the largest exporter of petroleum. The petroleum sector typically accounts for 75 percent of budget revenues, 45 percent of GDP, and 90 percent of export earnings. The government is trying to diversify the economy and joined the WTO in 2005.

The Saudi Arabian government is a close ally of the U.S., but this relationship is not very popular with a large segment of the population. Osama bin Laden, lest we forget, is a member of a prominent Saudi construction family.

The market

Saudi Arabia has been one of the most important international markets for North American firms for decades. In particular, after the OPEC-led rise in oil prices in the 1970s, Saudi Arabia went on a building spree that resulted in major commissions for many U.S. and Canadian firms.

In recent years, the demand for North American design services has lessened but is still strong. With the rise in oil prices—as this book was being written—an acceleration in building is likely.

Religious restrictions, security concerns, the climate, uneven business practices, and other factors make Saudi Arabia a challenging market for any Western firm. Nevertheless, many architects have designed projects there and have enjoyed the experience. The kingdom is likely to remain a mecca for design professionals.

Reasons to be there

Saudi Arabia has offered some of the most challenging design opportunities for over three decades. In addition, design professionals with Saudi experience cite the following reasons to be there:

- The country's oil wealth makes it a major buyer of services—including design services—from the U.S. and other developed countries.
- Saudi clients are not only major investors in their own country but also in projects in many other countries.
- For those who like the desert, Saudi Arabia has many beautiful areas, and the Saudis are a hospitable people. Some North American architects have established lifelong friendships there.
- Saudi clients have, at times, been supportive of good design on large, complex projects.

Reasons to be cautious

There are many reasons to be cautious. Among the most important are the following:

- It can be an expensive, time-consuming, and frustrating place to work.
- With the exception of a few high-profile commissions (SOM's Haj terminal, CRS's College of Petroleum, and a few others), projects in Saudi Arabia are rarely covered in the West. Some architects have complained that the time they spent there goes unrecognized and unappreciated in North America.
- Security concerns have been rising; those issues, combined with the kingdom's harsh legal system, make personal safety a real concern.

Who is operating there now?

Over the last 30 years, most of the large firms—as well as many smaller North

American design firms—have worked for Saudi clients.

Languages and communications
Arabic is the official language. The telecommunications system is modern.

Licensing and legal issues
Licensing requirements are as follows:

- *Is a license required?* Yes.
- *Licensing requirements:* A degree in architecture from a recognized authority and three years of practical experience.
- *What agency licenses?* Ministry of Commerce.
- *What is the professional architectural organization?* Engineering Committee and Al Umran Saudi Association.
- *To practice, is a local representative required?* Yes, a local representative who is a citizen of Saudi Arabia is required. Information on arrangements for local representation can be obtained through the Engineering Committee.

Sources of information
U.S. Embassy, Saudi Arabia
Telephone: 966-1-488-3800
E-mail:
    USEmbRiyadhWebSite@state.gov
Web site: http://riyadh.usembassy.gov

Al-Umran Saudi Association

Syria
Syria is one of the larger countries in the region, and it emerged as a nation after the breakup of the Ottoman Empire during World War I. France administered the country until 1946. The country was politically unstable for its first 25 years of independence. Hafiz al-Asad seized power in 1970 and stabilized the country. He died in 2000 and has been succeeded by his son, Bashar.

The country's international and economic policies have gotten it into trouble on a regular basis and have helped keep Syria poor. Disastrous wars with Israel, support of terrorism, interference in Lebanon, and other factors have kept it relatively isolated internationally. Its government-controlled economy has performed poorly, in spite of having some petroleum revenues, and badly needs reform. The net result is that it is a poor country with a lot of problems.

The market
Until Syria decides to reform its international politics and economy, it is a very limited market for Western firms. As the man seated next to me remarked as we entered Damascus, "No wonder they always want to fight, they have nothing to lose."

If Syria ever cleans up its act, though, it could become a potential market for North American firms. Until then, it is one of the least attractive places to work in the Middle East.

Languages and communications
Arabic is the official language, but other languages, including English and French, are also used by part of the population. Kurdish, Armenian, Aramaic, and Circassian are widely understood. The telecommunications infrastructure is limited but is being modernized.

Sources of information
U.S. Embassy, Syria
Telephone: 963-11-333-1342
E-mail: damasweb-query@state.gov
Web site: http://damascus.usembassy.gov

Order of Syrian Engineers and Architects

Fig. 4–53: *Metrocity, Istanbul, Turkey. Architects: Anthony Belluschi Architects with Dogan Tekeli and Sami Sisa. Photograph by Kadir Kir, Dogan Tekeli.*

The market

As a modernizing country, Turkey is a potential market for firms with the relevant interest and skills. It has suffered through a major financial crisis in 2001, as well as other problems. At the time this book was being written, it was growing again and attracting significant outside investment. According to an article in the *International Herald Tribune* (July 7, 2006), "Real estate purchases by foreigners have increased by 83 percent since 2003." Some of this is going to develop the country's spectacular tourism assets.

Turkey has approximately 30,000 licensed architects, and there is some resistance to the employment of international firms. Nevertheless, a number of firms (e.g., Swanke Hayden, Hillier, Anthony Belluschi, and others) have obtained major commissions, and if and when Turkey joins the EU, the door will open even wider. Swanke Hayden maintains an office in Turkey. But currently most of the work done in that office is in support of other offices (see "Case Studies," Chapter 3).

Licensing and legal issues

Licensing requirements are as follows:

- *Is a license required?* Yes.
- *Licensing requirements:* An applicant for a license must have a degree from a recognized school of architecture. This is required for the initial licensing of indigenous and foreign architects in Turkey.
- *What agency licenses?* The Chamber of Turkish Architects is responsible for licensing. Architects wanting to work with government agencies should also present a file of references to the Ministry of Public Works and Settlement.
- *To practice, is a local representative required?* Yes. Only architects with Turk-

Turkey

Turkey is a country that wants to be a member of the European Union, but it is also a bridge to the Islamic countries of the Middle East. It is a sophisticated country of over 70 million people with a rich culture and history that stretches back to the beginning of Western Civilization. Since the early twentieth century and the fall of the Ottoman Empire, Turkey has tried to be a secular state, but its current government still must reflect the fact that the country is 99.8 percent Muslim.

ish citizenship can practice independently (i.e. sign drawings and construction documents). Foreign contractors or foreign entities who are commissioned by a state or private body can employ foreign architects within the limits of a specific contract upon review and recommendation of the Union of Chamber of Engineers and Architects and the approval of the Ministry of Public Works.

Sources of information
U.S. Embassy, Turkey
Telephone: 90-312-455-5555
E-mail: webmaster_ankara@state.gov
Web site: http://ankara.usembassy.gov

Turkiye Mimardar Odasi (The Chamber
   of Architects of Turkey)
Telephone: 90-312-417-3727
Fax: 90-312-418-0361
E-mail: info@mo.org.tr
Web site: www.mo.org.tr

Bayindirilik Ve Iskan Bakanligi
   (The Ministry of Public Works
   and Settlement)
E-mail: yapidenetim@bayindirlik.gov.tr
Web site: http://ydk.bayindirlik.gov.tr

United Arab Emirates
The United Arab Emirates (UAE) are a federation of seven states: Abu Dhabi, Dubai, Sharjah, 'Ajman, Al Fujayrah, Ra's al Khaymah, and Umm al Qaywayn. The population of these seven states is estimated to be 2,602,00; but the numbers vary, as over 70 percent of the total population are non-nationals. The best available breakdown on the population of the different states is as follows.

Abu Dhabi (purportedly 40 percent of population is here): 1,850,000

Dubai: 1,400,000
Sharjah: 750,000
'Ajman: 275,000
Ra's al Khaymah: 230,000
Al Fujayrah: 130,000
Umm al Qaywayn: 75,000[21]

Abu Dhabi has large oil reserves (approximately 8 percent of the world's confirmed reserves) and helps fund the budgets of the other six emirates. Dubai, the other major economy in the UAE, has moved beyond oil to become a major tourism, financial, and shopping center. The combined GDP is estimated to be over $129.4 billion in 2006, 30 percent of which comes from its oil and gas revenues. The UAE is one of the safest and most liberal parts of the Middle East, and it has begun a

Fig. 4–54: *Sabanci Center, Istanbul, Turkey. Architects: Swanke Hayden Connell Architects with Koray/Haluk Tumay. Courtesy of Swanke Hayden Connell Architects.*

period of rapid development. In recent years, the most visible development has taken place in Dubai, which has been transformed into an international, financial, tourism, and shopping destination. Now, Abu Dhabi has begun to increase its own plans, and the smaller emirates also have major plans.

With high oil prices and Middle East investors' interest in investing in the region, the building boom in the UAE is almost certain to continue for years. Since the scale and complexity of the projects exceed the capacity of the firms in the region, there will be a major role for international design firms.

The market

The leaders of the ruling Maktuum clan, including the recent and current rulers Sheik Maktuum and Sheikh Mohammad of Dubai, endorsed a plan to make this emirate a major tourism destination as well as a regional business center. In short order, luxurious hotels, resorts, and vacation residences were developed, huge new shopping malls offering duty-free merchandise from around the world were opened, and a number of policies were put in place to attract international businesses. This was done assuming, "If we build it, they will come," and they were right. The hotels, resorts, retail malls, condominium towers, offices, and other developments have prospered. After 9/11 additional investment flowed in from other oil-rich neighboring countries concerned about placing funds in the West. Today Dubai is a city of about 1.2 million, almost 80 percent of whom are not nationals. This population is expected to double in five years and triple by 2020, if the Crown Prince's growth plans are achieved. The U.S. Department of Commerce estimates that $20 billion will be spent on construction over the next three to five years.

Dubai's success has stimulated its neighboring emirates to follow suit. With the death of the conservative ruler of Abu Dhabi in 2005, this emirate—the richest and most populous—has begun to move forward with an ambitious development program. These plans now also include hospitals, schools, and other major institutional facilities, as well as still more resorts, malls, condominium towers, and of-

Fig. 4–55: *Al Raha Beach Hotel and Resort, Abu Dhabi, United Arab Emirates. Architect: Perkins Eastman. Courtesy of Perkins Eastman.*

fice buildings.

The other emirates are smaller and less developed. In addition, some are much more observant of traditional restrictions on female dress, drinking, and western influences. Nevertheless, they, too, have ambitious development plans.

Reasons to be there

The UAE have rapidly emerged as an attractive market for North American design professionals. Among the many reasons firms cite for their interest are the following:

- The projects are bigger and more challenging than those available in most other parts of the world. Large manmade resort islands shaped like palm trees, towers that will be the tallest in the world, multimillion-square-foot malls (one with an indoor ski slope), hotels shaped like spinnaker sails, and many other unique projects have been part of this boom.
- Contrary to many peoples' expectations, Dubai and the region have become a major tourism destination, and they are planning for many more visitors. A June 2006 article in *Vanity Fair* reports that, "His Highness is speaking of 15 million people coming to Dubai every year." The article goes on to note that this number is, "more than three times the number of foreign tourists who visit New York City each year" (Nick Tosches, "Dubai's the Limit").
- It also wants to be the health care and education choice for the region.
- There is a lot of work, and it can be profitable. Payment is, on average, better than in most developing countries.
- There is strong competition, but a serious effort can result in work.
- It is more business–oriented than most countries in the region. Dubai, for example, is sometime referred to as "Dubai Inc." or the "Delaware of the Middle East," according to Peter Moriarty of Burt Hill (personal correspondence).
- Moriarty also states that he hears repeatedly that there is a preference "to work with American professionals, because we are practical, straightforward, reasonable, responsible, service oriented, and easy to deal with compared to Europeans and other nationalities." (personal correspondence)
- Many of us enjoy the region and its people, and we find it a fascinating place to work.
- The U. S. government has encouraged American firms to locate or work in the region.
- It is a relatively safe place to work. In spite of the movie *Syriana* (set partly in Dubai), the emirates are relatively free of the ethnic and religious tensions that inflame so much of the region. In addition, it has been in the interest of neighboring states to have a safe, nearby playground that is also a reasonable place for them to invest their growing oil revenues.

Reasons to be cautious

All work in the Middle East has its problems.

- The challenging projects there can, at times, be too challenging.
- The schedules can be too compressed, the design expectations unrealistic, and the staffing required beyond most firms' capabilities.
- It is far enough away to make the

travel physically demanding and communication with the home office difficult.

- It is hard to get staff who want to travel to and work anywhere in the Middle East.
- The weather can be brutal many months of the year. Daytime temperatures in excess of 110°F are common in the summer.
- If things go wrong or the client refuses

to pay, there is little legal recourse.

- It is a relatively expensive place to seek and do work, unless one has access to the large pool of low-priced south Asian and Asian professionals.

Skills and capabilities that are important

Among the skills and capabilities that are essential for success in the UAE, several are particularly important:

Fundamental is the ability to staff the work. We had to turn down our first opportunity because we could not staff it. In addition, as Peter Moriarty noted, "To maintain an A-level visa to work in Dubai, we have to have at least 10 percent come from Europe and North America. Dubai is sensitive about all of the staff coming from Asia" (personal correspondence).

Possessing the required skills to do the project are also important. The best clients are looking for expertise, and they are sophisticated enough to find it.

As in some other parts of the world, the business-development process often requires some conceptual design. Thus, the ability to do quick, appealing presentations is important.

It is essential to be able to communicate in Arabic and to understand the business traditions and sensitivities in both the region and the UAE.

Who is operating there now?

Many firms have recognized the opportunities and are pursuing or working in the UAE. Among the North American firms actively engaged in the UAE are SOM, P&W, TVSA, Burt Hill, The Pei Partnership, HOK, RTKL, Hillier, Perkins Eastman and many others. Burt Hill is one of

Fig. 4–56: *Ghurair City Centre, Dubai, United Arab Emirates. Architect: RTKL.*

the few North American design firms to establish a full office, and it has grown rapidly to over 200 people, rivaling the already-established British and European firms with local offices.

Who are the clients?

The UAE has opportunities across the full range of project and client types: housing, retail, office, hospitality, and mixed use for both local and international developers; public buildings, hospitals, and other institutional projects for a variety of government entities; and projects ranging from biomedical research parks to university buildings for quasi-governmental and institutional clients. Due to the shortage of local design professionals, virtually all major projects might consider international design teams.

What is the process for getting work?

Almost every selection method is used. One of the most common—and annoying—is the unpaid, or minimally paid, design competition. Clients will ask for a couple of renderings for a complex project that often has only a sketchy program. Many projects, however, use something that resembles a qualification-based selection system. In these, it is often important to have a local or regional partner.

Languages and communications

The official language is Arabic. While many speak some English, most business is conducted in Arabic. Persian, Urdu, and Hindi are also spoken by parts of the population. Most of the telecommunications infrastructure is quite modern.

Licensing and legal issues

Working in the UAE is facilitated by being properly registered. It is possible to work as a consultant without being registered, but local registration is strongly encouraged. Registration typically requires the help of one of the several attorneys who specialize in this field. It is a time-consuming and frustrating process, but in the end it is manageable. It requires some modest fees and an office lease.

Scope of services

Many firms only provide design services with documentation- and construction-phase services provided by local firms or design-build organizations. Others, however, provide the equivalent of full services.

Fee levels, payment terms, and taxes

Fee levels no longer have much of a built-in premium. There are a lot of firms operating there, and fees usually have to be competitive. Payment terms should be negotiated with the contract advice outlined in Chapter 2 in mind. There is limited recourse when a client decides not to pay. Services there are not taxed.

Major contract issues

Almost all of the recommendations in Chapter 2 apply to work in the Middle East. Negotiating acceptable contracts can be achieved, but it often requires both patience and a willingness to walk away.

A major contract provision for contracts in the region (and a common problem for all contract work in the region) is the requirement that all parties to the contract comply with the boycott of Israel. U.S. firms are forbidden by law from agreeing to abide by their boycott, but some firms ignore this prohibition. It does not appear in all contracts, but it is still common.

Local resources

There are a large number of architectural and other design firms operating in the region, but they are of very uneven quality. Picking a local associate team must be done with care. There is also an array of support services (printers, etc.)—again, of varied quality.

Design issues

To look at what is being built, it would be easy to conclude that there are no strong design traditions. The whole region has buildings in many different styles. Nevertheless, the climate and traditional Islamic design themes are a significant influence on many projects.

Typical schedules

All of the jokes that "Inshallah means the same as mañana without the implied sense of urgency" do not always apply in the oil-rich Gulf states. There is a desire to modernize and/or get to market as soon as possible. Thus, even extremely large projects are expected to be designed and documented on highly compressed schedules that even rival projects in China. It is not unusual for programming and concept design to have a 60-day schedule followed by only 6–12 months for design development and construction documentation for a multi-million-square-foot, mixed-use development. On the other hand, many projects—particularly government projects—can stop, start and take as long as their counterparts in other countries.

Local construction capabilities

Many of the major international construction companies, such as Turner Construction, have major offices in the region. This, combined with extensive, imported labor, means that even large, complex projects can be constructed.

Personal safety and health issues

The UAE (as well as Bahrain, Qatar, Oman, and Kuwait) are all relatively safe places. Some normal dietary precautions should be observed; but, in general, foreign visitors should not encounter health or safety problems.

Pete Moriarty of Burt Hill noted, however, that even though the area is relatively safe, Dubai and other countries in

Fig. 4–57: *DIFC Gate Building, Dubai, United Arab Emirates. Architect: Gensler. Photograph by Hufton & Crow.*

Fig. 4–58: *Abu Dhabi Court Complex, Abu Dhabi, United Arab Emirates. Architect: Perkins Eastman. Courtesy of Perkins Eastman.*

the region present firms with a number of special health and safety issues:

- "With a proliferation of drivers from 30 plus countries, traffic is now not only maddening, but it is dangerous."
- "Since it is customary for the driver of a fatal pedestrian accident to pay compensation to the deceased's family, this has become a popular method of suicide." One of their staff had to pay a fine and spend four weeks in jail, even though the accident was not her fault.
- "To date, the available health care does not meet American standards...Our expats need to have a service available 24/7 that will get the best available treatment (for a serious medical condition) ASAP" (personal correspondence).

Sources of information
U.S. Embassy, United Arab Emirates

Telephone: 971-2-414-2200
Web site: http://uae.usembassy.gov

Yemen
The Republic of Yemen is a small country with a relatively large population (over 21 million) located on the southern border of Saudi Arabia. Yemen became independent following World War I but was split into North and South Yemen until unified in 1990.

It is one of the poorest countries in the Arab world with a per capita GDP of only $900. It has some oil revenues, but poor government policies and rampant corruption have inhibited improvement in the economy.

The market
Yemen is an unlikely market for North American firms.

Languages and communications
The national language is Arabic. The

ASIA, OCEANIA, AND THE SOUTH PACIFIC

This region has emerged as a very important market for North American design services. According to the 2003 AIA survey, it is a close second to the Americas as the most common location for U.S. firms' international projects. During the recession that began at the end of the 1980s, many firms looked to the region for the projects that would tide them over. For some of these firms, the experience was—at best—mixed, and for those caught in the Asian fiscal crisis it was costly.

This diverse region has been divided into four areas: India, Pakistan and the adjacent nations; China, Hong Kong, Macao, Taiwan, Japan and Korea; Indonesia and Southeast Asia; and Australia, New Zealand, and the South Pacific. As in the other regions, longer descriptions are done for the countries that have shown the most potential for international design firms.

This region is likely to grow in importance over time. Several of the world's fastest growing economies are there, and the desire to create modern societies, the need to employ the large pools of unskilled labor, and many other factors have fueled a long building boom in many countries. Since the technical requirements of these building programs often exceed the capacity of the local design professionals, there have been thousands of opportunities for international firms. Many of these have been in China, the largest market for international design services; but other countries in the region have many opportunities for firms with the right capabilities, contacts, and interest.

Southern Asia

This region includes one of the world's two population giants, India. India is poised to be a large market for interna-

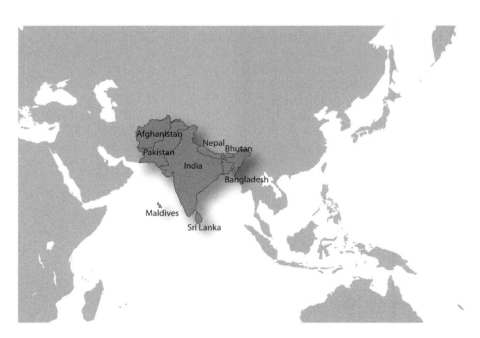

tional design firms, but in 2007 this is more potential than reality.

India is surrounded by six countries— Afghanistan, Pakistan, Bangladesh, Bhutan, Nepal, and Sri Lanka (plus China, see p. 240))—all of which are very poor. Two of these countries—Afghanistan and Pakistan—are important allies of the United States and therefore, potential markets for firms working on projects with U.S. support. The remainder have limited potential for firms other than those involved in developing the region's considerable tourism potential. This region also includes a small island nation, the Maldives, which is primarily of interest as a growing tourism destination.

Afghanistan

Afghanistan is a desperately poor, mountainous, and chronically politically unstable country that may finally be emerging from decades of strife. The U.S.-backed groups that ousted the fundamentalist Taliban regime after September 11, 2001, are trying hard to stabilize this fractious country. With a population of approximately 31 million and a GDP estimated to be only $21.5 billion ($800 per capita), however, it is an extremely poor country that is unlikely, on its own, to retain international design services.

The U.S. and other parts of the international community have pledged significant amounts of aid to help with reconstruction and modernization. Some of this is going for planning and design services for the basic physical infrastructure, including educational and health-care facilities. Since there is very little local capability, much of this work will go to international teams.

The potential of this work must be balanced against the hazards of working in Afghanistan. It is a difficult place to get to

Contents

Countries in bold type receive longer descriptive sections.

Table 4.12 Southern Asia Population and Economic Statistics[22]

Country	Population	Population Growth Rate (%)	GDP—Purchasing Power Parity*	GDP—Official Exchange Rate*	GDP— Per Capita ($)
Afghanistan	31,057,000	2.67	21.5	7.10	800
Bangladesh	147,365,000	2.09	330.8	69.02	2,200
Bhutan	2,280,000	2.1	2.9	840.5	1,400
India	1,095,352,000	1.38	4.042 trillion	796.1	3,700
Maldives	359,000	2.78	1.25	817	3,900
Nepal	28,287,000	2.17	41.92	7.15	1,500
Pakistan	165,804,000	2.09	427.3	124	2,600
Sri Lanka	20,222,000	0.78	93.33	23.52	4,600

In billions of U.S. dollars unless otherwise noted.

and to work in, it has all of the health hazards of a minimally developed country, and of course, it is still in an armed conflict to control the Taliban, Al Qaeda, local warlords, and the drug trade.

Languages and communications

Afghan, Persian or Dari, and Pashtu are official languages, but over 30 minor languages are also spoken. The telecommunications infrastructure is primitive.

Bangladesh

When India achieved independence in 1947, Bangladesh was partitioned off as East Pakistan. In 1971, Bangladesh—with Indian military assistance—fought for independence from Pakistan and won.

Today Bangladesh is a country of more than 147 million people and a GDP of only $330 billion. It is one of the poorest countries in Asia and an unlikely market for international architectural services, especially as almost one-third of the country floods each rainy season. Its Parliament Building, however, was one of Louis Kahn's most important projects.

Languages and communications

Bengali and English are both considered official languages. The telecommunications infrastructure is inadequate for a modern country's needs.

Bhutan

Bhutan is a tiny, scenic country located between China and India. Population estimates vary widely, with the official numbers being around 2,280,000, but some estimates are as low as 810,000. The GDP is estimated at $2.9 billion (as of 2003). It is an unlikely market for international design firms.

It is a monarchy but seems to be making a peaceful transition to a democratic form of government. With liberalization there could be some investment in tourism and other areas that might generate a few opportunities for firms interested in the region.

Languages and communications

The official language is Dzongkha, but some Tibetan and Nepalese dialects are also spoken. Although wireless service

has been available in the country since 2003, the density of phone lines in the country is extremely limited, and overall the state of the telecommunications industry is poor.

India

India is the second most populous country in the world, with a population approaching 1.1 billion. While two-thirds of the workforce remain in agriculture and other rural occupations, India has many large and growing, nonagricultural economic sectors. India has capitalized on its large numbers of well-educated people skilled in the English language to become a major provider of software and outsourcing services. Many North American businesses—including some architects—have outsourced work to India.

India's economy has had over 10 years of strong growth, and its GDP now exceeds $4 trillion. Nevertheless, many international organizations worry about the need for significant reform if the recent growth is to continue. According to one source, approximately one-third of the world's population living in poverty live in India, and 380 million Indians still live on less than a dollar a day. In the United Nations Human Development Report, India ranks as the 127th poorest country, just two rungs above Myanmar and more than 70 below Cuba and Mexico. Many of the very poor live in the tens of thousands of villages, which have changed little in the last several hundred years. Overall, seventy percent of the population is rural.[23]

India also has a legendary bureaucracy, not necessarily one of the better legacies

Fig. 4–59: *American University of Afghanistan, Kabul, Afghanistan. Architects: Yost Grube Hall Architecture with Studio Zarnegar. Courtesy of Yost Grube Hall Architecture and Studio Zarnegar.*

Fig. 4–60: *Khalsa Heritage Memorial Complex, Anandpur Sahib, Punjab, India. Architects: Moshe Safdie & Associates with Ashok Dhawan Architects. Courtesy of Moshe Safdie & Associates.*

of the British Raj, which is often blamed as a brake on development. India is a market economy, but it has a very large state sector. There is a dynamic, high-tech sector operating side by side with inefficient state industries and a general economy subject to heavy government regulation.

Urbanization, however, is beginning to accelerate. India's educated class regularly produces brilliant scientists, professionals, and businessmen, and a recent study quoted in *Business Today* (February 12, 2006) noted that 71 percent of urban housewives and 41 percent of those in rural households were literate, up from 69 percent and 35 percent, respectively, in 2000. However, caste and other invisible barriers block the futures of many.

India is a physically large country—even without Pakistan and Bangladesh, which were part of India prior to 1947—

and has a very varied geography. For example, it has the rich agricultural areas of the Punjab in the north, the towering Himalayas that form the country's northern border, arid Rajistan, and the tropical southern states such as Kerala.

Overall, it is a complex, fascinating, frustrating, and important country with both enormous problems and potential.

The market

In the late 1990s it appeared that India was about to become a market for international design firms, but it did not happen. Now there is a lot of talk again that a major building program is about to begin. To date, India has not had a national building boom comparable to China's; but as a large, growing country, there are an increasing number of opportunities for international design professionals. For example, even though India's "retail sector is largely sealed off from foreign competition,"[24] there are impending signs of change with foreign chain stores readying to enter the market and firms such as Callison are actively designing retail centers in several cities.

An article in *The Economic Times New Delhi* (January 29, 2006) quoted Cushman & Wakefield's list of 12 new malls underway in the capital region. A later article in the same newspaper (February 1, 2006) noted that India had only 70 million square feet of Class A–office space. It assumed such a small amount for so large a country would both drive up rents and spur new development.

In fact, one of the impressions left by a visit to India is how little international-class, modern architecture exists. The airports are old and inefficient, there are very few modern office buildings, and almost all the hospitals are in obvious need of modernization. In general, there is only limited evidence of the modern building boom so common elsewhere in Asia's stronger economies.

Even in Bangalore, which because of the influx of more than 1,000 international technology companies in the last 15 years is referred to as India's Silicon Valley, the new technology parks are small and the infrastructure deficient compared to the ones in some other developing countries.

Hotels—one of the few building types in India currently employing international design teams—help illustrate India's potential. In spite of its spectacular assets, India has only a small fraction of the tourism of China and other comparable destinations. Moreover, it only has 110,000 hotel rooms. This number is the equivalent of the total in the New York metropolitan area, only 10 percent of the number in China and only 2.5 percent of the U.S. total.[25] The limited number of first-class hotels is not able to serve a significant increase in either tourism or business travel, and many new hotels are being planned by the leading hotel chains.

The rise of education and the increase in literacy is also having a large impact on development and building. With the government and private sectors opening many new schools, universities, and training centers, there has been a large influx of people into cities and towns. Towns on the outskirts of rural areas are becoming larger. There has also been a marked increase in the numbers of middle-class Indians, who are demanding more housing, schools, and shopping centers (as shopping is a favorite pastime of the middle-class Indian community).

These are just a few of the potential markets for design services for modern, Western building types. If the economy continues to develop rapidly, the demand for modern offices, research faculties, hospitals, airports, etc., is likely to follow.

As in China, a rapid increase in demand for experienced design teams will probably exceed the capacity of the local Indian firms. Most local firms are already very busy. India has many sophisticated architects and other design professionals, but not enough—at this time—to service a major boom in complex buildings built to modern, international standards.

Reasons to be there

While India is not a big market for North American architectural services in 2007—the year this book was written—it is a very large potential market. This potential, if combined with one or more of the following reasons, could justify a sustained effort:

- India will need the modern buildings that are the core of North American design expertise as it modernizes. This process is just beginning, and the future could see a significant building boom requiring experienced international firms' services.
- India is a fascinating country and became addictive to many British and other Europeans in the colonial era. It can still captivate today.
- India is one of the most logical locations to build an outsourcing-support capability. The educated classes' use of the English language and the large numbers of intelligent, educated, and low-paid professionals make it an appropriate and logical location for this capability. Some U.S. firms are already in India for this reason.
- A rapidly growing number of Americans are of Indian ancestry, which can provide an entrée and make being there more than a business goal.
- More Indian clients are beginning to understand that they have to pay reasonable fees to get quality.

Reasons to be cautious

For most firms, cautions concerning work in India should be the guide:

- India is far away and a difficult trip that is likely to take its toll on all but the most hardy. As one architect noted, "It wears you out."
- In part because of the distance, it can be an expensive place to seek work.
- It is not yet a hot market for international design services. While this has the advantage of reducing the amount of competition, it means that marketing efforts must be carefully targeted. Without preparation and introduc-

tions, unfocused approaches are likely to be unproductive.
- It is a country where bureaucracy and inefficiency can be extremely frustrating and time consuming.
- Except in the tourism sector, many clients are not yet committed to quality, and, as a result, some projects can be disappointing.
- India still has strong ties to Britain, which can give U.K. and Commonwealth firms a competitive advantage.
- A lot of firms see India as the next big market and are beginning to market heavily.
- Business practices can be opaque. One architect reported being asked to study the same site by three different clients— all of whom claimed to own the property. This architect went on to advise: "If you do not know the market, only go in with a player (developer, operator, etc.) who has done the legwork on the landowner and the property" (personal correspondence, 2007).
- As in any foreign country, a word of caution must be given regarding fee collection—especially when using local middlemen. It is best if a direct contract can be negotiated with the client in the U.S., preferably one that can be enforced in U.S. courts, should that be necessary.

Skills and capabilities that are important

Among the key skills and capabilities cited by those who work in India as necessary are the following:

- A good guide to doing business in India, as well as a source of introductions. Most business is done with personal recommendations.

- An interest in and appreciation of India and Indian culture.
- A knowledge of the design issues inherent in India's often extreme climate.
- The ability to communicate in Hindi or the primary regional language where the firm is working.
- Extreme patience.
- An understanding of and access to the lower cost local resources (associate architects, consultants, staff, printers, etc.).
- Specialized expertise in the building types—particularly large complex projects—that are not served by local design professionals.

Who is operating there now?

A growing number of international firms are active in India. As would be expected, many are from England or from other parts of the former British Empire—Singapore, Australia, etc. A growing number of North American firms are also engaged in India. For example, Freeman-White has an office in India; WATG has been working on hospitality projects (many of them unbuilt) for over a decade; Cannon has both industrial and health-care work; Pei Cobb Fried has a project in Hyderabad; Shepley Bulfinch is developing health-care and higher-education projects; Callison has worked on several retail malls; KPF has a luxury residential tower in Mumbai; and some New York firms, including FX Fowle (one of whose partners is from India), are beginning to do some commercial projects in the country. One of Delhi's newest landmarks is the Baha'i House of Worship, a project won by Toronto architect Fariburz Sahba in an international competition.

Who are the clients?

As of 2006, some of the major existing and potential clients for North American architects include:

- International corporations building operations in India.
- Indian development companies seeking specific expertise—particularly in hospitality, mixed-use, retail, entertainment, and large-scale housing development.
- Hospitality companies developing projects that serve the country's rapidly growing tourism industry.
- Technically complex projects such as airports, hospitals, and research facilities.
- Indian architects looking to strengthen their capabilities and competitive position.
- Public projects, institutions, housing, and most other more routine projects are currently (in 2007) served almost exclusively by Indian architects.

What is the process for getting work?

To date, most of the clients have been from the private sector seeking firms with specific skills and qualifications. Thus, successful firms have focused on meeting key clients rather than more broad-based marketing efforts.

Languages and communications

One of the important legacies of the British period is a common language: English. Indians use 14 to 19 (different sources give different figures) major native languages, over 4,000 major dialects, and thousands move minor dialects. Following independence in 1947, the government tried to make Hindi the official language and to phase out the official use of English.

Hindi, however, is a northern language, and people in the south strenuously objected. As a result, English has increasingly become the "unofficial official" language. North American firms can have contracts in English and do business in English, but the ability to communicate in Hindi and some other major regional languages can be important. In many parts of the country a significant number of people will only speak the local language and neither Hindi nor English will suffice.

One of the dividends from the wide use of English has been its role in helping India become a leader in outsourcing and information technology. In spite of India's sophisticated technology, communications technology is not consistent. It can range from the most advanced to the most primitive, depending on the location.

Licensing and legal issues

Indian nationals can receive a license to practice nationally following completion of an architectural degree. It is possible for a foreigner to receive a license, but few find it necessary. Most international firms work as design consultants with an Indian firm that carries out the tasks requiring a license.

Moreover, few international firms want to get too enmeshed in India. As the February 13, 2006 issue of *India Today* noted on page 27, for a typical business in India "[i]t takes 11 steps and 71 days to set up a business. Licensing and permit requirements take 20 steps and 270 days. It takes…40 steps to enforce contracts. Closing down a business could take up to 10 years. Hiring and firing are equally cumbersome." Any significant involvement in India is likely to bring a firm into contact with India's legendary bureaucracy.

Licensing requirements are as follows:

- *Is a license required?* No, but professional registration is necessary with the Council of Architecture, New Delhi.
- *Licensing requirements:* Any degree or diploma in architecture from any university in India or abroad and some examination boards recognized by the Council of Architecture. Professional experience is also necessary for registration.
- *What agency licenses?* Council of Architecture.
- *What is the professional architectural organization?* The Indian Institute of Architecture (IIA).
- *To practice, is a local representative required?* Yes.

Scope of Services

As noted earlier, most international firms restrict their role to planning and design.

Fee levels, payment terms, and taxes

The COAC Web site states that the Indian Institute of Architects publishes a compulsory fee scale; however, because of the much lower professional salaries in India, it is hard for a North American firm to compete if price is an issue. The firms that have found a way to work in India have usually focused on services that justify a premium (for example, the planning and design phases of a luxury-resort project) and made maximum use of local resources. Beyond this, it is hard to generalize about Indian fees.

Firms working only as consultants face minimal tax issues.

Local resources

India has sophisticated architects and engineers available to work in association with international firms. In addition, the other support services—printers, model shops, etc.—exist in the major cities. Coordination has improved with the computer. As one experienced architect noted: "The dimensions of our projects do not change as much now that our local associates are basing their construction documents (CDs) on our CAD files."

Design issues
India has a long architectural and urban planning history, which is often swamped by the chaos of most urban areas. While the number of modern buildings employing the materials, forms, and design vocabulary of international, modern architecture is increasing, most Indian architecture reflects three major influences: India's climate, its building traditions and capabilities, and its traditional decorative arts.

- First of all, most of India is very hot for a large part of the year. Thick walls, flat roofs, deep roof overhangs, solar screening, and light colors are basic parts of the architectural vocabulary.
- As in virtually all developing countries, most construction uses labor-intensive systems: poured-in-place concrete frames, masonry walls, and plaster and stucco exterior finishes.
- Historically, Indian architecture was highly decorative, and some of the trades and traditions continue. Carved stone, decorative plaster finishes, elaborate metalwork, marble inlays, and other crafts are often featured in new buildings. Some of the new luxury hotels, designed by international teams, for example, make extensive use of these design traditions.

Code and regulatory issues
There is a new master plan for development in Delhi that is being released with major changes in zoning. Similar changes are being made in Bombay (Mumbai), Bangalore, Chandigarh, and other cities.

Typical schedules
The labor exists to move quickly, as in China, but bureaucracy and chaos stretch out most project schedules.

Local construction capabilities
India has a large construction industry capable of building sophisticated structures. However, most construction is relatively crude and similar to that found in other countries where labor is plentiful and cheap. Structures are typically poured-in-place concrete, and partitions and exterior walls are a combination of tile, masonry, plaster, and stucco—all traditionally labor-intensive trades. In Bangalore you can watch women carry concrete blocks on their heads, one at a time, up to the masons building the new offices of international technology companies. Most building systems, such as curtain walls, glass technology, metal panels, and stone that are made locally in India, are not the same quality as in the West, although there is a lot of opportunity for customization within each building trade. The quality level of typical construction projects is often mixed, and consistent, high quality can only be achieved with extensive supervision.

Personal safety and health issues
India is a relatively safe place to live and work if one observes normal precautions. "Delhi belly" is just one of the gastrointestinal problems that come if the precautions are not followed. In addition,

exposure to more serious diseases, including malaria, should have visitors consulting their doctors and taking appropriate cautions before traveling in India. When possible, it is best to avoid travel to India in the summer, even though most commercial buildings are air-conditioned.

India has some terrorism and urban-crime problems, but these do not affect most international visitors and expatriate residents. As in most parts of the world, if one avoids the known problem areas, personal safety should not be a major issue.

Sources of information
U.S. Embassy, India
Telephone: 91-11-2419-8000
E-mail: ndcentral@state.gov
Web site: http://newdelhi.usembassy.gov

Council of Architecture
Telephone: 91-11-2465-4172
E-mail: coa@ndf.vsnl.net.il
Web site:
   www.coa-india.org/home/home.htm

The Indian Institute of Architects (IIA)
Telephone: 91-22-2204-6972
E-mail: iia@vsnl.com
Web site: www.IIA-india.org

Maldives
The Maldives are an archipelago off the coast of Sri Lanka. There are 1,190 coral islands clustered in the 26 natural atolls—all less than two meters above sea level. Only 200 of the islands are inhabited, and the total population is just 359,000. The Maldives achieved independence in 1965 after a long period as a British protectorate. It is a republic, but the President in 2006 was serving his sixth term.

Because of its climate, minimalist beauty, and a number of ancient Buddhist and Hindu temples (for those wanting a little culture on their vacation), the Maldives are becoming a popular tourist destination. Tourism accounts for 20 percent of the Maldives' $1.25 billion GDP, 60 percent of its foreign-exchange receipts, and 90 percent of government revenues. According to *The World Factbook*, "Maldivian authorities worry about the impact of erosion and possible global warming on their low-lying country; 80 percent of the area is one meter or less above sea level. In late December 2004, a major tsunami left more than 100 dead, 12,000 displaced, and property damage exceeding $300 million." Over the past decade, real GDP growth averaged over 7.5 percent per year. As a result of the tsunami, the GDP contracted by about 5.5 percent in 2005.

The market
The Maldives are only an occasional market for firms with a proven specialty in resort planning and design.

Languages and communications
The population is Sunni Muslim, and the official language is Maldivian Dhivehi (a dialect of Sinhala, script derived from Arabic). English is spoken by most government officials. The communications industry is minimal.

Nepal
Nepal is similar to Bhutan in that it is small (population 28,287,000, as estimated in 2006), landlocked in the Himalayas between India and China, and poor (a GDP estimated to be only $41.92 billion as of 2006). Unlike Bhutan, however, it has been having a rough transition from monarchy to a more democratic form of government. The occasionally violent unrest has hurt the country's best known in-

dustry—tourism. If and when the political future of the country is resolved, Nepal is very likely to be the site for a handful of projects of interest to the international design community.

Languages and communications

Nepali is the dominant language, although there are others and multiple dialects. Many in government and business do speak English. Although the telecommunications infrastructure is poor, there is a fair mobile telecommunications network and the beginnings of Internet use.

Sources of information

The Society of Nepalese Architects
   (SONA)
Telephone: 977-1-4262252
E-mail: sona@htp.com.np
Web site: www.sona.org.np

Pakistan

Pakistan was part of British India until independence in 1947. Its population is predominantly Muslim and has deep divisions between the large fundamentalist segments and the more modern groups (including the Army) who dominate the government.

It also remains a very poor country, which has not had the same recent economic success of its large neighbor—and occasional foe—to the east. Its GDP is only $427.3 billion (as estimated in 2006) but it currently has a real-growth rate of 6.6 percent. *The World Factbook* notes of Pakistan, "In the near term, growth probably cannot be sustained at the 7 percent level; however, massive international aid, increased government spending, lower taxes, and pay increases for government workers will help Pakistan maintain strong GDP growth over the longer term." As an important U.S. ally now, the U.S. tries to support some positive development.

As in Afghanistan, however, any interest in Pakistan as a location for international design work must be balanced by the physical strain of travel and work there, the health hazards, and the physical danger.

Languages and communications

There are numerous languages and dialects in Pakistan, the dominant one being Punjabi, but with Urdu as the official language. English is also an official language and the lingua franca of the Pakistani elite and most government ministries.

Sources of information

The Institute of Architects Pakistan
   (IAP)
Telephone: 92-21-5883865-6
Fax: 92-21-5885060
E-mail: info@iap.com.pk
Web site : www.iap.com.pk

Sri Lanka

Sri Lanka (formerly known as Ceylon) is a large island nation located southeast of India. It became independent in 1948. The country has a population of 20,222,000 (2006 estimate) and a GDP of $86 billion (2005 estimate). Sri Lanka has transitioned from a primarily agricultural economy to one where the most dynamic sectors now are food processing, textiles and apparel, food and beverages, telecommunications, and insurance and banking.

The December 2004 tsunami had a dramatic effect on the country, with tens of thousands dead, missing, and displaced, and with over $1.5 billion in property damage. Additionally, Sri Lanka has suffered from the effects of a decades-old war (beginning in 1983) with Tamil separatist groups who are seeking independence for their part of the country. At the time this book was being written, the conflict had escalated into a period of heavy fighting. Until the Tamil issue is resolved, Sri Lanka's development is likely to be slow, and its potential for North American design firms is likely to be minimal.

Languages and communications

Sinhala is the official and national language, spoken by the majority of the population, with Tamil as a second national language. English is commonly used in government, however, and is spoken competently by about 10 percent of the population. The telecommunications industry is poor, although it was privatized relatively recently and is beginning to see improvements.

Licensing and legal issues

Foreign architects may only work in collaboration with a local registered architec-

tural practice, according to the COAC Web site.

Sources of information

Sri Lanka Institute Of Architects
Web site: www.slia.lk

East Asia

East Asia includes several countries that have been important markets for North American design firms. China is currently the most important market, but many firms have had major projects in Hong Kong, Macao, South Korea, Taiwan, and Japan.

China

As of the publication date of this book, China has become one of the largest—if not the largest—market for international design firms. The country is the most populous in the world with over 1.3 billion people. It is also the fastest growing of the

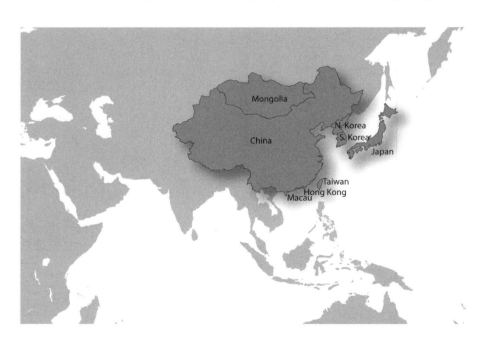

Table 4.13 East Asia Population and Economic Statistics[26]

Country	Population	Population Growth Rate (%)	GDP—Purchasing Power Parity*	GDP—Official Exchange Rate*	GDP— Per Capita ($)
China	1,313,974,000	0.59	10 trillion	2.512 trillion	7,600
Hong Kong	6,940,000	0.59	253.1	187.1	36,500
Japan	127,464,000	0.02	4.22 trillion	4.91 trillion	33,100
Korea, North	23,113,000	0.84	40	NA	1,800
Korea, South	48,847,000	0.42	1.18 trillion	768.5	24,200
Macao	453,000	0.86	10	11.56	24,300
Mongolia	2,832,000	1.46	5.78	1.54	2,000
Taiwan	23,036,000	0.61	668.3	353.9	29,000

* In billions of U.S. dollars unless otherwise noted.

Fig. 4–61: *The Johns Hopkins Center for Chinese and American Studies at Nanjing University, Nanjing, China. Architect: Perkins Eastman Architects. Photograph by Tim Griffith.*

world's major economies. In 2005 it had a GDP of over $2 trillion ($10 trillion in purchasing-power parity in 2006, according to *The World Factbook*), and it has sustained a growth rate of over 9.5 percent since it began reforming its economy almost 30 years ago. It is now the fourth largest economy in the world (after the U.S., Japan, and Germany); and if its current growth continues, it will be the largest economy before 2040.

Over the next 15 to 20 years, it is projected that over 300 million people will move from the countryside into the cities. This huge migration—equal to the population of the U.S.—has combined with a public policy committed to rapid modernization, a torrid real estate boom, and the construction necessary to support economic growth. Together, these factors have fueled an unprecedented demand for new construction. In Shanghai (one of the 100 Chinese cities with a population of over one million) over 360 million square feet of construction was completed in 2003 alone. A 2004 report in *Architectural Record* also noted that the Chinese were consuming 54.7 percent of the concrete and 36.1 percent of the steel produced in the world.

While China is a one-party dictatorship that is still nominally communist, communism (as an economic doctrine) is fading rapidly. Nowhere is this more evident than in the country's overheated real estate industry. Even many of the state-

Fig. 4–62: *Chongqing Library, Chongqing, China. Chongqing Land Properties Group. Architect: Perkins Eastman Architects. Photograph by ZhiHui Gu.*

owned industries are engaged in large scale, for-profit real estate development. In 2006 many of the estimated 15 billionaires and 320,000 millionaires (in U.S. dollars) made their fortunes, at least in part, in real estate.[27] I have asked my Chinese friends more than once, "Who ever thought the Chinese could be communist?"

This demand has overwhelmed the local design resources and created a widespread interest in the experience and capabilities of firms in North America, Europe, Hong Kong, Japan, Australia, and other more developed areas.

While China has a rapidly expanding group of talented design professionals, most are too young or too inexperienced with modern-building types to lead the design of all of the thousands of challenging projects being commissioned. Thus, for a time, there is a large, constant demand for the services offered by firms from North America as well as other developed regions.

Until recently, many of the highest profile projects have been in Beijing, Shanghai, and a few other major cities. Today, many of the other cities and regions are the sites for projects similar to those already built in Beijing and Shanghai.

Reasons to be there

The market opportunity is clear, but the firms active in China often cite the following reasons to do business in China:

1. The scale, complexity, and professional challenges of the projects.
2. Many clients are open to innovative, modern design solutions that push the envelope.
3. The ability to obtain projects that are unavailable or too hard to win in North America.
4. The ability to obtain experience, which can enhance a firm's ability to get related projects in North America.
5. The exposure to China's rich culture and history.
6. To gain revenues and profits to balance those from domestic clients.
7. The opportunity to travel in one of the most interesting countries in the world.
8. The potential for long-term growth (the chairman of one large firm predicts that in 10 years Shanghai will house their largest office).
9. As Don Goo of WATG noted, a growing reason is because "China is rapidly becoming a source of investment capital for projects elsewhere in the world. It is becoming increasingly common to have a Chinese client say, 'I am looking at a project in London, will you look at it with me?'"

Reasons to be cautious

1. The first commission(s) typically require a significant (several hundred-thousand dollar) investment.
2. Typically, getting work in China requires a sustained effort over years. It is not a place where it is easy to go, win, and do well on a single project.
3. There is little legal recourse if things go wrong.
4. Fee margins have narrowed to North American levels with far greater risks.
5. It is a physical drain on the firm's most senior resources and diverts them from domestic priorities. Few trips can be for less than 7 to 10 days.
6. Many projects never get off the ground due to the inexperience of the clients.
7. There is a growing backlash against some of the avant-garde designs by western architects. Peng Pei Gen was

Fig. 4–63: *Linked Hybrid, Beijing, China. Architect: Steven Holl Architects. Courtesy of Steven Holl Architects.*

quoted in the *New York Times Magazine* (May 21, 2006, p. 146): "They are using the Chinese as their new weapons test field."

8. Codes are often arbitrarily interpreted and can cause pain and additional work.

9. The local Chinese institutes and firms are getting more competent and confident. In the future they are likely to be politically connected, low-cost competitors on an increasing percentage of the projects.

Skills and capabilities that are important

Among the skills and capabilities required for successful practice are the following:

• A Mandarin-speaking senior staff member or adviser who understands working in China.

• A sophisticated technology infrastructure that permits staff in China to work with the home office 24/7.

• An organization that can spare and support the senior principals and staff that clients expect to see in China.

• An organization with the resources and skills to win the design competitions that are the start of many projects.

• Real expertise in the project types you are seeking.

• An understanding of Chinese business practices, contract forms, tax regulations, fees, etc.

• An understanding and appreciation of Chinese history and culture.

• An understanding and contact with the many excellent resources—printers, renderers, local design professionals, etc.—available in China.

- The judgment to know when to turn down an opportunity.
- The ability and willingness to eat and drink almost anything since many important meetings take place over multicourse meals.

The two qualities, however, that most experienced China hands say are essential are flexibility and patience. If the firm is to succeed in China, the project leaders must have the patience and flexibility to adapt when almost everything fails to go as planned.

Who is operating there now?

A majority of the largest firms are active in China as well as many medium-sized firms. Unless a small firm (with a staff of 30 or less) has an international reputation in a specialized area or a strong personal connection to China, it is probably not an appropriate place to seek work. There are, however, smaller firms—such as that headed by Ben Woods—that have been so successful in China that it has become the primary focus of their practices.

Who are the clients?

As one would expect in a large, complex economy, there are many different types of clients. The ones most likely to hire international design firms include:

- Government agencies, such as municipal governments, and government-sponsored entities, such as the 2008 Olympic Organization, the Shanghai World Expo 2010, and the Academy of Sciences.
- Current and former state-owned enterprises, such as power companies and major industrial concerns, with real estate–development arms.
- Chinese real estate–development companies (which is the group to approach with the most caution), successful corporations, and individuals who make up China's growing private sector.
- International corporations and development companies—in most cases Asian companies with strong links to China.
- Some of the larger institutions, including major medical centers and universities (although most cannot pay international level fees).

Fig. 4–64: *Shanghai World Expo 2010, Public Events Center, Shanghai, China. Architects: Perkins Eastman with Beijing Institute of Architectural Design (BIAD). Courtesy of Perkins Eastman.*

- And, somewhat to my surprise, local design institutes and firms seeking the additional expertise and design skills they need to compete for some major commissions.

These clients are commissioning major design assignments across a wide range of building types including:

- Office, retail, and mixed use.
- Hotels and resorts (in 2006, of the 386 hotels being developed throughout Asia, 188 were in China and 134 of these were rated as four- or five-star hotels or resorts, according to *Lodging Economics*).
- Housing (although most housing is designed by local firms or firms from Hong Kong and other nearby countries).
- University buildings.
- Sports facilities.
- Hospitals.
- Major public buildings, including libraries, performing arts centers, convention centers, museums, etc.
- Master planning and urban design (this is one of the places in the world that routinely commissions major master plans and urban design studies).

While the major international civil engineering firms are active in China, much of the work being commissioned is limited to planning, architecture, landscape architecture, and urban design. If the team is to include international mechanical and electrical or structural engineers and/or specialty consultants, this typically must be sold to Chinese clients up front. Many do not yet recognize the value of paying a premium for these other services.

What is the process for getting work?

The process of getting work is not dissimilar to that in North America. Normal networking and follow-up of leads are basic to the process; but to be successful, a firm must typically:

- Find a well-connected advisor to guide them during the courtship of major clients and to advise on everything from which prospects are worth pursuing to contract negotiation and fee collection.
- Learn how to be invited into and then win the design competitions that are part of the typical selection process (and mandatory on most projects funded directly or indirectly by the government).
- Learn how to sort out the good from the bad clients. As Scott Kilbourn, co-head of RTKL's Shanghai office, noted, "it is best to follow the client, not the project."

Without a good advisor, and without the skills to win a reasonable percentage of the inevitable design competitions, a North American firm is likely to find the search for work expensive and unrewarding.

Languages and communications

There are many Chinese dialects, but Mandarin is the official language and essential for doing business in China. A growing number of people speak English—and many projects are presented in both languages—but Mandarin governs. Thus, the ability to communicate and present in Mandarin is essential. Cantonese is often the primary language in the south and in and around Hong Kong, but even there Mandarin is the official language.

Fig. 4–65: *City Crossing, Shenzhen, China. Architect: RTKL. Photograph by Tim Griffith.*

It is also essential that the person doing the translation have a command of technical terms. It is common for serious misunderstandings to arise from inexact translations or, as the Chinese say, "chickens talking to ducks."

The major cities—and local staff—have sophisticated computer capabilities, and cell phone services are better than in North America. Landlines are often less important than mobile phones for communication.

Licensing and legal issues

As Brent Hannan reported in his article "Business in China Can Pose Pitfalls"[28]: "Among the many problems that bedevil foreign businesses in China, most seem to stem from this state of economic immaturity: Regulations that aren't effectively written, promulgated or enforced, because the regulatory framework is a work in progress; suppliers that can't deliver quality, due to lack of experience; an acute shortage of qualified staff, because the necessary skills are so rare. But for each of these problems, the answer is the same: The business environment is improving, but the process will take many more years. As a result, in conversations with foreign businesses operating in China, a word that comes up frequently is 'time.'"

At this time, western firms cannot yet provide full architectural services. This is restricted to Chinese firms, but this will probably change in the future. Therefore, most North American firms use one of three options:

1. Many firms—particularly as they are starting—only look for projects that can be done in North America, in the home office, and that will be paid in dollars. If local staff help is needed, this help can be retained on a consultant basis.

2. The least difficult of the other options is to open a *representative office*. The registration process is relatively simple, and the firm can have local employees. However, a representative office cannot sign contracts or provide more than local liaison services. Contracts are signed by the parent firm, and the services are supposed to be provided offshore. In summary, this option's main characteristics are as follows:
   - *Function*: Liaison, marketing, employee training
   - *Time to register*: Usually less than 60 days but can be much longer
   - *Renewal*: Annually
   - *Cost to register*: Approximately $5,000 for consultant help and government disbursement fees
   - *Contracts*: Must be signed by parent company
   - *Restrictions*: Cannot invoice or collect money

   - *Taxes*: Ten percent tax on yearly costs
   - *Space requirement*: Must have a lease in a grade-A building to apply
   - *Staff*: Staff need to be retained through an employment service such as the Foreign Enterprise Human Resources Service Co. Ltd. (FESCO).

3. For firms who want to sign contracts that are paid in local currency (a large percentage of the available work) and who want to do work using local staff, the main option is to establish a *wholly foreign-owned enterprise* (or WFOE, pronounced WOOFY). This requires a long registration process, the investment of capital, and development of a tax strategy. The local profits of WFOEs can be repatriated once each year after payment of taxes. Management of local tax exposure is complex and can be the difference between actually making a profit and a real loss.
   - *Function*: Same as representative office plus planning, design, production.
   - *Time to register*: Approximately three (3) months.
   - *Renewal*: Twenty-year license.
   - *Cost to register*: Requires investment of capital that can be used to fund local operations. Amount varies from city to city, but it is often about $150,000. In addition, consultant help in registering can cost approximately $10,000.
   - *Contracts*: Can sign contracts. Requires an additional license from Ministry of Construction for Architectural Consulting License.
   - *Restrictions*: Can invoice and collect local currency (an important issue for many clients) but cannot seal drawings.

Fig. 4–66: *Jinan South City, Jinan, China. Architect: Perkins Eastman. Courtesy of Perkins Eastman.*

- *Taxes:* Requires professional guidance. Taxes include a 5 percent business tax on collections and 15–33 percent earned-income tax.
- *Space requirement:* An office in a class-A building.
- *Staff:* Can hire staff directly.

As in most rapidly developing areas, there is a growing body of consultants who are in business to guide firms through the thicket of evolving regulations.

Licensing requirements are as follows:

- *Is a license required?* Yes. American NCARB-certified architects are now able to practice in China in collaboration with a local architect.

- *What agency licenses?* National Administration Board of Architectural Registration.
- *To practice, is a local representative required?* Yes. The requirements for establishing local representation include: (1) Registering capital; (2) applying for a business license at the National Bureau of Industrial and Commercial Administration; (3) registering with the Taxation Bureau; and (4) registering with the authoritative construction organizations.

Scope of services

One experienced Chinese developer described the difference between the Chinese and American process. "In the U.S.," he said, the team starts with "Da Wenti" (big problem) and with effort moves to "Mei Wenti" (no problem), while in China they start by saying "Mei Wenti" and eventually discover that it is really "Da Wenti." The Chinese process often assumes even the largest, most complex projects can be planned and designed within a very limited time frame and with limited program input.

It is typical for international firms to do a master plan and/or concept design as an initial phase of work. This master plan may go into a second planning phase, where the zoning and code issues are detailed and approved. Each planning phase is often limited to 60 days.

Ten to fifteen years ago, the international firm's scope might extend through full schematic design and then end. Now, it is more typical for services to extend through design development.

During these initial phases, the local design institute or licensed local team members typically provide zoning and code analysis, preparation of the drawings required for preliminary public approvals, and most, if not all, engineering. More recently—as the capabilities of local firms have developed—they have begun to seek a more substantive role in design.

Because of the often incomplete nature of the typical construction documentation and the limited construction-phase quality control provided by the local institutes and firms, some international firms are being asked to extend their services through all phases. This additional scope can involve overseeing the local design team, providing supplemental drawings as required, and other quality-control services.

On many projects, international firms find that they are expected to provide more than "basic services." It is common for clients to expect urban planning, functional programming, feasibility-analysis services, specialized guidance on such issues as curtain-wall design, and many other tasks as part of "basic services."

Fee levels, payment terms, and taxes

Fee levels for work in China should be at least 20 percent higher than the compensation for a comparable project in North America, but they rarely are. In recent years, many fees have shrunk to or below North American levels. Moreover, some projects are subject to the normal domestic fee levels, which are often a fraction of what a North American firm needs to do the work. Only the compressed schedules, the large size of many projects, the ability to use inexpensive local resources, and an experienced team make it possible to be profitable. Once a project is underway, getting payment on schedule requires a constant effort.

Clients who make the effort can often pay in dollars by wire transfer. Many clients, however, can only pay in local currency, which is difficult to convert. Moreover, repatriation of profits from local currency payments can only be done once a year after payment of taxes. Many clients expect travel and other out-of-pocket direct costs to be included in the lump-sum fee quote. Management of these costs is a major challenge.

The tax bureau often assumes your profit to be 15 percent and then taxes fee volume at 34 percent. All taxes can be as much as 10 to 15 percent of gross fees, and minimizing this potential cost requires a significant effort.

Payment terms are also a problem. All experienced firms try to get a retainer and to stay ahead of their clients, but most find

this difficult. Moreover, final payments are often hard to collect.

Major contract issues

The major contract issues include virtually all of the ones listed in "Getting Those First Contracts" and the sidebars in Chapter 2 as well as in "Contracts," Chapter 3. In China, however, 10 of the most common issues are the following:

1. Develop standard contract forms with all of the boilerplate text in English *and* Chinese. If these standard provisions are reasonable, it will often reduce contract discussions to scope, schedule, fee, and payment.
2. Most Chinese clients want an all-inclusive lump-sum fee. Reimbursable expenses and hourly charges are unusual—in part because some fee payments require government approval and take time. Thus, clients prefer simple, predictable billing, and payment terms.
3. Be very specific about your scope, including the number of trips included, the deliverables (number and type of drawings, renderings, models, etc.), and other variables. Many Chinese clients will use vague language as the basis for asking for more.
4. Be very clear when the contract scope for each phase is complete. The measure of "complete" should not be client approval. Again, many Chinese clients will keep asking for more and more. For example, you may only have been hired for schematic design, but you will find yourself being asked for clarifying drawings at the design development (DD) or construction document (CD)

Fig. 4–67: *CyberGarden, Beijing, China. Architect: Perkins Eastman. Courtesy of Perkins Eastman.*

level of key components such as the exterior wall. Later you will be asked to comment on material samples, shop drawings, and mock-ups.

5. Try to protect yourself from the tendency for projects to suddenly go on hold due to some problem in the approval process, land clearance, or financing. Few clients, particularly Chinese clients, understand the costs associated with this problem.

Fig. 4–68: *Bank of China Head Office Building, Beijing, China. Architect: Pei Partnership Architects. Photography by Kerun Ip.*

6. Additional services are very difficult to negotiate unless the contract clearly defines when they are justified.

7. Clearly define the task allocation between the international design team and the Chinese Design Institute. One typical method is a matrix that lists which firm leads and which supports each task. In addition, clarify how you will be compensated if you must correct or supplement inadequate work by the Design Institute—a common problem.

8. Make sure the method and timing of payments are clearly defined. Everyone advises getting paid in advance and staying ahead of your clients, but this is very hard to do. Most Chinese projects are on very compressed schedules, and any wiggle room in the payment terms will result in the client getting ahead of you. The typical excuse is the project must start now, but the retainer will be delayed due to the need for approval from the tax authorities.

9. Be sure that the responsibility for taxes is clear. In the best case, taxes—if any—are paid by the client. It is not unusual to have relatively arbitrary income taxes assessed before a payment is made—even on the minimal fees (that often do not fully cover the direct costs) of the ubiquitous design competitions.

10. Do not assume you will get much comfort from whatever dispute-resolution terms are in the contract. If it is a mainland Chinese client, your chances of a successful outcome are minimal.

Local resources
There are a rapidly growing number of good, bilingual local design professionals.

Due to the societal chaos of the Cultural Revolution that cost China a generation of educated leaders, among other losses, most of these professionals are under 40 years old. The best are also very busy, and it is important to establish relationships with design institutes and other local firms where you will have access to the best professionals. Most experienced firms can tell one or more stories about problems caused by inexperienced or incompetent local team members.

On the other hand, most experienced firms have learned that some local resources—in particular, computer rendering and animation, printing, translation services, and several others—are high quality, fast, and inexpensive.

Design issues

I. M. Pei used to discuss the need for China to develop a modern architectural language appropriate to its history and culture. It has not happened yet, and China's long architectural history has been largely ignored in the rush to modernize. There are many issues that influence successful designs in China, and some of them vary from region to region within the country. Sensitivity to these issues can be very important. Among the more commonly referred to are the following:

- *Orientation:* For understandable reasons, there is a strong preference in most of China for residential buildings (as well as some other building types, such as hospitals) to face south. In some cities, such as Shanghai, this orientation is mandated by code, and in others it is a strong market preference. Given the cost of heating, the shortages of the past, and the ubiquitous practice of drying laundry outside the living-room window, this tradition can hamper good design. For example, it can make it hard to create urban spaces, since planning encourages a well-ordered parade of single-loaded, south-facing slabs.

- *Sunlight:* The south-facing design preference is combined with strong restrictions against creating shadows that fall on neighboring residences and other building types. We had to completely redesign an office building when it was discovered that it would cast a shadow on 12 apartments in an approved—but not yet built—residential tower to the north of our site. Sunlight protection is built into many local planning and zoning approval process.

- *Entrances:* Traditionally, main entrances are on the south or east facades.

- *Kitchens and bathrooms:* In part, due to unreliable mechanical ventilation and (in some regions) the use of garlic and other items with strong odors in cooking, there is a strong preference for both bathrooms and kitchens to have a window for natural ventilation.

- *Colors:* Colors can have very strong meanings in China. For example, white and black can be associated with death; yellow was a color reserved for use by the Emperor; a client's zodiac color may be important to incorporate; etc.

- *Feng shui:* This arcane Chinese art, which translates literally as "wind and water," is used to interpret the surroundings of a particular environment as auspicious or inauspicious and, then, to create imbalances of energy flow. It is an extremely complicated subject, and usually requires a feng-shui master to determine the suitability and/or need for redesign of a building or space.

It is a very important consideration in Southern China and Hong Kong, but it can also be a factor in many other parts of the country as well. It may seem to be so much hocus pocus to a Westerner, but even many highly educated Chinese take it very seriously.

• *Symbolism:* The symbolic interpretation of a building form can be critical to acceptance. Herzog & de Meuron's happy choice of a "bird's nest" (a luxury food in China) to describe its Olympic stadium was a major aid in its acceptance. On the other hand, KPF's use of a circular void at the top of the tallest building in Shanghai almost derailed the approval. The project was financed by the Japanese, and the circular void evoked the image of the rising sun of Japan over Shanghai—an image with very negative connotations from World War II. The circle became a rectangle and the project proceeded.

Typical schedules

While many Chinese projects stop and start like their western equivalents, most move on very short schedules. It is typical for a client to expect the equivalent of full master planning, programming, and schematic design for a complex building 60 days after commissioning. Following approval of schematics, many clients then expect to be in the ground within three or four months. Many western firms find these schedules can cause staff burnout and a compromised design process. As Chris Choa of EDAW (and former head of HLW's Shanghai office) notes: "The compressed schedules often limit design to an incomplete refinement of the architect's first concept" (personal correspondence, 2006).

Code and regulatory issues

Yung Ho Chang of the Massachusetts Institute of Technology commented in the

Fig. 4–69: *Wanliu Shopping Center, Beijing, China. Architect: Perkins Eastman with Beijing Institute of Architectural Design (BIAD). Courtesy of Perkins Eastman.*

New York Times Magazine that "[i]t's not that we [China] don't have systems; we have incomplete systems. We have this super-progressive energy code, but a decades-old structure code. It is pretty easy for the bureaucrats to make exceptions, which they love to do. They think every case is unique, so *they* will break the code. Not *you*. It's this kind of incomplete changeable system."[29]

China and many Chinese municipalities have their own codes and regulations that have many unique daylighting, fire-safety, and other special provisions. Local advice is essential since many of these regulations are negotiable or subject to several interpretations. Typical of the issues that North American firms must learn when designing in China are the following:

- There are significant variations in the codes between cities and provinces. Moreover, there are great differences in the sophistication and flexibility of those reviewing the codes. A local design professional with knowledge and connections is almost always very important.
- In most cities where the winters can be cold, there is a strong market preference for south-facing residential units. In some cities, such as Shanghai, this preference is written into the local code. The principal rooms—master bedroom and living room—must get 90 minutes of direct sun on the shortest day of the year.
- The sunlight provisions also extend to control of shadows. A new building in most cities cannot block the sunlight of an existing residential building.
- A portion of the basement space—in particular, in below-grade garages—must be designed to serve as a bomb shelter.

- Much of China is in active seismic zones, and the structural codes and construction procedures reflect this.
- Fire safety is taken very seriously, and the codes can be very restrictive. In some cases, however, these restrictions can be relaxed if there is a convincing demonstration that the design follows best international practices.
- The related code reviews for anything other than routine design require considerable time in addition to the normal schedule.
- Fire safety is also one of the issues that can impact site plans. Traffic control is another. For example, many large buildings require circulation around—and through—the site for fire trucks and other emergency vehicles.

Local construction capabilities

Most construction is done by Chinese construction companies. The Chinese can, and do, build anything. Most major buildings are built of poured-in-place concrete with tile, stucco, masonry, stone, or simple curtain-wall exteriors. Quality is an issue but can be achieved if strictly monitored.

Nikolaus Goetze, of the major German firm GMP, wrote of Chinese construction in his Progress Report on "Von Gerkan, Mark and Partner" in *Building Projects in China: A Manual for Architects and Engineers* (Bielefeld and Rusch 2006, 133), noting:

> I am…constantly fascinated by the contrast between the antiquated building methods—managing completely without machinery but needing a proportionately larger workforce—and the highly technical work for which the most recent technologies are used, as in façade design, for example…

Most Common Problems

- Getting paid
- Scope creep without additional compensation
- Local design institutes that do not carry their part of the load
- Expensive competitions that do not lead to projects
- Inexperienced clients
- Impossible schedules and staff burnout
- Individuals who falsely claim to have relationships that will lead to work
- Poor translations that cause significant misunderstanding
- Vague and variable code interpretations
- Arbitrary and excessive tax assessments

The pile foundations [for the 90,000-square-meter Nanning International Convention and Exhibition Center] were sunk by countless married couples: the man drilled into the ground meter by meter with his hand tools, assembled by his wife, who pulled the soil up in a basket, and then provided him with something to eat and drink as well....The shell of the building was erected by inexperienced migrant workers from western China, who lived on the building site during the building period as if as a matter of course. Here talented improvisation compensated for the lack of craft skills. Much to our regret, this often shows in the structural quality of the building. In contrast with this, extremely bold membrane structures were erected without difficulty with the assistance of foreign firms...

Personal safety and health issues

China is very safe. In addition, if normal dietary precautions about the water, unpeeled fruit, raw vegetables, and certain strange dishes are observed, food-related illnesses can be avoided. And, of course, there are occasional outbreaks of epidemics such as SARS (Severe Acute Respiratory Syndrome) and avian flu.

Key pieces of advice

- Find an experienced advisor
- Recognize that developing work in China requires a long-term commitment
- Recognize the risks
- Be prepared to walk away
- Be clear about the potential costs and benefits of each project before pursuing it

- Organize to win design competitions, create the technology infrastructure necessary, and learn to use local resources
- Avoid unpaid or very poorly compensated competitions
- Negotiate clear and complete contracts
- Use a good translator
- Do not go there if you do not really enjoy China and the Chinese

Sources of information

There has been a great deal written on doing business in China, providing many other resources, including:

Bielefeld, Bert, and Lars-Phillip Rusch, eds. 2006. *Building Projects in China: A Manual for Architects and Engineers.* Basel and Boston: Birkhäuser.

Fishman, Ted C. 2006. *China, Inc.: How the Rise of the Next Superpower Challenges America and the World.* New York: Scribner.

Lieberthal, Kenneth, et al. 2006. "China Tomorrow: Prospects and Perils." *Harvard Business Review* (March).

Lubow, Arthur. "The China Syndrome." *New York Times Magazine*, May 21, 2006, 68.

Walter, Derek. 1991. *The Feng-Shui Handbook: A Practical Guide to Chinese Geomancy and Environmental Harmony.* New York: Thornsons.

Wong, Eva. 1996. *Feng-Shui.* Boston: Shambhala.

Wong, Eva. 2001. *A Master Course in Feng-Shui.* Boston: Shambhala.

Fig. 4–70: *Shanghai International Medical Zone, Shanghai, China. Architect: Perkins Eastman. Courtesy of Perkins Eastman.*

"Working with China" articles from a special advertising series published in the *Asian Wall Street Journal* and the *Wall Street Journal Europe*, http://www.questionsforthefuture.tv/ws5/index.htm

U.S. Embassy—China
Telephone: 86-10-6532-3831
E-mail: ircacee@state.gov
Web site:
    http://beijing.usembassy-china.org.cn

Ministry of Construction P.R.C.
Telephone: 86-10-589-33-575
E-mail: cin@mail.cin.gov.cn
Web site: www.cin.gov.cn

Architectural Society of China
Telephone: 86-10-880-82-224
E-mail: asc@mail.cin.gov.cn
Web site:
    www.chinaasc.org/english/asc.php

National Administration Board of Architectural Registration (NABAR)

National Board of Architectural Accreditation

Hong Kong and Macao

Hong Kong, which Britain occupied in 1841, was returned to China in 1997 as a Special Administrative Region (SAR). China controls it under its "one country, two systems" formula. It remains a bastion of capitalism under a layer of governmental control from Beijing.

Macao, which the Portuguese colonized in the sixteenth century, became a SAR in 1999. It, too, remains a capitalist outpost, with the unique position of being the major center for legal gambling in the region.

Hong Kong is by far the larger of the two regions, with a population of at least 6.9 million and a $253 billion economy.

This economy rests on Hong Kong's position as a major port and trading center as well as a major international financial center. While it suffered temporary setbacks in 1998 and 2000/2001 as well as during the SARS epidemic, it has resumed strong growth.

Macao, only has about 450,000 people and a GDP of about $10 billion. Its traditional textile business is moving to the mainland, but it is being replaced with a surge in tourism and an expanding gaming industry. International gaming companies have been allowed in and are investing billions of dollars in new casinos. Growth is very strong right now, but it—and government revenues—is heavily dependent on this single industry.

The market

Hong Kong and Macao have used international firms—including many North American firms for a wide variety of projects. Before China opened up, some of the large firms—HOK, SOM, RTKL, Leo Daly and others—based their Asian practices in Hong Kong. Since the opening of the mainland, many firms have shifted the core of at least their China practice to Shanghai or Beijing. Nevertheless, North American firms remain active in the two Special Administrative Regions, and for firms with the right skills there are still projects of potential interest.

Because of gaming, Macao is very busy as this book is being written—international firms are hard at work on new casinos and hotels. Hong Kong, however, is—to quote a Canadian who had his firm there—"a mature market." In the 1980s and early to mid-1990s, Hong Kong was seen as a good base to serve mainland China and other parts of Asia. It also offered a number of major project opportunities.

Two things changed the perception of Hong Kong as a market—the opening up of the mainland and the Asian financial crisis of the late 1990s. The former made it more appropriate for firms to locate in Shanghai or Beijing; the latter eliminated most of the local demand for international architects. As a former principal of HOK said, "Our firm set two records. We were the first to have over 100 staff in Hong Kong and the first to have to downsize by 100." (personal correspondence)

Fig. 4–71: *40 Peak Road, Hong Kong, China. Architect: Hellmuth, Obata + Kassabaum, Inc. (HOK). Photograph by Kerun Ip.*

Although on a smaller scale, other firms experienced the same parabolic ride.

Today, only a few North American firms remain active in Hong Kong and a few others—primarily hotel and casino specialists—are finding work in Macao. Most of the work, however, is now being done by Hong Kong offices and other firms in the region. Thus, two Special Administrative Regions are an occasional market, but they are not the architectural meccas of the past.

Reasons to be there

Among the continuing reasons to consider Hong Kong and Macao include the following:

- It is the base for some of the most important and richest development companies in the world. Sun Hung Kai, for example, is the world's largest development organization, with 20,000 employees and millions of square feet of real estate. Even more important than SHK's and other developers' developments in the SARs are these companies' involvement in major developments throughout Asia.
- There are still a few important projects, some of which are open to North American firms.
- Hong Kong is still—along with Singapore—one of the most attractive and sophisticated business bases in Asia.

Reasons to be cautious

Among the caveats, several of the most commonly cited are the following:

- Hong Kong is a very expensive place to live and work. Mainland options are far less expensive and more centrally located to the bulk of the Chinese projects.
- Hong Kong is the base for many large, sophisticated and aggressive Chinese design firms that do not feel there is any need for international firm involvement. They do most of the local work and operate at fees that North American firms typically cannot match.
- As a gaming center, Macao has attracted some of the same unsavory individuals and organizations that have traditionally plagued this business.

Skills and capabilities that are important

Among the many skills and capabilities required for success at this time, some of the most important are the following:

- The ability to communicate fluently in both Cantonese and Mandarin.
- A tie to, or a specific specialty required by, local clients. Some of the remaining firms active in Hong Kong and Macao are there because of strong ties to major developers or specialized capabilities in hotel and casino design.
- An established relationship with, or the ability to work with, a local firm with the appropriate license.

Who is operating there now?

Many international firms have shifted most of their China practices to the mainland, but a few North American firms remain as of 2006. SOM, HOK, John Portman, and Leo Daly established themselves before the fallout in the late 1990s and still keep a small presence serving both clients in the SARs as well as in other regions. Other firms continue to work there as well, but they do so with teams commuting from the home offices or offices elsewhere in the region.

Who are the clients?

In 2006 the major potential and existing clients include:

1. Developers of office, retail, hotels, and mixed-use developments. Housing, however, is typically done by local firms.
2. Hong Kong–based companies developing buildings in the mainland and elsewhere in the region.
3. Gaming companies.
4. A limited number of public and institutional clients for specialized services related to major transportation, health-care, or cultural projects.
5. International corporations and organizations requiring facilities in the two SARs.

Languages and communications

As noted above, in spite of the long British influence over Hong Kong and Portuguese over Macao; the ability to communicate fluently in both Cantonese and Mandarin is essential. The telecommunications systems are modern.

Licensing and legal issues

Licensing requirements are as follows:

- *Is a license required?* Yes. Currently, only those admitted into the Architects Register maintained by the Architects Registration Board Hong Kong can call themselves architects. The protection of title is covered under the Architects Registration Ordinance of Hong Kong. Hong Kong differentiates between practicing architecture and the act of submitting plans. The Government main-

tains an Authorized Persons (AP) Register; only those admitted into the Register are authorized to submit plans to the government for approval. The AP list consists of authorized persons list I (architect), list II (engineer), or list III (surveyor). Hong Kong does not differentiate between local and foreign persons.

- *Licensing requirements:* Under the purview of the Buildings Department of the Hong Kong Special Administrative Region (HKSAR).
- *What agency licenses?* The Architects Registration Board.
- *What is the professional architectural organization?* Hong Kong Institute of Architects.
- *To practice, is a local representative required?* No. Submission of building plans to the government for approval would need signatures from professionals belonging to the Authorized Persons List as governed by the Buildings Department of the HKSAR.

Fee levels, payment terms, and taxes

Hong Kong has a compulsory fee scale by the Hong Kong Institute of Architects. Macao has a recommended scale published by the government.

Sources of information

American Consulate General, Hong Kong
Telephone: 852-2523-9011
E-mail: uscghk@pacific.net.hk and
uscghk@pacific.net.hk
Web site:
http://hongkong.usconsulate.gov

Hong Kong Institute of Architects
(HKIA)
Telephone: 852-2511-6323
E-mail: hkiasec@hkia.org.hk
Web site: www.hkia.net

Architects Registration Board
Telephone: 852-2511-5794
Fax: 852-2519-6011
Web site: www.arb.org.hk

Hong Kong Housing Authority
   Headquarters
Telephone: 852-2712-2712
E-mail: hkha@housingauthority.gov.hk
Web site:
   www.housingauthority.gov.hk/en

Associação dos Arquitectos de Macau
   (Association of the Architects of
   Macao)

Japan

In spite of its well-documented economic problems, Japan still has the world's second largest economy. It has a hard working, highly educated population of over 127 million and a very technologically advanced economy with a GDP of more than $4.2 trillion. Japan has a large, sophisticated design and construction community that exports these services around the world. Japan, however, still imports some design expertise for building types where international experience is relevant.

The market

Japanese clients hired a large number of North American architects during the 1980s when their economy was doing well. Many of the large firms—HOK, KMD, RTKL, Jerde, for example—had multiple projects as did emerging design stars such as Frank Gehry and Morphosis. This work slowed dramatically in the 1990s, when Japan's economy went into a long period of stagnation.

As noted above, however, Japan still is the world's second-largest economy and has a large, active need for new buildings.

Moreover, in spite of the sophistication of Japan's own design community, there is still a steady need for international design expertise. As in the U.S., however, it is now largely limited to specialized expertise or the occasional prestige project that justifies an international star.

Even though Japan's economy appears to be recovering, Japan is not likely to return to being the major market it was in the 1980s. It will, however, continue to offer a number of interesting opportunities for interested North American firms with the right skills and/or reputations.

Reasons to be there

The main reason to be in Japan is the opportunity to work on large, challenging projects in an environment where a quality result is far more likely than in most other international locales. In our case, we have had an opportunity to work in one of our major specialized areas—senior living—on a series of projects that have more challenging design goals, more adequate budgets, and better construction quality than our comparable work in North America. In addition, Japan has a long, rich culture and history, and it is an important and often enjoyable place in which to work and travel for any international architect.

Reasons to be cautious

A major caveat about seeking work in Japan is the cost. Japan is one of the most expensive countries to work in or visit. Therefore, most firms interested in Japan limit their efforts to following up on strong leads and contacts. In addition, it is a very formal country, and productive new business efforts usually require carefully arranged introductions. Unlike some other Asian countries, such as China, one

Fig. 4–72: *Sun City Ginza East, exterior. Tokyo, Japan. Architect: Perkins Eastman. Photograph by Milroy & McAleer Photography.*

- An understanding of Japanese business etiquette.
- The ability to be a team player.
- The ability to communicate in Japanese.
- Patience—decision making can be constipated and often moves very slowly. One RTKL principal said he worked on a project that had been in schematics for 10 years.

Who is operating there now?

After the boom years of the 1980s, most North American firms active in Japan reduced their presence. HOK maintains a small presence, as does RTKL. Gensler has about 40 people in its Tokyo office in large part to service Western companies in Japan.

Who are the clients?

North American architects have worked for a wide variety of clients in Japan: Japanese developers, international developers, Japanese and international corporations, and some institutions. Most of the clients come from the private sector. In recent years, North American architects have designed everything from office buildings and shopping centers to golf clubs and retirement communities.

cannot just show up and expect something to happen.

Skills and capabilities that are important

Firms working in Japan list the following as the basic skills required:

- A recognized design specialty or reputation for design excellence.
- The ability to get your client to define your role and authority clearly to the rest of the team.

What is the process for getting work?

Most firms that have been successful in Japan have approached the prospect carefully. For some, including my firm, our first opportunity came from an invitation to meet the chairman of Japan's first major developer of retirement communities. As with other sophisticated developers and corporations in Japan, his staff had researched the design firms with the most experience. We were one of several invited over to present our experience and then given a test project. The first project went well, and we have been working there ever since.

For other firms, the approach came because of their expertise in high-rise office, shopping centers, or other building types. For still others, the invitation has come because of an international design reputation. Japan is very brand conscious and is willing to pay a premium for what they consider a brand name. Once there, many firms—ourselves included—have looked to develop other clients by more traditional networking techniques.

Languages and communications

Communications technology is, of course, very advanced in Japan. Normal interpersonal communication is not. Business is conducted in Japanese on a very formal basis. Many Japanese will only speak English if they feel they can do it well.

Technical sessions and project meetings are typically translated back and forth, and as my partners note, it is "very helpful and important to have a Japanese (or Japanese-speaking) architect on your side with you." There is a funny scene in the movie *Lost in Translation* (2003) that rings true to many of us who have worked in Japan and Asia. Bill Murray's character asks for a translation of a long blast of Japanese, whereupon the translator responds with two words: "More intensity." Without a bilingual person on your side, you will miss a great deal.

My partner, David Hance, who has been in charge of our Japanese projects, noted some of the cultural and language issues he has experienced in his frequent trips to Japan:

- "You learn to assume nothing. It's a dangerous enough practice in the U.S., but when the others around the table oper-

Fig. 4–73: *Sun City Ginza East, interior. Tokyo, Japan. Architect: Perkins Eastman. Interiors by Barry Design. Photograph by Milroy & McAleer Photography.*

ate from a different base on issues such as design processes and priorities, protocol, personal opportunity, and acceptance of the status quo (to generalize, American architects tend to question everything; the innovation that results is at the core of the value we bring to these projects), you learn to organize your thoughts and words into basic, bite-sized concepts and images. State positions clearly, and build on that base.

- If the person you are explaining your position to is nodding their head and

"We published our own in-house guide to Conducting Business in Japan....[It] covers everything from proper business dress to meeting protocol and gift-giving...

- Business cards are very important tools. They must be correct, and you must handle others' cards with respect.

- Body language can be crucial. It's wise to have an observer on your team who watches reactions while you continue to talk.

- You'll never hear 'no,' but you will hear the polite equivalent. You must learn to recognize it.

- No one is 'equal' in Asia. There is a hierarchy for every situation and a pecking order to be followed.

- Touching someone of the opposite sex—however casually—is inappropriate. These are formal cultures in which personal matters are not discussed and people do not express anger openly or loudly."

—Harold L. Adams, RTKL, "The Practice of Architecture in Southeast Asia." Keynote addresses presented at the Southeast Asia Architectural Markets and Practice Conference, Hong Kong and Shenzhen, China, November 5–11, 1994 (Washington, DC: American Institute of Architects, 1995), p. 12.

saying 'Hai, hai, hai' (Yes, yes, yes), they may not be agreeing with you, but merely letting you know that they are hearing you. We've left more than one meeting thinking that we had reached a resolution, only to find that it all unraveled later.

- Japanese place a high value on punctuality. American architects are not always so good at this trait, although I just found out about it. Our local staff was very embarrassed during a recent trip because our early morning taxi, train, train, taxi trip to the job site got us there 20 minutes late. Being typical Americans, we gave a quick apology and *assumed* that they would, of course, understand that these things happen.

- Even after two and a half years, our local staff is still not comfortable calling me by my first name. Japanese seek to settle the relative positions of others when they first meet, and title and age are key signifiers. Not putting *san* (equivalent of ' Mr.') or *sama* (a very respectful version of *san*) after my name just does not sound right to them.

- Size 13 shoes are quite the novelty in Japan. I've had a couple of humorous experiences at Japanese bathhouses where one is to leave their shoes inside an individual locker before entering the changing areas. Size 13s don't fit Japanese-sized lockers, and this can lead to considerable commotion and many *sumimasens* (excuse me's) on both sides before finding just the right place for my shoes to reside while I'm bathing."

There is also a great deal of importance placed on ceremony. As David went on to write for a local AIA newsletter, formal

With a hearty "Aye! Aye! Aye!" and three swings of the cedar sickle, Hoglund-san attacks the vegetation protruding from the top of the sand cone. By this "clearing" of the land to make way for the new building, the site is prepared for the great changes that are in store.

Twenty-one months have passed since we began work on Sun City Takatsuki, the latest project by our client, Half Century More, to meet the great demand for more and better care for the elderly of Japan. The challenges are huge for this nation of 125 million, as nothing short of a reinvention of their senior-care model is envisioned. Our own lengthy design process has offered no small insight into the formidable task of changing from a government-provided to a market-driven model essentially overnight. But no one is thinking today of the many challenges ahead or the trials that we have overcome already to get to this day. On this breezy, cold January day in Osaka, we have come to participate in the Jichinsai (site purification ceremony).

A large red and white tent has been erected for the day's events. We arrive early with the client's representative for rehearsal, as there are roles in the Shinto ceremony for the owner, the contractor, and the architect. Dave, as ichiban of the Perkins Eastman contingent, gets the architect's lead. Patience is extended by all as Dave runs through "put on white gloves, rise, bow to the owner, accept the sickle, bow to the altar, bow to everyone, approach the cone" and so forth. And that's just Act One.

The others have arrived in the meantime, and at 9:30 we begin by having water ladled over our hands for cleansing of the body before reentering the shrine end of the tent. The priest, dressed in full splendor from shoes to hat, leads us through a series of purifications, invitations to the gods, and offerings of sake, salt, rice, and cotton. Dave then "clears the site," followed by the placing of a gift into the earth by the owner and priest and then by the symbolic start of construction by the contractor, as he breaks down the sand cone with a cedar hoe. The owner, architect, and contractor then take turns offering a laurel branch to the altar. Audience participation is required for this part, and when each of the respective leads steps back from the altar, the other members of his contingent join in first two, then one, handclaps to summon the gods.

A communal sharing of the sacred sake rounds out the ceremony, and we file out with optimism for the eighteen months before us. Toasts and sushi are shared at the opposite end of the tent, small gifts are given to everyone, and taxis arrive to whisk us off for Construction Meeting #1.

—*David Hance, Perkins Eastman*

ceremonies are woven into the life of a project (see sidebar).

Licensing and legal issues
RTKL, for example, is registered as a business in Japan. When it has had registered architects in the office, it could practice as an architect; but for reasons expanded on below, there is little incentive to provide full services that require sealing documents. Thus, many of us just act as design consultants, which does

cific design process that requires a license is determined on a case-by-case basis. Licensing requires on the job training and written examination and demonstration of technical skills. The term *Kenchikushi* combines the Architect and Building Engineer. The title of Architect is equivalent to "1st class *Kenchikushi*."

- *What agency licenses?* For the first-class license, the Ministry of Construction is responsible for licensing; for the second-class license, the respective prefectural governor is responsible.
- *What is the professional architectural organization?* Japan Federation of Architects and Building Engineers Association; Japan Institute of Architects.
- *To practice, is a local representative required?* In order to practice in Japan, a U.S. architectural firm must establish a Japanese office with a founder and a licensed person. Japanese architectural law requires the registration of any individual or firm wishing to open an architectural office. In the case of Tokyo, a registration application and other required documents should be submitted to the building policy section. A licensed *Kenchikushi* architect must be responsible for the operations of a U.S. architectural firm's Japanese office.

Fig. 4–74: *Nadya Park International Design Center, Nagoya, Japan. Architects: Kaplan McLaughlin Diaz (KMD) with Daiken Sekkai. Photograph by Isao Harukami.*

not require a license or other special approval.

Licensing requirements are as follows:

- *Is a license required?* Yes.
- *Licensing requirements:* In Japan, architectural designers and construction supervisors are required to obtain licenses of first-class architects or second-class architects, depending on the use, scale, and type of structures involved. A spe-

Scope of services
International architects are usually hired to go through schematic design or design development. After that, the project is often taken over by one of Japan's many capable builders, who often finish it on a design-build basis. To complete a successful project, however, it is often important to stay involved on a periodic basis in the later phases to make sure the design is properly documented and implemented.

Fig. 4–75: *Disney Ambassador Hotel, Tokyo, Japan. Architects: Robert A.M. Stern Architects with Nikken Sekkei Architects. Photograph by Peter Aaron/Esto.*

Fee levels, payment terms, and taxes

Fee levels are usually reasonable as are payment terms. The Ministry of Construction has developed a recommended fee scale.

Major contract issues

Japanese contracts are relatively sophisticated but somewhat less legalistic than those in the U.S. The negotiations can be very numbers or formula driven. It is important to look for mutual benefits and win-win results. Thus, the key issues are the normal ones: scope, division of responsibilities, compensation, schedule, etc. As my partner David Hance noted: "There are few pitfalls that are Japan-specific. We have learned (in contract negotiations) to hang tough. There is a very strong 'customer is always right' ethic at work in Japan, and getting additional fees for changes of mind or exploration of options is almost unheard of in our experience. Once you sign up, you're not done until they are happy."

On the other hand, agreements are honored and payments are timely in most cases.

Local resources

Japan has sophisticated—although often expensive—support services from model shops and printers to engineers and associate architects.

Design issues

Japan has extremely advanced and highly developed aesthetic traditions. Somewhere after World War II, they seemed to have lost touch with large parts of these traditions. Japanese cities often suffer from visual cacophony as modern buildings of uneven quality are inserted into the historic urban fabric. Nowhere is this more striking than in Kyoto, where ugly modern buildings and chaotic urban planning coexist with some of the greatest achievements in building and landscape design in this former imperial capital of Japan.

On the other hand, Japanese clients are usually seeking high-quality modern design from international designers. This expectation—combined with a sophisticated construction industry—makes it possible for western architects to do some of their best work.

On a more detailed level, Japan shares a number of design details and planning preferences with its neighboring countries, such as wide use of tile as an exterior wall surface material, a strong residential demand for south-facing units, and a number of other regional traditions.

Code and regulatory issues

Japan's severe earthquake threat is the best-known feature of its complex codes, and others typically lead to massive structural frames. Most other issues are familiar to architects with international experience. One Japan-specific issue, however, is the emphasis on smoke evacuation. Rated partitions are also important, but getting smoke out of corridors and common spaces is a central issue. For example, there are maximum distances from any point to a "smoke window" that drops open when a smoke alarm activates.

Typical schedules

There is no such thing as a typical schedule. As noted earlier, slow decision-making can stretch out schedules. Projects where decisions go immediately to the top man, however, can move quickly.

Local construction capabilities

As noted above, Japan's sophisticated construction capabilities make it possible to build high-quality, complex buildings.

Personal safety and health issues

Japan is a very safe place to visit and work.

Unless one is allergic to raw fish, it is also a place with limited health issues.

Sources of information

U.S. Embassy, Japan
Telephone: 81-3-3224-5000
Web site: http://tokyo.usembassy.gov

Japan Institute of Architects
Telephone: 81-3-3408-7125
E-mail: ktakano@jia.or.jp
Web site: www.jia.or.jp

Japan Federation of Architects and
   Building Engineers Association
Web site:
   www.jaeic.or.jp/k-seidozenpan-e.htm

Japan Architectural Education and
   Information Center (JAEIC)
Web site: www.jaeic.or.jp/index_e.htm

The Ministry of Land, Infrastructure
   and Transportation
Web site: www.mlit.go.jp/english/

Mongolia

This country was the home of one of the great empires: the Mongols, in the thirteenth century. Later this region came under Chinese rule, but Mongolia regained independence in 1921, with Soviet backing. Today, it has a parliamentary government with a significant communist flavor.

The market

Mongolia is small (fewer than 3 million people), poor (per capita GDP of $1,900), and remote. It is an unlikely market for North American design services.

Languages and communications

Khalkha Mongol is the dominant language. The telecommunications infrastructure is limited but improving.

North Korea

North Korea is an impoverished, backward country of 23 million plus people and a GDP of only $40 billion. Hopefully, someday its benighted leadership will move on, the two Koreas will reunite, relations with the U.S. will normalize, and the North will begin to share in the growth and prosperity of its immediate neighbors—China, Japan, and South Korea. Until then, there is no reason for North American firms to consider North Korea as a place to work.

South Korea

South Korea is a relatively small country (almost 49 million people) with a remarkable economy. The country was occupied by Japan for most of the first half of the twentieth century. Liberation was quickly followed by the Korean War. By the end of the war in 1953, Korea was physically and economically devastated. As recently as 40 years ago, Korea was a very poor country; but today its GDP is approaching $1 trillion, making it one of the more successful economies in the world. It benefits from a highly educated, hardworking population. It suffered a sharp setback during the 1997–99 Asian financial crisis, but the economy has resumed growing since then. Over a quarter of the population lives in Seoul, and most Koreans live in dense urban settings. The country is very mountainous, with limited developable land. The future of North Korea, of course, is a major unknown, and the potential for war remains. Virtually all of Seoul is within range of North Korea's artillery. If reunification is eventually achieved peacefully, it should reinforce

one of the world's most successful models of modernization.

South Korea has had strong links to the U.S. ever since the 1950–53 Korean War. As Korea has developed, many North American design professionals have worked on projects throughout the country. Korea has its own sophisticated design and construction community, but many international firms continue to be involved in a wide variety of projects.

Korea has experienced a radical economic transformation from an agricultural- and industrial-based economy to the current technology-based economy throughout the last few decades. Continuing the current development momentum, Korea is focusing its effort to become the hub of Northeast Asia, where various types of business and culture intersect. As one Korean architect noted: "In order to accommodate such effort, both Korean government officials and business leaders have realized that the construction of infrastructure is critical" (personal correspondence). As a result, building culture has shifted from economical solutions to quality solutions. High design quality architecture and planning are now accepted as standard, not as an option. The building market in Korea is now embracing international firms equipped with high-end design and cutting-edge technology.

Reasons to be there

Korea is an attractive market for several reasons:

- It has strong ties to the U.S. and has shown a consistent interest in North American design expertise.
- It is easy to service if the firm is already active in China and/or Japan, which are only two hours away by air.

Fig. 4–76: *KINEX—Korean International Exhibition Center, Koyang, South Korea. Architects: DeStefano & Partners with Junglim Architecture, Space Group, Kunwon Architects Planners, and Wonyang Architects & Engineers. Courtesy of DeStefano & Partners and Junglim Architecture.*

- It has strong local resources—both for design and construction.
- It has a highly educated, hardworking workforce.
- And it is an interesting, safe, and challenging place to work.

Reasons to be cautious

Balancing the reasons to be there are several other issues:

- It is a very expensive place to operate. In my hotel, during a recent trip, a cup of tea cost $18, and a cab to the airport was $140.
- There is a lot of sophisticated local competition. The Seoul yellow pages have a 10-page listing of architects.
- It is not a big enough market to sustain a continuous presence by all but a few firms.

Skills and capabilities that are important

Among the important skills and capabilities are the following:

- *A design reputation or special area of expertise relevant to the project.* This is a sophisticated market capable of seeking out and picking a firm based on relevant qualifications.
- *The ability to communicate fluently in Korean and to adapt to Korean business practices.* Many Koreans speak some English, but business is conducted in Korean. Moreover, doing business in Korea can be very formal, and to be successful one must learn to be sensitive to Korean ways of communicating and doing business.
- *The ability to win in a competition format.* As in China and some other countries, many architect selection processes are done by competition. The firm must know how to do winning competitions effectively.

Fig. 4–77: *Rodin Museum, Samsung Headquarters, Seoul, South Korea. Architects: Kohn Pedersen Fox Associates (KPF) with Samoo Architects & Engineers. Photograph by Timothy Hursley.*

- *An understanding of local resources.* To be successful a firm must know how to work efficiently with local resources—especially local Korean architects and engineers.
- *A sophisticated technology infrastructure.* Korea is technologically sophisticated, and Korean clients expect their architects to have advanced technical capabilities.
- *Patience.* As with all international work, work in Korea requires patience. Nothing goes as planned, although Korea is more organized than most countries.

Who is operating there now?

HLW International had a virtual office in Seoul in association with a local firm for several years, and at least one other U.S. firm reportedly maintains a small presence as well. Today, there are many firms with recent experience in Korea, but virtually all of the major work by North American architects is done by offshore teams. Standing in an office building overlooking Seoul's downtown, one can see buildings designed by KPF, SOM, de Stefano, Yamasaki, Viñoly, Pelli, and others. KPF is designing a new city near the Inchon international airport and many other firms have challenging projects.

Who are the clients?

The unique feature about the economy in Korea is the economic dominance by a few conglomerates. For instance, Samsung, one of the well-known corporations, owns highly successful subordinate firms such as Samsung Electronics, Samsung Insurance,

Samsung Motors, Samsung Engineering & Construction, and many other diversified subsidiaries. This applies identically to other conglomerates such as LG and Hyundai. When these corporations decide to erect a building either for their own use or an investment purpose, they are likely to use their own subordinate construction firm. According to some Korean architects, when these corporations seek designers for new construction, most consider international designers, hoping to create an icon that can reflect their corporate image. There are many local architects whom they do consider as well; however, many corporations have a biased perception of local architects. They, at times, feel local firms lack experience on large-scale projects. As a result, many conglomerates search out and hire international firms to design their projects. They trust international firms equipped with experienced staff, which can incorporate advanced technology in design. If an international firm gets a project from one of these conglomerates and delivers a good building, the firm will often be invited again for projects in the future.

In addition, international firms could be invited to collaborate in the design process by local architects. Due to a perceived lack of experience and/or human resources, local architects often seek overseas partners. In two competitions in which we worked, many of the teams partnered U.S. architects with Korean offices. In both, the competition our team won and in the other, which we lost, the U.S. team took the design lead.

Invited competitions and open international competitions, which are also used to design for important government or official buildings, often adapt one of these two forms for new construction. Most recently, Seoul held an international competition for the new Seoul Opera House, first, in the form of an open international competition and, second, as a closed competition with a few well-known international architects. On the Seoul City Hall expansion, Korean builders were invited to a design-build competition, and they in turn often used design teams that combined Korean and international architects.

Thus, potential Korean clients and project types include all of the ones you would expect in a sophisticated country:

- Major corporations and real estate developers building everything from department stores and mixed-use projects to retirement communities and housing. Many of the most active and important are South Korea's large conglomerates, such as Samsung, that have large real estate interests in addition to their many other businesses.
- Some government clients with major projects (airports, major municipal buildings, etc.) requiring international expertise.
- Some institutions, including hospitals.
- Korean architects seeking North American expertise to make them more competitive.
- U.S. corporations doing business in Korea.

What is the process for getting work? When seeking work in Korea, it is important to observe Korean protocol. Much of this is quite similar to Harold Adams' description of doing business in Japan (see sidebar on p. 264). As my Perkins Eastman colleague, Jihoon Kim, noted, architectural selection can be influenced by what he calls the "Starbucks effect."

When one gets a cup of Starbucks coffee either in New York or Seoul, one expects the same taste and quality. The consumer is well aware of the fact that Starbucks uses the same ingredients and production process, resulting in uniformity in every product. When a globalized product is expected to be identical in any location, I would call the phenomenon the "Starbucks effect." The Korean building industry is not an exception. When a Korean developer or an investor sees and experiences an extraordinary work of architecture in another part of the globe, they often want it in the context of Korea and expect the same quality. That is why there are many buildings designed by international firms in Korea. It is only a matter of delivering a good example. There is a long list of international architects from SOM to OMA who have already built in Korea and are being asked to build more.

Brand names are important in Korea. As Jihoon Kim explains: "Many clients want a well-established brand providing

Fig. 4–78: *Sun Tower, Seoul, South Korea. Architect: Morphosis. Photograph by Young-Il Kim.*

the same taste as that constructed abroad. Samsung even built a museum with three architects in collaboration: Rem Koolhaas, Jean Nouvel, and Mario Botta each built a building, and Koolhaas also created the circulation link for the three individual pieces. The museum is as awkward as Disneyland, but people like this icon. If an international firm can create a brand or an example to be seen by Korean eyes, the firm will be invited to design."

Kim also noted that: "Doing well in the context of China is also important because of its close proximity to Korea. If an iconic tower is constructed or a well-designed master plan is created in China, these will be observed by possible clients in Korea."

In addition to branding, international firms with design specialties, such a health care, hotels, senior living, etc., are sought in Korea. Both developers and local architects often seek international expertise. In the latter case, bringing in an international firm is often seen as gaining a competitive edge when a Korean firm is vying for a project.

Languages and communications

Business is conducted in Korean, and the ability to communicate fluently is essential. There are excellent telecommunications and IT capabilities in place.

Licensing and legal issues

Licensing requirements are as follows:

- *Is a license required?* Yes. Only Korean firms can be licensed, but foreign design firms may act as consultants.
- *Licensing requirements:* A bachelor's degree in architecture, an associate's degree in architecture from a two year-college, or a high school diploma from a vocational school with an architecture major. Five years of internship is the minimum in order to be eligible to take the architect license qualifying exam.
- *What agency licenses?* Ministry of Construction and Transportation, a governmental agency.
- *What is the professional architectural organization?* The Korean Institute of Architects (KIA) and The Korean Institute of Registered Architects (KIRA).
- *To practice, is a local representative required?* Yes, unless you have a Korean license or your license in your own jurisdiction is validated and registered by the ministry of construction and transportation of Korea. The representative must be an architect who has a Korean license, and he or she must be properly registered.

Scope of services

International architects are typically retained for planning, programming, and schematic design. For complex projects, services might extend through design development and even subsequent phases. Given the sophistication of Korean design firms and builders, however, involvement in the later phases may not be requested or required.

Fee levels, payment terms, and taxes

Most fees can be paid in dollars without local tax. There are no recommended fee scales.

Major contract issues

See Chapters 2 and 3 for typical contract issues.

Local resources

Korea—in particular Seoul—has a wide range of capable local resources from architects and engineers to printers, renderers, and model builders. Advanced computer capability is common, and the design professions have a great deal of construction sophistication.

Design issues

Korea shares Chinese design roots with other Asian countries, but it has its own strong, historical traditions. International architects, however, are retained for their ability to produce good modern buildings. Korean modernist taste is more conservative than China's and some other Asian countries.

Korean traditional elements are valued, yet not forced in building design. Global-ization is a common word in all industries in Korea, and modern, technologically integrated designs are widely embraced. If a Korean client hires an international architect, the client often wants to see what has been done in other parts of the globe. In other words, international design concepts and elements are expected. However, if traditional elements or site-specific contextual elements can be abstractly incorporated throughout the design process, it would probably be embraced.

Code and regulatory issues

Korea has a sophisticated set of planning and building regulations. It also has its own unique requirements, which foreign

Fig. 4–79: *Tangent, Seoul, South Korea. Architect: Studio Daniel Libeskind. Photograph by Bitter Bredt Photographie.*

firms often find out too late to prevent redesign. For example: Buildings in Seoul can no longer have a facade that exceeds 55 meters in unbroken length or width.

Typical schedules
As in many places, project schedules often follow a "hurry-up-and-wait" cycle. Projects often begin with intense 60–90 day competitions.

Local construction capabilities
Korea exports construction talent to the Middle East and other regions. Today, Korea has a very sophisticated construction industry capable of building almost any project.

Similar to other industries in Korea, this industry is also dominated by large corporations. Samsung Engineer & Construction, SK E & C, Hyundai E & C, and a few others are good examples. They take on the role as a contractor for their own buildings, civil, corporate, and infrastructure projects. Samsung E & C, for example, has accumulated experience through large-scale projects in the Middle East, Southeast Asia, and Korea. (For instance, Clarke Pelli's Petronas Towers in Kuala Lumpur, Malaysia; TFC 101 Tower in Taipei, Taiwan; and SOM's Dubai Tower, UAE, were or are being constructed by Samsung E & C.) In general, their construction quality is very high.

Personal safety and health issues
If normal dietary cautions are observed, and North Korea remains quiet, South Korea is a very safe place to work.

Sources of information
U.S. Embassy, South Korea
Telephone: 82-2-397-4114

E-mail: seoul_acs@state.gov
Web site: http://seoul.usembassy.gov

Korean Institute of Architects (KIA)
Telephone: 82-2-744-8050
Fax: 82-2-743-5363
E-mail: kia@kia.or.kr
Web site: www.kia.or.kr

The Korea Institute of Registered Architects (KIRA)
Telephone: 82-2-581-5711
Web site: www.kira.or.kr

Architectural Institute of Korea
Telephone: 82-2-525-1841-4
Fax: 82-2-525-1845
E-mail: webmaster@aik.or.kr
Web site: www.aik.or.kr

Taiwan
From 1895 until the end of World War II, Japan controlled Taiwan (Republic of China). Following the war, the island reverted to China's control. In 1949 two million mainland Chinese fled to Taiwan following the Communist victory on the mainland. Over the last 50 years, Taiwan has become a dynamic economy and has moved slowly toward real democracy. Relations with the People's Republic of China and the issues of eventual unification dominate much of the public debate.

Taiwan has a population of approximately 23 million and a GDP of over $668 billion. It has a very strong export-oriented economy, and the Taiwanese are major investors throughout Asia. Its economy is increasingly linked to mainland China's, but it also has strong economic ties to the U.S.

The market
Taiwan has been a market for a few North American firms; but at this time, the num-

ber of significant design opportunities is limited. As with many countries, most of the opportunities go to international specialists or firms with ties to this island nation. New York's J. M. Lin, for example, recently completed a small award-winning project for the Taiwan Foundation for Democracy in Taipei. Local firms, however, do almost all of the work.

Licensing and legal issues
Licensing requirements are as follows:

- *Is a license required?* Yes.
- *Licensing requirements:* There are two steps to the licensing process. First, a Taiwan citizen must pass the architect examination. Those who pass this examination may practice architecture under the supervision of a certified architect. Second, a Taiwan citizen who has passed the architect examination and has more than two years of work experience under a certified architect may apply for a certificate to practice as a certified architect. A foreigner may be allowed to participate in Taiwan's architect examination provided that a citizen of Taiwan is allowed to practice as an architect in the foreigner's country according to the laws of his or her country. A foreigner who has passed the examination and received an architect's license may apply to Taiwan's Ministry of Interior (MOI) for approval to practice in Taiwan.
- *What agency licenses?* Construction and Planning Administration, MOI.
- *What is the professional architectural organization?* The National Union of Architect Associations, ROC; The Taiwan Architect Association; The Taipei Architect Association; The Kaohsiung Architect Association.

- *To practice, is a local representative required?* A U.S. architectural firm must have a local representative in order to practice in Taiwan, and the local representative must be a locally certified architect. Local participation of a certified architect is needed to certify (legalize) the architectural and engineering drawings and specifications or other documents that the architect is committed to design and/or to perform any other activities in connection with the construction. Foreign engineering fees and the payment of architectural construction documents prepared outside Taiwan for a project inside Taiwan would be considered as royalty and taxed at a rate of 20 percent of the gross contract value. However, if a foreign engineering firm or an architectural firm makes an application to the Ministry of Finance for a 3.75 percent tax rate prior to signing a contract, the Ministry of Finance would automatically grant the 3.75 percent tax rate to engineering and architectural firms because of the difficulty in assessing expenses for individual projects. The Ministry of Finance allows foreign firms to estimate the net as 15 percent of the gross and then applies a 25 percent corporate tax rate to the 15 percent, amounting to a 3.75 percent tax rate.

Sources of information
American Institute in Taiwan, Trade Center
Telephone: 886-2-720-1550
E-mail: aitcomm@arc.org.tw
Web site: www.ait.org.tw

Construction & Planning Administration, MOI
Telephone: 886-2-2356-5000

Web site: www.moi.gov.tw/outline/
Construction.asp

Kaohsiung Architect Association

National Union of Architect
Associations, ROC

Taipei Architect Association

Taiwan Architect Association

Taiwan Green Building Council
Web site: www.taiwangbc.org.tw

Southeast Asia

Southeast Asia is a heavily populated region that contains twelve countries. These range from small, highly sophisticated countries—such as Singapore—to large, potentially strong countries such as Vietnam and Indonesia. It also includes a number of poor undeveloped areas as well. This region has been—and should continue to be—a major market for North American design services. This market was painfully disrupted in the Asian Fiscal Crises in 1997–98, and many of the pioneering North American design firms lost their appetite for the region. Nevertheless, new opportunities in recent years have encouraged a growing number of firms to seek work in the region.

Brunei

The Sultanate of Brunei has been ruled by the same family for six centuries. It became a British protectorate in the late nineteenth century and gained independence in 1984. It has extensive oil and gas resources that account for half of the GDP and 90 percent of the government revenues. The government provides free health care and education as well as heavy food and housing subsidies. The oil revenues have made the country prosperous, and there are efforts to broaden the economic base.

Table 4.14 Southeast Asia Population and Economic Statistics[30]

Country	Population	Population Growth Rate (%)	GDP—Purchasing Power Parity*	GDP—Official Exchange Rate*	GDP— Per Capita ($)
Burma (Myanmar)	47,383,000	0.81	83.84	7.85	1,800
Brunei	379,000	1.87	6.842	5.49	23,600
Cambodia	13,881,000	1.78	36.78	5.12	2,600
East Timor	1,063,000	2.08	0.37	0.35	800
Indonesia	245,453,000	1.41	935	264.4	3,800
Laos	6,368,000	2.39	13.43	2.77	2,100
Malaysia	24,386,000	1.78	308.8	131.8	12,700
Philippines	89,469,000	1.80	443.1	98.48	5,000
Papua New Guinea	5,670,000	2.21	15.13	4.15	2,700
Singapore	4,492,000	1.42	138.6	121.5	30,900
Thailand	64,632,000	.68	585.9	196.6	9,100
Vietnam	84,403,000	1.02	258.6	48.26	3,100

In billions of U.S. dollars unless otherwise noted.

The market

In spite of the country's relative prosperity and occasional projects for the ruling family and international oil companies, this is a tiny potential market.

Languages and communications

Malay is the official language, but English and Chinese are also spoken by parts of the population. The telecommunications industry is "excellent," according to *The World Factbook.*

Cambodia

Cambodia became part of French Indochina in 1887. It was occupied by Japan during World War II and gained full independence in 1953. It got caught up in the Vietnam War, and following the American withdrawal, things got worse. After a five-year civil war, the Communist Khmer Rouge captured Phnom Penh, the capital, and began evacuating the cities and towns. This nightmare period saw at least 1.5 million die from execution, starvation, or forced labor. This period was ended by a Vietnamese invasion and occupation. A thirteen-year civil war finally ended in the late 1990s, and since then Cambodia has achieved a fragile independence and stability.

Fully 75 percent of the population is engaged in subsistence agriculture, and the economy faces many challenges. Most of the population lacks the education and skills to compete in a global economy.

The market

The one bright spot is a rapidly growing tourism sector, which is also creating some planning and design opportunities. Other than this however, it is a very limited market for international design firms.

Languages and communications

Khmer is the main language, although English and French are spoken by some of the country's small, educated class. The telecommunications infrastructure is improving. My BlackBerry worked even in remote rural areas.

East Timor

This country is located in the eastern islands of the Indonesian archipelago. It was a Portuguese colony for centuries. It was invaded by Indonesia in 1975 and finally achieved independence in 2002. It is one of only two predominantly Roman Catholic countries in Asia. It is also, by some measures, the poorest country in the world with a per capita GDP of $400.

The market

It has suffered periods of violence—most recently in 2006—and travelers are encouraged to avoid it. Overall, it is an unlikely market for North American design professionals.

Languages and communications

Tetum and Portuguese are the official languages. The telecommunications infrastructure is very limited.

Indonesia

Indonesia is a large and complex country that has been the site for many projects designed by North American firms. With a population of over 245 million and a GDP of approximately $935 billion, it is likely to continue to need international design expertise.

Much of the international design presence slowed sharply during the Asian fiscal crisis in the late 1990s. Since the crisis, the country's many problems—endemic corruption, highly visible terrorist incidents, declining oil production, a poor investment climate, high unemployment, a fragile banking sector, inadequate infrastructure, etc.—have made this a less interesting place for North American design professionals.

The market

In spite of its problems, Indonesia is a very large country with a number of sectors that will still need to import design services. Therefore, it will remain a market for those firms who can deal with the risks. Few firms will want to establish a permanent presence in the country; but for those active elsewhere in the region, it may be worth establishing local relationships and tracking potential clients and projects in Indonesia.

Languages and communications

A number of languages are used, with Javanese being the most widely understood. The telecommunications infrastructure is "fair," according to *The World Factbook*.

Licensing and legal issues

Licensing requirements are as follows:

- *Is a license required?* Yes, but the NCARB Web site gives no further information on specific requirements.
- *What agency licenses?* The provincial and municipal government.
- *What is the professional architectural organization?* Indonesian Institute of Architects.
- *To practice, is a local representative required?* Yes.

Fee levels, payment terms, and taxes

The government has a compulsory fee scale for government projects, and the Indonesian Institute of Architects puts out a compulsory fee scale for private projects.

Sources of information
U.S. Embassy, Indonesia
Telephone: 62-21-3435-9000
Web site: www.usembassyjakarta.org

Ikatan Arsitek Indonesia (Indonesian
   Institute of Architects)
Telephone: 62-21-530-4715
E-mail: sinfar@iai.or.id
Web site: www.iai-jakarta.org

Laos
Laos became part of French Indochina in the nineteenth century. In 1975, the communist Pathet Lao ended the country's ancient monarchy and allied with Vietnam. Laos is still officially Communist, but there has been a gradual return to a more market-based economy. The economy has been growing, but from a very low base. Over 80 percent of the population is engaged in subsistence agriculture.

The market
This country is too small, poor, and remote to be a significant market for international design services.

Languages and communications
Lao is the official language, but some French and English are spoken. The telecommunications infrastructure is "poor but improving," according to *The World Factbook*.

Malaysia
Great Britain had a number of colonies and protectorates in the Malay Peninsula up until Japanese occupation during World War II. In 1948 these British-ruled territories formed the Federation of Malaya, which achieved independence in 1957. Singapore, which was originally part of the federation, seceded in 1965.

Malaysia was a producer of raw materials but has moved steadily to become an export-oriented, multisector economy. It is also an exporter of oil and gas. As a result, it has become one of the more prosperous countries in the region.

Fig. 4–80: *Menara Karya (Tower of Towers), Jakarta, Indonesia. Architect: Arquitectonica. Courtesy of Arquitectonica.*

The market

The national oil company, Petronas, commissioned Cesar Pelli to design its headquarters, which was briefly the tallest office building in the world. Other major North American firms have had work there as well—some from the international corporations that have established operations there. In recent years, since the 1997–98 Asian fiscal crisis, it has not been a particularly significant market for North American design firms. This could change as the economy grows.

Languages and communications

Behasa Melayu is the official language, and English, several Chinese dialects, and a number of other regional languages are also spoken. The telecommunications infrastructure is modern.

Licensing and legal issues

Licensing requirements are as follows:

- *Is a license required?* Yes
- *Licensing requirements:* Requirements include a degree, practical work experience, and examinations.
- *What agency licenses?* Board of Architects Malaysia.
- *What is the professional architectural organization?* Pertubuhan Akitek Malaysia (PAM).
- *To practice, is a local representative required?* Yes, although foreign architects can receive temporary registration for intergovernmental-sponsored ventures.

Fee levels, payment terms, and taxes

The Board of Architects of Malaysia publishes a compulsory fee scale.

Sources of information

U.S. Embassy, Malaysia
Telephone: 60-03-2168-5000
E-mail: klconsular@state.gov
Web site: http://malaysia.usembassy.gov

Lembaga Arkitek Malaysia (Board of Architects Malaysia)
Telephone: 60-3-2698-2878
E-mail: info@lam.gov.my
Web site: www.lam.gov.my

Pertubuhan Akitek Malaysia (PAM)
Telephone: 60-3-2693-4182
E-mail: info@pam.org.my
Web site: www.pam.org.my

Myanmar (formerly Burma)

Burma was conquered by Britain and incorporated as a province in the Indian Empire. It became a separate colony in 1937 and independent in 1948. The country has been dominated by a repressive military junta for most of its post-independence history.

The market

The country is resource rich, but the economy has been chronically mismanaged. Oil, gas, mining, and timber are the most productive sectors; but most other parts of the economy are hampered by inadequate infrastructure, erratic government policies, deteriorating health and education, corruption, and some economic sanctions. Most foreign aid ceased in 1988 due to the junta's efforts to suppress democracy. The U.S. bans imports of Burmese products as well as the provision of financial services by U.S. citizens.

These factors make Myanmar (Burma) an unlikely market in the near future. A change in government and more competent management of the economy could change this in the future.

Languages and communications
The predominant language is Burmese. The telecommunications infrastructure is poor.

Papua New Guinea
Papua New Guinea occupies the eastern half of the island of New Guinea (the western half is part of Indonesia) as well as a number of smaller islands. It was colonized in the nineteenth century but finally achieved independence from Australia in 1975. Most of the population is rural, and, in spite of rich natural resources, the country is ranked by the UN as a member of the "least developed" category.

The market
This is not a market for North American design professionals at this time. What little work there is will almost certainly be done by Australians. Australian aid accounts for about 20 percent of the national budget.

Language and communications
English, Tok Pisin, and Hiri Motu are the official languages, but over 850 indigenous languages are used by most of the population. The telecommunications infrastructure is very limited.

Philippines
The Republic of the Philippines consists of over 7,000 islands lying between the South China Sea and the Pacific Ocean. At a population of 89.5 million people, it is one the 12 most populated countries in the world. The Philippines will reach a population of 115 million by 2025. How-

ever, it is a small country, in area about the size of the state of Arizona, making it one of the world's densest at 769 people per square mile. The capital, Manila, with a metropolitan population of 10.7 million, is the 20th largest city in the world. The country is experiencing rapid growth at 5.5 percent in economic terms during the last decade. It is also the third largest English-speaking country in the world.

The Philippine Islands were a Spanish colony from 1565 to 1898. On April 25, 1898, the United States declared war on Spain and the Secretary of the Navy, Theodore Roosevelt, ordered Admiral Dewey to attack the Spanish fleet in the Philippines. The Battle of Manila Bay was won by the U.S., and in 1898 Spain ceded the Philippines to the United States in accordance with the Treaty of Paris. An American colony was created from 1901 to 1941 with the Philippines in a commonwealth form of government. After World War II, this commonwealth status changed when independence was granted in 1946 by the U.S. Ever since, the Republic of the Philippines has had a close political, military, cultural, and business relationship with the United States.

Today, there are concerns about political instability; former president Joseph Estrada was impeached on charges of corruption in 2000 and current president Gloria Macapagal Arroyo has had limited success reigning in the Moro Islamic Liberation Front. As a result, development opportunities in the Philippines are limited. Traditionally, politics and business in the Philippines have always gone hand in hand. Cronyism has flourished in the past and is likely to do so in the future. The center of economic power has shifted from the Spanish mestizo (Spanish-Malay)

Fig. 4–81: *1332 Roxas Boulevard, Manila, Philippines. Architects: Architecture International with GF & Partners. Rendering by Phil Ishimaru.*

elite to the Filipino Chinese, who, although accounting for only 5 percent of the population, control as much as 60 percent of the country's banking and commerce.

Filipinos are very open and friendly toward foreigners, and a strongly pro-American bias is evident in the Philippines in everything from the structure of government and the courts to the adversarial role of the press. Filipinos comprise one of the largest Asian communities in the U.S., and personal contacts between the two countries are frequent. But, beneath the surface, Filipinos remain passionate Malays with a rich tradition of Spanish and pre-Spanish mystical beliefs.

In business, personal connections are all important and personal "face" should always be respected. Appearances are everything. Nothing is more important than a Filipino's sense of "face," or dignity, in his community. Filipinos are particularly sensitive to anything that may be construed as a personal rejection or insult.

The family is the center of Philippine life, and families are closely knit and help each other financially. Filipinos are also said to be the most church-going Christians in the world. Nearly 85 percent of the population is Roman Catholic, with 10 percent belonging to other Christian sects, and 5 percent Muslim. Filipinos also form a strong bond with school classmates that become the basis of a lifelong network for business dealings.

Gift giving is a strong Filipino custom; resident expatriates returning from a trip abroad are expected to bring some token of affection. No custom is more important than that of *utang na loob* (lifelong debt of gratitude). Much of Philippines business and politics is meaningless without appreciating this element. A very small favor on the part of a foreigner (such as helping to arrange an immigration visa for someone's nephew) can reap enormous benefits in return.

Almost every Filipino is given a nickname as a child and keeps it for life, even in business. The Filipino prefers to address a foreigner by his or her nickname, which helps to establish a friendly and more binding relationship. Filipinos are also particularly fastidious about titles. An architect is addressed as "Architect So-and-so," which offers a higher level of respect for the profession than in the U.S.

The market

The Philippines is in need of new commercial development, with only 2 percent of the market belonging to shopping centers and department stores. It is one of the biggest countries in Asia, but more than 37 percent of Filipinos live below the poverty line, subsisting on $2 a day, and wouldn't be able to afford Western goods even if they wanted to. The country is spread over 7,107 islands, with about 90 percent of the population in the major cities of Manila, Quezon City, Makati City, and Cebu.

More than 90 percent of all investment is concentrated in the capital region of Manila, and the U.S holds the largest share of registered foreign investment. Foreign companies are allowed only investments up to 40 percent; theoretically, this also applies to the limit of architects' fees for work in the Philippines. Educational standards are high (88 percent literacy rate), but wages are among the lowest in Asia; university graduates sometimes end up serving in cocktail bars or driving taxis.

A February 2006 article by Adam Dalgliesh on the Philippine market in *Urban Land* noted that Philippine real estate and construction have not fully recovered from the Asian fiscal crisis of the late 1990s.[31] Political and economic uncertainty, a weak currency and sovereign debt, an inadequate infrastructure, restrictions of foreign investment, and bureaucratic issues have also slowed new development.

Nevertheless, there are some major, direct foreign investments being made by international parties, including Marriott and the Hong Kong–Singapore Kuok family. Moreover, the office sector seems set to embark on a new cycle of growth. According to Dalgliesh, "the key demand drivers…are the Business Process Outsourcing (BPO) and call center industries."

At the time this book was written, there was still a market for North American design services, but it is likely to be limited for the reasons noted above.

Reasons to be there

There are many good reasons for a firm to be active in the Philippines:

- It is a strong ally of the U.S.
- Its educational system and constitution are based on U.S. models.
- Clients have respect for American talent and trends.
- English is spoken as the second language, and the country has a high literacy rate.
- The people are friendly and welcoming to foreigners.
- There is a large expat community, especially in Makati, the business center.
- The Philippines has a low cost of living for long-term stays.
- There are good support firms in terms of architectural and engineering technical skills. Design skills, however, are limited.

Reasons to be cautious

The country has a recent history of unstable government with periodic coup attempts.

- There is a recent history of kidnapping of wealthy Filipino family members as well as foreigners.
- Terrorism, seated mostly in the south, has disrupted Metro Manila urban areas in recent years.
- Travel time from most U.S. cities can take its toll.

- It is a hot, tropical climate that is also subject to typhoons, earthquakes, and volcanic eruptions.

Skills and capabilities that are important
Among the skills needed to be a success in the Philippines are:

- A respect for the local culture and mix of heritages.
- A strong design reputation or real expertise in particular project types.
- A respect for the local architectural and engineering professions.
- A willingness to make the commitment of principals of the firm to service the clients in a personal way.

Who is operating there now?
In the 1980s and 1990s, dozens of new buildings from American architects in association with Philippine architectural firms mushroomed throughout the Metro Manila area. Among them: Skidmore Owings & Merrill's Ayala Tower One on the Ayala Triangle; Kohn Pederson Fox's ICEC/LKG Tower; Arquitectonica's Pacific Place; Callison Partnership's Ayala Center Greenbelt shopping center; Pei Cobb Freed's residential towers; and Moore Ruble Yudell's mixed-use, residential project in Fort Bonifacio. Even postmodern architecture came to the Philippines via Michael Graves's World Trade Exchange Center in Binando.

In addition, some Hong Kong and Australian firms have not only been active in local projects but have also established local offices. Most of the smaller firms that gain entrée into the Philippines do so through specialized design expertise, such as hospitality and resort design.

Many large and small firms have had experience in the Philippines, but not all have stayed, having fled during the downturn in the late 1990s. In recent years, Architecture International of San Francisco founded by William Higgins, Sherry Caplan, and John Sheehy has been the leading American firm working in association with prominent Filipino architectural firms. They have completed many residential high-rise, office, mixed-use, and retail projects, among them: The Residences at Greenbelt, 1322 Roxas Boulevard Condominiums, Ayala Center Cebu, Filipinas Heritage Center, Ayala Center Glorietta, Oakwood Hotel, One Legaspi Park Condominium, Market! Market! Retail Center, and the CitiBank Manila Headquarters.

Who are the clients?
Many of the project opportunities in the Philippines revolve around real estate development, primarily in the metro Manila areas of Ortigas, Makati, and Fort Bonifacio. Opportunities are found in the following ways:

- A few hundred families control all business and wealth, most of it inherited. No foreigner can hope to do big business without one of the elite as a partner.
- Real estate development firms that specialize in housing, retail, mixed-use; call centers, hotels, and resorts: Ayala Land, Inc; Filinvest Development Corp.; and Rockwell Land.
- Retail and real estate tycoons: Henry Sy of SM Group and John Gokongwei of JG Summit Holdings.
- Infrastructure and transportation design projects through the government and design-build consortiums.

- Civic, religious, educational, and cultural design work is mostly done by local architects with periodic participation by foreign consultants.
- Architecture, master planning, landscape design, and interior design are the main design services that are looked for in foreign consultants.

What is the process for getting work?

The process for getting work is similar to that in the U.S. A firm's go or no-go decision process for pursuing work in the Philippines should consider the following attributes:

- Proactive marketing: U.S. expertise in specific project types, especially large complex projects.
- Networking with both U.S. and Filipino architects and engineers.
- Entering some competitions, but proceeding with caution regarding compensation and judging process.
- Following U.S. companies (corporate, health care, real estate) to the Philippines.
- Publicizing notable work: Brand names are important in the Philippines, so experience in a landmark U.S. project will open doors.
- Learning to say no and how to sort out bad from good clients.
- Remembering allegiance and professional commitment to the client is extremely important; it is the professional kiss of death to work for the competition.

Languages and communications

Business is conducted in English, as are contracts and communications. Tagalog is the native language, and it is spoken amongst professionals in a casual way and may be part of a meeting dialogue. There is a solid telecommunications infrastructure.

Licensing and legal issues

Foreign design firms perform services as consultants, even deleting the reference to architecture, i.e., design consultant, visual consultant versus architectural consultant. Local professionals can partner with foreign professionals as long as the foreign professionals are registered and licensed. There is no discrimination against U.S. professional practitioners, providing they have the necessary qualifications and the license required by law.

However, in an attempt to protect the local profession, a new law created in 2004 (Republic Act No. 9266) requires that foreign architects register with the Board of Architecture in order to practice architecture or engage in preparing architectural plans and specifications for the erection of a building in the Philippines. According to the Act, violators will be criminally prosecuted and subject to fines; however, the Board has yet to formulate a process to implement this Act.

The Professional Regulation Commission (PRC) is responsible for licensing professionals in the country. The accredited professional architectural organization in the Philippines is the United Architects of the Philippines (UAP), an organization founded in 1975.

Licensing requirements are as follows:

- *Is a license required?* Yes. A professional license to practice architecture issued by the Professional Regulation Commission (PRC) is required by law.
- *Licensing requirements:* The following qualifications are necessary to take the board examinations for architects as

provided by RA 545: that he or she is at least 21 years of age; that he or she is of good reputation and moral character; that he or she has completed the high school course or its equivalent; that he or she is a graduate of a four-year course in architecture or its equivalent of a school, college, academy, or institute duly recognized by the government and in addition, has a specific record of at least two years of diversified experience as an architectural draftsman, clerk-of-work, specification writer, or superintendent, provided, however, that an applicant holding a master's degree in architecture from a school, college, university, or institute recognized by the government or the state in which it is established, shall be credited one year in his or her practical experience. The UAP logbook provides specific requirements for diversified training.

- *What agency licenses?* The Professional Regulation Commission (PRC) is responsible for licensing professionals in the country.
- *What is the professional architectural organization?* The United Architects of the Philippines (UAP) is the accredited professional organization (APO).
- *To practice, is a local representative required?* No. Local professionals can partner with foreign professionals only if the foreign professionals are registered, certificated, and licensed.

Scope of services

The COAC Web site states that foreign architects may be allowed to practice under reciprocity agreements with the country of origin. Outstanding experts or well-known specialists may be allowed to practice, provided it will be to the benefit of the Philippines and not impair Filipino professionals.

International architects are typically retained for planning, programming, and schematic design. For complex projects, services might extend through design development. In later phases, the foreign consultant usually performs a design intent and documentation quality control review. The local architect is usually responsible for all zoning, building code, and life safety issues and is the architect of record. Other associated disciplines that are occasionally outsourced to foreign consultants are: structural engineer, landscape architect, elevator consultant, lighting consultant, and graphics consultant.

Projects in the Philippines follow the U.S. model of the design phases from schematic design through construction administration. Most large projects have a construction manager as part of the team to provide scheduling and costing services at the various phases. Some projects utilize a design-build delivery system, a guaranteed maximum price (GMP) format, and in the case of many transportation or infrastructure projects, a BOT (build/operate/transfer) delivery method is used.

Design documents are written in English and use the metric system for measures, although one will inevitably hear discussion about measurements in feet and inches.

Fee levels, payment terms, and taxes

The COAC Web site states that the United Architects of the Philippines publishes a compulsory fee schedule. Fees are generally lower than in the U.S., and with the exchange rate escalating over the past decade, most U.S. firms' scope of services is limited to master planning, schematic design, and, in some instances, design de-

Fig. 4–82: *GSIS Headquarters, Manila, Philippines. Architects: The Architects Collaborative with Jorge Ramos & Associates. Rendering by Steve Oles.*

velopment. This could change in the future as more firms enter the market.

Fees can be paid in U.S. dollars without local or national government taxes. The U.S. has a tax treaty with the Philippines that allows for work performed in the U.S. for projects in the Philippines to be exempt from Filipino taxes.

Payment terms usually include a retainer with monthly progress payments based on a percentage of completion. Filipino clients generally prefer to have lump-sum contracts that also include general project expenses of printing, courier, telephone, etc. Travel is generally reimbursed for business-class airfare and business hotels.

Major contract issues

In many cases, the proposal with professional scope of services and fee becomes the basis for a short-form contract. Long-form contracts with a lot of legalese are seldom used. The new AIA B611 or B621 Agreements for international projects are not yet widely used, but the matrix of responsibilities associated with these documents is a useful tool in describing the corresponding responsibilities among the foreign consultant, the local architect, and the owner.

Due to market conditions, exchange rates and local fee structures in the Philippines, most contracts with international architects do involve fee negotiations; this can be a challenge for the U.S. firm to match the scope of services with the costs of doing work internationally. Always anticipate a "negotiation factor" when submitting fee proposals. Additional services should be defined up front as part of the contract so that there are no misunderstandings when a client asks for services not included in the contract and expects the U.S. firm to perform the services in due course.

Local resources

The Philippines has a history of good local architects and engineers; although not cutting edge from a design perspective, they are sophisticated and technically proficient. Construction documents are generally thorough, however moderately detailed, and most local firms use the latest version of CAD software. Many of the local firms have upgraded their business practices learned from U.S. firms, because sophisticated clients expect it as the norm.

Support services—such as architectural illustrators, by computer and by hand—

Fig. 4–83: *Pacific Plaza Towers, Manila Philippines. Architect: Arquitectonica. Photograph by John K. Chua.*

are quite good and affordable. There is also a good support network of model makers and graphic firms. Other local disciplines available for project-consulting support are construction management and marketing consultants.

Design issues

The long colonial history of Spain established a Spanish colonial architectural heritage that changed with the new American colony. American modernization started in 1904, based on Daniel Burnham's "City Beautiful" planning—the idea of making Manila the "Pearl of Orient," a city made of lively streets and squares. Burnham was commissioned by the U.S. government to design plans for Manila, Quezon City, and Baguio, details of which appear in *The Chicago Plan* publication of 1909. This publication was considered the first example of a comprehensive planning document in the nation and often called the "White City." It popularized neoclassical architecture in a monumental and rational European beaux-arts tradition. In 1912 Burnham went on to design the Manila Hotel and the Central Post Office and other important government buildings.

For the most part, the great Spanish colonial and European beaux-arts architecture in Manila was destroyed by the Japanese in the last 100 days of World War II. After Philippine independence, the 1950s was considered a period of intense building in the manner of the "International Style." In the 1950s and 1960s, American architects ushered in modern architecture to the Philippines, including the original Philam Life by Lawrence B. Anderson and Herbert Beckwith. And Dean Pietro Belluschi of MIT designed the Magsasay Foundation on Roxas Boulevard in Manila.

By the 1970s, a search for a distinctive Philippine style inspired the Architects Collaborative of Cambridge, Massachusetts, to produce the award-winning GSIS Government Insurance Headquarters on the Manila waterfront. The GSIS set an example in energy-conscious design and influenced many others around the world due to its early published articles and energy awards.

The use of traditional and local materials such as bamboo, capiz shell, rattan, and other native woods and marbles are still widely used in interior residential construction. However, modern design and technological advances are embraced in much of the new architecture. Many materials for interior finishes are now imported, especially from China.

All Filipinos are superstitious and will never do business in a house with steps in multiples of three; all tall buildings deny the existence of a thirteenth floor. Feng shui (Filipino style) is followed either because of belief in the practice or because the market place requires adherence, especially in multifamily residential design. Elements such as beams over the bed, unit doors facing opposite each other, positioning of furniture, etc., are scrutinized during the design process.

The Philippines, a tropical climate at 14 degrees above the equator, has a strong tradition in their historic housing for designing in response to climate. Verandas, overhangs, and window shades are a norm, for sunlight is seen as an enemy in terms of heat, versus a source of light and possible form giver to the architecture. Many Filipino architects excel in maintaining the vernacular architecture of their heritage. Moreover, several architectural schools are refocusing their syllabi on "green" architecture and aspects of the heritage and urban context of emerging Asian and Philippine architecture.

Typical schedules

Many projects start off with a hurry-up attitude and deadlines, but then slow due to client indecision, local issues, holidays, politics, and, in some cases, natural disasters. Typical design schedules are similar to the United States, with the usual fast-track efforts. Most projects follow the schematic design (SD), design development (DD), construction documents (CD) phases practiced by the American Institute of Architects and U.S. firms. Payments of foreign consultant firms are generally by percentage of completion by phase, but lapses can occur regularly so beware.

Code and regulatory issues

The Filipino Code, the National Building Code of the Philippines, is modeled after the U.S. code; but not all elements of the code are strictly followed. The code does have provisions to enhance mobility of disabled persons; but, again, it is not strictly followed. Making matters more complicated, local municipal code officials are frequently bribed, resulting in some provisions being implemented or not, at their discretion.

Local construction capabilities

Most construction is done by local companies with local labor or, occasionally, by an international consortium for larger complex projects, such as the new international terminal or transit system. A few foreign (Japanese, Australian, or British) firms have attempted to make inroads into the local construction industry but none have made a long-term impact. Nearly all projects have construction or project managers (some local, some British or Australian), which are helpful for most projects by U.S. architectural firms.

Most construction materials are imported from Asia or Europe; sometimes this allows for more advanced items to be available for consideration than even in the U.S. Many local materials, such as the

Fig. 4–84: *JTC Summit, Jurong East, Singapore. Architect: Hellmuth, Obata + Kassabaum, Inc. (HOK). Photograph by Kerun Ip.*

safety before travel, for many coup attempts, kidnappings, and terrorist bombings have occurred over the years, especially in the urban areas. One has to be cautious, adhere to embassy warnings, stay at 5-star hotels, not explore outlying areas; use hotel taxis only, and avoid street taxis.

Dietary concerns include stomach illnesses that can result from eating food from street vendors and from certain shellfish. In addition, be cautious of drinking water in lower-class establishments, including the ice to chill your soft drink. Most business-class hotels and restaurants are safe, however.

Sources of information
U.S. Embassy, Philippines
Telephone: 63-2-528-6300
Web site: http://manila.usembassy.gov

United Architects of the Philippines
Telephone: 63-2-412-6403
E-mail: uapnational@yahoo.com
Web site: www.united-architects.org

Singapore
Singapore is a tiny country (a population of less than 4.5 million and a land area of less than 700 square kilometers) with a highly developed and successful free-market economy. Today, on a per capita basis, Singapore is comparable to the major economies of Western Europe.

As a former British colony, a stable and open economy, and a regional crossroads, it has always attracted international design and development firms. International institutions have also found it to be an appropriate base for their operations in the region.

Singapore is a base for a number of international design firms, but it also has been the site for many major projects designed by firms from other countries.

native stones and indigenous woods, are used widely, but they are either becoming rare or are of inferior quality. It is an inexpensive labor market, but budgets remain tight due to higher material prices, especially for imports.

Personal safety and health issues
One must proceed with caution when traveling to the Philippines for both safety and health reasons. Always check and evaluate the State Department warnings on country

The market

In spite of its small size and strong local design community, Singapore is a steady market for international design firms. Most, however, are firms already active in the region or firms with design reputations or specialties relevant to Singapore's projects. As this book was being written, the biggest new projects were the major casino and tourism projects just approved by the government. As with many other large projects in Singapore, these, too, involve major U.S. design firms.

Licensing and legal issues

Licensing requirements are as follows:

- *Is a license required?* Yes.
- *Licensing requirements:* A bachelor of art's degree in architecture. Practical experience in an architect's firm (de-pending on the category chosen). There are three categories of professional registration. *Category One:* Graduates with 2 years of practical experience consisting of at least 12 consecutive months in Singapore and who have passed such professional practice examination as may be prescribed or approved by the board, which includes two written papers and one oral examination. *Category Two:* Those with 5 years practical experience, of which 2 are in Singapore, as well as a professional interview. *Category Three:* Those with 10 years practical experience plus an interview.
- *What agency licenses?* Board of Architects.
- *What is the professional architectural organization?* Singapore Institute of Architects (SIA).

Fig. 4–85: *Water Place, Singapore. Architect: Arquitectonica. Photograph by Far East Organization.*

- *To practice, is a local representative required?* Yes. However, a U.S. architect registered with the Board of Architects does not require a local representative. Architectural firms can be partnerships, sole proprietorships, or licensed corporations. For licensed corporations, the chairman and at least two-thirds of the directors of the corporation should be registered architects and allied professionals.

Sources of information
U.S. Embassy, Singapore
Telephone: 65-6476-9100
E-mail: SingaporeACS@state.gov
Web site: http://singapore.usembassy.gov

Board of Architects
Telephone: 65-6222-5295
E-mail: boarch@singnet.com.sg
Web site: www.boa.gov.sg

Singapore Institute of Architects
Telephone: 65-6226-2668
E-mail: info@sia.org.sg
Web site: www.sia.org.sg/new

Thailand
Thailand (formerly Siam) is the only Southeast Asian country to avoid colonization by a European power. A unified Thai kingdom was established in the fourteenth century, and Thailand became a constitutional monarchy in 1932. It is a U.S. ally and has had a comparatively peaceful history. It is, however, dealing with armed violence in the Muslim-majority region in south of the country.

The market
Thailand has a free-enterprise economy with pro-investment policies. It had a major building boom that came to a screeching halt during the 1997–98 Asian fiscal crisis. Many of the design firms working in the country had to deal with bankrupt clients and incomplete projects. The economy recovered after 1997–98, except during the period right after the December 2004 tsunami. The government has implemented expansionist economic policies, and the country is growing again. Thailand faces many of the issues of other developing countries, but it appears to have a promising future that will continue to generate significant design commissions.

Some of the opportunities are in and around Bangkok, the capital, and run the full range of urban projects. Others are generated by the country's growing tourism sector. And, in the 1960s and 1970s, the U.S. invested heavily in Thailand as a base that supported the war in Vietnam.

Who is operating there now?
The firms working in Thailand have varied from year to year, since few can sustain a continuous presence.

Languages and communications
Thai is the predominant language, but English is also used by many of the country's business and government elite. The country has a high-quality telecommunications infrastructure, according to *The World Factbook.*

Licensing and legal issues
Licensing requirements are as follows:
- *Is a license required?* Yes. A practicing architect who designs, supervises, and provides consulting service on professional architectural work is required to be licensed. Foreign practicing architects are required by law to have a license and work permits.

- *Licensing requirements:* An educational degree in architecture and examinations are legally required for the initial licensing (associate) of both indigenous and foreign architects.
- *What agency licenses?* Office of the Board of Control of Engineering and Architectural Professions, Office of the Permanent Secretary, Ministry of Interior.
- *What is the professional architectural organization?* The Association of Siamese Architects under the Royal Patronage.
- *To practice, is a local representative required?* The information on the NCARB Web site states the following: "By law with the exception of government projects, no foreign architect is allowed to practice in any private sector project. However, there are some major government projects that require a foreign architectural firm to form a joint venture with a local firm. By law with the exception of government projects, no foreign architect is allowed to practice in any private sector project. However, there are some major government projects that require a foreign architectural firm to form a joint venture with a local firm."

Sources of information
U.S. Embassy, Thailand
Telephone: 66-2-205-4000
E-mail: acsbkk@state.gov
Web site: http://bangkok.usembassy.gov

Association of Siamese Architects (ASA)
Telephone: 662-319-6555
E-mail: office@asa.or.th
Web site: www.asa.or.th/home.htm

Vietnam
France conquered Vietnam in the nineteenth century. It was occupied by Japan during World War II, and Vietnam then fought a war of independence from France that ended in a partial victory in 1954. The country was divided in two, which set off a struggle that became the Vietnam War in the 1960s. The North won the war and unified the country in 1973.

Postwar Vietnam stagnated economically until the late 1980s when liberalization set off a period of significant growth. Due to the ravages of almost 50 years of war, however, Vietnam started from a very low base and remains poor.

It has a hardworking, largely literate population that is surprisingly friendly to the U.S. Most of us who have experienced working in the country expect Vietnam to continue to develop successfully.

The market
Due to its size and many strengths, Vietnam has the potential to be a real market for North American design services in the future. Some firms such as SOM and KPF have already had projects there, and international investment in a growing Vietnam should help create more opportunities in the future.

Languages and communications
Vietnamese is the official language, but English is increasingly favored as a second language. There is a major effort underway to modernize the telecommunications infrastructure.

Licensing and legal issues
According to the COAC Web site, a foreign architect may not practice independently in Vietnam. A joint venture with a local architect is necessary. Any liabilities of the foreign architect will be taken on by the local firm.

Sources of information
Vietnam Architects Association
23 Dinh Tien Hoang Street
Hoan Kiem District
Hanoi
E-mail: hoiktsvn@hn.vnn.vn

Oceania and the South Pacific

Australia
Australia has had opportunities for North American design firms since at least 1912 when my grandfather's cousins, Marion Mahony and Walter Burley Griffin, won the design competition for Australia's new capital, Canberra. Approximately 70 years later, Romaldo Giurgola of Mitchell Giurgola won his most important commission, the Parliament building at Canberra. More recently HOK, KPF, Anthony Belluschi,

EDAW, and other North American firms have had one or more projects there. These are just a few of the North American firms that have had major opportunities in Australia. Some, including HOK and EDAW, even maintain offices in the country.

The market
Australia, however, is a physically large country with a small population. In the summer of 2006 the population was estimated at 20,264,000 and the GDP was $635.5 billion (2005 estimate). The economy is doing well due to strong demand from China and Asia for Australia's exports. Australia, however, is far, far away. The trip from the U.S. is longer than the trip to China. Thus, most North American firms that work in Australia do so only when invited. It is not a country to target

Table 4.15 Oceania and Pacific Island Population and Economic Statistics[32]

Country	Population	Population Growth Rate (%)	GDP—Purchasing Power Parity*	GDP—Official Exchange Rate*	GDP— Per Capita ($)
Australia	20,264,000	0.85	666.3	645.3	32,900
Fiji	906,000	1.4	5.50	2.04	6,100
New Zealand	4,076,000	0.99	106	98.77	26,000
Samoa	176,908	-0.20	1	399 million	2,100
Tonga	114,689	2.01	1.785 million	244 million	2,200

* In billions of U.S. dollars unless otherwise noted.

as a deep market, but it has been an attractive market for a number of firms with the right areas of expertise, local contacts, and principals willing to take long trips.

Reasons to be there

David Moore of WATG noted several reasons why his firm has found Australia a rewarding place to work:

- There is a real need for some areas of specialized design expertise, particularly for large-scale project planning, which can often lead to an architectural commission in the future.
- The economy is currently doing well and generating a variety of architectural opportunities.
- The local associate firms and construction industry are both technically competent and responsive.
- Australians tend to be nice people to work with.
- It is an interesting place to visit and to work and travel in.

Reasons to be cautious

There are reasons to be cautious:

- It is a relatively small market that is very remote for most firms. As a result,

it can be a very expensive and time-consuming place to develop work.
- Australian design professionals are nationalistic and tend to resent foreign firms taking work.
- The Australian dollar is relatively weak versus the U.S. dollar, which exacerbates pressure on fees.

Skills and capabilities that are important

Among the most important are the following:

- A specialized expertise or design reputation that is not seen to be available in Australia.
- Contacts with companies (developers, hotel operators, etc.) seeking to do projects in Australia.
- One or more relationships with strong local associates.

Who is operating there now?

Most of the firms who have worked there are the large international firms with skills attractive to private clients seeking specialized or high-profile design expertise.

Fig. 4–86: *Chifley Tower, Sydney, Australia. Architects: Kohn Pedersen Fox Associates (KPF) with Travis Partners Pty, Ltd. Photograph by Eric Sierins.*

Who are the clients?

As noted above, most of the clients are private-sector clients, such as developers, hotel companies, etc.

What is the process for getting work?

Most selections of international firms are qualifications based.

Languages and communications

A unique form of English is, of course, the language, and the telecommunications infrastructure is sophisticated.

Licensing and legal issues

Most firms limit their services to schematic design planning (SD), design development consulting (DD) and construction documents (CD) review. As a result, a license is not required. Licensing requirements are as follows:

- *Is a license required?* Yes. It is the law in Australia that any person who uses the title *architect* and who offers his or her services to the public as an architect must be registered. Under Australia's federal system of government, each state is legislatively autonomous and has its own statutes for the registration of architects, although these statutes are similar as they relate to individual architects. There is greater variation among states in the requirements for registration of architectural firms.
- *Licensing requirements:* Certified copies of an original degree and official transcripts,; evidence of employment experiences; references relating to professional work; evidence of registration and licensure, if any; evidence of residence status in Australia; and evidence of professional assessment.
- *What agency licenses?* Architects who seek registration must do so with the Architects Registration Board in the state or territory in which they wish to practice. Each registration board is independent, and each administers its state or territorial registration act. Architects registered in one state or territory in Australia are not necessarily accepted for registration in another.
- *What is the professional architectural or-*

ganization? The Royal Australian Institute of Architects is the country's professional architectural organization. It serves the Architects Registration Boards in an advisory capacity in the accreditation process, but they are separate entities.

• *To practice, is a local representative required?* No, but in New South Wales, one-third of the directors of the practice must be registered architects; in Victoria, two-thirds of the directors must be registered architects.

Fee levels, payment terms, and taxes
Because of the distance and Australian dollar, project margins can be slim, but general fee levels and payment terms are not unreasonable. Most experienced firms negotiate contracts that call for the client to pay any local taxes. The Royal Australian Institute of Architects does publish a recommended fee scale.

Major contract issues
International firms, such as WATG, report that they can usually get their clients to sign their normal contract forms. Thus, the normal negotiation issues are those faced on most projects in developed countries with a reasonable legal system.

Local resources
Local associates and other resources, which are mostly in the major cities along the coast, are competent and relatively sophisticated.

Design issues
Australian design falls within the normal boundaries of current international practice. One thing that firms working there note, however, is a deep interest in sustainable, environmentally sensitive design.

Code and regulatory issues
As noted above, environmental sensitivity is a major issue in the approval process. Projects typically require both state and shire (local) land-use approvals. In general, however, Australia is a typical developed-country set of codes and regulations.

Local construction capabilities
Australia has sophisticated contractors capable of building complex projects. A major issue, however, is the cost and difficulty of building in remote locations—a common issue in the large, sparsely populated areas in much of the country. In those areas, creative design solutions that minimize labor, use local materials, or facilitate prefabrication are often required for project feasibility.

Personal safety and health issues
Australia does not present significant health and safety issues.

Sources of information
U.S. Embassy, Australia
Telephone: 61-2-9373-9200
E-mail:
   info@usembassy-australia.state.gov
Web site: http://canberra.usembassy.gov/
   sydney/index.html

Architects Board of South Australia
Telephone: 61-8-8373-2766
E-mail: msarunic@gtsa.com.au
Web site: www.archboardsa.org.au

Architects Board of Western Australia
Telephone: 61-8-9287-9920
E-mail: info@architectsboard.org.au
Web site: www.architectsboard.org.au

Architects Registration Board of Victoria
Telephone: 61-3-9417-4444
E-mail: registrar@arbv.vic.gov.au
Web site: www.arbv.vic.gov.au

Australian Capital Territory Architects
    Board
Telephone: 61-2-6207-6288
E-mail: jodie.rosewarne@act.gov.au
Web site: www.actpla.act.gov.au/
    industry/architects-board

Board of Architects of Queensland
Telephone: 61-7-3224-4482
E-mail: douglasl@boaq.qld.gov.au
Web site: www.boaq.qld.gov.au

Board of Architects of Tasmania
Telephone: 61-3-6234-2399
E-mail: gharper@engineersaustralia.org.au

Northern Territory Architects Board
Telephone: 61-8-8999-8905
E-mail: Bernadette.McKirdy@nt.gov.au

NSW Architects Registration Board
Telephone: 61-2-9241-4033
E-mail: mail@architects.nsw.gov.au
Web site: www.architects.nsw.gov.au

Royal Australian Institute of Architects
E-mail: national@raia.com.au
Web site: www.architecture.com.au

New Zealand

New Zealand is a spectacularly beautiful
country that is far, far away. It is also a
very small island nation with a population
of just over 4 million. Its GDP (in purchasing power parity terms) is now about
$106 billion, making it reasonably pros-
perous. However, the combination of its
remote location, its small size, and the sophisticated design firms of neighboring

Australia make this an unlikely market for
North American design services, except
possibly for an occasional project requiring some specialized experience. HOK
and a few other firms have worked as design consultants to New Zealand firms.
Moreover, WATG is finding the number
of opportunities for their specialized hospitality expertise increasing, but overall
the opportunities are very limited for
North American firms.

Licensing and legal issues

Licensing requirements are as follows:

- *Is a license required?* In order to use the
  title *architect*, a person must be registered as an architect with the Architects Education and Registration Board
  and hold a current annual practicing
  certificate.
- *Licensing requirements:* For the purposes
  of this section, the term *recognized certificate* means a certificate, diploma,
  membership, degree, license, letters,
  testimonial, or other public institution
  in New Zealand or elsewhere, which is
  recognized by the Architects Education
  and Registration Board as furnishing a
  sufficient assurance of the possession by
  the holder of knowledge and skill requisite for efficient practice of architecture in New Zealand. The practical experience prescribed by the Board is a
  term of 140 weeks of on-the-job experience. The Practical Experience Examination, which must be taken by all
  applicants for registration, with the exception of Australian-registered architects, is an oral examination. It should
  be noted that the Registration Board
  has a reciprocal registration agreement
  with Australia through the Architects
  Accreditation Council of Australia.

- *What agency licenses?* Architects Education and Registration Board.
- *What is the professional architectural organization?* New Zealand Institute of Architects, Inc.
- *To practice, is a local representative required?* If the principals of a U.S. architectural firm are registered with the New Zealand Registration Board, they can practice in New Zealand without local representation. Any local or U.S. citizen can practice as a designer without registration; but to use the title *architect*, the individual must be registered.

Sources of information

U.S. Embassy, New Zealand
Telephone: 64-4-462-6000
Web site: http://wellington.usembassy.gov

Architects Education and Registration
   Board
Telephone: 64-4-801-8972
E-mail: registrar@aerb.org.nz
Web site: www.aerb.org.nz

New Zealand Institute of Architects
Telephone: 64-9-623-6080
Web site: www.nzia.co.nz

The Island Nations of the South Pacific

There are hundreds of islands in the South Pacific, many of which have few or no inhabitants. A small number are large, beautiful, populated, and the sites for occasional architectural design opportunities. Most of these opportunities are limited to tourism planning and design projects for such traditional destinations as Fiji, Tahiti, Bora Bora, Bali (part of Indonesia), Pago Pago, and others. Tourism in some of these areas is improving, generating interest in new projects. The region is so large and the opportunities so few that this market is largely limited to the established international hospitality specialists who are brought to most projects by the clients.

Chapter 5
The Future

Any predictions about the future should be treated with great skepticism. Nevertheless, there are some major trends that will almost certainly result in changes in international architectural practice. Therefore, this chapter discusses some of the more likely results of current trends and then follows that with a discussion of things far less certain, even wild guesses about the future of international practice for North American firms.

1. *Globalization will continue:* The most certain prediction is that globalization will continue and will have an increasing impact on all aspects of the economy in North America, including the design professions. Clients for professional services will seek out the highest quality, most responsive, lowest cost providers, no matter where in the world they are based.

2. *Communications barriers will continue to evaporate:* The growing use of English (e.g., it is now the required second language in China's and many other countries' schools) will erode some existing barriers, and advances in technology will deal with many of the others. It is not hard to envision teams in several countries working on the same project via reliable video, voice, and building modeling technology links. Multicountry teams are a basic trend in globalization.

3. *Steady downward pressure on the cost of services:* The design professions have been experiencing steady downward pressure on fees ever since set fee curves were declared illegal in the U.S. This trend will continue and is likely to accelerate as more overseas professionals compete with North American firms for many of the major commissions.

4. *Outsourcing will become more common:* One approach to cost reduction will be the increased use of outsourcing. This practice, combined with increasingly sophisticated CAD (computer-aided design) software, will begin to have a noticeable impact on the amount of time spent on drafting by design professionals in North America. Drafting rooms will probably shrink as time is refocused on research, quality control, and design. (The challenge, of course, will be to get clients to pay for this increased emphasis on high value-added time rather than taking the savings and running.)

5. *Specialized knowledge-based practices will grow:* Cost reduction, growing complexity, reduced schedules and market expectations will all encourage firms to move toward specialized and knowledge-based practices. Clients have always wanted their design professionals to bring real expertise to their projects, but in the future it will be ever easier for them to seek out and retain firms with demonstrated specialized expertise. Cost reduction, reduced schedules, and greater complexity will reinforce this same trend. The time available for analysis of a design problem has been shrinking for years. Specialized expertise is one of the best

ways to reduce the cost and time required to move from data gathering and analysis into design.

6. *Large firms will continue to dominate international practice:* The costs, complexity, and demands of international practice will continue to make most international projects a large-firm game. More firms will have offices overseas, and even the U.S. offices will continue to become more ethnically diverse. My own firm, as of 2007, had principals and senior staff born in 51 different countries. Ten years from now that number is almost certain to increase.

7. *Many small firms will continue to prosper:* Any predictions that large firms will dominate all aspects of the design professions are certainly wrong. Large firms continue to struggle to provide consistent, high-quality service on many design assignments, and clients will continue to seek out the principal-led personal service that smaller firms deliver. What is more, there will always be clients for firms offering superior design quality, a new approach, or a needed specialization.

8. *More competition will come from overseas:* As was the case after the 1980s, foreign firms will learn from us and then compete with us. By the 1990s, English, French, Japanese, and other foreign firms were increasingly frequent competitors for North American commissions. In 2007 China and many other countries need to import design expertise, but in 10 years they are likely to be exporting expertise as well. If their sizable cost advantages are maintained, they will be formidable competitors.

9. *Many design commissions will not be affected:* Distance, language, local knowledge, and many other factors will keep many design commissions local. The major impact of globalization will be felt on larger projects.

10. *New countries will emerge as markets for design services:* Some new countries will emerge as potential markets for North American design services. Some of these are likely to be oil-rich countries, such as Kazakhstan, because they want to accelerate their development. Others will probably be countries that attract extensive outside investment, such as the United Arab Emirates today. Still others might be former markets, such as Cuba and Iran, reopening to North American firms in the future. Firms that identify these emerging clients early will benefit the most.

11. *Some existing markets will cool off or dry up:* For those of us who work in China, we expect that in 10 years Chinese clients will no longer be willing to pay the premium required to retain design services from North America and other developed countries. Their domestic design professionals will have learned enough from us to replace us on most commissions.

12. *Offices must evolve to remain in a foreign market:* As a foreign market matures, the foreign firms that want to continue to work there will have to find a way to integrate themselves into the local service economy. As was the case with firms that set up offices in Europe in the 1980s with a significant number of U.S. staff, by the 1990s, most of the staff and office leadership were local. In the future some of the larger international firms

will see their leadership take on a multinational complexion.

13. *In an increasingly competitive global economy, North American firms can continue to lead:* The design professions in North America have traditionally provided a significant percentage of the world leaders. This was due in part to America's economic strength, the quality of our higher educational system, and the fact that we built more of the buildings that other countries—for better or worse—decided they wanted. U.S. firms had the training and extensive practical experience to design skyscrapers, shopping centers, research laboratories, airports, hospitals, and other specialized building types. A growing number of foreign-based firms have emerged to compete for—and in some cases lead—these specialized fields. Nevertheless, if North American firms continue to build on their strengths and accumulated experiences, they can continue to lead.

14. *Developers will not evolve as a client type:* One thing that probably will not change is the character and payment pattern of real estate developers. No matter what passport they carry or what country they work in, they will continue to use other people's money and pay erratically.

15. *Change will accelerate:* The next 10 to 20 years will be a very challenging time for the design professions. As globalization continues, change will accelerate. New, strong competitors will emerge; the economics of practice will require rapid improvements in productivity; schedules will continue to shrink; and new skills will be required.

For those firms that think they can continue to practice as they do today, I predict the future will be difficult. For those that evolve and adapt to these trends, as well as to the many other changes not foreseen here, the next decades can be an interesting and profitable period.

Appendix A

Union Internationale des Architectes • International Union of Architects

UIA Accord on Recommended International Standards of Professionalism in Architectural Practice

Third Edition
Adopted by the XXI UIA Assembly
Beijing, China, June 28, 1999
Preamble Adopted by XXII UIA Assembly
Berlin, Germany, July 27, 2002

UIA Professional Practice Program Joint Secretariat

The American Institute of Architects
Co-Director James A. Scheeler, FAIA
1735 New York Avenue, NW
Washington, DC 20006
Telephone: 202 626 7315
Facsimile: 202 626 7421

The Architectural Society of China
Co-Director Zhang Qinnan, Vice President
Bai Wan Zhuang, West District
Beijing, China 100835
Telephone: 86 10 6839 3428
Facsimile: 86 10 6831 1585

Contents

Note: Guideline Documents have been prepared and approved for the following Policy
Issues of the Accord:

         Accreditation/Validation/Recognition
         Practical Experience/Training/Internship
         Demonstration of Professional Knowledge and Ability
         Registration/Licensing/Certification
         Procurement – Qualification Based Selection
         Ethics and Conduct
         Continuing Professional Development
         Practice in a Host Nation
         Intellectual Property and Copyright

Preamble

As professionals, architects have a primary duty of care to the communities they serve. This duty prevails over their personal interest and the interests of their clients.

In a world where trade in professional services is rapidly increasing and architects are regularly serving communities other than their own, the International Union of Architects believes that there is a need for International Standards of Professionalism in Architectural Practice. Architects who meet the standards defined in this Accord will, by virtue of their education, competence and ethical behavior, be capable of protecting the best interests of the communities they serve.

Introduction

The UIA Council established the Professional Practice Commission and approved its program in 1994. Following some 25 months of intensive activity by the Commission during the 1993-1996 triennium, the UIA Assembly unanimously adopted the first edition of the Proposed UIA Accord on Recommended International Standards of Professionalism in Architectural Practice in Barcelona, Spain in July 1996. By this action of the UIA Assembly, the Accord was established as policy recommendations to guide the ongoing work of the UIA and the UIA Professional Practice Commission.

The first edition of the Accord was transmitted to all member sections of the UIA with the request for their comments and cooperation in the further development of the policy framework for presentation to the XXI UIA Assembly in Beijing, China, in 1999. The 1997-1999 Professional Practice program focused on responding to comments and recommendations received from Council members, UIA member sections, and members of the Commission on the Accord and its policies. The first edition of the Accord was modified in response to those comments and as a result of Commission debate of the policy issue guideline documents being developed to flesh out the bare bones policy framework of the Accord.

The Accord and guidelines recognize the sovereignty of each UIA member section, allow flexibility for principles of equivalency, and are structured to allow for the addition of requirements reflecting local conditions of a UIA member section.

It is not the intention of the Accord to establish obligatory standards set by negotiated agreements between competing interests. Rather, the Accord is the result of the co-operative endeavor of the international community of architects to objectively establish standards and practices that will best serve community interests. The Accord and Guideline documents are intended to define what is considered best practice for the architectural profession and the standards to which the profession aspires. These are living documents and will be subject to ongoing review and modification as the weight of opinion and experience dictates. Whilst respecting the sovereignty of UIA member sections, they are invited and encouraged to promote the adoption of the Accord and the Guidelines and, if appropriate, seek the modification of existing customs and laws.

It is intended that the Accord and guidelines will provide practical guidance for governments, negotiating entities, or other entities entering mutual recognition negotiations on architectural services. The Accord and guidelines will make it easier for parties to negotiate recognition agreements. The most common way to achieve recognition has been through bilateral agreements, recognized as permissible under Article VII of the GATS. There are differences in education and examination standards, experience requirements, regulatory influence etc., all of which make implementing recognition on a multilateral basis extremely difficult. Bilateral negotiations will facilitate focus on key issues relating to two specific environments. However, once achieved, bilateral reciprocal agreements should lead to others, which will ultimately extend mutual recognition more broadly.

The Accord begins with a statement of "Principles of Professionalism," followed by a series of policy issues. Each policy issue opens with a definition of the subject policy, followed by a statement of background and the policy.

The XXI UIA Assembly in Beijing, China unanimously adopted the Accord in June 1999. A copy of the Resolution of Adoption is attached as Appendix A.

UIA Accord on Recommended International Standards of Professionalism in Architectural Practice

Principles of Professionalism

Members of the architectural profession are dedicated to standards of professionalism, integrity, and competence, and thereby bring to society unique skills and aptitudes essential to the sustainable development of the built environment and the welfare of their societies and cultures. Principles of professionalism are established in legislation, as well as in codes of ethics and regulations defining professional conduct:

Expertise: Architects possess a systematic body of knowledge, skills, and theory developed through education, graduate and post-graduate training, and experience. The process of architectural education, training, and examination is structured to assure the public that when an architect is engaged to perform professional services, that architect has met acceptable standards enabling proper performance of those services. Furthermore, members of most professional societies of architects and indeed, the UIA, are charged to maintain and advance their knowledge of the art and science of architecture, to respect the body of architectural accomplishment, and to contribute to its growth.

Autonomy: Architects provide objective expert advice to the client and/or the users. Architects are charged to uphold the ideal that learned and uncompromised professional judgment should take precedence over any other motive in the pursuit of the art and science of architecture.

Architects are also charged to embrace the spirit and letter of the laws governing their professional affairs and to thoughtfully consider the social and environmental impact of their professional activities.

Commitment: Architects bring a high level of selfless dedication to the work done on behalf of their clients and society. Members of the profession are charged to serve their clients in a competent and professional manner and to exercise unprejudiced and unbiased judgment on their behalf.

Accountability: Architects are aware of their responsibility for the independent and, if necessary, critical advice provided to their clients and for the effects of their work on society and the environment. Architects undertake to perform professional services only when they, together with those whom they may engage as consultants, are qualified by education, training, and/or experience in the specific technical areas involved.

The UIA, through the programs of its national sections and the Professional Practice Commission, seeks to establish principles of professionalism and professional standards in the interest of public health, safety, welfare, and culture, and supports the position that inter-recognition of standards of professionalism and competence is in the public interest as well as in the interest of maintaining the credibility of the profession.

The principles and standards of the UIA are aimed at the thorough education and practical training of architects so that they are able to fulfill their fundamental professional requirements. These standards recognize different national educational traditions and, therefore, allow for factors of equivalency.

Practice of Architecture

Definition:

The practice of architecture consists of the provision of professional services in connection with town planning and the design, construction, enlargement, conservation, restoration, or alteration of a building or group of buildings. These professional services include, but are not limited to, planning and land-use planning, urban design, provision of preliminary studies, designs, models, drawings, specifications and technical documentation, coordination of technical documentation prepared by others (consulting engineers, urban planners, landscape architects and other specialist consultants) as appropriate and without limitation, construction economics, contract administration, monitoring of construction (referred to as "supervision" in some countries), and project management.

Background:

Architects have been practicing their art and science since antiquity. The profession as we know it today has undergone extensive growth and change. The profile of architects' work has become more demanding, clients' requirements and technological advances have become more complex, and social and ecological imperatives have grown more pressing. These changes have spawned changes in services and collaboration among the many parties involved in the design and construction process.

Policy:

That the practice of architecture as defined above be adopted for use in the development of UIA International Standards.

Architect

Definition:

The designation "architect" is generally reserved by law or custom to a person who is professionally and academically qualified and generally registered/licensed/certified to practice architecture in the jurisdiction in which he or she practices and is responsible for advocating the fair and sustainable development, welfare, and the cultural expression of society's habitat in terms of space, forms, and historical context.

Background:

Architects are part of the public and private sectors involved in a larger property development, building, and construction economic sector peopled by those commissioning, conserving, designing, building, furnishing, financing, regulating, and operating our built environment to meet the needs of society. Architects work in a variety of situations and organizational structures. For example, they may work on their own or as members of private or public offices.

Policy:

That the UIA adopt the definition of an "architect" as stated above for use in developing UIA International Standards.

Fundamental Requirements of an Architect

Definition:

The fundamental requirements for registration/licensing/certification as an architect as defined above, are the knowledge, skills, and abilities listed below that must be mastered through recognized education and training, and demonstrable knowledge, capability, and experience in order to be considered professionally qualified to practice architecture.

Background:

In August 1985, for the first time, a group of countries came together to set down the fundamental knowledge and abilities of an architect (*). These include:

- Ability to create architectural designs that satisfy both aesthetic and technical requirements, and which aim to be environmentally sustainable;
- Adequate knowledge of the history and theories of architecture and related arts, technologies, and human sciences;
- Knowledge of the fine arts as an influence on the quality of architectural design;
- Adequate knowledge of urban design, planning, and the skills involved in the planning process;
- Understanding of the relationship between people and buildings and between buildings and their environments, and of the need to relate buildings and the spaces between them to human needs and scale;
- An adequate knowledge of the means of achieving environmentally sustainable design;
- Understanding of the profession of architecture and the role of architects in society, in particular in preparing briefs that account for social factors;
- Understanding of the methods of investigation and preparation of the brief for a design project;
- Understanding of the structural design, construction, and engineering problems associated with building design;
- Adequate knowledge of physical problems and technologies and of the function of buildings so as to provide them with internal conditions of comfort and protection against climate;
- Necessary design skills to meet building users' requirements within the constraints imposed by cost factors and building regulations;
- Adequate knowledge of the industries, organizations, regulations, and procedures involved in translating design concepts into buildings and integrating plans into overall planning;
- Adequate knowledge of project financing, project management, and cost control.

Policy:

That the UIA adopt a statement of fundamental requirements as set out above as the minimum basis for development of UIA International Standards and seek to ensure that these particular requirements are given adequate emphasis in the architectural curriculum. The UIA will also seek to ensure that the fundamental requirements will be constantly kept under review so that they remain relevant as the architectural profession and society evolve.

(* Cf. Derived from Directive 85/384/EEC of the Commission of the European Communities)

Education

Definition:

Architectural education should ensure that all graduates have knowledge and ability in architectural design, including technical systems and requirements as well as consideration of health, safety, and ecological balance; that they understand the cultural, intellectual, historical, social, economic, and environmental context for architecture; and that they comprehend thoroughly the architects' roles and responsibilities in society, which depend on a cultivated, analytical and creative mind.

Background:

In most countries, architectural education is conventionally delivered by 4-6 years full-time academic education at a university (followed, in some countries, by a period of practical experience/training/internship), though historically there have been important variations (part-time routes, work experience etc.).

Policy:

In accordance with the UIA/UNESCO Charter for Architectural Education, the UIA advocate that education for architects (apart from practical experience/training/internship) be of no less than 5 years duration, delivered on a full-time basis in an accredited/validated/recognized architectural program in an accredited/validated/recognized university, while allowing variety in their pedagogic approach and in their responses to local contexts, and flexibility for equivalency.

Accreditation/Validation/Recognition

Definition:

This is the process that establishes that an educational program meets an established standard of achievement. Its purpose is to assure the maintenance and enhancement of an appropriate educational foundation.

Background:

Validated criteria and procedures for accreditation/validation/recognition by an independent organization help to develop well integrated and coordinated programs of architectural education. Experience shows that standards may be harmonized and promoted by regular, external monitoring, in some countries, in addition to internal quality assurance audits.

Policy:

That courses must be accredited/validated/recognized by an independent relevant authority, external to the university at reasonable time intervals (usually no more than 5-years), and that the UIA, in association with the relevant national organizations of higher education, develop standards for the content of an architect's professional education that are academically structured, intellectually coherent, performance-based and outcome-oriented, with procedures that are guided by good practice.

Practical Experience/Training/Internship

Definition:

Practical experience/training/internship is a directed and structured activity in the practice of architecture during architectural education and/or following receipt of a professional degree but prior to registration/licensing/certification.

Background:

To complement academic preparation in order to protect the public, applicants for registration/licensing/certification must integrate their formal education through practical training.

Policy:

That graduates of architecture will be required to have completed at least 2 years of acceptable experience/training/internship prior to registration/licensing/certification to practice as an architect (but with the objective of working towards 3 years) while allowing flexibility for equivalency.

Demonstration of Professional Knowledge and Ability

Definition:

Every applicant for registration/licensing/certification as an architect is required to demonstrate an acceptable level of professional knowledge and ability to the relevant national authority.

Background:

The public is assured of an architect's knowledge and ability only after he or she has acquired the requisite education and practical experience/training/internship, and demonstrated minimum knowledge and ability in the comprehensive practice of architecture. These qualifications have to be demonstrated by examination and/or other evidence.

Policy:

That the acquired knowledge and ability of an architect have to be proven by providing adequate evidence. This evidence must include the successful completion of at least one examination at the end of the practical experience/training/internship. Necessary components of professional practice knowledge and ability that are not subject to an examination have to be proven by other adequate evidence. These include such subjects as business administration and relevant legal requirements.

Registration/Licensing/Certification

Definition:

Registration/licensing/certification is the official legal recognition of an individual's qualification allowing her or him to practice as an architect, associated with regulations preventing unqualified persons from performing certain functions.

Background:

Given the public interest in a quality, sustainable built environment and the dangers and consequences associated with the development of that environment, it is important that architectural services are provided by properly qualified professionals for the adequate protection of the public.

Policy:

That the UIA promote the registration/licensing/certification of the function of architects in all countries. In the public interest, provision for such registration/licensing/certification should be by statute.

Procurement

Definition:

The process by which architectural services are commissioned.

Background:

Architects (through their codes of conduct) uphold the interests of their clients and society at large before their own interests. In order to ensure they have adequate resources to perform their functions to the standards required in the public interest, they are traditionally remunerated in accordance with either mandatory or recommended professional fee-scales.

There are international rules, such as the General Procurement Agreement (WTO) and the EU Services Directive, that aim to guarantee the objective and fair selection of architects. However, there has been an increasing tendency recently to select architects, for both public and private work, on the basis of price alone. Price-based selection forces architects to reduce the services provided to clients, which in turn compromises design quality and therefore the quality, amenity and social/economic value of the built environment.

Policy:

To ensure the ecologically sustainable development of the built environment and to protect the social, cultural, and economic value of society, governments should apply procurement procedures for the appointment of architects that are directed to the selection of the most suitable architect for projects. Conditional upon adequate resources being agreed among the parties, this is best achieved by one of the following methods:
- Architectural design competitions conducted in accordance with the principles defined by the UNESCO-UIA international competitions guidelines and approved by national authorities and/or architectural professional associations.
- A qualification based selection (QBS) procedure as set out in the UIA guidelines;
- Direct negotiation based on a complete brief defining the scope and quality of architectural services;

Ethics and Conduct

Definition:

A code of ethics and conduct establishes a professional standard of behavior that guides architects in the conduct of their practices. Architects should observe and follow the code of ethics and conduct for each jurisdiction in which they practice.

Background:

Rules of ethics and conduct have as their primary object the protection of the public, caring for the less powerful and the general social welfare, as well as the advancement of the interests of the profession of architecture.

Policy:

The existing UIA International Code of Ethics on Consulting Services remains in force. Member Sections of the UIA are encouraged to introduce into their own codes of ethics and conduct the recommended Accord Guidelines and a requirement that their members abide by the codes of ethics and conduct in force in the countries and jurisdictions in which they provide professional services, so long as they are not prohibited by international law or the laws of the architect's own country.

Continuing Professional Development

Definition:

Continuing Professional Development is a lifelong learning process that maintains, enhances, or increases the knowledge and continuing ability of architects.

Background:
More and more professional bodies and regulatory authorities require their members to devote time (typically at least 35 hours per year) to maintaining existing skills, broadening knowledge, and exploring new areas. This is increasingly important to keep abreast with new technologies, methods of practice, and changing social and ecological conditions. Continuing professional development may be required by professional organizations for renewal and continuation of membership.

Policy:

That UIA urge its member sections to establish regimes of continuing professional development as a duty of membership, in the public interest. Architects must be sure they are capable of providing the services they offer, and codes of conduct must oblige architects to maintain a known standard in a variety of areas described under the "Fundamental Requirements of an Architect" and in future variations thereof. In the meantime, the UIA must monitor the developments in continuing professional development for registration renewal, recommend guidelines among all nations to facilitate reciprocity and continue to develop policy on this subject.

Scope of Practice

Definition:

This is the provision of design and management services in connection with land-use planning, urban design, and building projects.

Background:

As society has evolved, the creation of the urban and built environment has become more complex. Architects have to deal with an increasingly wide range of urban, aesthetic, technical, and legal considerations. A coordinated approach to building design has proved to

be necessary to ensure that legal, technical, and practical requirements are met and that society's needs and demands are satisfied.

Policy:

That the UIA encourage and promote the continuing extension of the boundaries of architectural practice, limited only by the provisions of codes of ethics and conduct, and strive to ensure the corresponding extension of the knowledge and skills necessary to deal with any extension of boundaries.

Form of Practice

Definition:

The legal entity through which the architect provides architectural services.

Background:

Traditionally, architects have practiced as individuals, or in partnerships or in employment within public or private institutions. More recently, the demands of practice have led to various forms of association, for example: limited and unlimited liability companies, cooperative practices, university-based project offices, community architecture, although not all are allowed in all countries. These forms of association may also include members of other disciplines.

Policy:

That architects should be allowed to practice in any form legally acceptable in the country in which the service is offered, but always subject to prevailing ethical and conduct requirements. The UIA, as it deems necessary, will develop and modify its policies and standards to take account of alternative forms of practice and varied local conditions where these alternatives are thought to extend the positive and creative role of the architectural profession in the interests of society.

Practice in a Host Nation

Definition:

Practice in a host nation occurs when an individual architect or corporate entity of architects either seeks a commission or has been commissioned to design a project or offer a service in a country other than his/her/its own.

Background:

There is an interest in increasing the responsible mobility of architects and their ability to provide services in foreign jurisdictions. There is also a need to promote the awareness of local environmental, social, and cultural factors and ethical and legal standards.

Policy:

Architects providing architectural services on a project in a country in which they are not registered shall collaborate with a local architect to ensure that proper and effective understanding is given to legal, environmental, social, cultural, and heritage factors. The conditions of the association should be determined by the parties alone in accordance with UIA ethical standards and local statutes and laws.

Intellectual Property and Copyright

Definition:

Intellectual property encompasses the three legal areas of patent, copyright, and trademark. It refers to the right (sometimes guaranteed under the law of some nation states) of designers, inventors, authors, and producers, to their ideas, designs, inventions, works of authorship, and the identification of sources of products and services.

Background:

While many countries have some legal protection covering the architect's design, that protection is often inadequate. It is not unusual for the architect to discuss ideas and concepts with a prospective client, subsequently not be hired, and later find that the client has used the architect's ideas with no recompense. The intellectual property of architects is, to some extent, protected by international regulations. In the context of the GATS, this is the agreement on trade-related aspects of intellectual property rights, including trade in counterfeit goods (TRIPS). The World Copyright Convention of September 16, 1955 is also of international significance. In Europe, the Revised Berne Agreement of 1886 is binding in most states.

Policy:

That the national law of a UIA member section should entitle an architect to practice his/her profession without detriment to his/her authority and responsibility, and to retain ownership of the intellectual property and copyright of his/her work.

Role of Professional Institutes of Architects

Definition:

Professions are generally controlled by a governing body that sets standards (e.g. of education, ethical rules, and professional standards to be observed). The rules and standards are designed for the benefit of the public and not the private advantage of the members. In some countries, certain types of work are reserved to the profession by statute, not in order to favor members but because such work should be carried out only by persons with requisite education, training, standards and discipline, for the protection of the public. Institutes have been established for the advancement of architecture, promotion of knowledge and--by ensuring that their members perform to a known standard--protection of the public interest.

Background:

Depending on whether a country has protection of title or function, (or both, or neither), the role and responsibilities of professional institutes varies considerably. In some countries, the statutory bodies also represent the profession; in others, these functions are separate.

 It is customary for members of professional institutes to be expected to maintain a known standard. This is achieved by adhering to codes of conduct promulgated by the professional institutes, and fulfilling other requirements of membership, e.g. continuing professional development.

Policy

In countries where professional institutes do not exist, the UIA should encourage members of the architectural profession to form such institutes in the public interest.

Professional Institutes should seek to ensure that their members adhere to the UIA international standards, the minimum requirements of the UIA-UNESCO Architectural Education Charter, and UIA International Code of Ethics and Conduct; keep up to date their knowledge and skills as required by the list of "Fundamental Requirements" (both current, and as they evolve in the future); and generally contribute to the development of architectural culture and knowledge as well as the society they serve.

Appendix A

RESOLUTION OF ADOPTION (Number 17) OF THE UIA ACCORD ON
RECOMMENDED INTERNATIONAL STANDARDS ON PROFESSIONALISM IN
ARCHITECTURAL PRACTICE

Adopted by the XXI UIA Assembly
Beijing, China, July 28, 1999

The Assembly unanimously resolved that it adopts the Second Edition of the UIA Accord on
Recommended International Standards of Professionalism in Architectural Practice as an
advisory document intended to be used by member sections in setting and reviewing their own
standards. The Accord and Guidelines will also make it easier for UIA member sections to
negotiate mutual recognition agreements.

The Assembly asks that the Accord be transmitted to all UIA member sections with the
request for their cooperation and participation in the further development of this policy
framework for presentation at the XXII UIA Assembly (Berlin 2002).

The Assembly recognizes the mandate of Council to adopt Accord Policy Guideline
documents and commend them to the UIA member sections.

The Assembly recognizes that there are differences in the cultures, practices and conditions in
different member sections and encourages the member sections to use the documents as
advisory documents intended to be adapted to local conditions.

The Assembly acknowledges that the sovereignty of each UIA member section must be
respected in negotiations of mutual recognition agreements and notices that the guidelines are
intended to allow flexibility for principles of equivalency and reciprocity and are structured to
allow for the addition of requirements reflecting local conditions of a UIA member section.

The Assembly authorizes the UIA President and Secretary General to submit the Accord to
the World Trade Organization, to other interested institutions and organizations as the basis
for mutual recognition negotiations and to the Government of a country on the specific
request of the UIA member section of the country in question.

The Assembly requests that the Professional Practice Commission analyze all the comments
expressed during the General Assembly during its meeting in Prague (October 1999) in order
to check on whether or not it is opportune to integrate them in the documents approved by the
Beijing Assembly.

The Assembly authorizes the UIA Council to develop a policy to communicate the Accord
and Guideline documents to interested parties.

The Assembly recommends to UIA member sections that following the use of these
Standards, they inform the Commission Secretariat of their experience, in order that it can be
taken into account for the improvement and evolution of these basic documents.

Appendix B

Union Internationale des Architectes · International Union of Architects

Recommended Guidelines for the UIA Accord On Recommended International Standards of Professionalism in Architectural Practice Policy on Practice in a Host Nation

As approved by Council during the 95th Session held in Barcelona, Spain, February 26-28, 2002 and amended during the 100th Session held in Villahermosa, Tabasco, Mexico, May 26, 2004.

UIA Professional Practice Program Joint Secretariat

The American Institute of Architects	The Architectural Society of China
Co-Director Russell V. Keune, FAIA	Co-Director Xu Anzhi
1735 New York Avenue, NW	The Architectural Design and Research Institute
Washington, DC 20006	Shenzhen University
	Shenzhen, Guangdong Province
	China 518060
Telephone: 202 626 7566	Telephone: 86 755 653 4644
Facsimile: 202 626 7426	Facsimile: 86 755 653 4674

Accord Policy on Practice in a Host Nation

Architects providing architectural services on a project in a country in which they are not registered shall collaborate with a local architect to ensure that proper and effective understanding is given to legal, environmental, social, cultural, and heritage factors. The conditions of the association should be determined by the parties alone in accordance with UIA ethical standards and local statutes and laws.

Recommended Guidelines for the Accord Policy on Practice in a Host Nation

Preamble

The UIA is committed to the encouragement of bilateral and multilateral recognition agreements within the context of the General Agreement on Tariffs and Trade (GATT), The General Agreement on Trade in Services (GATS) and the World Trade Organization (WTO). Experience in the development of mutual recognition and/or free trade agreements for the architectural profession suggests that the process requires identification of gaps between the elements of the foreign professional qualifications standards and those of the local qualification standards, and the negotiation of means to bridge these gaps through establishment of equivalencies. It is a process that must recognize the sovereign right of each jurisdiction to establish its professional standards at whatever level it deems appropriate for the environmental, social, cultural, public health, safety, and welfare interests of its citizens.

The Accord acknowledges that there are differences in the standards, practices and conditions reflecting the diversity of cultures of the countries of UIA member sections and that the Accord represents a first step in an effort by representatives of the international community of architects to reach consensus on standards and practices that will best serve community interests. The UIA recognizes that bilateral and multilateral mutual recognition and/or free trade agreements may take time to negotiate and bring into operation, and therefore there is a need to provide sector specific guidelines and protocols for conditions where mutual recognition and/or free trade agreements do not yet exist.

The Accord Policy on Practice in a Host Nation is intended to include equal standing between the associated architects and provide a bridge to the time when mutual recognition and/or free trade agreements are prevalent rather than a rarity, as is now the case. The following guideline suggests provisions for a protocol recommended for adoption by UIA member sections seeking to provide an appropriate mechanism for recognizing practice in a host nation by a foreign architect.

Introduction

In most jurisdictions architects must be registered, licensed, or certified in order to practice architecture. Practice in a Host Nation covers the situation when individual architects or corporate entities of architects have been commissioned to design projects in a country in which they are not registered, licensed, or certified.

The UIA recognizes the need for the responsible mobility of architects and their ability to provide services in foreign jurisdictions. It is the goal of the UIA that an architect recognized by the relevant authority of the nation/state in any UIA member section should be recognized as being able to be registered, licensed, or certified through bilateral or multilateral agreements and be able to establish in those nation/states as an architect by the relevant authorities in the nations/states of all UIA member sections.

The UIA also recognizes a need to promote the awareness of local environmental, social, and cultural factors and ethical and legal standards. To this end, the UIA Assembly has approved the Second Edition of the UIA Accord on Recommended International Standards of Professionalism in Architectural Practice. While the Accord and related Policy Guidelines are intended to define best practice for the architectural profession and the standards to which the profession aspires, they are also intended to make it easier for interested parties to negotiate mutual recognition and/or free trade agreements allowing portability of architectural credentials and/or services.

The long established UIA International Code of Ethics on Consulting Services requires that "every consultant from a foreign country…shall associate and work harmoniously with consultants or professionals of the country where the project is located."

Guidelines for Practice in a Host Nation

It is recommended that the member sections or nation/states of the International Union of Architects adopting this guideline agree that the UIA Accord on Recommended International Standards of Professionalism in Architectural Practice (referred hereafter as the Accord) establishes a policy framework for the negotiation of agreements under which local and foreign architects collaborate.

While the UIA Accord and related guidelines attempt to establish standards for the international practice of architecture, it is recognized that there are differences in the traditions and practices of the UIA member section countries.

Architects entering into 'Practice in a Host Nation' agreements should agree 1) that arrangements affecting professional liability, insurance, the jurisdiction of the courts, and similar issues are covered by local statutes or considered business arrangements and most appropriately negotiated by the local architect, the foreign architect, and the client and should be formalized in the agreements between and among the parties; 2) that public liability, statutes, and laws affecting the conduct of the architect and the practice of architecture are matters to be appraised by and the responsibility of both architects; and 3) that the following conditions shall apply for the practice of architecture by foreign architects in local jurisdictions:

1. In this guideline an architect is a professional recognized and registered/licensed/certified by a relevant authority in a nation/state. A local architect is the entity registered/licensed/certified and practicing in the nation where the project is located. A foreign architect is the entity registered/licensed/certified and practicing in a jurisdiction/country but is not registered/licensed/certified in the jurisdiction where the project is located.

2. Where there is no mutual recognition or free trade agreement between the relevant authorities of the host country and that of the foreign architects' country:

   ☐ Foreign architects registered/licensed/certified by a relevant authority in their own countries but not in the host country should be admitted individually and permitted to practice in association with registered/licensed/certified local architects, in accordance with local laws and practices.
   ☐ Foreign architects coming from nation/states that do not have relevant authorities dealing with issues of registration/licensing/certification should be required to be subjected to the registration/licensing/certification standards in force in the nation/states where the projects are located.
   ☐ A foreign architect should not be permitted to enter into an arrangement to provide services in another jurisdiction without the meaningful and substantial participation and contribution of a local architect in the provision of the design, documentation and contract administrative services of the project. Foreign architects entering an international competition in a country where they do not hold a license should be required to enter into such an arrangement only when they win the competition and are commissioned to proceed with the project.

2.1 Foreign architects should:

   a. Be prepared to demonstrate to the national or international relevant authority that they hold a current registration/license/certification from a relevant authority of a jurisdiction, which allows them to use the title "architect" and to engage in the unlimited practice of architecture in that jurisdiction.
   b. Provide proof of their qualifications.
   c. Certify that they are not subject to any criminal/ethical conviction.

2.2 Promptly after being selected as architect for a project in which a foreign architect is to be involved, the local architect should be required to provide a document to the relevant authority establishing the local architect's relationship with the foreign architects to include their qualifications, and a description of the specific project for which this arrangement has been made.

2.3 Foreign and local architects should make sure that in their collaboration they both have the necessary expertise and experience to meet the needs of the project.

2.4 Professional services rendered by the associated architects should jointly and severally be rendered by the foreign and qualified local architects involved in the project.

2.5 In any documents and when claiming credit for the project, the local architect and the foreign architect shall accurately represent their respective responsibilities on the project.

2.6 Upon request from a local relevant authority, it is expected that the foreign relevant authority of the UIA member section will agree to confirm the status of the foreign architect as suggested in paragraph 2.1.

2.7 A foreign architect should be required to agree to follow the laws, codes of ethics and conduct, building codes, etc. of the local jurisdiction.

2.8 Foreign and local architects forming collaborations should be required to enter into formal, fair and equitable agreements that uphold the ethical standards of the UIA. Numerous model documents and books have been developed that cover the principles involved and issues to be considered when developing an agreement between collaborating architects.

3. Where a mutual recognition agreement exists between the relevant authorities of two countries, this guideline is not relevant.

Practice in a Host Nation Drafting Panel

James A. Scheeler, Chairman
Luis M. Rossi
Carlos Maximiliano B. Fayet
Andreas Gottlieb Hempel
Tillman Prinz
Dato' Hahi Esa Bin Mohamed
Artur Jasinski
Edward D'Silva
Susan M. Allen

Appendix C: AIA International Contract Documents

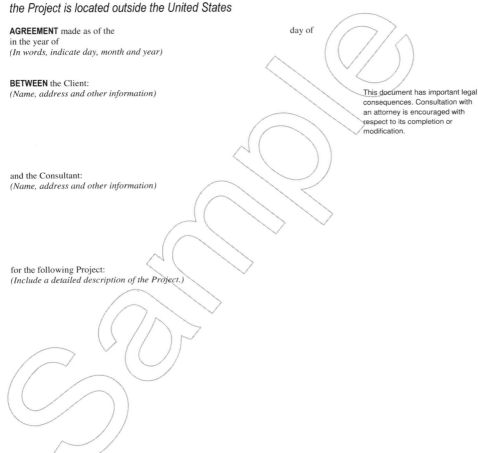

▲AIA® Document B161™ – 2002

Standard Form of Agreement Between Client and Consultant *for use where*
the Project is located outside the United States

AGREEMENT made as of the
in the year of
(In words, indicate day, month and year)

day of

BETWEEN the Client:
(Name, address and other information)

This document has important legal
consequences. Consultation with
an attorney is encouraged with
respect to its completion or
modification.

and the Consultant:
(Name, address and other information)

for the following Project:
(Include a detailed description of the Project.)

The Client and Consultant agree as follows:

ARTICLE 1   INITIAL INFORMATION
This Agreement is based on the following information and assumptions:

§ 1.1 PROJECT PARAMETERS
§ 1.1.1 The objective or use is:
(Identify or describe, if appropriate, the proposed use or Project goals.)

§ 1.1.2 The site is:
(Identify or describe, if appropriate, size, location, dimensions or other pertinent information, such as geotechnical reports about the site.)

§ 1.1.3 The Client's Program is:
(Identify documentation or state the manner in which the program will be developed.)

§ 1.1.4 The pertinent legal information is:
(Identify information such as land surveys, legal descriptions and restrictions of the site.)

§ 1.1.5 The Client's budget for the Cost of the Work is:

§ 1.1.6 The time considerations are:
(Identify, if appropriate, milestone dates, duration or fast-track scheduling. Coordinate with Exhibit E, Consultant's Services Matrix, if used.)

§ 1.1.7 The proposed procurement or delivery method for the Project is:
(Identify the method, such as competitive bid, negotiated contract, or construction management.)

§ 1.1.8 Other considerations are:
(Identify special characteristics or needs of the Project, such as energy, environmental or historic preservation requirements.)

§ 1.2 PROJECT TEAM
§ 1.2.1 The Client's Designated Representative, authorized to act on behalf of the Client in all matters, is:
(Name, address and other information)

§ 1.2.2 The Local Architect to be retained by the Client is:
(Name, address and other information)

§ 1.2.3 The Cost Consultant to be retained by the Client is:
(Name, address and other information)

§ 1.2.4 Other Project Team members to be retained by the Client are:
(List disciplines and, if known, identify members by name and address.)

§ 1.2.5 The subconsultants to be retained at the Consultant's expense are:
(List disciplines and, if known, identify subconsultants by name and address.)

§ 1.2.6 The Client shall provide services of consultants other than those designated in Section 1.2.5 or shall authorize the Local Architect or Consultant to provide them as a Change in Services when such services are requested by the Consultant and are reasonably required by the scope of the Project.

ARTICLE 2 SERVICES PROVIDED BY THE CONSULTANT

§ **2.1** The Consultant shall consult with the Client and Local Architect, review applicable design criteria with the Local Architect, attend project meetings, communicate with members of the Project Team and issue progress reports. The Consultant shall coordinate the services provided by the Consultant and its subconsultants with those services provided by the Client and Client's consultants.

§ **2.2** The Consultant shall prepare and periodically update the Consultant's Services Schedule that shall identify milestone dates for decisions required of the Client, design services provided by the Consultant, completion of documentation provided by the Consultant and anticipated commencement of construction and Substantial Completion of the Work as defined in Article 8.

§ **2.3** In accordance with the Consultant's Services Schedule, the Consultant shall make presentations to explain the design of the Project to the Client. The Consultant shall submit design documents to the Client at intervals appropriate to the design process for purposes of evaluation and approval by the Client. The Consultant shall be entitled to rely upon approvals received from the Client in the further development of design.

ARTICLE 3 SERVICES PROVIDED BY THE CLIENT

§ **3.1** The Client shall provide a program setting forth the Client's objectives, schedule, constraints and criteria, including space requirements and relationships, special equipment, systems and site requirements.

§ **3.2** The Client shall retain a qualified Local Architect to provide the services described in Article 4. These services shall be incorporated into the Client's agreement with the Local Architect.

§ **3.3** The Client shall provide surveys to describe physical characteristics, legal limitations and utility locations for the site of the Project and a written legal description of the site. The surveys and legal information shall include, as applicable, grades and lines of streets, alleys, pavements and adjoining properties and structures; adjacent drainage; rights-of-way, restrictions, easements, encroachments, zoning, deed restrictions, boundaries and contours of the site; locations, dimensions and necessary data with respect to existing buildings, other improvements and trees; and information concerning available utility services and lines, both public and private, above and below grade, including inverts and depths. All the information on the survey shall be referenced to a Project benchmark.

§ **3.4** When requested by the Consultant, the Client shall provide services of geotechnical engineers, which may include but are not limited to test borings, test pits, determinations of soil bearing values, percolation tests, evaluations of hazardous materials, ground corrosion tests and resistivity tests, including necessary operations for anticipating subsoil conditions, with reports and appropriate recommendations.

§ **3.5** When the program requirements have been sufficiently identified, the Cost Consultant employed by the Client shall prepare a preliminary estimate of the Cost of the Work. The Cost Consultant shall be experienced in cost estimating in the locality of the Project. As the design process progresses through the end of the preparation of the Construction Documents, the Cost Consultant shall update and refine the preliminary estimate of the Cost of the Work. The Cost Consultant shall advise the Client and Consultant of any adjustments to previous estimates of the Cost of the Work indicated by changes in project requirements or general market conditions.

§ **3.6** If the estimated cost exceeds the budget, the Client shall:
  .1 increase the budget for the Cost of the Work
  .2 cooperate in revising the Project scope and quality as required to reduce the Cost of the Work and authorize a Change in Services in accordance with Section 6.2
  .3 terminate the Project in accordance with Section 6.6

§ **3.7** Unless otherwise provided for in this Agreement, the Client shall provide tests, inspections and reports required by law or the Construction Documents, such as structural, mechanical and chemical tests, tests for air and water pollution, and tests for hazardous materials.

ARTICLE 4   SERVICES OF THE LOCAL ARCHITECT

§ 4.1 The Client shall retain a qualified Local Architect who shall be the Architect of Record under applicable law and who shall be contractually obligated to the Client to provide the following services to support the work of the Consultant. The Consultant shall be entitled to rely upon the adequacy and accuracy of the services provided by the Local Architect.

§ 4.2 The Local Architect shall attend meetings between the Consultant and Client to maintain awareness of the status of the Project. The Local Architect shall advise the Consultant and Client of any local requirements or potential issues that may affect the Project. During meetings, the Local Architect shall provide translation to and from English as necessary.

§ 4.3 The Local Architect shall identify applicable codes, regulations and requirements affecting the Project, including those of entities providing utilities and services to the site and those related to cultural and religious issues affecting the Project. The Local Architect shall inform the Consultant as to the application of these codes, regulations and requirements to this Project. The Local Architect shall forward copies of English language versions of all such material to the Consultant. If English language versions are not available, the Local Architect shall provide the content of the applicable portions to the Consultant by written translation, diagrams or sketches.

§ 4.4 The Local Architect shall provide copies of maps and photographs of the site and its surroundings to familiarize the Consultant and Consultant's home office staff with the site.

§ 4.5 The Local Architect shall meet and correspond with all authorities and organizations whose agreement is legally required for the approval of the Project design, construction and occupancy to determine their requirements for this Project and to assist the Client in obtaining the necessary agreements and approvals. The Local Architect shall submit such applications and materials as are required. If drawings prepared by the Consultant are required for such submittals, the Local Architect shall advise the Consultant as to any requirements as to format, scales, colors and specific information to be shown.

§ 4.6 If the Agreement, the Client or any local or national authority requires that drawings, reports, letters or other material prepared by the Consultant be submitted in a language other than English, the Local Architect shall translate and prepare such material in the finished form required for submission. In the case of drawings, the Local Architect shall add the translated material to the drawings provided by the Consultant. The Local Architect shall translate into English any letters or other materials received by the Consultant from the Client or from national or local authorities in connection with the Project.

§ 4.7 The Local Architect shall advise the Consultant of the availability of construction materials and their relative costs at the location of the Project, and of any special issues related to their use at that location.

§ 4.8 As the Consultant's work proceeds, the Local Architect shall review the Consultant's sketches, drawings and other presentations for each phase of services to determine that the design, as proposed, will satisfy the Client's program. The Local Architect shall inform the Consultant promptly of any necessary changes.

§ 4.9 The Local Architect shall provide drafting and conference room space and administrative support for the Consultant's staff during visits to the country.

§ 4.10 The Local Architect shall, in addition, provide the following services:
(*If other services are required of the Local Architect, describe them here.*)

ARTICLE 5   RESPONSIBILITIES OF THE PARTIES
§ 5.1 CLIENT
§ 5.1.1 The Client shall provide full and timely information regarding requirements for, and limitations on, the Project and shall render decisions to avoid delay in the orderly and sequential progress of the Consultant's services.

§ 5.1.3 The Client shall review and provide approvals in accordance with Exhibit E, Consultant's Services Matrix. Such approvals shall be in writing.

§ 5.2 CONSULTANT

§ 5.2.1 The services performed by the Consultant shall be as described in Articles 2 and 4 and as indicated in Section 9.2.

§ 5.2.2 The Consultant's standard of care shall be to exercise reasonable skill, care and diligence in the performance of its obligations under this Agreement.

§ 5.2.3 Except with the Client's knowledge and consent, the Consultant shall not knowingly engage in any activity, or accept any employment, interest or contribution that would, or would reasonably appear to, compromise the Consultant's professional judgment with respect to this Project. The Consultant shall not engage in any activity that would, or would reasonably appear to, conflict with laws or regulations applicable to the Consultant's services.

§ 5.2.4 The Consultant shall be entitled to rely upon the accuracy, timeliness and completeness of services and information furnished by the Client, the Local Architect and the Client's Consultants.

ARTICLE 6   TERMS AND CONDITIONS
§ 6.1 INSTRUMENTS OF SERVICE

§ 6.1.1 Drawings, Specifications, documentation and other materials, including those in electronic form, prepared by the Consultant and Consultant's subconsultants are Instruments of Service for use solely with respect to this Project. The Consultant and Consultant's subconsultants shall be deemed the authors and owners of their respective Instruments of Service and shall retain all rights accorded under applicable law, including copyrights.

§ 6.1.2 Upon execution of this Agreement, the Consultant grants to the Client a nonexclusive license to reproduce the Consultant's Instruments of Service solely for purposes of constructing, using and maintaining the Project, provided that the Client shall comply with all obligations, including prompt payment of all sums when due, under this Agreement. No other license or right shall be deemed granted or implied under this Agreement. The Client shall not assign or otherwise transfer any license herein to another party without the prior written agreement of the Consultant.

§ 6.1.3 The Client shall not use the Instruments of Service for future additions or alterations to this Project or for other projects, unless the Client obtains the prior written agreement of the Consultant and Consultant's subconsultants. Any unauthorized use of the Instruments of Service shall be at the Client's sole risk and without liability to the Consultant and Consultant's subconsultants.

§ 6.2 CHANGE IN SERVICES

§ 6.2.1 The Consultant shall be entitled to an appropriate adjustment in the Consultant's Services Schedule and Payment as described in Article 7 and to any Reimbursable Expense described in Section 7.10, should the Consultant's services be affected by circumstances which may include, but are not limited to, the following:

- .1 Changes to instructions or approvals previously given by the Client that require revisions in the Instruments of Service
- .2 Enactment or revision of codes, laws, regulations, or official interpretations that require changes to previously prepared Instruments of Service
- .3 Decisions of the Client not rendered in a timely manner
- .4 Significant changes in the Project, including but not limited to size, quality, complexity, the Client's schedule or budget, or procurement method
- .5 Failure of performance on the part of the Client, the Local Architect, or Client's Consultants or contractors
- .6 Preparation for and attendance at a public hearing, a dispute resolution proceeding, or a legal proceeding, except where the Consultant is a party thereto
- .7 Change in the information contained in Section 1.2
- .8 Providing more than   (   ) reviews of an individual Shop Drawing, Product Data item, sample or similar submittal of the Contractor
- .9 Providing more than   (   ) site visits during the construction phase
- .10 Reviewing a Contractor's submittal out of sequence from the submittal schedule agreed to by the Consultant

.11 Responding to the Contractor's requests for information where such information is available to the Contractor from a careful study and comparison of the Construction Documents, field conditions, other Client-provided information, Contractor-prepared coordination drawings, or prior Project correspondence or documentation

.12 Processing Change Orders requiring evaluation of proposals, including preparation or revision of the Contract Documents

.13 Providing consultation concerning replacement of Work resulting from fire or other cause during construction

.14 Evaluating an extensive number of claims submitted by the Client's Consultants, the Contractor or others in connection with the Work

.15 Evaluating substitutions or changes proposed by the Client, Client's Consultants or Contractors and making subsequent revisions to Instruments of Service

.16 Preparing design and documentation for alternate bids or proposals requested by the Client

.17 Providing Construction Phase Services 60 days after the date of Substantial Completion of the Work

§ 6.3 MEDIATION

§ 6.3.1 The Consultant and Client shall endeavor to resolve claims, disputes and other matters in question between them through mediation, which shall be conducted by a mutually selected mediator who is fluent in English.

§ 6.3.2 The parties shall equally share mediation costs and filing fees. The mediation shall be held in the place where the Project is located, unless another location is mutually agreed upon. Mediation proceedings shall be confidential. Agreements reached in mediation shall be enforceable as settlement agreements in any court having jurisdiction thereof.

§ 6.4 ARBITRATION

§ 6.4.1 Claims, disputes and other matters in question between the parties that are not resolved through mediation shall be decided by arbitration unless the parties mutually agree otherwise. Arbitration shall be in accordance with rules of the United Nations Commission on International Trade Law (UNCITRAL) in effect as of the date of this Agreement. The demand for arbitration shall be filed in writing with the other party to this Agreement and with the UNCITRAL.

§ 6.4.2 A demand for arbitration shall be made within a reasonable time after the claim, dispute or other matter in which question has arisen. In no event shall the demand for arbitration be made after the date when institution of legal or equitable proceedings based on such claim, dispute or other matter in question would be barred by any applicable statute or the provisions of Section 6.5.3.

§ 6.4.3 The arbitration proceeding shall be conducted in the English language and shall take place in a neutral location to be determined by the arbitrator(s).

§ 6.4.4 Any award rendered by the arbitrator(s) shall be final, and judgment may be entered upon it in any court having jurisdiction. This Agreement and any award rendered under it shall be governed by the Convention on the Recognition and Enforcement of Foreign Arbitration Awards.

§ 6.5 MISCELLANEOUS PROVISIONS

§ 6.5.1 This Agreement shall be governed by the law of the principal place of business of the Consultant, unless otherwise provided in Section 9.3. Language in this Agreement shall be interpreted in accordance with the standard usage of English in the United States.

§ 6.5.2 The Client and Consultant, respectively, bind themselves, their partners, successors, assigns and representatives to the other party to this Agreement and to the partners, successors, assigns and legal representatives of such other party with respect to all covenants of this Agreement. Neither the Client nor Consultant shall assign this Agreement without the written consent of the other.

§ 6.5.3 The Consultant and Consultant's subconsultants shall not be liable for any loss or damage unless a claim is formally made upon the Consultant before the expiration of six years after the date of final completion of the Consultant's services on the Project or the date of Substantial Completion of the Project, whichever is earlier, or such earlier date as may be prescribed by applicable law.

§ 6.5.4 To the maximum extent permitted by the law, the Consultant's and Consultant's subconsultant's liability to the Client for any loss or damage shall be limited to the amount of applicable insurance coverage available to pay the award at the time of settlement or judgment or, in the event of an uninsured claim, to the amount of payment received by the Consultant under this Agreement.

§ 6.6 TERMINATION OR SUSPENSION

§ 6.6.1 Failure of the Client to make payments to the Consultant in accordance with this Agreement shall be considered cause for termination or, at the Consultant's option, cause for suspension of performance of services under this Agreement. In such event, the Consultant shall have the right to immediately withhold the Consultant's Instruments of Service without notice. Prior to suspending services, the Consultant shall give seven days written notice to the Client. In the event of a suspension of services due to failure of the Client to make payments to the Consultant, the Consultant shall have no liability to the Client for delay or damage caused to the Client because of such suspension of services. Before resuming services, the Consultant shall be paid all sums due prior to suspension and any expenses incurred in the interruption and resumption of the Consultant's services. The Consultant's fees for the remaining services and the time schedules shall be equitably adjusted.

§ 6.6.2 If the Client, for more than 30 consecutive days, suspends the Project, the Consultant shall be paid for services performed prior to notice of such suspension. When the Project is resumed, the Consultant shall be paid for expenses incurred as a result of the interruption and resumption of the Consultant's services. The Consultant's fees for the remaining services and the time schedules shall be equitably adjusted.

§ 6.6.3 If the Project is suspended or the Consultant's services are suspended for more than 90 consecutive days, the Consultant may terminate this Agreement by giving not less than seven days written notice.

§ 6.6.4 This Agreement may be terminated by either party upon not less than seven days written notice should the other party fail substantially to perform in accordance with the terms of this Agreement through no fault of the party initiating the termination.

§ 6.6.5 In the event of termination not the fault of the Consultant, the Consultant shall be entitled to payment for services performed prior to termination, together with Reimbursable Expenses then due. Additionally, the Consultant shall be paid for expenses directly attributable to termination for which the Consultant is not otherwise paid, plus an amount for the Consultant's anticipated profit on the value of the services not performed by the Consultant.

ARTICLE 7 PAYMENTS TO THE CONSULTANT

§ 7.1 For the Consultant's services as described in this Agreement, payment shall be made in United States dollars, and fees shall be computed as follows:

§ 7.2 If the services of the Consultant are changed as described in Section 6.2, the Consultant's payments shall be equitably adjusted in conformance with the Consultant's Table of Hourly Rates, Exhibit G.

§ 7.3 For a Change in Services of the Consultant's subconsultants, payments shall be computed as a multiple of ( ) times the amounts billed to the Consultant for such services.

§ 7.4 For Reimbursable Expenses as described in Section 7.10, payments shall be computed as a multiple of ( ) times the expenses incurred by the Consultant, the Consultant's employees and subconsultants. Reimbursable Expenses shall be paid in United States dollars and computed at a conversion rate in effect at the time the expense is incurred.

§ 7.5 The hourly rates and multiples for services of the Consultant and Consultant's subconsultants as set forth in this Agreement shall be adjusted in accordance with their normal salary review practices or as agreed upon between the Client and the Consultant.

§ 7.6 An initial payment of   Dollars ($) shall be made upon execution of this Agreement and is the minimum payment under this Agreement. It shall be credited to the Client's account at final payment. Subsequent payments for services shall be made monthly and, where applicable, shall be in proportion to services performed on the basis set forth in this Agreement.

§ 7.7 Payments are due and payable ( ) days from the date of the Consultant's invoice. Amounts unpaid ( ) days after the invoice date shall bear interest at the rate entered below. *(Insert rate of interest agreed upon.)*

§ 7.8 If the services covered by this Agreement have not been completed within ( ) months of the date hereof through no fault of the Consultant, extension of the Consultant's services beyond that time shall be paid as provided in Section 7.2.

§ 7.9 Payments on account of services rendered and for Reimbursable Expenses incurred shall be made monthly upon presentation of the Consultant's statement of services.

§ 7.10 Reimbursable Expenses are in addition to fees for the services and include expenses incurred by the Consultant and Consultant's employees and subconsultants directly related to the Project. These Reimbursable Expenses are identified as follows:

.1 Transportation in connection with the Project, authorized out-of-town travel as further described in Exhibit F, meals and lodging, and telecommunications
.2 Reproductions, printing of electronic drawings, standard form documents, postage, couriers, and handling and delivery of Instruments of Service
.3 Expense of overtime work requiring higher than regular rates if authorized in advance by the Client
.4 Renderings, models and mock-ups requested by the Client
.5 Expense of professional liability insurance requested by the Client dedicated exclusively to this Project, or the expense of additional insurance coverage or limits in excess of that normally carried by the Consultant and Consultant's subconsultants
.6 Other similar direct Project-related expenditures

§ 7.11 Sale, value added, duties, withholdings and other government imposed taxes on the amounts payable for the Consultant's services and Reimbursable Expenses are not included in the Consultant's payment hereunder. No deductions shall be made from payments to the Consultant because of such obligations.

§ 7.12 The Client shall be solely obligated to pay and remit to the appropriate governmental authority such sales, value added, duties, withholding or other taxes on the Consultant's services without reduction of the Consultant's payment. The Client shall provide the Consultant photocopies of all forms sent to such governmental authorities evidencing payment of these taxes.

§ 7.13 Payments for services and Reimbursable Expenses shall be transmitted by the Client as follows: *(Insert instructions for payments, wire transfer, etc.)*

ARTICLE 8 DEFINITIONS
§ 8.1 Construction Documents. Drawings, Specifications and Contract Documents prepared by the Consultant or Local Architect that set forth, in detail, the requirements for construction of the Project.

§ 8.2 Contractor. Entity responsible for construction of the Project.

§ 8.3 Cost of the Work. The total cost or, to the extent the Project is not completed, the estimated cost to the Client of all elements of the Project designed or specified by the Project Team. Cost of the Work does not include the compensation of the Consultant or Local Architect or the subconsultants of either, the costs of the land and financing, or other costs that are the responsibility of the Client.

§ 8.4 Day. "Day" as used in the documents shall mean calendar day unless otherwise specifically defined.

§ 8.5 Payment. Distribution of money in return for services or other obligations.

§ 8.6 Product Data. Product Data are illustrations, standard schedules, performance charts, instructions, brochures, diagrams, and other information furnished by the Contractor to illustrate materials or equipment for some portion of the Work.

§ 8.7 Samples. Samples are physical examples that illustrate materials, equipment or workmanship and establish standards by which the Work will be judged.

§ 8.8 Shop Drawings. Shop Drawings are drawings, diagrams, schedules and other data specially prepared for the Work by the Contractor or a subcontractor, subsubcontractor, manufacturer, supplier or distributor to illustrate some portion of the Work.

§ 8.9 Substantial Completion. Substantial Completion is the stage in the progress of the Work when the Work or designated portion thereof is sufficiently complete in accordance with the contractual requirements so that the Client can occupy or utilize the Work for its intended use.

§ 8.10 Work. Work means the construction and services required by the contractual requirements, whether completed or partially completed, and includes all other labor, materials, equipment and services provided, or to be provided, by the Contractor to fulfill the Contractor's obligations. The Work may constitute the whole or a part of the Project.

ARTICLE 9 COMPONENTS OF THE AGREEMENT AND OTHER SPECIAL TERMS AND CONDITIONS
§ 9.1 This Agreement consists of this AIA Document B161™–2002, Standard Form of Agreement Between Client and Consultant, and:
(List other documents, if any, forming part of the Agreement.)

§ 9.2 Services and Additional Information
(Check off the exhibits delineating the Consultant's Scope of Services. List any other documents in the space below.):

- ☐ B161™–2002/Exhibit A, Evaluation and Planning Services
- ☐ B161™–2002/Exhibit B, Schematic Design/Design Development Services
- ☐ B161™–2002/Exhibit C, Construction Documents Services
- ☐ B161™–2002/Exhibit D, Construction Procurement/Construction Services
- ☐ B161™–2002/Exhibit E, Consultant's Services Matrix
- ☐ B161™–2002/Exhibit F, Projected Travel Costs
- ☐ B161™–2002/Exhibit G, Table of Hourly Rates

§ 9.3 Special terms and conditions that modify this Agreement are as follows:

§ 9.4 This Agreement represents the entire and integrated Agreement between the Client and Consultant and supersedes all prior negotiations, representations or agreements, either written or oral. This Agreement may be amended only by written instrument signed by both the Client and Consultant.

This Agreement entered into as of the day and year first written above.

CLIENT *(Signature)*   **CONSULTANT** *(Signature)*

(Printed name and title)   *(Printed name and title)*

CAUTION: You should sign an original AIA Contract Document, on which this text appears in RED. An original assures that changes will not be obscured.

▓AIA® Document B161™ – 2002 Exhibit A

Evaluation and Planning Services

§ A.1 The Consultant shall provide a preliminary evaluation of the information furnished by the Client under this Agreement. The Consultant shall review such information to ascertain that it is consistent with the requirements of the Project and shall notify the Client of any other information or consulting services that may be reasonably needed for the Project.

§ A.2 The Consultant shall provide a preliminary evaluation of the Client's site for the Project based on the information provided by the Client of site conditions and the Client's program, schedule and budget for the Cost of the Work.

§ A.3 The Consultant shall review the Client's proposed method of contracting for construction services and shall notify the Client of anticipated impacts such method may have on the Project.

CLIENT *(initials)* _____   **CONSULTANT** *(initials)* _____

▓AIA® Document B161™ – 2002 Exhibit B

Schematic Design/Design Development Services

§ B.1 SCHEMATIC DESIGN SERVICES
§ B.1.1 The Consultant shall provide, with the assistance of the Local Architect, Schematic Design Documents based on the mutually agreed-upon program and schedule. The documents shall establish the conceptual design of the Project, illustrating the scale of and relationship among the Project components. The Schematic Design Documents shall include a conceptual site plan, if appropriate, and preliminary building plans, sections and elevations.

§ B.2 DESIGN DEVELOPMENT SERVICES
§ B.2.1 The Consultant shall provide, with the assistance of the Local Architect, Design Development Documents based on the approved Schematic Design Documents. The Design Development Documents shall illustrate and describe the refinement of the design of the Project, establishing the scope, relationships, forms, size and appearance of the Project by means of plans, sections and elevations, selected construction details and equipment layouts. The Design Development Documents shall include specifications that identify major materials and systems and establish, in general, their quality levels.

CLIENT *(initials)* _____   CONSULTANT *(initials)* _____

AIA Document B161™ – 2002 Exhibit C

Construction Documents Services

§ **C.1** The Consultant shall provide, with the assistance of the Local Architect, Construction Documents based on the approved Design Development Documents. The Construction Documents shall set forth in detail the requirements for construction of the Project. The Construction Documents shall include drawings and specifications that establish in detail the quality levels of materials and systems required for the Project.

CLIENT *(initials)* _____   **CONSULTANT** *(initials)* _____

◢▰AIA® Document B161™ – 2002 Exhibit D

Construction Procurement/Construction Services

§ D.1 CONSTRUCTION PROCUREMENT SERVICES
§ D.1.1 The Consultant shall provide Construction Procurement Services as described below:
(Insert scope text for procurement services, depending upon delivery method.)

§ D.1.2 All Construction Procurement Services other than those required under AIA Document B161–2002 shall be performed at a location selected by the Consultant.

§ D.2 CONSTRUCTION SERVICES
§ D.2.1 GENERAL ADMINISTRATION
§ D.2.1.1 The Consultant shall provide construction services as set forth within this exhibit, which shall be incorporated as part of the Contract between the Client and Contractor. Modifications, additions or deletions to the provisions, when incorporated into the Agreement between the Client and Contractor, shall be enforceable under this Agreement only to the extent that they are consistent with the Agreement and are approved in writing by the Consultant.

§ D.2.1.2 The Consultant shall be a representative of, and shall advise and consult with, the Client during the provision of the Construction Services. The Consultant shall have authority to act on behalf of the Client only to the extent provided in this Agreement.

§ D.2.1.3 The Consultant shall review and respond to properly prepared requests presented in a timely manner by the Contractor for additional information about the Construction Documents.

§ D.2.1.4 Upon written request of either the Client or Contractor, the Consultant shall interpret and decide matters concerning the performance of the Client and Contractor under the requirements of the Construction Documents. The Consultant's response to such requests shall be made in writing and in a timely manner. The Consultant shall render initial decisions on claims, disputes or other matters in question between the Client and Contractor.

§ D.2.2 EVALUATIONS OF THE WORK
§ D.2.2.1 The Consultant, as a representative of the Client, shall visit the site at intervals as agreed to by the Client and Consultant to (1) become generally familiar with and to keep the Client informed about the design quality of the portion of the Work completed; (2) endeavor to guard the Client against defects and deficiencies in the Work; and (3) determine in general if the Work is being performed in a manner indicating that the Work, when fully completed, will be in accordance with the Construction Documents. However, the Consultant shall not be required to make exhaustive or continuous on-site inspections to check the quality or quantity of the Work. The Consultant shall not have control over, charge of or responsibility for the construction means, methods, techniques, sequences or procedures, or for safety precautions and programs in connection with the Work, since these are solely the Contractor's rights and responsibilities. Nor shall the Consultant be responsible for acts or omissions of the Contractor, Subcontractors, or their agents or employees or of any other persons or entities performing portions of the Work.

§ D.2.2.2 The Consultant shall, at all times, have access to the Work wherever it is in preparation or progress.

§ D.2.2.3 The Client shall endeavor to communicate with the Contractor through the Consultant about matters arising out of or relating to the Construction Documents. Communications by and with the Consultant's subconsultants shall be through the Consultant.

§ D.2.2.4 The Consultant shall have the authority to reject Work that does not conform to the Construction Documents. Whenever the Consultant considers it necessary or advisable, the Consultant will have authority to require inspection or testing of the Work, whether or not such Work is fabricated, installed or completed. However, neither this authority of the Consultant, nor a decision made in good faith either to exercise or not to exercise such authority, shall give rise to a duty

1

or responsibility of the Consultant to the Contractor, subcontractors, material and equipment suppliers, their agents or employees or other persons or entities performing portions of the Work.

§ D.2.3 CERTIFICATION OF PAYMENTS TO THE CONTRACTOR

Unless the Client has retained a Cost Consultant identified in Section 1.3.3 to provide such review and certification, the Consultant shall review and certify the amounts due the Contractor and shall issue Certificates for Payment in such amounts.

§ D.2.4 SUBMITTALS

§ D.2.4.1 The Consultant shall review and approve or take other appropriate action upon the Contractor's submittals, such as Shop Drawings, Product Data and Samples, but only for the limited purpose of checking for conformance with information given and the design concept expressed in the Construction Documents. Review of such submittals is not conducted for the purpose of determining the accuracy and completeness of details, such as dimensions and quantities, or for substantiating instructions for installation or performance of equipment or systems. The Consultant's review shall not constitute approval of safety precautions, construction means, methods, techniques, sequences or procedures. The Consultant's approval of a specific item shall not indicate approval of an assembly of which the item is a component.

§ D.2.4.2 The Consultant shall maintain a record of submittals and copies of submittals supplied by the Contractor.

§ D.2.4.3 The Consultant shall be entitled to rely upon the adequacy, accuracy and completeness of the services, certifications or approvals performed by any consultants retained by the Contractor.

§ D.2.5 CHANGES IN THE WORK

§ D.2.5.1 The Consultant shall prepare Change Orders for the Client's approval and execution. The Consultant may authorize minor changes in the Work not involving an adjustment in Contract Sum or an extension of Contract Time that are consistent with the intent of the Construction Documents.

§ D.2.5.2 The Consultant shall review requests by the Client or Contractor for changes in the Work when such requests are accompanied by sufficient supporting data and information to permit the Consultant to make a reasonable determination without extensive investigation or preparation of additional drawings or specifications.

§ D.2.5.3 If the Consultant determines that implementation of the requested changes would result in a material change to the Contract, the Client may authorize further investigation of such change. Upon such authorization, and based upon information furnished by the Contractor, if any, the Consultant shall obtain from the Cost Consultant an estimate of the additional cost and time that might result from such change, and shall include any additional costs attributable to a Change in Services of the Consultant. The Consultant shall then incorporate those estimates into a Change Order for the Client's execution or negotiation with the Contractor.

§ D.2.5.4 The Consultant shall maintain records relative to changes in the Work.

§ D.2.6 PROJECT COMPLETION

§ D.2.6.1 The Consultant shall conduct inspections to determine the date or dates of Substantial Completion and the date of final completion; shall receive from the Contractor and forward to the Client for the Client's review and records, written warranties and related documents required by the Construction Documents and assembled by the Contractor; and shall issue a final Certificate for Payment based upon a final inspection indicating that, to the best of the Consultant's knowledge and belief, the Work complies with the requirements of the Construction Documents.

§ D.2.6.2 The Consultant's inspection shall be conducted with the Client's Designated Representative to check for conformance of the Work with the requirements of the Construction Documents and to review and amend, if appropriate, the list submitted by the Contractor of Work to be completed or corrected.

§ D.2.6.3 When the Work is found to be substantially complete, the Consultant shall inform the Client about the balance of the Contract Sum remaining to be paid to the Contractor, including any amounts needed to be paid for final completion or correction of the Work.

CLIENT *(initials)* _____   CONSULTANT *(initials)* _____

2

AIA® Document B161™ – 2002 Exhibit E

Consultant's Services Matrix

§ E.1 The Consultant shall perform its work in accordance with the scope and schedule outlined below.

§ E.2 The Consultant shall not be responsible for delays due to causes outside the Consultant's control. Should the schedule extend beyond the timeframes described below, the Consultant shall be entitled to an adjustment in its compensation unless the extension is a direct result of its failure to adhere to provisions in this Agreement. This schedule has been mutually determined by the Client and Consultant and shall be modified only by mutual agreement of the Consultant and Client.

Legend:

Primary Responsibility	= P
Support Responsibility	= S
No Responsibility	= N

Pre-Design Services	Client	Consultant	Local Architect	Not Applicable	Reference Note No.	Schedule
Project management						
Project administration						
Site investigation and analysis						
Utilities investigation						
Compilation of site surveys						
Compilation of existing conditions						
Soils investigation coordination						
Final program budget for construction cost						
Presentations to client						
Preparation of project concept diagrams						
(insert deliverable products)						
(insert deliverable products)						
(insert deliverable products)						
(insert deliverable products)						
Preparation of detailed building program						
Zoning/Planning/Calculations						
Final presentations						

Insert notes as referenced within the matrix:

CLIENT *(initials)* _____   **CONSULTANT** *(initials)* _____

1

Appendices

Schematic Design (SD)s	Client	Consultant	Local Architect	Not Applicable	Reference Note No.	Schedule
Project management						
Project administration						
DD mockup and cartoon set						
Client and team coordination						
Client conferences						
Special presentations						
Refine design phasing schedule						
Evaluate, integrate construction schedule/phasing						
Planning and zoning analysis						
Code/Life safety analysis						
Coordinate civil engineers and soil testing						
Develop architectural forms and select materials						
Develop interior and support spaces						
Develop structural and MEP systems						
Interim progress presentations						
Review interim cost plan						
Preparation of SD Documents						
(insert deliverable products)						
Prepare and distribute engineering backgrounds						
Coordinate MEP and structural services						
Coordinate other project consultants						
Coordinate special photos, renderings, models						
Collate complete SD documents						
Prepare and evaluate final preliminary estimate						
Present schematic documents						
Review SD with local agencies						
Accounting/Invoicing/Disbursements						

Insert notes as referenced within the matrix:

CLIENT *(initials)* _____   **CONSULTANT** *(initials)* _____

2

Legend:

Primary Responsibility	= P
Support Responsibility	= S
No Responsibility	= N

Design Development (DD)	Client	Consultant	Local Architect	Not Applicable	Reference Note No.	Schedule
Project management						
Project administration						
Participate in client and team conferences						
Update project schedule, phasing approach						
Schedule and conduct user and client meetings						
Review and confirm space allocations, layouts						
Develop exterior and interior design concept options						
Curtainwalls						
Wall sections						
Landscape and site design						
Primary public lobbies and corridors						
Secondary public lobbies and corridors						
Selection of exterior and interior materials						
Signage						
Prepare room data sheets						
Coordinate engineer services (SE, MEP, CE)						
Coordinate other consultant services						
Review interim cost plan						
Present interim documents						
Preparation of DD documents						
(insert list of deliverables)						
Coordinate and collate DD documents						
Select DD materials, finishes and colors						
Coordinate special photos, renderings and models						
Prepare DD cost estimate						
Review DD documents with state and local agencies						
Present final DD to user and client						
Conduct constructibility review and packaging						

Insert notes as referenced within the matrix:

CLIENT *(initials)* _____   **CONSULTANT** *(initials)* _____

3

Appendices

Construction Documents	Client	Consultant	Local Architect	Not Applicable	Reference Note No.	Schedule
Project management						
Project administration						
Participate in client and team conferences						
Conduct special presentations						
Update project schedule/refine construction schedule						
Conduct technical refinement of exterior and interior details						
Verify final materials, finishes and colors						
Prepare CDs (Drawings, Specs) *See DD list, repeat the date*						
Coordinate CD work of engineer services (SE, MEP, CE)						
Present interim documents to the user and client						
Review cost check						
Conduct QA/QC check of documents						
Present CD design intent review						
Coordinate, assemble, print final CDs						
Review CD documents with local and state agencies						
Transmit pre-bid documents to client for comments						
Prepare final 100% CD cost estimate						
Coordinate the permit process						
Incorporate revisions from the client review						
Coordinate client review of bid documents						
Bidding/Negotiation						
Project management						
Project administration						
Respond to questions regarding CDs						
Prepare and issue addenda						
Assist client and CM in evaluation of bids						

Insert notes as referenced within the matrix:

CLIENT *(initials)* _____   **CONSULTANT** *(initials)* _____

4

Legend:
Primary Responsibility = P
Support Responsibility = S
No Responsibility = N

Construction Contract Administration	Client	Consultant	Local Architect	Not Applicable	Reference Note No.	Schedule
Project management						
Project administration						
Coordinate engineer services						
Coordinate construction observation services						
Attend construction job meetings						
Coordinate and process submittals review						
Shop Drawings						
Product Data						
Samples						
Mock-ups						
Other submittals						
Issuance of sketches for clarification						
Review change orders						
Process payment certificates or requests						
Travel to manufacturers/fabricators for materials/ mock-ups						
Review and comment: mock-ups						
Review and coordinate punch list						
Review for substantial completion						
Review for final completion						
Coordinate warranties, manuals, Client documents, commission						

Insert notes as referenced within the matrix:

CLIENT _(initials)_ _____   **CONSULTANT** _(initials)_ _____

5

Document B161™ – 2002 Exhibit F

Projected Travel Costs

(Use this exhibit to establish the number and frequency of trips and their projected costs, if necessary.)

The Client and Consultant have developed the Project schedule in accordance with Exhibit E and further agree that the total number of required trips and associated travel expenses shall be as follows:
(Complete the chart below)

Total Cost per Person/Trip
(Compute total cost, including travel time, airfare, ground transportation, hotel, etc.)

Service *(Insert services and compute total costs)*	Days in Country	Total Trips	Total Cost

Total trip cost per person is computed based on the following rates:

Should the indicated costs materially change during the term of the Project, payment to the Consultant for travel costs shall be equitably adjusted.

CLIENT *(initials)* _____   **CONSULTANT** *(initials)* _____

▦AIA® Document B161™ – 2002 Exhibit G

Table of Hourly Rates

(Use this Exhibit to tabulate hourly billing rates.)

When applicable, the Consultant shall be paid on the basis of the following schedule of hourly rates:

Employee or Category	Rate

Rates are computed in United States dollars, are effective as of the date of this Agreement and shall be adjusted in accordance with the salary review procedure of the Consultant.

CLIENT *(initials)* _____   **CONSULTANT** *(initials)* _____

▓AIA® Document B162™ – 2002

Abbreviated Form of Agreement Between Client and Consultant
For use where the Project is located outside the United States

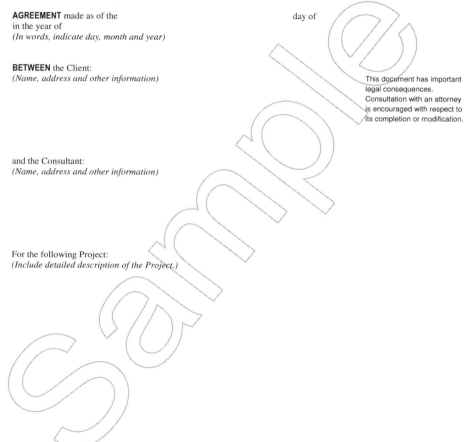

AGREEMENT made as of the   day of
in the year of
(In words, indicate day, month and year)

BETWEEN the Client:
(Name, address and other information)

This document has important legal consequences. Consultation with an attorney is encouraged with respect to its completion or modification.

and the Consultant:
(Name, address and other information)

For the following Project:
(Include detailed description of the Project.)

The Client and Consultant agree as follows:

ARTICLE 1 RESPONSIBILITIES OF THE PARTIES
§ 1.1 The Client shall, in a timely manner, provide full information regarding requirements for and limitations on the Project, and shall render timely decisions.

The Client shall retain all necessary consultants, including the Local Architect, Cost Consultant and contractors required for the Project.

The Consultant shall exercise reasonable skill, care and diligence in the performance of its obligations under this Agreement.

ARTICLE 2 DESCRIPTION OF SERVICES
(Insert a brief description of the services to be provided by the Consultant.)

ARTICLE 3 CHANGE IN SERVICES
§ 3.1 Any change in the services of the Consultant mutually agreed upon in writing by the Client and Consultant shall entitle the Consultant to an adjustment in payment.

ARTICLE 4 PAYMENTS
§ 4.1 The Consultant shall be paid on the following basis:
(Describe the basis of initial payment, payment for services, change in services and reimbursable expenses.)

§ 4.2 The Client shall make monthly payments in U.S. dollars upon presentation of the Consultant's statement, without deductions for sales, income, value added, duties and other government-imposed taxes. The Client shall be responsible for all such obligations.

§ 4.3 Payments shall be transmitted by the Client as follows:
(Insert instructions for the method of payment.)

ARTICLE 5 INSTRUMENTS OF SERVICE
§ 5.1 Drawings, Specifications and other documents, including those in electronic form, prepared by the Consultant are Instruments of Service for use solely with respect to this Project. The Consultant shall be deemed the author and owner of such Instruments of Service and shall retain all rights accorded under applicable law, including copyrights under the Berne Convention. Upon execution of this Agreement, the Consultant grants to the Client a nonexclusive license to reproduce the Consultant's Instruments of Service solely for use with this Project, provided that the Client shall comply with all obligations, including prompt payment of all sums when due, under this Agreement. The Consultant shall have the right to withhold the Instruments of Service in the event the Client fails to make payments in a timely manner.

ARTICLE 6 DISPUTE RESOLUTION
§ 6.1 Any claim, dispute or other matter in question arising out of or related to this Agreement shall be subject to mediation as a condition precedent to arbitration. The Client and Consultant shall share mediation costs equally. If mediation fails to bring resolution, matters still in question shall be decided by arbitration in accordance with the rules of United Nations Commission on International Trade Law (UNCITRAL). Mediation shall be held at the site, arbitration shall be held in a neutral location and each shall be conducted in English. Agreements reached shall be enforceable as settlement agreements in any court having jurisdiction thereof. Any arbitration award shall be governed by the Convention on the Recognition and Enforcement of Foreign Arbitration Awards.

2

Appendices

ARTICLE 7 TERMINATION

§ 7.1 This Agreement may be terminated by either party upon not less than seven days written notice should the other party fail substantially to perform its obligations in accordance with the terms of this Agreement. In the event of termination not the fault of the Consultant, the Consultant shall be entitled to payment for services performed prior to termination, together with reimbursable expenses then due.

ARTICLE 8 MISCELLANEOUS PROVISIONS

§ 8.1 This Agreement shall be governed by the law in the principal place of business of the Consultant and may be amended only by mutual written agreement.

ARTICLE 9 OTHER TERMS AND CONDITIONS

(Insert a description of any other terms or conditions)

This Agreement entered into as of the day and year first written above.

_____ _____
CLIENT *(Signature)* **CONSULTANT** *(Signature)*

_____ _____
(Printed name and title) *(Printed name and title)*

CAUTION: You should sign an original AIA Contract Document, on which this text appears in RED. An original assures that changes will not be obscured.

4

Appendix D: Foreign Corrupt Practices Act Antibribery Provisions[1]

United States Department of Justice
Fraud Section, Criminal Division
10th & Constitution Avenue, NW
(Bond 4th fl.)
Washington, D.C. 20530
Telephone: (202) 514-7023
Fax: (202) 514-7021
Internet: www.usdoj.gov/criminal/fraud/
fcpa/fcpa.html
E-mail: FCPA.fraud@usdoj.gov

United States Department of Commerce
Office of the Chief Counsel for International Commerce
14th Street and Constitution Avenue, NW
Room 5882
Washington, D.C. 20230
Telephone: (202) 482-0937
Fax: (202) 482-4076
Internet: www.ita.doc.gov/legal

INTRODUCTION

The 1988 Trade Act directed the Attorney General to provide guidance concerning the Department of Justice's enforcement policy with respect to the Foreign Corrupt Practices Act of 1977 ("FCPA"), 15 U.S.C. §§ 78dd-1, et seq., to potential exporters and small businesses that are unable to obtain specialized counsel on issues related to the FCPA. The guidance is limited to responses to requests under the Department of Justice's Foreign Corrupt Practices Act Opinion Procedure (described below at p. 10) and to general explanations of compliance responsibilities and potential liabilities under the FCPA. This brochure constitutes the Department of Justice's general explanation of the FCPA.

U.S. firms seeking to do business in foreign markets must be familiar with the FCPA. In general, the FCPA prohibits corrupt payments to foreign officials for the purpose of obtaining or keeping business. In addition, other statutes such as the mail and wire fraud statutes, 18 U.S.C. § 1341, 1343, and the Travel Act, 18 U.S.C. § 1952, which provides for federal prosecution of violations of state commercial bribery statutes, may also apply to such conduct.

The Department of Justice is the chief enforcement agency, with a coordinate role played by the Securities and Exchange Commission (SEC). The Office of General Counsel of the Department of Commerce also answers general questions from U.S. exporters concerning the FCPA's basic requirements and constraints.

This brochure is intended to provide a general description of the FCPA and is not intended to substitute for the advice of private counsel on specific issues related to the FCPA. Moreover, material in this brochure is not intended to set forth the present enforcement intentions of the Department of Justice or the SEC with respect to particular fact situations.

BACKGROUND

As a result of SEC investigations in the mid-1970's, over 400 U.S. companies admitted making questionable or illegal payments in excess of $300 million to foreign government officials, politicians, and political parties. The abuses ran the gamut from bribery of high foreign officials to secure some type of favorable action by a

---

[1] This document is available at: http://www.usdoj.gov/criminal/fraud/fcpa/dojdocb.htm (accessed 2/2007).

foreign government to so-called facilitating payments that allegedly were made to ensure that government functionaries discharged certain ministerial or clerical duties. Congress enacted the FCPA to bring a halt to the bribery of foreign officials and to restore public confidence in the integrity of the American business system.

The FCPA was intended to have and has had an enormous impact on the way American firms do business. Several firms that paid bribes to foreign officials have been the subject of criminal and civil enforcement actions, resulting in large fines and suspension and debarment from federal procurement contracting, and their employees and officers have gone to jail. To avoid such consequences, many firms have implemented detailed compliance programs intended to prevent and to detect any improper payments by employees and agents.

Following the passage of the FCPA, the Congress became concerned that American companies were operating at a disadvantage compared to foreign companies who routinely paid bribes and, in some countries, were permitted to deduct the cost of such bribes as business expenses on their taxes. Accordingly, in 1988, the Congress directed the Executive Branch to commence negotiations in the Organization of Economic Cooperation and Development (OECD) to obtain the agreement of the United States' major trading partners to enact legislation similar to the FCPA. In 1997, almost ten years later, the United States and thirty-three other countries signed the OECD Convention on Combating Bribery of Foreign Public Officials in International Business Transactions. The United States ratified this Convention and enacted implementing legislation in 1998. *See* Convention and Commentaries on the DOJ Web site.

The antibribery provisions of the FCPA make it unlawful for a U.S. person, and certain foreign issuers of securities, to make a corrupt payment to a foreign official for the purpose of obtaining or retaining business for or with, or directing business to, any person. Since 1998, they also apply to foreign firms and persons who take any act in furtherance of such a corrupt payment while in the United States.

The FCPA also requires companies whose securities are listed in the United States to meet its accounting provisions. *See* 15 U.S.C. § 78m. These accounting provisions, which were designed to operate in tandem with the antibribery provisions of the FCPA, require corporations covered by the provisions to make and keep books and records that accurately and fairly reflect the transactions of the corporation and to devise and maintain an adequate system of internal accounting controls. This brochure discusses only the antibribery provisions.

ENFORCEMENT

The Department of Justice is responsible for all criminal enforcement and for civil enforcement of the antibribery provisions with respect to domestic concerns and foreign companies and nationals. The SEC is responsible for civil enforcement of the antibribery provisions with respect to issuers.

ANTIBRIBERY PROVISIONS

Basic Prohibition

The FCPA makes it unlawful to bribe foreign government officials to obtain or retain business. With respect to the basic prohibition, there are five elements which must be met to constitute a violation of the Act:

A. *Who*—The FCPA potentially applies to *any* individual, firm, officer, director, employee, or agent of a firm and any stockholder acting on behalf of a firm. Individuals and firms may also be penalized if they order, authorize, or assist someone else to violate the antibribery provisions or if they conspire to violate those provisions.

Under the FCPA, U.S. jurisdiction over corrupt payments to foreign officials depends upon whether the violator is an "issuer," a "domestic concern," or a foreign national or business.

An "issuer" is a corporation that has issued securities that have been registered in the United States or who is required to file periodic reports with the SEC. A "domestic concern" is any individual who is a citizen, national, or resident of the United States, or any corporation, partnership, association, joint-stock company, business trust, unincorporated organization, or sole proprietorship which has its principal place of business in the United States, or which is organized under the laws of a State of the United States, or a territory, possession, or commonwealth of the United States.

Issuers and domestic concerns may be held liable under the FCPA under *either* territorial or nationality jurisdiction principles. For acts taken within the territory of the United States, issuers and domestic concerns are liable if they take an act in furtherance of a corrupt payment to a foreign official using the U.S. mails or other means or instrumentalities of interstate commerce. Such means or instrumentalities include telephone calls, facsimile transmissions, wire transfers, and interstate or international travel. In ad-

dition, issuers and domestic concerns may be held liable for any act in furtherance of a corrupt payment taken *outside* the United States. Thus, a U.S. company or national may be held liable for a corrupt payment authorized by employees or agents operating entirely outside the United States, using money from foreign bank accounts, and without any involvement by personnel located within the United States.

Prior to 1998, foreign companies, with the exception of those who qualified as "issuers," and foreign nationals were not covered by the FCPA. The 1998 amendments expanded the FCPA to assert territorial jurisdiction over foreign companies and nationals. A foreign company or person is now subject to the FCPA if it causes, directly or through agents, an act in furtherance of the corrupt payment to take place within the territory of the United States. There is, however, no requirement that such act make use of the U.S. mails or other means or instrumentalities of interstate commerce.

Finally, U.S. parent corporations may be held liable for the acts of foreign subsidiaries where they authorized, directed, or controlled the activity in question, as can U.S. citizens or residents, themselves "domestic concerns," who were employed by or acting on behalf of such foreign-incorporated subsidiaries.

B. *Corrupt intent*—The person making or authorizing the payment must have a corrupt intent, and the payment must be intended to induce the recipient to misuse his official position to direct business wrongfully to the payer or to any other person. You should note that the FCPA does not require that a corrupt act succeed in its purpose. The *offer* or *promise* of a corrupt payment can constitute a violation of the statute. The FCPA prohibits any corrupt payment intended to *influence* any act or decision of a foreign official in his or her official capacity, to induce the official to do or omit to do any act in violation of his or her lawful duty, to obtain any improper advantage, or to *induce* a foreign official to use his or her influence improperly to affect or influence any act or decision.

C. *Payment*—The FCPA prohibits paying, offering, promising to pay (or authorizing to pay or offer) money or anything of value.

D. *Recipient*—The prohibition extends only to corrupt payments to a *foreign official*, a *foreign political party* or *party official*, or any *candidate* for foreign political office. A "foreign official" means any officer or employee of a foreign government, a public international organization, or any department or agency thereof, or any person acting in an official capacity. You should consider utilizing the Department of Justice's Foreign Corrupt Practices Act Opinion Procedure for particular questions as to the definition of a "foreign official," such as whether a member of a royal family, a member of a legislative body, or an official of a state-owned business enterprise would be considered a "foreign official."

The FCPA applies to payments to *any* public official, regardless of rank or position. The FCPA focuses on the *purpose* of the payment instead of the particular duties of the official receiving the payment, offer, or promise of payment, and there are exceptions to the antibribery provision for "facilitating payments for routine governmental action" (see below).

E. *Business Purpose Test*—The FCPA prohibits payments made in order to assist the firm in *obtaining* or *retaining business* for or with, or *directing business* to, any person. The Department of Justice interprets "obtaining or retaining business" broadly, such that the term encompasses more than the mere award or renewal of a contract. It should be noted that the business to be obtained or retained does *not* need to be with a foreign government or foreign government instrumentality.

Third Party Payments

The FCPA prohibits corrupt payments through intermediaries. It is unlawful to make a payment to a third party, while knowing that all or a portion of the payment will go directly or indirectly to a foreign official. *The term "knowing" includes conscious disregard and deliberate ignorance.* The elements of an offense are essentially the same as described above, except that in this case the "recipient" is the intermediary who is making the payment to the requisite "foreign official."

Intermediaries may include joint venture partners or agents. To avoid being held liable for corrupt third party payments, U.S. companies are encouraged to exercise due diligence and to take all necessary precautions to ensure that they have formed a business relationship with reputable and qualified partners and representatives. Such due diligence may include investigating potential foreign representatives and joint venture partners to determine if they are in fact qualified for the position, whether they have personal or professional ties to the government, the number and reputation of their clientele, and their reputation with the U.S. Embassy or Consulate and with local bankers, clients, and other business associates. In addition, in negotiating a business relationship, the U.S. firm should be aware of so-called "red flags," *i.e.*, unusual payment patterns or financial arrangements, a history of corruption in the country, a refusal by the foreign joint venture partner or representative to provide a certification that it will not take any action in furtherance of an unlawful offer, promise, or payment to a foreign public official and not take any act that would cause the U.S. firm to be in violation of the FCPA, unusually high commissions, lack of transparency in expenses and accounting records, apparent lack of qualifications or resources on the part of the joint venture partner or representative to perform the services offered, and whether the joint venture partner or representative has been recommended by an official of the potential governmental customer.

You should seek the advice of counsel and consider utilizing the Department of Justice's Foreign Corrupt Practices Act Opinion Procedure for particular questions relating to third party payments.

PERMISSIBLE PAYMENTS AND AFFIRMATIVE DEFENSES

The FCPA contains an explicit exception to the bribery prohibition for "facilitating payments" for "routine governmental action" and provides affirmative defenses which can be used to defend against alleged violations of the FCPA.

Facilitating Payments for Routine Governmental Actions

There is an exception to the antibribery prohibition for payments to facilitate or expedite performance of a "routine governmental action." The statute lists the following examples: obtaining permits, licenses, or other official documents; processing governmental papers, such as visas and work orders; providing police protection, mail pick-up and delivery; providing phone service, power and water supply, loading and unloading cargo, or protecting perishable products; and scheduling inspections associated with contract performance or transit of goods across country.

Actions "similar" to these are also covered by this exception. If you have a question about whether a payment falls within the exception, you should consult with counsel. You should also consider whether to utilize the Justice Department's Foreign Corrupt Practices Opinion Procedure, described below on p. 10.

"Routine governmental action" does *not* include any decision by a foreign official to award new business or to continue business with a particular party.

Affirmative Defenses

A person charged with a violation of the FCPA's antibribery provisions may assert as a defense that the payment was lawful under the written laws of the foreign country or that the money was spent as part of demonstrating a product or performing a contractual obligation.

Whether a payment was lawful under the written laws of the foreign country may be difficult to determine. You should consider seeking the advice of counsel or utilizing the Department of Justice's Foreign Corrupt Practices Act Opinion Procedure when faced with an issue of the legality of such a payment.

Moreover, because these defenses are "affirmative defenses," the defendant is required to show in the first instance that the payment met these requirements. The prosecution does not bear the burden of demonstrating in the first instance that the payments did not constitute this type of payment.

SANCTIONS AGAINST BRIBERY

Criminal

The following criminal penalties may be imposed for violations of the FCPA's antibribery provisions: corporations and other business entities are subject to a fine of up to $2,000,000; officers, directors, stockholders, employees, and agents are subject to a fine of up to $100,000 and imprisonment for up to five years. Moreover, under the Alternative Fines Act, these fines may be actually quite higher — the actual fine may be up to twice the benefit that the defendant sought to obtain by making the corrupt payment. You should also be aware that fines imposed on individuals may *not* be paid by their employer or principal.

Civil

The Attorney General or the SEC, as appropriate, may bring a civil action for a fine of up to $10,000 against any firm *as well as* any officer, director, employee, or agent of a firm, or stockholder acting on behalf of the firm, who violates the antibribery provisions. In addition, in an SEC enforcement action, the court may impose an additional fine not to exceed the greater of (i) the gross amount of the pecuniary gain to the defendant as a result of the violation, or (ii) a specified dollar lim-

itation. The specified dollar limitations are based on the egregiousness of the violation, ranging from $5,000 to $100,000 for a natural person and $50,000 to $500,000 for any other person.

The Attorney General or the SEC, as appropriate, may also bring a civil action to enjoin any act or practice of a firm whenever it appears that the firm (or an officer, director, employee, agent, or stockholder acting on behalf of the firm) is in violation (or about to be) of the antibribery provisions.

Other Governmental Action

Under guidelines issued by the Office of Management and Budget, a person or firm found in violation of the FCPA may be barred from doing business with the Federal government. *Indictment alone can lead to suspension of the right to do business with the government.* The President has directed that no executive agency shall allow any party to participate in any procurement or nonprocurement activity if any agency has debarred, suspended, or otherwise excluded that party from participation in a procurement or nonprocurement activity.

In addition, a person or firm found guilty of violating the FCPA may be ruled ineligible to receive export licenses; the SEC may suspend or bar persons from the securities business and impose civil penalties on persons in the securities business for violations of the FCPA; the Commodity Futures Trading Commission and the Overseas Private Investment Corporation both provide for possible suspension or debarment from agency programs for violation of the FCPA; and a payment made to a foreign government official that is unlawful under the FCPA cannot be deducted under the tax laws as a business expense.

Private Cause of Action

Conduct that violates the antibribery provisions of the FCPA may also give rise to a private cause of action for treble damages under the Racketeer Influenced and Corrupt Organizations Act (RICO), or to actions under other federal or state laws. For example, an action might be brought under RICO by a competitor who alleges that the bribery caused the defendant to win a foreign contract.

GUIDANCE FROM THE GOVERNMENT

The Department of Justice has established a Foreign Corrupt Practices Act Opinion Procedure by which any U.S. company or national may request a statement of the Justice Department's present enforcement intentions under the antibribery provisions of the FCPA regarding any proposed business conduct. The details of the opinion procedure may be found at 28 CFR Part 80. Under this procedure, the Attorney General will issue an opinion in response to a specific inquiry from a person or firm within thirty days of the request. (The thirty-day period does not run until the Department of Justice has received all the information it requires to issue the opinion.) Conduct for which the Department of Justice has issued an opinion stating that the conduct conforms with current enforcement policy will be entitled to a presumption, in any subsequent enforcement action, of conformity with the FCPA. Copies of releases issued regarding previous opinions are available on the Department of Justice's FCPA Web site.

For further information from the Department of Justice about the FCPA and the Foreign Corrupt Practices Act Opinion Procedure, contact Mark F. Mendelsohn, Deputy Chief, Fraud Section, at (202) 514-1721.

Although the Department of Commerce has no enforcement role with respect to the FCPA, it supplies general guidance to U.S. exporters who have questions about the FCPA and about international developments concerning the FCPA. For further information from the Department of Commerce about the FCPA contact Eleanor Roberts Lewis, Chief Counsel for International Commerce, or Arthur Aronoff, Senior Counsel, Office of the Chief Counsel for International Commerce, U.S. Department of Commerce, Room 5882, 14th Street and Constitution Avenue, N.W., Washington, D.C. 20230, (202) 482-0937.

Last Updated: November 2006
usdoj/criminal/fraud/mm:dlj

Notes

CHAPTER 2

[1] Harold L. Adams, "Keynote Address : The Practice of Architecture in *Southeast Asia," in Southeast Asia Architectural Markets and Practice Conference, Hong Kong and Shenzhen, China, November 5–11, 1994* (Washington, D.C.: American Institute of Architects, 1995), p. 13.

CHAPTER 3

[1] Stephen A. Kliment, *Writing for Design Professionals: A Guide to Writing Successful Proposals, Letters, Brochures, Portfolios, Reports, Presentations, and Job Applications* (New York: Norton, 2006), p. 210.

CHAPTER 4

[1] Central Intelligence Agency. *The World Factbook*, https://www.cia.gov/library/publications/the-world-factbook/ (accessed January 2007).

[2] Population statistics are from Statistics Canada and www.infoplease.com/ipa/A0107390.html (accessed January 2007).

[3] Miguel Villa and Jorge Rodríguez, "Demographic trends in Latin America's metropolises, 1950–1990," *The Mega-City in Latin America*, ed. Alan Gilbert (New York: United Nations University Press, 1996), www.unu.edu/unupress/unupbooks/uu23me/uu23me05.htm,

[4] Síntesis de Resultados del Conteo 2005, http://en.wikipedia.org/wiki/Greater_Mexico_City.

[5] Central Intelligence Agency. *The World Factbook*, https://www.cia.gov/cia/publications/factbook/ (accessed January 2007).

[6] Central Intelligence Agency, *The World Factbook*, https://www.cia.gov/cia/publications/factbook/ (accessed January 2007).

[7] Central Intelligence Agency. *The World Factbook*, https://www.cia.gov/cia/publications/factbook/ (accessed January 2007).

[8] Background history for Brasília, http://en.wikipedia.org/wiki/Brasilia. (January 2007)

[9] Censo 2005, Departmento Administrativo Nacional de Estadisticas, Colombia, www.dane.gov.co/files/censo2005/resultados_am_municipios.pdf (accessed February, 2007). Statistics given for cities rather than greater metropolitan area.

[10] Thomas Brinkhoff, "City Population," www.citypopulation.de (accessed February, 2007).

[11] *The World Factbook*, https://www.cia.gov/cia/publications/factbook/ (accessed January 2007)

[12] Giancarlo Alhadeff, "Practicing in Italy," in *Europe: Architectural Markets and Practice April 25-28, 1996 Paris* (Washington D.C.: American Institute of Architects, 1997), p. 19.

Notes

13 Central Intelligence Agency, *The World Factbook*, https://www.cia.gov/cia/ publications/factbook (accessed January 2007).

14 Central Intelligence Agency, *The World Factbook*, https://www.cia.gov/cia/ publications/factbook (accessed January 2007).

15 Patricia S. Kuehn. "The Practice and Business of Architecture in Russia", 1997. *Europe: Architectural Markets and Practice April 25-28, 1996 Paris.* Washington D.C.: American Institute of Architects. 37)

16 Central Intelligence Agency, *The World Factbook*, https://www.cia.gov/cia/ publications/factbook (accessed January 2007).

17 Central Intelligence Agency, *The World Factbook*, https://www.cia.gov/cia/ publications/factbook (accessed January 2007).

18 Central Intelligence Agency, *The World Factbook*, https://www.cia.gov/cia/ publications/factbook (accessed January 2007).

19 Central Intelligence Agency, *The World Factbook*, https://www.cia.gov/cia/ publications/factbook (accessed January 2007).

20 Combined statistics from *The World Factbook* (Central Intelligence Agency 2007) entries on the West Bank and Gaza Strip.

21 See the following for population details: http://lexicorient.com/e.o/uae.htm (accessed March 2006).

22 Central Intelligence Agency, *The World Factbook*, https://www.cia.gov/cia/ publications/factbook (accessed January 2007).

23 Pankaj Mishra, "The Myth of the New India," *New York Times*, July 6, Op-Ed.

24 Joyhan Larkin and Eric Bellman, "Reliance to Invest $750 million in Indian retailing," *Wall Street Journal* (January 24, 2006).

25 Anand Giridharada, "Addressing a Shortage of Hotel Rooms, Not People," *The New York Times* (December 12, 2006): Section C.

26 Central Intelligence Agency, *The World Factbook*, https://www.cia.gov/cia/ publications/factbook/ (accessed January 2007).

27 Gary Bowerman, "The Year of the Mega IPO," *Shanghai Business Review*, December 2006, p. 26.

28 Brent Hannan, "Business in China Can Pose Pitfalls, "*Asian Wall Street Journal*, September 20, 2005, and *Wall Street Journal Europe*, September 20, 2005.

29 Arthur Lubow, "The China Syndrome," *New York Times Magazine* (May 21, 2006), p. 74.

30 Central Intelligence Agency, *The World Factbook*, https://www.cia.gov/cia/ publications/factbook/ (accessed January 2007).

31 Alan Dalgleish, "The Philippines Market," *Urban Land* (February 2006): 111–112.

32 Central Intelligence Agency *The World Factbook*, www.cia.gov/cia/publications/ factbook/ (accessed January 2007).

References, Further Reading, and Resources

REFERENCES AND FURTHER READING

Abelsky, Paul. 2005. "The Americans Were Coming." In *Russia Profile* II, 9 (November 7): 26. http://www.russiaprofile.org/culture/article.wbp?article-id=302B09D8-0619-4F1E-8E84-7F2793B2EA33

Abercrombie, Stanley. 1997. "Doing Business in the Pacific." *Interior Design* (August). Bennett, Paul. 2003. "When in Rome: Richard Meier Helps the Vatican Celebrate the Millennium." *Architecture* (December).

Bielefeld, Bert, and Lars-Phillip Rusch, eds. 2006. *Building Projects in China: A Manual for Architects and Engineers*. Basel and Boston: Birkhäuser.

Claybaker, Paul M. 2004. "Offshore Production: Trend of the Month or Industry Transformation?" *AIA/DC News* (September). Demkin, Joseph A., ed. 2001, 2006. *The Architect's Handbook of Professional Practice*, 13th ed. and 2006 update. New York: John Wiley & Sons.

"European Practice Not for the Faint of Heart." 1996. *Architectural Record* (July).

Fathy, Hassan. 2000. *Architecture for the Poor: An Experiment in Rural Egypt*. Chicago, IL: University of Chicago Press.

Fishman, Ted C. 2006. *China, Inc.: How the Rise of the Next Superpower Challenges America and the World*. New York: Scribner.

Forward, The Quarterly Journal of the National Associates Committee. 2006. "Feedback: Response to 'Our Shrinking World'." (April).
http://www.aia.org/ep2_template.cfm?pagename=nacq_a_060427_fb_outsource

Friedman, Thomas L. 2005. *The World Is Flat: A Brief History of the Twenty-First Century*. New York: Farrar, Straus and Giroux.

Hall, Kevin G. 2005. "Offshoring affects more complex U.S. jobs: Work done by junior architects and lawyers can now be done overseas faster or more cheaply." *Philadelphia Inquirer*, Washington Bureau, December 29.

Ivy, Robert. 2004. "China Business Blitz." *Architectural Record* (March), page 114.

Lieberthal, Kenneth, et al. 2006. *China Tomorrow: Prospects and Perils*. 2nd ed. Cambridge, MA: Harvard Business School Publishing Corp.

Lubow, Arthur. 2006. "The China Syndrome." *New York Times Magazine*, May 21, page 68.

Martin, Frank Edgerton. 2001. "Crossing the Border: Working Abroad Simpler than Landscape Architects Realize." *Landscape Architecture* (September), page 84.

Mehta, Suketu. 2005. "A Passage From India." *New York Times*, July 12.

Miller, George H. 2003. "Innovations and Competitions." *Oculus* (Fall).

Morrison, Terri, and Wayne A. Conaway. 2006. *Kiss, Bow, or Shake Hands: The Bestselling Guide to Doing Business in More Than 60 Countries*. Avon, MA: Adams Media.

"New Overseas Markets." 1997. *Architecture* (October):

Ramnarayan, Abhinav. 2006. "Architectural Outsourcing—Drawing a New Design." *The Hindu Business Line*, January 23.
http://www.thehindubusinessline.com/2006/01/24/stories/2006012402740300.htm

Scheer, David R. 1992. "Critical Differences: Notes on a Comparison of Architectural Practice in France and the U.S." *Practices* (Spring).

Siems, Thomas F. 2006. "Beyond the Outsourcing Angst: Making America More Productive." *Economic Letter: Insights from the Federal Reserve Bank of Dallas* 1:2 (February). http://www.dallasfed.org/research/eclett/2006/el0602.pdf

Slatin, Peter. 1996. "International Practice." *Architectural Record* (July).

Solomon, Nancy B., and Charles Linn. 2005. "Are We Exporting Architecture Jobs?" *Architectural Record* (January), page 82.

Soota, Ashok, and Marcus Courtney. 2006. "Resolved: Offshoring is Good for America." *Fast Company* (January/February). Issue 102, 108.

Tombesi, Paolo, Bharat Dave, and Peter Scriver. 2003. "Routine Production or Symbolic Analysis? India and the Globalization of Architectural Services." *The Journal of Architecture* 8(1): 63–94.

Walter, Derek. 1991. *The Feng-Shui Handbook: A Practical Guide to Chinese Geomancy and Environmental Harmony*. New York: Thornsons.

Wendover, Jess. 2006. "Our Shrinking World." *Forward, The Quarterly Journal of the National Associates Committee* (January): xx. http://www.aia.org/ep2_template.cfm?pagename=nacq_a_060112_editorial_ shrinking_world_wendover

Williams, Roger B., and C. Richard Meyer. 2001. "Practicing in a Global Market." In *The Architect's Handbook of Professional Practice*, 13th ed., ed. Joseph A. Demkin, 100–108. New York: John Wiley & Sons.

Wong, Eva. 1996. *Feng-Shui*. Boston: Shambhala.

———. 2001. *A Master Course in Feng-Shui*. Boston: Shambhala

PROFESSIONAL ORGANIZATIONS AND INFORMATION RESOURCES

American Consulting Engineers Council (ACEC)
1015 15th Street, NW, Suite 802
Washington, DC 20005
Telephone: (203) 347-7474
Fax: (202) 898-0068
E-mail: acec@acec.org
Web site: www.acec.org

American Institute of Architects (AIA)
1735 New York Avenue, NW
Washington, DC 20006-5292
Telephone: (202) 626-7300
Fax: (202) 626-7426

E-mail: infocentral@aia.org
Web site: www.aia.org

American Planning Association (APA)
1776 Massachusetts Avenue, NW
Washington, DC 20036
Telephone: (202) 872-0611
Fax: (202) 872-0643
E-mail: customerservice@planning.org
Web site: www.planning.org

American Society of Civil Engineers (ASCE)
1801 Alexander Bell Drive

Reston, VA 20191
Telephone: (800) 548-2723
Fax: (703) 295-6222
E-mail: member@asce.org
Web site: www.asce.org

American Society of Interior Designers (ASID)

608 Massachusetts Avenue, NE
Washington, DC 20002-6006
Telephone: (202) 546-3480
Fax: (202) 546-3240
E-mail: network@asid.org
Web site: www.asid.org

American Society of Landscape Architects (ASLA)

636 Eye Street, NW
Washington, DC 20001-3736
Telephone: (202) 898-2444
Fax: (202) 898-1185
E-mail: membership@asla.org
Web site: www.asla.org

Association of Collegiate Schools of Architecture (ACSA)

1735 New York Avenue, NW
Washington, DC 20006-5292
Telephone: (202) 785-2324
Fax: (202) 626-0448
E-mail: info@acsa-arch.org
Web site: www.acsa-arch.org

National Council of Architectural Registration Boards (NCARB)

1801 K Street, NW, Suite 1100
Washington, DC 20006
Telephone: (202) 783-6500
Fax: (202) 783-0290
E-mail: customerservice@ncarb.org
Web site: www.ncarb.org

National Society of Professional Engineers (NSPE)

1420 King Street
Alexandria, VA 22314
Telephone: (703) 684-2800
Fax: (703) 836-4875
E-mail: customer.service@nspe.org
Web site: www.nspe.org

American Institute of Architects (AIA) Resources

American Institute of Architects International Committee and International Practice Committee, www.aia.org

American Institute of Architects. 1995. *Southeast Asia Architectural Markets and Practice.* Conference proceedings from Hong Kong and Shenzhen, China, November 5–11, 1994. Washington, DC: American Institute of Architects.

American Institute of Architects. 1997. *Europe: Architectural Markets and Practice.* Conference proceedings from Paris, France, April 1996. Washington, DC: The American Institute of Architects International Committee.

American Institute of Architects. 2006. *AIA International Committee Offshore Outsourcing Roundtable Reader.* Washington, DC: American Institute of Architects.

American Institute of Architects. *The Business of Architecture: 2003–2005 AIA Firm Survey.* Washington, DC: AIA Economics and Market Research Department.

Of particular interest is the summary of the International Chapter on Offshore Outsourcing.

American Institute of Architects. *The Business of Architecture: 2000-2002 AIA Firm Survey.* Washington, DC: AIA Economics and Market Research Department.

Of particular interest is Chapter 7 on "International Work."

Many of the AIA "Best Practices" series, which are available on the AIA Web site are useful, including many of the following from section 06.04 on Practice in a Global Market and section 06.03 Strategic Alliances:

06.03.01: "Forming Strategic Alliances." Victor O. Schinnerer & Company Inc., November 2006. http://www.aia.org/SiteObjects/files/bp_06_03_01.pdf

06.04.01: "Getting Paid for International Work," November 2006. http://www.aia.org/SiteObjects/files/bestpractice_06_04_01.pdf

06.04.02: "Managing International Teams." Dean W. Engel. November 2006. http://www.aia.org/SiteObjects/files/bestpractice_06_04_02.pdf

06.04.03: "International Videoconferencing." William J. Higgins. November 2006. http://www.aia.org/SiteObjects/files/bestpractice_06_04_03.pdf

06.04.04: "International Practices Checklist." http://www.aia.org/SiteObjects/files/06-04-04.pdf

Vonier, Thomas. 2006. "Exporting Architectural Services: Considerations for U.S. Architecture Firms." http://www.aia.org/SiteObjects/files/US_firms_exporting.pdf

Williams, Roger B., and C. Richard Meyer. 2001. "Practicing in a Global Market." In *The Architect's Handbook of Professional Practice*, 13th ed., ed. Joseph A. Demkin, 100–108. New York: John Wiley & Sons.

Online Resources

1. Central Intelligence Agency, *The World Factbook*, https://www.cia.gov/cia/publications/factbook

2. Collegi d'Arquitectes de Catalunya (COAC), or Architects' Association of Catalonia, http://www.coac.net

3. Foreign Commercial Service, U.S. Department of Commerce, http://www.commerce.gov/index.html

4. International Trade Administrator, U.S. Department of Commerce, http://www.ita.doc.gov

5. International Union of Architects (L'Union Internationale des Architectes), http://www.uia-architectes.org

6. National Council of Architectural Registration Boards (NCARB), http://www.ncarb.org/overseas/index.html

7. U.S. State Department, http://www.state.gov

Index

Index

Index

Index